W9-BSA-604

DATE DUE			MAY 04
GAYLORD			PRINTED IN U.S.A.

CELEF

CELEBRITY-IN-CHIEF

✦✦✦✦

How Show Business
Took Over the White House

ALAN SCHROEDER

Westview
PRESS

A Member of the Perseus Books Group

WITHDRAWN
Damaged, Obsolete, or Surplus

JACKSON COUNTY LIBRARY SERVICES
Jackson County Library Services
MEDFORD OREGON 97501

All rights reserved. Printed in the United States of America. No part of this publication may be reproduced or transmitted in any form or by any means, electronic or mechanical, including photocopy, recording, or any information storage and retrieval system, without permission in writing from the publisher.

Copyright © 2004 by Alan Schroeder

Published in the United States of America by Westview Press, A Member of the Perseus Books Group, 5500 Central Avenue, Boulder, Colorado 80301-2877, and in the United Kingdom by Westview Press, 12 Hid's Copse Road, Cumnor Hill, Oxford OX2 9JJ.

Find us on the World Wide Web at www.westviewpress.com.

Westview Press books are available at special discounts for bulk purchases in the United States by corporations, institutions, and other organizations. For more information, please contact the Special Markets Department at the Perseus Books Group, 11 Cambridge Center, Cambridge, MA 02142, or call (617) 252-5298, (800) 255-1514 or e-mail specialmarkets@perseusbooks.com.

Library of Congress Cataloging-in-Publication Data
Schroeder, Alan, 1954-
  Celebrity-in-chief : how show business took over the White House / by Alan Schroeder.
    p. cm.
Includes bibliographical references (p. 305) and index.
  ISBN 0-8133-4137-X (alk. paper)
  1. Presidents—United States—History—20th century. 2. Public relations and politics—United States—History—20th century. 3. Political culture—United States—History—20th century. 4. United States—Politics and government—20th century. 5. Celebrities—United States—History—20th century. 6. Entertainers—United States—History—20th century. 7. Performing arts—Political aspects—United States—History—20th century. 8. Popular culture—Political aspects—United States—History—20th century. 9. Political culture—Washington (D.C.)—History—20th century. 10. Washington (D.C.)—Social life and customs—20th century. I. Title.
  E176.1.S3525 2004
  352.23'2748'0973—dc22

                                2003025806

The paper used in this publication meets the requirements of the American National Standard for Permanence of Paper for Printed Library Materials Z39.48-1984.

Designed by *Reginald R. Thompson*

Set in 11-point AGaramond by the Perseus Books Group.

10   9   8   7   6   5   4   3   2   1

For my mother,
who took me to President Eisenhower's funeral

CONTENTS

✤✤✤✤

CELEBRITY-IN-CHIEF

Bill Clinton in New York City, November 2000.
(Clinton Presidential Materials Project)

Introduction

✱✱✱✱

The Showbiz Presidency

On a Saturday evening in the Map Room of the White House the president and his closest aides gathered for a last-minute run-through of an event soon to commence in a hotel ballroom a few blocks away. Clad in tuxedos and formalwear, the men and women surrounded their leader as he prepared to march into battle—a battle of wits known as the White House Correspondents Association dinner. The dinner, and specifically the lighthearted presentations that followed, served as the climax to Washington's annual "humor season," a trifecta of springtime soirees hosted by journalists and loomed over by whichever president holds office. During the relentlessly entertaining administration of Bill Clinton, the dinners had become an especially hot ticket, and now, on the night of April 29, 2000, Clinton was headlining his final bash.

Into the Map Room, fresh from an editing room in Virginia, rushed a wired man with a six-minute videotape: Philip Rosenthal, executive producer of the television series *Everybody Loves Raymond*, and, more to the point, director and cowriter of the first comedy short subject ever made by a sitting president of the United States. All day long Rosenthal had been putting the final touches on his magnum opus; now it was time to unveil the finished product for the star. If the video did not pass muster with its leading man, it would not be screened at the dinner.

Rosenthal had written jokes for Clinton before, but this was his first time attending a correspondents dinner. Rosenthal's connection to the White House came through a high school friend named Mark Katz, a figure much admired among Washington insiders for his ability to make politicians sound funnier than they really are. As a writer, the New York–based Katz specialized in jokes for Democrats; over the years many of President Clinton's best lines had come from Katz. Rosenthal and Katz had long dreamed of shooting a comedy piece for Clinton to contribute to the correspondents dinner, but the president's crowded schedule always precluded production. Now, as a lame duck, Clinton had time, which in turn supplied the conceptual joke behind the video.

The premise of *The Final Days* is simple: Bill Clinton, in his waning weeks as the most powerful man on earth, has too little to do. Sound bites from journalists and White House associates are intercut with scenes of Clinton battling lame-duck ennui: waiting for his laundry to dry, mowing the grass, watching movies in the screening room with Buddy the dog, chasing after Hillary's limousine with a brown-bag lunch. This sad-sack montage ends with the president standing before a mirror holding an Oscar statue in his hand. "I want to thank the Academy for this tremendous honor," Clinton intones. "Ever since I was a little boy I've wanted to be a real—"

Into the frame steps a man in black tie with a disapproving scowl on his face: Kevin Spacey, who six weeks earlier had won the Academy Award as Best Actor.

"Actor," Clinton finishes.

Wordlessly, Spacey motions with his fingers for Clinton to hand over the Oscar. Clinton does. Still saying nothing, Spacey fires one last scathing look and makes his exit.

Originally White House schedulers had given Rosenthal only half an hour of production time with the president, nowhere near enough for so complicated a shoot. But Clinton the actor enjoyed himself, and by the end of the week two additional half-hours had magically materialized on the schedule. On the day the video premiered Rosenthal and his crew were still shooting; Spacey and Clinton taped their scene with the Oscar the morning of the party.

As ideal as Spacey proved to be in his part, the role of Clinton's *Final Days* costar might instead have gone to Robert De Niro. Phil Rosenthal had the inspiration to include a big-name cameo appearance while scouting locations at the executive mansion. The day was Easter Sunday, and De Niro and his family happened to be among those taking part in the annual egg roll on the White House lawn. Rosenthal approached the actor about contributing to the project. Although De Niro was game, a scheduling conflict prevented his participation. Scouring the list of actors who would be traveling to Washington for the correspondents dinner, Rosenthal came across the name of Kevin Spacey, a friend of

Bill Clinton. Spacey agreed to do the bit and brought along his real Oscar for use as a prop. It was Spacey's idea to don a tux for his on-camera exchange with the president.

According to Rosenthal, Clinton proved to be as skilled a performer as Kevin Spacey, nailing each of his scenes in one or two takes. For the shot in which he watches his laundry spinning in the dryer, Clinton improvised an eye roll that corresponded to the circular motion of the machine. "There's a way to do that too much," Rosenthal said. "There's the Jerry Lewis version, or there's the subtle funny version—which is the way he did it."

Back in the Map Room, with only a few minutes to spare before the dinner, President Clinton began to watch the tape. Rosenthal, a bundle of nerves, stood next to him. For the first twenty seconds Clinton did not laugh. "And so of course," Rosenthal recalled, "when the president's not laughing, no one else is laughing." But then Bill Clinton let out a chuckle. Then another and another. "By the end he was laughing hysterically and so was everyone else," Rosenthal said. Bill and Hillary Clinton hugged Rosenthal; others in the room added their congratulations. Then, in a streak, the entire room emptied out for the ride to dinner in the presidential motorcade.

At the Washington Hilton, the audience of journalists, government officials, and lobbyists rubbed elbows with a platoon of invaders from Hollywood: Kevin Spacey, Tobey Maguire, Martin Sheen, Rob Lowe, Morgan Fairchild, Billy Baldwin, Bo Derek. When *The Final Days* had its screening, the response in the ballroom was as enthusiastic as it had been in the Map Room. Rob Lowe told a reporter afterward that President Clinton "upstaged us all and that's as it should be." Lowe added that both he and his tablemate Spacey were "amazed" at Clinton's comic timing. "I said to Kevin, 'Maybe we should call up our agents!'"

✳✳✳✳

The *Final Days* comedy video provides an exceptionally vivid example of the intersection of show business and the White House. Not only does it illustrate the degree to which presidents and entertainers occupy the same social milieu, it also suggests a shift in the presidential job description. As a baseline requirement of the position, a modern chief executive must now be able to present a version of himself that is as audience-friendly as the persona of an entertainment star. In addition to his more solemn duties, the president of the United States is expected to perform the functions of a professional showman.

With the *Final Days* video, the conflation of entertainment and politics, well under way before Bill Clinton, hit a plateau. No longer does a president stand apart on a remote civic pedestal, isolated from the hurly-burly; instead the powerful forces of the American celebrity circus have dragged him into the tent and asked him to put on a show. The position has always been demanding, but now there is an added demand: a president must know how to "fill the frame."

A number of factors have lured our First Citizens into the showbiz arena. Presidents themselves have actively cultivated relationships with performers. As early as 1918, Woodrow Wilson was rubbing shoulders with the superstars of silent film. Franklin Roosevelt summoned to the White House every marquee attraction from Shirley Temple to Orson Welles. John F. Kennedy held honorary membership in Frank Sinatra's Rat Pack and romanced some of the silver screen's most stunning beauties. Ronald Reagan, literally a show business president, maintained close ties to old-line Hollywood after he got to Washington. Bill Clinton took appreciation for movie royalty to unprecedented heights, crooning with Barbra Streisand, trading wisecracks with Whoopi Goldberg, hosting Tom Hanks at White House sleepovers. Even George W. Bush, a figure not known for his celebrity ties, has appeared alongside a range of entertainers.

For their part, performers have eagerly reciprocated the interest accorded them by the White House. In show business terms, the president of the United States is the ultimate name above the title. No matter how successful, mere actors can never match the stellar firepower of a sitting chief of state. Entertainers gain credibility, to say nothing of access and publicity, from their links to the world's most powerful person. Their egos are stroked. Their political views are taken seriously. Some serve as friends and trusted advisers. And at least briefly, they exit the realm of make-believe and perform on a stage where real-life history is made.

As entertainers have gravitated toward politics, so have politicians gravitated toward entertainment. Presidents in particular have co-opted the performance and publicity techniques of their showbiz counterparts. Like the elite names of Hollywood, modern presidents surround themselves with hair stylists, makeup artists, lighting technicians, set designers, location scouts, voice coaches, scriptwriters, producers, and directors. The White House spin machine operates like the studio publicity departments of yore, concocting a ceaselessly flattering image of the leading man in order to stoke audience approval. As a means of staying close to the public, presidents and their families willingly place themselves in every imaginable entertainment context: situation comedies, talk shows, awards ceremonies, *Christmas at the White House* TV specials. George W. Bush went so far as to emulate Tom Cruise in *Top Gun* for a photo opportunity aboard an aircraft carrier.

The mass media, taking a cue from presidential behavior, have helped redefine the White House as a Washington-based branch of the entertainment industry. The executive mansion and its denizens now supply endless fodder for comedians, writers, actors, and film directors, further eroding the separation of show business and state. Presidents and their families alternate between participating in these media depictions and feeling targeted by them.

For the body politic the union between presidents and entertainers serves as both a source of amusement and a cautionary tale. With a cast of characters drawn from the nation's two most exotic tribes, the spectacle cannot help but be compelling. At the same time, too much chumminess between the gods and goddesses of politics and showbiz has the potential to do the public a disservice.

Americans recognize only two branches of royalty: presidents and entertainers. *Celebrity-in-Chief* examines what happens when these aristocrats join forces.

Hollywood stars pose with Eleanor Roosevelt in the White House Blue Room, January 1940. (AP/Wide World Photos, reprinted by permission)

1
✴✴✴✴
Gilt by Association

HOW ENTERTAINERS ARE
GOOD FOR PRESIDENTS

O N JANUARY 30, 1940, the golden age of Hollywood slipped into perfect
alignment with the golden age of Franklin Delano Roosevelt. Like visiting
nobility from a faraway duchy, eighteen of Tinsel Town's brightest stars had journeyed east to pay their respects at the white-columned mansion at the opposite
end of the continent. The troupers came to Washington for more than social reasons; they had been invited to lead a nationwide birthday celebration for the
beloved thirty-second president of the United States.

At midday on this cold, gray January Friday, the actors made their way to the
White House for a welcome luncheon hosted by the first lady. The all-star cast of
performers represented the most glittering critical mass the White House had ever
attracted: nineteen-year-old Mickey Rooney, reigning king of the American box
office; Jimmy Cagney, who two years later won the Academy Award as Best Actor
(for *Yankee Doodle Dandy*, a film in which an FDR look-alike plays FDR); leading
lady Olivia de Havilland; heartthrob Tyrone Power; jungle siren Dorothy Lamour;
tough guy Edward G. Robinson; singing cowboy Gene Autry; even character actors like Edward Everett Horton and Elsa Lanchester, the bride of Frankenstein.

As the stars arrived, they gathered in the Blue Room to pose for a group portrait with First Lady Eleanor Roosevelt. Looking at the shot today, one is struck

by the amateur quality of the staging: all the women, plus a handful of the shorter men, sit uncomfortably on the floor on either side of Eleanor; the rest of the men stand in line behind them. To the immediate right of Mrs. Roosevelt, Dorothy Lamour has staked out the shot's most valuable piece of real estate; next to Lamour sits Edward G. Robinson. On the back row, Gene Autry in his western suit and kerchief cuts a vivid figure, as does angel-faced Rooney, two full heads shorter than Red Skelton.

The picture-taking over, Mrs. Roosevelt ushered her guests into the State Dining Room. The event was billed as an informal luncheon, but no luncheon invitation to the White House can be taken lightly, especially by first-time visitors from a place as insecure as Hollywood. The president and his wife were seated across from each other at a long oval table decorated with flowers. Flanking the host and hostess on either side sat eighteen stars of screen and stage, plus a sprinkling of spouses and miscellaneous guests.

As the meal proceeded the wheelchair-bound president circumnavigated the table, spending a few minutes with each of his visitors. When FDR got to Mickey Rooney, the topic turned to the actor's fictional alter ego, Andy Hardy. "The nation had adopted the Hardy family as its own ideal American family," Rooney wrote in his memoir, "and President Roosevelt had apparently done so, too."

FDR, an avid movie fan, offered his young guest some good-natured advice about his character's love life: "You'd better stick with that Polly Benedict."

Summoning up his best Andy Hardy, Rooney put on an earnest face. "Golly, I sure will, Mr. President."

Rooney was not the only joker at the table. At one point during the gathering comedian Red Skelton grabbed a glass out of Roosevelt's hand. "Careful what you drink, Mr. President," Skelton quipped. "I once got rolled in a joint like this." FDR roared with laughter.

Much as Roosevelt loved a party, at the end of lunch he excused himself to attend to affairs of state, specifically the writing of the birthday address he would deliver that evening to the nation. When the first lady asked her glamorous guests if they would like a tour of the White House, they eagerly accepted.

As Mrs. Roosevelt escorted the stars through the historic rooms, Tyrone Power stuck close behind Dorothy Lamour. "Every time Mrs. Roosevelt stopped to make a comment, he'd whisper some shockingly funny aside in my ear," Lamour recalled. "When I looked him in the eyes, his face always bore the most innocent expression, and I'd start to laugh. Mrs. Roosevelt must have thought I was a little daft."

According to a journalist who accompanied the tour, White House stenographers and secretaries "created a mild riot" when the parade came traipsing through the mansion's office quarters. "Presence of such almost mythical characters as Tyrone Power, Dorothy Lamour, Gene Autry, Olivia de Havilland, and others was too much for clerical and stenographic austerity," the reporter noted.

Their sightseeing completed, the celebrities returned to their hotels to grab a few hours' rest. That evening, at 6:00 P.M. sharp, they embarked on the main event: a social marathon of public appearances at venues around the city to raise funds for FDR's pet charity, the National Foundation for Infantile Paralysis. This was their gift—Hollywood's gift—to an esteemed president.

The entertainers followed a meticulously choreographed route through a succession of hotel ballrooms and theaters. Accompanied by flying wedges of policemen, they pushed their way from one event to the next. Maneuvering this precious cargo through the starstruck city proved to be a challenge of military proportions. As the *New York Times* reported, "Ermine-mantled queens of the film capital ran down alleys, dodged through hotel kitchens and rode freight elevators to pant their greetings to the fans."

All over Washington the parties were jammed. In the ballroom of the Mayflower Hotel, fifteen hundred couples made what the *Times* called "a gallant effort at dancing." Behind heavy guard ropes in the five-hundred-foot lobby another thousand fans strained for a glimpse of the celebrities. A cluster of stars would pop up at one hotel, work the room for a frenzied ten minutes, then scurry off to the next engagement. "Hello, good-bye, I'm in a hurry," Pat O'Brien told the Mayflower audience. "I'm in a hurry, hurry, hurry. I'm going. I'm coming. Hello, good-bye, where do we go from here?"

A rotating slate of performers accompanied the indefatigable Eleanor Roosevelt, who led them through the city like a human pace car. At every stop the cheers for the president's wife matched those for the movie stars. Washington photographers, accustomed to the drab doings of government bureaucrats, found themselves swept up in the glamour of Hollywood. How could they resist a shot of Mrs. R exchanging grins with Jimmy Cagney? Or Dorothy Lamour dancing with Franklin Delano Roosevelt Jr.?

The undisputed superstar of the 1940 birthday ball was Mickey Rooney. "Clowning, mugging, kissing, lap-sitting and otherwise exhibiting his screen personality, Rooney easily stole the Washington show," wrote *Life* magazine. A three-photo spread in the magazine shows Mickey making merry with a series of D.C. dowagers. First he smooches a portly matron from Baltimore. Then he locks lips with the wife of the secretary of the navy. In the final, and largest, shot, Mickey has leapt into the lap of stunned socialite Mrs. Jock Hay Whitney. "It was, after all, a birthday party," Rooney said. "So I did my best to enjoy myself and bring all the others along with me on the joy ride."

At the end of the evening the visitors were rewarded with a return invitation to the White House, this time to watch FDR give his birthday radio address. For Rooney other plans interfered. At the Mayflower Hotel a "sleek, sophisticated brunette in a long silver gown" caught the young star's eye. The two exchanged meaningful glances across the ballroom, then met in the middle of the dance floor. Instead of returning to the White House, Mickey Rooney did what any nineteen-year-old Hollywood prince would do: he got laid.

✹✹✹✹

By 1940 FDR's birthday observance had become a fixed point on the national compass, the reliable moment of the year when the nation's two dominant branches of celebrity intertwined for twenty-four hours of mutual admiration. Unlike modern interactions between performers and presidents, which revolve primarily around campaign fund-raising, the Roosevelt birthday celebrations favored a loftier goal: helping sick children. Screen idols could bask in the glow of a popular president while simultaneously doing their bit for charity.

The first birthday ball took place in 1934, with Will Rogers leading a roster of relatively low-wattage acts at Washington's Shoreham Hotel. The idea caught the public's fancy, and within a few years the party had blossomed into an all-night, all-city blowout that raised millions of dollars for the cause. Over the next decade of birthday ball celebrations, as the star power grew ever brighter, a tradition took shape: sometime around FDR's real birthdate of January 31, Washington, D.C., would supplant Hollywood and New York as the entertainment capital of America. A brigade of top-name performers would come to town and sprinkle their stardust on what *Daily Variety* called the "national capital yokels." Not to be outdone, Los Angeles and New York threw their own celebrity-studded fetes, as did scores of other cities across the country. At their height, more than eight thousand such parties were held around the United States.

But Washington was the epicenter, and few showbiz aristocrats could resist the invitation to be part of the social bull's-eye. In 1936 Ginger Rogers became the first big glamour star to headline at Washington's birthday balls. A staunch Republican, Rogers had to be pressured by her studio into making the trip east. As her traveling companion she took along her mother, the even more conservative Lela Rogers, who for decades loomed as the doyenne of right-wing Hollywood.

Upon their arrival at Union Station, the Rogers women hit the ground running. Hustled to the Mayflower Hotel, Ginger had only an hour to freshen up before she was due at the White House, where she and her mother had been invited to sit in on President Roosevelt's radio broadcast from the Oval Office. They took their chairs next to Secretary of Labor Frances Perkins, another of the fifteen or so guests in the room. As technicians fiddled with the broadcast equipment around the president's desk, one of the radio men told FDR his speech would begin in ten minutes. Meanwhile, music was being piped into the Oval Office from hotel ballrooms around the nation where early birthday celebrations had already begun.

The music gave FDR an idea. He summoned an aide and whispered something in his ear. Ginger saw them looking at her. The aide then approached Ginger and said, "The president would like you to dance for him."

"But where would I dance?" the incredulous star asked, surveying what she described as the room's "two-inch sink-your-heels-into-it type carpet." The aide pointed toward a modest stretch of marble floor fronting a set of French doors.

Against her better judgment, Ginger Rogers made her way to the impromptu stage, which she realized at once was dangerously slick. Ginger sketched the scene in her autobiography:

> I started to move in a graceful manner. Suddenly, the announcer broke in, saying, "And now we come to you from San Francisco." The slow waltz was immediately replaced by "Running Wild" at a breakneck speed. The rhythm truly was wild, and I couldn't possibly keep up with it. I thought to myself, "If this is dancing, I don't know how to spell it."
>
> Striving to find a middle ground of rhythm, I came dangerously close to the two-inch rug facing me. In whirling, I lost my balance and though I didn't fall, the shoulder strap which held the heavy orchids on my left shoulder fell, dragging the front of the dress down with it. I grabbed the dress as fast as I could, to keep from standing half-naked in front of my audience. But I was not quick enough. Holding my corsage up, I curtsied and made straight for my chair. I was embarrassed beyond words. The applause from the mini-audience in the Oval Office made me even more embarrassed.

Ginger took particular notice of the president's subdued response: "six noiseless pats." Seconds later, FDR got his cue from the radio men and began to speak, giving Ginger a chance to compose herself. At the end of the broadcast, after the other guests had streamed out, a smiling President Roosevelt beckoned to his Hollywood visitor. "I realize asking you to dance on the spur of the moment was an imposition," he told her. "And you did it very graciously."

As he spoke, Roosevelt scribbled an inscription on the typewritten radio speech he had just delivered and handed the document to Miss Rogers: "This is for you." Ginger later learned that she had just been gifted with one of the few original texts ever released from FDR's personal files, a "precious memento of a visit to Washington that I didn't want to accept and a dance that I didn't want to do."

Years later, FDR's secretary, Grace Tully, was still fuming over this breach of protocol, for it was her job to see that the originals got saved for the archives. "The Boss was given something of a scolding later for his casual surrender of a document which might have historic value," she wrote. "When Miss Rogers later appeared as one of the anti-Roosevelt film politicians he was chided further." (Tully took an equally dim view of Ginger's impromptu performance: "I had seen Miss Rogers dance in the movies with Fred Astaire and I thought she was excellent. This night, however, she seemed as if she had lead in her shoes.")

A year after Ginger Rogers's visit to Washington, Jean Harlow and Robert Taylor headlined the capital city's 1937 birthday celebration. Harlow, Taylor, and three lesser-known Hollywood actors—Mitzi Green, Marsha Hunt, and John Trent—ate lunch at the White House with the first lady, met the president in his study (according to one eyewitness, Harlow was "terrified"), and watched him film a spot for the newsreel photographers. *Daily Variety* recounted the moment:

> He looked up when it was completed and said "Okay?"
> "Okay," was the response.
> "One take Frankie, eh?" said a girl's voice.
> "Who said that?" the president asked and laughed. Marsha Hunt, youngest Hollywooder in the room, admitted with some trepidation it was she. He laughed again and assured her he was highly flattered.

At the evening balls Jean Harlow was joined onstage by Eleanor Roosevelt. Transfixed by the incongruity of the pairing, photographers could scarcely shoot fast enough. Harlow was giddy, telling partyers at the Wardman Park Hotel that visiting Washington was "the highlight of my whole life." Six months later, Jean Harlow was dead of uremic poisoning at age twenty-six.

Each year's birthday balls tended to feature what in show business argot is called a "breakout performer." In 1938 actress Janet Gaynor took the honors when FDR pronounced her "cute as a button" and made sure she sat next to him at lunch. Twenty-year-old starlet Lana Turner was the media darling of 1941, eroticizing a city that desperately needed it. Everywhere Lana went in Washington, males of all ages and stations in life—from delinquent boys to the president of the United States—found themselves irresistibly drawn.

At one hotel an eleven-year-old named Tony Batista broke through police lines in an attempt to make physical contact with Miss Turner. Though officers nabbed him before he reached his target, the child pleaded so convincingly they took him to meet the actress. After she graciously shook his hand, Tony asked if he could touch her a second time. "Her escorts told him one touch was enough," reported the *Washington Post*.

Earlier that day at the White House, all the stars were invited to file past the wheelchair-bound president for an individual greeting. When Lana reached him, FDR put out his hand and said, "You are Miss Lana Turner." Turner described the meeting in her memoir:

> What made me do it, I don't know, but I pulled back my coat so that he could see the lovely dress I was wearing.
>
> "My," he said, "you are a beautiful young woman."
>
> "Thank you, Mr. President."
>
> "I understand you are all going dancing."
>
> "I believe so, sir."
>
> As he smiled, his eyes twinkled at me. Then he said, "Oh, how I wish I could go with you."

The confusion of the evening led to press reports that Lana Turner had shoved a child out of camera range during a photo opportunity. Eleanor Roosevelt, in her newspaper column "My Day," sprang to Lana's defense: "I remember that particular meeting and picture-taking quite well. There were crowds all around us, the cameramen were telling us what to do every minute, and I am rather surprised that we did not actually knock each other down." Mrs. Roosevelt went on to tut-tut those who would criticize: "The movie stars who came on for the party did so to help the cause of infantile paralysis and I do not think they should receive unfavorable criticism."

The following year, 1942, featured a return to the White House by Mickey Rooney, this time accompanied by his bride of several weeks, Ava Gardner. Gardner could not believe the sudden transformation in her life. "Six months ago I was in Wilson, North Carolina, worrying about what sort of secretarial job I might get, and here I am in the White House being introduced to the President of the United States and the First Lady." Jimmy Stewart, Robert Montgomery, and Douglas Fairbanks Jr. showed up in uniform that year, and pinup girls Betty Grable and Dorothy Lamour lent the requisite glamour. A page-one photo in the *Washington Post* shows Lamour posing with a sour-faced little boy, a four-year-old poster child from New York's Hell's Kitchen named Gerry King. When Lamour asked the boy for a kiss, he demurred, saying, "I don't want that red stuff on me." When the star kissed him anyway, Gerry punched her in the nose.

Young actors had always been part of the birthday ball events in Washington; in 1943 the youth contingent was represented by Roddy McDowall and Bonita Granville, whose mothers accompanied them to the Roosevelt luncheon. (Granville, the teenage star of Nancy Drew mystery films, returned to Washington in the 1980s as the producer of Ronald Reagan's Kennedy Center Honors galas.) At the cake-cutting ceremony that evening, the first lady indulged in a mock competition with ventriloquist's puppet Charlie McCarthy over who got to blow out the birthday candles; Eleanor prevailed.

Franklin Roosevelt did not attend the final birthday ball luncheon of his presidency, held three months before his death in 1945. Because he was traveling on a secret wartime mission the president missed meeting his favorite movie star of all, Myrna Loy. He never got another chance.

At the time she accepted her invitation to Washington, Loy did not realize Roosevelt would be away. She was so excited about meeting her "hero" that her psychiatrist warned the actress not to expect perfection. Loy was as fluttery as a freshman at her first prom. "I'm going down to the White House to meet the president," she told her dressmaker, "and I want something that will really knock him out."

Myrna Loy showed up for the luncheon in a dramatic ensemble of black dress and white hat. When she reached the mansion she searched in vain for the president, finding only Mrs. Roosevelt. Loy remembered the moment in her memoir: "She looked at this glamour girl all done up and said, 'Oh, my dear, my husband is going to be so distressed!' And I thought, Well, you're something! I fell in love with her then and there."

Another visitor that year was sultry movie star Veronica Lake, who shared a lunch table with Eleanor Roosevelt, Harry Truman, and Truman's daughter,

Margaret. At the end of the meal Veronica leaned over to the first lady. "You know what I'd love, Mrs. Roosevelt?" Lake asked.

"No. What is it?"

"A spoon. A spoon from the White House."

Eleanor Roosevelt laughed, discreetly slipped Veronica Lake a spoon from the table, and excused herself to mingle with her other guests. As Lake fell into conversation with the Trumans, the outspoken vice president complained about the bum rap he'd been getting from the press. "I agreed, of course," the actress recalled, "but wanted to say that perhaps if Margaret and Bess dressed a little better, the press might be more kind. I've never seen any mother and daughter dressed in such bad taste."

For Hollywood-obsessed Miss Truman, mixing with Veronica Lake and the other stars in the room—Joe E. Brown, Linda Darnell, Danny Kaye, Gene Kelly, Alan Ladd, and Jane Wyman—constituted a dream come true. "It was my first close-up look at movie stars," Margaret said. "As one of America's leading movie fans from the age of four, I really enjoyed it."

It was another Margaret—Margaret O'Brien—who came in for heightened attention at the 1945 birthday celebrations. The eight-year-old actress had arrived in Washington a few days early to kick off the annual infantile paralysis campaign with a radio broadcast from the White House. "Our fathers and mothers can protect us from most bad things," Margaret declaimed, in a speech she had spent the whole day memorizing, "but parents can't protect us from infantile paralysis." Watching the broadcast, mesmerized, were Eleanor Roosevelt and her grandchildren.

Everywhere she went Miss O'Brien captivated her audiences. At the Mayflower Hotel banquet, the tiny star was lifted to the tabletop to recite "The Story of the Nativity." Newspapers remarked upon the "ethereal quality" of the performance. Margaret O'Brien, wrote one critic, "stole the show lock, stock, and both barrels."

Veronica Lake, observing the diminutive star at the White House luncheon, came to the conclusion that "Mrs. Roosevelt wanted to adopt her." Even a hard-bitten aide to the president, former newspaperman William Hassett, was smitten. Of the Hollywood visitors, Hassett noted in his diary: "On the whole a not too glamorous bunch at close range, nor camera-shy either—except little Margaret O'Brien."

After FDR's death, the new president, Harry Truman, extended the tradition one last year before retiring it into memory. Margaret O'Brien came back to town, along with William Bendix, Eddie Bracken, Charles Coburn, Paul Henreid, Van

Johnson, Dorothy Kilgallen, Angela Lansbury, Cesar Romero, Zachary Scott, and Alexis Smith. In its final incarnation, the 1946 President's Birthday Ball, minus the key ingredient of Franklin Roosevelt, fell apart. A story in *Weekly Variety* accurately predicted the tradition's demise: "With film and radio names doing a burn whose smoke could be detected all the way from New York to Hollywood—and particularly in Washington—on the treatment they received at the President's Birthday Ball . . . event may well turn out to have been the last of the annual shindigs."

What started off a respectful posthumous celebration degenerated into a behind-the-scenes pissing match, first between the movie stars and the radio stars and then among the movie stars themselves. The radio performers complained, justifiably, that they had been shut out of the annual picture-taking session at the White House. According to *Variety*, the "squawk of the pixites" was that Metro-Goldwyn-Mayer's Van Johnson and Margaret O'Brien drew more than their share of the limelight: "Papers carried stories and pix showing bobby-soxers swooning and fainting over Johnson" and "the little O'Brien gal" in rapt conversation with Harry Truman. At the evening's climactic cake-cutting ceremony, "the big picture was of Johnson holding Margaret O'Brien up to receive the first piece of cake. The other names were just extras in the scene." On this note of show business backbiting the birthday balls came to an inglorious end.

✳ ✳ ✳ ✳

The FDR birthday celebrations represent the first sustained effort by a president to forge a direct alliance with stars of the entertainment world. Previous occupants of the Oval Office had curried favor with Hollywood's studio bosses, as did Roosevelt himself. But this was something different: a deliberate, personal courting of the faces that lit up the nation's movie screens. In large part the birthday balls came about because of Roosevelt's status as a devoted fan of American pop culture, films in particular. Celebrating his birthday with the top stars of the day seemed appropriate to FDR because he understood the ways in which his job intersected with theirs. Without embarrassment, he recognized himself as a member of their firmament.

FDR, like only three other presidents in history—Kennedy, Reagan, and Clinton—spoke fluently the language of show business, and he had the natural temperament to get along with performers on a personal basis. Rosalind Russell, a birthday luncheon guest in 1942, recalled Roosevelt's remarkable ability to attend to his visitors individually. "To each person, he said something warm—'I'll see you later, don't go too far from me'—and as you left him, he followed you with his eyes until you were out of his vision. The great leonine head was the head of his photographs, but his charm was never caught by any camera." Tallulah Bankhead believed show people liked Roosevelt "for his eloquence, for his gifts as a phrase-maker, for his theatrics, for his ability to touch their hearts as well as their minds."

Yet for all his enthusiasm about actors, FDR approached the movie star visits with a sense of restraint which by today's standards seems quaint. Though perfectly willing to link the institution of the presidency with Hollywood for a good cause, he strictly limited his physical interaction with the out-of-town visitors. Few photos exist of Roosevelt with his celebrity guests, and he never appeared at a single birthday ball party. On only a handful of occasions did the president actually attend the White House luncheon with the stars.

Instead, the duties of dealing with the troupers from Hollywood fell to Eleanor. It is she who turns up smiling in the photographs, she who ran the gauntlet of public appearances, she who guided the notable guests through the presidential mansion. Perhaps FDR considered the actors to be a feminine responsibility; perhaps he did not want to diminish his office by appearing too chummy with them. Or perhaps, with world wars and a major depression to contend with, he simply lacked the opportunity to mingle.

Franklin Roosevelt was not the first president to mix with show business personalities, or to recognize their potency. Abraham Lincoln is said to have left a cabinet meeting in order to personally greet Tom Thumb and his bride, Lavinia, two superstars of the day. "The usual explanation is that Lincoln was looking for comic relief in the midst of the awful pressures of the Civil War," wrote Leo Braudy in his insightful study of fame, *The Frenzy of Renown*. "But he was also entertaining American celebrities whose faces and names were beginning to become at least as recognizable as his own."

Comedy actress Marie Dressler paid a social call on President Theodore Roosevelt during his years in the White House. Dressler, who in the early 1930s became an improbable box office favorite and Academy Award winner, considered TR "the most vigorous and magnetic" personality she had ever encountered. After introducing himself to Dressler, Roosevelt asked, "Now that we meet, what do you think of me?" "I think you have the strongest-looking neck I ever saw!" Dressler replied, to the president's amusement.

In April 1918 Woodrow Wilson welcomed to the White House four of the most popular entertainers of the day: Mary Pickford, Douglas Fairbanks, Charles Chaplin, and Marie Dressler. The quartet had been invited to Washington to launch a nationwide drive to sell war bonds; their schedule included a courtesy call on the chief executive. The gregarious Dressler mortified Pickford by telling President Wilson an off-color story. "As she moved to the denouement," Pickford recalled, "I kept wishing the parquet floor of the Blue Room would open up and swallow me. I could feel myself blushing all over." The president, according to Pickford, "neither smiled nor made a comment."

Whatever he thought of these vivacious visitors, the sober-minded Wilson could scarcely have missed the spell they cast on the nation's capital. Their appearance on the *Ellipse* to autograph war bond subscriptions caused a near riot as thousands of fans swamped the actors with pledge forms. According to the *Washington Post*, "Chaplin and Fairbanks mounted on the tops of trucks and kept the crowd shouting with merriment with many queer antics and characteristic remarks." Among the dignitaries the celebrity quartet encountered in Washington was a young, bespectacled assistant secretary of the navy named Franklin Roosevelt. Perched with the entertainers on a reviewing stand, Roosevelt accidentally took a tumble and fell through the railing, bringing Dressler down with him. It was a story FDR would dine out on for the rest of his life.

For most of the 1920s, even as radio and motion pictures revolutionized the delivery of entertainment to American audiences, presidents kept their distance from show folk. A few notable exceptions stand out. Warren Harding met the Gish sisters in 1922; he surprised Lillian by welcoming her with outstretched arms and a Hollywood greeting: "Darling!" Pickford and Fairbanks returned to the White House for lunch with President Coolidge in 1928, and radio stars Freeman F. Gosden and Charles J. Correll, better known as *Amos 'n' Andy*, called on Herbert Hoover two years later.

But it was Franklin Roosevelt who first perceived the power of association waiting to be harnessed in Hollywood stars. FDR was prescient enough to recognize that in a democratic society, elected officials had much to gain by embracing the people's choice. Millions of moviegoers—the same people who put Roosevelt in the White House—had ratified the popularity of the actors and actresses invited to the birthday balls. Combining forces with the big names of the screen could only enhance a politician's standing.

The Roosevelts made a concerted effort to align themselves with Shirley Temple, arguably the most adored entertainer of the 1930s. Eleanor Roosevelt first met the child star during a trip to Los Angeles in the spring of 1937. Mrs. Roosevelt dropped by the set of *Little Miss Broadway*, where the cast and crew broke from filming to greet the first lady in a receiving line. Shirley's leading man in the picture, Jimmy Durante, surprised Eleanor by asking her to dance. Ever the good sport, the gangly Mrs. Roosevelt played along, giggling at her own incompetence as she towered over Durante.

At the first lady's request Shirley took the distinguished visitor on a private tour of her on-set schoolroom. "Which do you like better," Mrs. Roosevelt asked, "school or making pictures?"

"I like them both," replied the child star. "But I guess I like geography best." Not a surprising choice—Shirley Temple went on to serve three presidents as a diplomat.

Shirley presented the first lady with a souvenir police badge and asked if she would sign her autograph book. As Mrs. Roosevelt scribbled, she told Shirley she would leave space for her husband to add his name.

"Do you like the president?" Mrs. Roosevelt asked.

Shirley, echoing a sentiment shared by millions of her compatriots, said she liked him "because he starts all his radio talks with 'My friends.'"

Before leaving, Eleanor Roosevelt invited Shirley to Washington. A year later the actress accepted. This time she got to meet the president—and the president got to meet her. Franklin Roosevelt and Shirley Temple talked about sailing ships and fishing. FDR asked why she wasn't smiling. "I thought you were famous for your smile." Shirley showed him why: she had just lost a tooth.

Shirley Temple had brought along her autograph book, and in the empty space left by his wife, Franklin Roosevelt added his message: "For Shirley, from her old friend."

Emerging from the meeting, the child star and her parents overheard someone remark that their visit had cut into a scheduled appointment between FDR and the secretary of the Treasury. Shirley protested: "But what we were talking about was important."

Shirley Temple's Roosevelt tour resumed two weeks later when the Temple family paid a call at Val-Kill, Eleanor Roosevelt's cottage at Hyde Park. In her newspaper column the first lady referred to the occasion as a "red-letter day" for herself and the Roosevelt grandchildren. Although journalists were eager to document this historic celebrity summit, newsreel photographers from Fox, Shirley's home studio, had been granted exclusive access. Mrs. Roosevelt recounted the scene: "I was amused when we walked out together for the first picture to have her tell me just what to do. 'We should walk,' she said, 'from far back and wave at the camera as we come out.' When I did not realize the camera was following us, she said, 'They are still taking us,' and we turned for a final wave together."

Ten-year-old Shirley Temple was teaching the president's wife the tricks of the trade.

✳✳✳✳

After Franklin D. Roosevelt, the next president to ally himself with American pop culture was John F. Kennedy, the son of a Hollywood film mogul. Like his father, Jack Kennedy developed an early appreciation of the uses of celebrity. In the late 1940s, visiting a friend who worked for actor Gary Cooper, JFK became fascinated by the connection between movie stars and their audiences. Kennedy and the friend, Chuck Spalding, would talk for hours about the popularity of various celebrities. "Jack was beginning to notice the parallels between people out there, like personalities drawing crowds," Spalding recalled. "Why did Cooper draw a crowd? And the other people out there: Spencer Tracy and Clark Gable and others who were floating through that world." Kennedy wondered about his own star quality. "He was always interested in seeing whether he had it—the magnetism—or didn't have it," Spalding said.

JFK's affinity for show business had much to do with his affinity for its female practitioners. But beyond romantic opportunities Kennedy, like Roosevelt, genuinely enjoyed the company of entertainers. This endeared the performing community to him, not just politically but emotionally as well. Actress June Havoc, emerging from a 1961 White House meeting with the president, excitedly told reporters that Kennedy's "vernacular is very theatrical. He talked show folk talk." It was an observation many other performers would repeat.

JFK's lifelong exposure to the movie industry and innate curiosity about show business made him unusually comfortable in the presence of entertainers. Other presidents, less inclined toward showmanship, have had to strain to achieve what came naturally to Jack Kennedy. Richard Nixon, the only president to spend his childhood in close proximity to the film studios of Southern California, seemed singularly ill at ease in the presence of performing artists. But Nixon saw in entertainers the next best thing to natural charisma: stardust by association. To Nixon, actors, comedians, and musicians could be deployed as a magic bullet against his own deficit of glamour.

Consider two remarkable gatherings President Nixon orchestrated less than a year apart at Casa Pacifica, his beachfront home in San Clemente, California. On August 27, 1972, Richard and Patricia Nixon invited four hundred entertainers of varying pedigrees to a late-afternoon outdoor "celebrity reception."

Most had publicly expressed their preference for the president's reelection, and the timing of the event was designed to shore up this support before election season kicked into high gear. But the party was neither a fund-raiser nor a media event. No contributions were solicited, and no news cameras recorded the scene. Rather, the celebrity reception was Richard Nixon's conception of a magical evening in lotus land. The ruler of the realm proudly assumed the lead role, ably supported by a brilliant cast of dramatis personae. No other president has ever thrown a party quite like it.

The guest list tilted toward the reliable Republican stars of yesteryear—June Allyson, Susan Hayward, Vic Damone, Connie Francis. From a higher plane of celebrity came perennials like Frank Sinatra, Jack Benny, and Charlton Heston. Governor Ronald Reagan was there with his wife Nancy, as were Freeman Gosden, who thirty years earlier had called on Herbert Hoover at the White House, and Jill St. John, on the arm of National Security Adviser Henry Kissinger. St. John confessed to reporters that after three years Kissinger had finally persuaded her to vote for Nixon. "And you guys thought I was just wasting my time out here," Kissinger deadpanned.

A handful of other younger celebrities with less predictably Republican inclinations mingled among the poolside talent: George Hamilton, who had dated the daughter of Democratic President Lyndon Johnson; Mary Tyler Moore, leaning toward Nixon after closely considering George McGovern; and red-hot film director Peter Bogdanovich, who told reporters, "I was invited to come and I thought it would be rude not to."

As in all Nixon social appearances, the reception unfolded with kabuki-like precision. Guests arrived at the valet parking stop to the bright sounds of a mariachi band. They then passed into a reception line, posed for a photograph with the Nixons in front of a fireplace, and were ushered to the poolside party area outside. Even visitors as distinguished as these were not permitted to enter the house.

Once everyone had convened, Nixon made his way to the cabana and greeted his guests with brief words of welcome. An advisory memo had preordained the tone: "Your remarks will be informal and casual . . . rather than substantive." The memo urged Nixon "not to hit the theme of how in standing up for a candidate they display courage by risking the alienation of part of their audience." White House speechwriters supplied the president with a number of suggested lines:

"It's not even sunset—and yet the stars are out already."

"If one were to make a list of the hundred Americans whose names and faces
are best known to the people of the world—that list could virtually begin
and end on this terrace."

"This looks like one of the biggest clusters of stars since the Milky Way—but
don't worry, we'll have something for you besides milk."

History does not record if any of these gems actually got uttered, but Nixon
took the occasion to pat himself on the back for having attracted such august
company. "If I ever told my old man I'd one day be talking to Jack Benny," the
president declared, "he'd have said I was crazy." Nixon gave his guests what they
wanted to hear. "I like my movies made in Hollywood, made in America,"
Nixon said, singling out Charlton Heston "and all those who are interested in
seeing that this great industry stays alive and remains strong."

If the objective of the first Casa Pacifica party was to reinforce Nixon's standing in the show business community and thus ensure support in the coming
election, a second reception nine months later enlisted the magic of Hollywood
to bedazzle a player on the international stage. As the finale to the 1973 Soviet-
American summit conference, President Nixon invited Leonid Brezhnev to a
"celebrity fiesta" at the Western White House. This time, some 175 famous Californians turned out, among them many who had attended the previous party,
including the Reagans, Frank Sinatra, and Red Skelton.

Meeting the Soviet secretary-general in the receiving line, Skelton could not
resist a quip. "Are you a card-carrying Communist?"

"Yes," said Brezhnev, laughing at the translation.

Pressed into service for this auspicious episode in East-West relations was a
group of actors associated with movie and TV westerns, including Clint Eastwood, Glenn Ford, Gene Autry, and Chuck Connors.

In his welcome Nixon told the guests that Brezhnev had expressed a fondness
for westerns, a genre to which the president himself was partial. "We have several
western movie stars here that you will recognize," Nixon said to Brezhnev. "But
because this is a house of peace every one of them has checked his holster belt
with the pistols at the door before he came in."

It was Connors, ex-professional baseball player and star of the television show
The Rifleman, who most favorably impressed the guest of honor. When Connors
reached Brezhnev in the receiving line, the interpreter reported that the Soviet
leader was a *Rifleman* fan. The two men instantly hit it off; a guest at the party,
Mrs. Burl Ives, described their conversation as being "so into the moment."

The next morning Connors returned to Casa Pacifica to see off his new best friend, Leonid Brezhnev. This time the star came bearing gifts: a cowboy hat and a pair of matching Colt .45 revolvers from the TV series *Branded*, presented "on behalf of everybody who ever made a western." Brezhnev, Connors remembered, "nearly went off the floor, he was so excited."

As photographers snapped away, the TV cowboy showed Brezhnev how to twirl the guns. Connors pretended to fire at him, and Brezhnev played dead. "Everybody falls (when shot) but everybody is alive," Brezhnev observed through his interpreter. Somewhere amid the horseplay, Brezhnev invited Connors to the USSR to make a movie, an invitation Connors accepted later that year.

When it came time for the Soviet president to depart, Nixon spoke his public farewell, and Brezhnev reciprocated with remarks of his own. Then, spotting Connors in the crowd, Brezhnev rushed over, threw his arms around him and gave him a bear hug. Connors returned the embrace and lifted Brezhnev off his feet. A wire service photographer captured the moment in a shot that hit hundreds of front pages all over the world.

Social critic John Strausbaugh found the camaraderie between Connors and Brezhnev "almost unseemly." Strausbaugh, author of *Alone with the President*, a photographic compilation of presidents with celebrities, detected deeper political meaning in the exchange: "The image of Connors arming Brezhnev with six-guns and teaching him the quick draw captures a bizarrely symbolic gesture of Cold War codependence, complete with Brezhnev's acquiescing to wearing the black hat."

Nixon seemed pleased by having engineered the Connors-Brezhnev shotgun diplomacy, and why not? Another celebrity had come through for the president, making a human connection that Nixon could not himself make.

❋ ❋ ❋ ❋

Presidents turn to different types of entertainers for different kinds of image compensation. One of the least likely partnerships in the history of American popular culture developed between Jimmy Carter with John Wayne, an alliance that kicked off the Carter presidency in 1977. Carter, a man not known for his interest in show business personalities, approached the relationship as a diplomatic challenge. John Wayne was, in a sense, a leader with his own constituency, a constituency Carter largely lacked. Wayne had campaigned against the Georgia governor, appearing with Gerald Ford on the campaign trail as he had previously appeared for Wendell Willkie, Thomas Dewey, Dwight Eisenhower, Richard Nixon, Barry Goldwater, and Ronald Reagan.

Soon after the election, Carter made a preemptive strike, inviting a surprised John Wayne to participate in the Carter inaugural gala. Impressed by the ballsiness of the offer, Wayne accepted the olive branch and flew to Washington to join a lineup of Democratic entertainers at the Kennedy Center extravaganza that took place the night before Carter's swearing in. Wayne left no doubt where he stood: he told the television audience he had come to the capital "to watch a common man take on uncommon responsibilities that he has won fair and square." Wayne continued: "I'm considered a member of the opposition, the loyal opposition. Accent on the 'loyal.' I'd have it no other way."

At a postgala reception for participating performers, the guests included some of the country's best-known show business liberals: Paul Newman, Shirley MacLaine, Bette Davis, and Lauren Bacall. But none of these supporters affected the president-elect the way John Wayne did. When Wayne entered the room, Carter broke out of the receiving line and strode over to greet him. "I've always been a fan of yours," Carter gushed, shaking the star's massive hand.

"It's a pleasure to meet you, Mr. President-elect," replied Wayne. "I guess you know I didn't vote for you—but don't forget, you're the president of all of us now."

In making an early and public peace with Wayne, Carter reaped a number of benefits. To a class of Americans who regarded Carter with suspicion, Wayne signaled his approval. Garry Wills, in the book *John Wayne's America*, makes the point that Wayne did not just hold political opinions, he embodied "a politics": "It was a politics of large meanings, not of little policies—a politics of gender (masculine), ideology (patriotism), character (self-reliance), and responsibility." By associating himself with the human icon who embodied these ideals, Carter gained stature, especially among those who, like Wayne, had not voted for him.

This inaugural goodwill served Carter well during the subsequent debate over the Panama Canal treaties. Most conservatives were harshly critical of Carter's position, branding the long-scheduled return of the canal a "giveaway." Among the most outspoken critics was Ronald Reagan, whose opposition to the proposal had become an article of faith in the 1976 Republican primaries. John Wayne, a lifelong aficionado of Latin America, wrote Reagan an angry letter: "I'll show you point by goddamn point in the treaty where you are misinforming people." Wayne did not take his endorsement of the Panama Canal treaties lightly, spending long hours studying the issue and drafting a seven-page position paper that he mailed to every member of Congress. It was, in the words of Wayne's wife, Pilar, "Duke's last political battle."

In April 1978, Carter invited Wayne to Washington for the ratification ceremonies, but by then the actor was too sick with cancer to attend. "You have my deep appreciation for your contribution to the successful conclusion of the Panama Canal Treaties," Carter wrote Wayne two months later. According to Pilar Wayne, President Carter called on her husband in the hospital near the end of his life; Carter was on the list of the actor's approved visitors. After Wayne died in June 1979, Jimmy Carter, in one of the last official acts of his presidency, presented him posthumously with the Medal of Freedom.

Image compensation between presidents and entertainers morphed from the political to the personal with George Herbert Walker Bush, forty-first president of the United States. As a counterpoint to an impossibly patrician upbringing, Bush undertook to wrap himself in the flag of country music. That Bush genuinely liked the music and its performers is not in doubt. But no president before or since has gone to such lengths to associate himself with a genre of show business for the purpose of political image building.

"If you ask Barbara," Bush liked to say, "she'll tell you that my favorite kind of music is a two-way tie between country and western." Bush campaigned with Nashville stars like Loretta Lynn, performed a Jimmy Dean imitation on Dean's Nashville Network TV show, and made a high-profile pilgrimage to the regional country music capital of Branson, Missouri. Visiting Branson, the president asserted, was "a dream come true."

Writing in *Country America* magazine, Bush expounded on his appreciation for the country-western genre; the essay later resurfaced as an op-ed column in the *Washington Post*. "Country music hits all the right chords," Bush wrote, "like caring for your family, remembering the good times and keeping faith in God." In justifying his preference for country music, Bush could not be accused of overanalysis: "So many country songs have that upbeat, optimistic sound to them, you can't help but tap your toes and hum along. When there's good country music playing, it's like a good game of horseshoes—I can't help but have fun and loosen up!"

President Bush's fascination with heartland music reached its apotheosis with a 1991 appearance at the Country Music Association awards, televised live from the Grand Ole Opry in Nashville. "What a shot in the arm for country music!" exclaimed mistress of ceremonies Reba McEntire as the show commenced, and throughout the evening George and Barbara Bush figured prominently in the camera shots. For the program's climax McEntire invited her "good buddy" George Bush to join her on the Opry stage. Here the president paid his by now familiar tribute to country music: "When I want to feel a surge of patriotism or turn nostalgic or even when I need a little free advice about Saddam Hussein I turn to country music." The audience of Nashville insiders required no translation: Bush was referring to Hank Williams Jr.'s "Don't Give Us a Reason," a song whose lyrics took direct aim at the Iraqi leader: "You can take that poison gas and stick it in your sassafras . . . "

Most of the country music establishment eagerly embraced George Bush, as they later supported his son. But not everyone jumped aboard the bandwagon. "Do these people ever actually listen to our songs?" lamented singer-songwriter Rodney Crowell. "Has this American art form fallen so low in self-esteem that we would just turn our award ceremony into a campaign event for a guy who doesn't even talk about any of our problems?"

Because it carried so little risk, Bush's public attachment to country music most likely accomplished its objective. "America loves country music because country music really loves America," the president told the audience at the award show, and he repeated the tautology at a campaign rally in Branson. In country-western music Bush discovered the performing arts equivalent of the flag factories he prominently visited in his 1988 run for the presidency. Overwhelmingly, the big names of Nashville did not mind being co-opted.

George Bush used entertainers to offset a second perceived deficiency as well. As Reagan's vice president, he had been depicted as a weakling—a famous 1987 *Newsweek* cover showed a photo of Bush over the caption "Fighting the Wimp Factor." As a countermeasure he recruited into his circle a formidable trio of Hollywood action film heroes: Arnold Schwarzenegger, Bruce Willis, and Chuck Norris.

Bush named Schwarzenegger chairman of the President's Council on Physical Fitness and Sports, and for three years in a row on the first day of May Schwarzenegger donned his sweats and came to the White House to preside over "The Great American Work-Out." The grounds of the executive mansion were transformed into an outdoor gym, with "workout stations" representing a variety of sporting pursuits. Joining Schwarzenegger and the president were celebrity athletes and an unpredictable roster of entertainers that ranged from Dick Van Patten to Mr. Potato Head. One year Milton Berle, wearing sweats, feigned a heart attack and fell into Schwarzenegger's arms.

Over the three-year run of the event, Bush's handlers seemed uncertain about the proper tone for the president to strike. The first year saw him in a sport jacket and dress shoes for his "workout" with Arnold; Bush looked uncomfortable as the two men rode fitness bikes, swung golf clubs, shot baskets, and pitched horseshoes. The second year a presidential windbreaker replaced the sports jacket, and instead of playing sports Bush casually checked out exercise machines with his wife, Barbara. The third year Bush showed up in a suit and tie and did no exercises at all. Instead, it was the full-figured Barbara who donned the workout suit and got physical.

✳✳✳✳

All presidents since Woodrow Wilson have seen fit to invite performers to the White House for quasi-official meetings of one sort or another. After Roosevelt, with the publicity value of entertainers firmly established, the pace of these visits picked up. Most encounters between presidents and performing artists constitute classic examples of what Daniel Boorstin called "pseudo-events"; generally there is a public relations rationale, though sometimes the meetings occur under the flimsiest of pretexts.

Harry Truman received a delegation of Hollywood actors at the White House in 1951 to commemorate the fiftieth anniversary of movies; among the troupers were future romantic rivals Elizabeth Taylor and Debbie Reynolds. Mary Pickford, still pushing government bonds, came to the White House four decades after her meeting with Woodrow Wilson to "sell" President Eisenhower the first savings bond of her twenty-six-city tour. A few months before his assassination, John F. Kennedy had an Oval Office meet-and-greet with Jerry Lewis and a Muscular Dystrophy Association poster child. Accompanying them was Patty Duke, whose hit TV series *The Patty Duke Show* just happened to be coproduced by JFK brother-in-law Peter Lawford.

Even nonhuman stars take their turn in the White House spotlight: Lady Bird Johnson costarred in a 1967 photo op with Lassie as part of her "Keep America Beautiful" campaign. "Not since Princess Margaret came for dinner," wrote Liz Carpenter, press secretary to the first lady, "had so many people called demanding an invitation." With a press corps of more than one hundred recording the event for posterity, Lassie put on a show for the cameras, picking up strategically placed litter on the lawn and dumping it in a nearby trash can. At the end of the proceedings, Lassie trotted up to Mrs. Johnson with a bouquet of flowers in his/her mouth.

Richard Nixon, as all the world knows, held a momentous tête-à-tête with a drug-addled Elvis Presley in December 1970; less familiar is Gerald Ford's meeting four Decembers later with ex-Beatle George Harrison. Harrison came to the White House at the invitation of Jack Ford, the president's twenty-two-year-old son, and brought along his father and fellow musicians Ravi Shankar, Billy Preston, and Tom Scott. Harrison, clad in a plaid jacket, bright orange pants, and red Tibetan boots, told reporters on his way in to the mansion, "I feel good vibes about the White House." Indeed good vibes appeared to be the order of the day. The group posed for portraits in the Oval Office, ate lunch in the family quarters with Jack, and got a tour of the mansion from Jack's sister, Susan. Jack introduced the visitors to his father, and George Harrison and Gerald Ford exchanged lapel buttons. The president gave Harrison a WIN button, a souvenir of Ford's ill-conceived campaign to "whip inflation now." Harrison, a devout Buddhist, gave Ford a button with an Asian character that transliterated as "Om."

Throughout the 1970s and beyond, prominent musicians made frequent social calls at the executive mansion. Dolly Parton joined other Nashville celebrities at the Carter White House for a 1979 reception honoring Country Music Month. When Parton stepped into position for her photograph with the president, a grinning Carter announced, "You're the one I've been waiting for," and surprised the singer with a smack on the lips. Smiling big, Dolly told the photographers: "Get a good'un now. My husband wants a picture of this, too." Carter's comeback was immediate: "It's the wrong time to bring up your husband."

Both Ronald Reagan and George Bush took time out from running the country to pose with Michael Jackson, then at the height of his enormous popularity. The 1984 meeting with Ronald and Nancy Reagan marks a particularly memorable encounter in the presidential-celebrity pantheon. Jackson showed up in full regalia: sunglasses; a spangled blue jacket decorated with gold braiding, epaulets, and sash; white-sequined socks, and a single glove. The Reagans stood in elegant contrast, Ronnie in black, Nancy in white. These three professional performers cut a striking visual ensemble for the cameras, which was of course the entire point of the exercise.

"Well, isn't this a thriller," Reagan told the hundreds of onlookers, mostly White House staffers and their families, who had assembled for the occasion on the South Lawn. "We haven't seen this many people since we left China." The ostensible purpose of Jackson's visit was to pick up a plaque, and the president got quickly to the point. Because Michael Jackson had permitted the use of his song "Beat It" in a traffic safety campaign, the twenty-five-year-old superstar received from Reagan a Presidential Public Safety Communication Award. The ceremony lasted only a few minutes, and Jackson spoke a mere two sentences: "I'm very,

very honored. Thank you very much, Mr. President and Mrs. Reagan." The whole thing was over almost before it began, the three stars slipping out of view inside the mansion. But preserved on videotape and film, this brief encounter forever remains a key moment in the Reagan pop cultural iconography.

Sometimes presidents associate with celebrities simply because they can. In his eight years in office Bill Clinton went sailing with James Taylor, sang oldies with Carly Simon, watched movies with Tom Hanks, took a road trip with Jimmy Buffett, partied after the State of the Union address with Whoopi Goldberg and Billy Baldwin, attended $100,000-a-couple dinner with Barbra Streisand and Frank Sinatra, and personally met most of the major performing artists in the land.

No president in the history of the republic took more delight in the company of entertainers than Bill Clinton. Where Roosevelt and Kennedy mixed their affection with a tinge of class-based condescension, Clinton sought only to please the show business community—and the devotion ran both ways. To an unprecedented degree, Clinton used his status as celebrity-in-chief to get acquainted with performers whose work he admired. After Clinton enjoyed a night on the town with Paul Newman and Joanne Woodward in 1993, press secretary Dee Dee Myers put the matter into perspective: "He grew up watching movies like *The Hustler*, *Hud*, and *Cat on a Hot Tin Roof* and he still gets genuinely blown away by spending time with some of these people. There's still a lot of the kid from Hope, Arkansas, in him."

For an unreconstructed aficionado of popular culture like Clinton, the White House provided the ultimate perk: entrée into a world which, at least on the surface, offered all of the glamour and none of the headaches of presidential politics. At a Beverly Hills fund-raiser during the 1992 campaign, at a point when he had not yet entered the stratosphere of fame, candidate Bill Clinton addressed an audience made up of some of the most famous faces on the planet. He appeared almost overwhelmed by the depth of the talent around him. "Warren Beatty said he hadn't known me a long time," Clinton told the crowd, "but I was sitting there thinking I have known many of you a long time. I have seen your movies or sung your songs and just imagined that life could be as it seems to be in the lyrics or up on the screen."

Even presidents need their illusions.

Lyndon Johnson gets an earful from Eartha Kitt at the White House, January 1969. (LBJ Library)

2

✵✵✵✵

Attack of the Cat Woman

How Entertainers Are
Bad for Presidents

THE OCCASION WAS ONE OF THOSE White House luncheons that are supposed to unfold as seamless and ultimately meaningless public relations
events, thrilling to the participants but otherwise destined to vanish into the va-
pors of history. On January 18, 1968, fifty women from around the country answered the call of Lady Bird Johnson to take part in a so-called Women Doers
luncheon discussion on the topic of citizen involvement in the fight against
crime. Most of the guests came from positions of civic authority. But among
them was a wild card, a Hollywood diva whose behavior reminded Washington
why some entertainers should carry a warning label.

Eartha Kitt, the sultry cabaret singer best known for her turn as Cat Woman
on the TV show *Batman*, had been invited on the basis of her work with African
American youth. Born into poverty in rural South Carolina, Kitt had achieved
modest stardom on Broadway and in Hollywood. Now, at thirty-nine, she found
herself in a career slump. For most entertainers in this position, a White House
invitation would come as good news. Not Eartha Kitt. Not at the height of the
Vietnam War. "I didn't want to go because I thought it would be a lot of non-
sense," she wrote in her autobiography. "I felt a con coming on."

A series of importunate calls from the White House persuaded Kitt to change her mind. She flew to the capital and took a limousine to 1600 Pennsylvania Avenue. The singer recalled her arrival: "I was nervous as I walked through the doors of the White House, greeted as I was by black faces with furrows of slavery still marking their brows. White gloved hands reached out to welcome me; the smiles on their faces showed a restrained kind of pride—at least we can come through the front door now."

Kitt joined her fellow guests at one of five tables in the Family Dining Room on the second floor of the presidential mansion. The women had just finished their meal of seafood bisque, chicken, and peppermint ice cream—"quite a delicious lunch," Mrs. Johnson noted in her diary, "a little on the sumptuous side." Just after dessert and just before the scheduled discussion of crime in the streets, an unannounced visitor strode into the room: President Lyndon Johnson, who regaled the women with brief, generic remarks about the need for greater police support and the value of parenting as a deterrent to juvenile delinquency. As Johnson turned to depart, Eartha Kitt rose from her chair, a violation of protocol that caught everyone in the room by surprise.

"Mr. President," she demanded, stopping him in his tracks, "what do you do about delinquent parents? Those who have to work and are too busy to look after their children?"

Startled, Johnson offered a halfhearted bureaucratic response about legislation to fund day care centers.

Kitt was not satisfied. "But what are we going to do?"

"That's something for you women to discuss here," Johnson answered, and beat a hasty retreat. The fireworks had begun.

After a series of short presentations Lady Bird opened the floor to questions; Kitt's hand shot up. Puffing on a cigarette and gesturing grandly, the singer set sail upon the performance of a lifetime. In the audience a quick-thinking woman with stenographic training grabbed a pen and began recording a transcript of what followed.

"I think we have missed the main point at this luncheon," Kitt said. "We have forgotten the main reason we have juvenile delinquency. The young people are angry and parents are angry because they are being so highly taxed and there's a war going on, and Americans don't know why." The forty-nine other guests sat in stunned silence; Mrs. Johnson thought to herself, Am I having a nightmare? "Boys I know across the nation feel it doesn't pay to be a good guy," Kitt went on. "They figure that with a (criminal) record they don't have to go off to Vietnam."

According to eyewitnesses, Kitt pointed a finger at Mrs. Johnson as she continued: "You are a mother, too, although you have had daughters and not sons. I am a mother and I know the feeling of having a baby come out of my gut. I have a baby and then you send him off to war." (In fact, Kitt had a five-year-old daughter.) "No wonder the kids rebel and take pot—and Mrs. Johnson, in case you don't understand the lingo, that's marijuana."

Betty Hughes, wife of the governor of New Jersey and mother of eight sons, punctured the awkward pause that followed. Declaring that she felt morally obligated to speak "in defense of war," Mrs. Hughes told the women that her first husband had been killed in World War II and that one of her sons now served in the air force. "None wants to go to Vietnam but all will go . . . they and their friends," she said, adding that anyone who smoked pot because of the war "is a kook."

In a quiet voice Mrs. Johnson offered her own remarks: "Because there is a war on . . . that still doesn't give us a free ticket not to try to work for better things." She began to directly address Kitt: "I cannot identify as much as I should. I have not lived the background you have nor can I speak as passionately and well. But we must keep our eyes and our hearts and our energies fixed on constructive areas and try to do something that will make this a happier, healthier, better-educated land." After three hours, the luncheon drew to an uncomfortable close.

As word of the incident spread, Eartha Kitt's upbraiding of the Johnsons rapidly became a cause célèbre. "I see nothing wrong with the way I handled myself," Kitt told reporters shortly afterward. "I can only hope it will do some good." Oblivious to the barrage of criticism that awaited her, Kitt held nothing back: "If Mrs. Johnson was embarrassed, that's her problem." And: "I should put on my claws because I am the Cat Woman of America."

In a memorandum to Lyndon Johnson written a few hours after the incident, Liz Carpenter, the first lady's press secretary, suggested that Kitt had staged the confrontation as a publicity stunt. "To keep a career going and to be in demand, a performer must stay constantly in the public eye or be forgotten," Carpenter noted. Others, including many in Hollywood, agreed with this explanation.

But if Kitt's goal was publicity, she instead reaped notoriety. For many years after the Johnson luncheon Eartha Kitt's career suffered. And though millions of Americans sympathized with the antiwar sentiments expressed that day in the White House, Kitt's unprecedented challenge to presidential dignity left an unpleasant aftertaste.

✳✳✳✳

Four years later, the war in Vietnam provoked a second, even stranger episode involving an entertainer at the White House. This time it did not take a big Hollywood name to embarrass the administration.

The occasion was a commemorative dinner at which President Richard Nixon presented the Medal of Freedom to DeWitt and Lila Wallace, cofounders of *Reader's Digest* magazine. Following the usual after-dinner custom the president's guests—a list that included Bob Hope, Billy Graham, Lionel Hampton, Charles Lindbergh, Alice Roosevelt Longworth, and Attorney General John Mitchell and his wife, Martha—adjourned to the East Room for coffee and musical entertainment. In keeping with the homespun tone of the evening, the headline act was the Ray Conniff Singers—a clean-cut, old-fashioned vocal chorus who specialized in the sort of middle-of-the-road fare Nixon favored. "If the music is square," the president announced in his introduction of the group, "it's because I like it square."

As Nixon returned to his seat in the front row, the singers—eight men and eight women, backed by a Marine Band combo—began filing into place for the show. Then, before the house lights dimmed, before anyone knew what was happening, one of the vocalists suddenly and dramatically departed from the script. Carole Feraci, a petite, dark-haired backup singer from Los Angeles who had been added to the choir as a last-minute substitute, stepped up to a microphone. From the fist of her hand, she unfurled a wadded-up, homemade banner that she had smuggled into the room. Originally Feraci had hidden the cloth inside her bodice; fearing security agents would mistake it for a weapon, she transferred it into her hand as the performers made their way into the East Room. Now she held up the banner for all the guests to read: "Stop the Killing."

"President Nixon," Feraci said, looking straight at Nixon a few feet away, "stop bombing human beings, animals, and vegetation." Richard Nixon was smiling, the sort of smile that freezes into position and stays put. "You go to church on Sundays and pray to Jesus Christ. If Jesus Christ were here tonight, you would not dare to drop another bomb."

By this time Ray Conniff had joined Feraci onstage. Although Conniff tried to snatch the banner away, Carole Feraci did not let go, folding the cloth back into a tight wad in her fist. "Bless the Berrigans and bless Daniel Ellsberg," Feraci said in quick conclusion, citing three prominent peace activists of the day.

Dumbfounded, Conniff struck up the first number: "Ma, He's Makin' Eyes at Me." With the banner still smashed into the palm of her hand, Feraci performed along with the rest of the choir. At the end of the song, which drew tepid applause, Conniff turned to the audience. "Thank you very much and good evening," he said. "I assure you, Mr. President, the first part of the program was as much a shock to me as it was to you." The guests applauded more enthusiastically.

A few rows behind Nixon a man shouted, "Throw her out!" and soon others voices joined the cry: "Throw her out!"

"I think it would be better if you left," Conniff told Feraci.

"Certainly," she said. She walked offstage and out the door, not even sure where she was going.

Trailing Feraci out of the East Room were Secret Service agents and stunned members of the press, who spoke with the singer in an impromptu news conference. Feraci told them she had gotten her inspiration as soon as she was hired for the gig. "I decided at that moment that I would make this speech," she said. "I made the sign myself and stuffed it down the bosom of my dress. I wrote the speech myself and I memorized it."

Feraci stressed that she was acting not on behalf of any organization but as an individual with fervent antiwar feelings. "I thought that it would make a nationwide impression if an oobie-doobie-doo girl like myself made this protest on a stage inside the White House."

Indeed. Feraci's outburst, like that of Eartha Kitt, made the front page of virtually every newspaper in the country. "I think she ought to be torn limb from limb," Martha Mitchell was quoted as saying. Though Feraci faced no charges, she, like Kitt, suffered immediate career repercussions.

Richard Nixon took the incident with equanimity, telephoning Ray Conniff a few days later to assuage the conductor's feelings. One of Conniff's choir members, the person responsible for hiring Carole Feraci, wrote the president to apologize. "In spite of the Incident," he said, "it is the consensus of the remainder of the chorus that performing at the White House was the highlight of our careers."

Reverend Norman Vincent Peale, who had been a guest at the party, also wrote to Nixon. "The incident of the foolish little girl cuts no ice," Peale said. "I had a hard time controlling my religion; I wanted to get up and throw her out myself."

✯✯✯✯

As both Kitt and Feraci discovered, entertainers who morally chide a president or first lady run serious risks, especially when the dressing-down occurs face-to-face in front of an audience. In such cases, the attempt at heroism diverts sympathy to the person being criticized; we are more likely to feel the public humiliation of Lady Bird Johnson and Richard Nixon than the certitude of Kitt and Feraci. Americans have no difficulty expressing disagreement with individual occupants of the office, but the institution of the presidency remains sacrosanct, off-limits to direct insult. The error of Eartha Kitt and Carole Feraci lay not in their objectives but in crossing that line.

More troublesome for presidents are entertainers whose opposition is tempered with restraint, or those whose standing with the audience brings a greater degree of credibility than a performer like Eartha Kitt. When an actor or a singer holds the high moral ground over a statesman—or believes he does—the situation carries the potential for political embarrassment.

During the Johnson administration, staff members in charge of lining up White House entertainment found their jobs increasingly complicated by the polarizing effect of the Vietnam War. "When you first get elected, everybody loves you," said Bess Abell, social secretary during the Johnson administration. "But, after a while, you run into problems. They (the performers) grandstand by 'regretting' publicly. Peter, Paul and Mary did a show for us in 1965. They wouldn't have come back by 1968." To avoid high-profile public rejections, Abell said, the Johnson White House booked an inordinate number of ballet dancers—"you're on pretty safe ground with them."

In July 1960, just as John F. Kennedy was clinching the Democratic presidential nomination in Los Angeles, John Wayne took out a three-page advertisement in *Life* magazine. The ostensible purpose of the spread was to publicize Wayne's film *The Alamo*, but the patriotic text subtly reflected harsh anti-Kennedy sentiment. "There were no ghostwriters at the Alamo—Only Men," the copy noted at one point, reminding readers of allegations that Kennedy had not authored *Profiles in Courage*. (Things could have been worse; in private Wayne dismissed JFK as a "snot-nosed kid who couldn't keep his dick in his pants.")

Because Wayne was so closely identified as a conservative Republican, it seems doubtful that his anti-Kennedy message changed many minds. Of greater value to political strategists are beloved entertainers whom the audience does not perceive as ideologues. A classic instance of this occurred in the 1984 presidential campaign, when Ronald Reagan unsuccessfully maneuvered to hitch his wagon to Bruce Springsteen's star. Springsteen at that point had achieved nearly iconic status as an American Everyman, his songs infused with authentic blue-collar ethos. Attempting to tap into Springsteen's resonance, Reagan invoked the singer's name at a campaign stop in Hammonton, New Jersey. "America's future rests in a thousand dreams inside your hearts," Reagan said. "It rests in the message of hope in songs so many young Americans admire: New Jersey's own Bruce Springsteen. And helping you make those dreams come true is what this job of mine is all about."

On several levels this foray into the contemporary pop culture proved to be perilous sledding for Ronald Reagan. When reporters asked campaign press aides which Springsteen song the president liked best, they initially came up empty-handed; by the end of the day, "Born to Run" had become the tune of choice. Reagan's opponent, Walter Mondale, poked fun at the transparency of White House attempts to hijack Springsteen, telling a New Jersey rally a few days later, "Bruce may have been born to run, but he wasn't born yesterday."

Republican interpretations of Springsteen's work betrayed a staggering degree of misapprehension. Conservative columnist and Reagan adviser George Will, after attending a Bruce Springsteen concert, wrote an encomium to the man audiences had dubbed "The Boss." Will seemed most impressed by the fact that "flags get waved at his concerts while he sings songs about hard times." According to Springsteen biographer Dave Marsh, it was Will who initiated the idea of involving Bruce Springsteen in the Reagan campaign. Through a series of back channels, the singer was invited to make a campaign appearance with President Reagan in New Jersey—an offer Springsteen had no difficulty declining. Looking back on the episode ten years later, Bruce Springsteen told an interviewer that his goal in the 1980s had been "to put forth an alternate vision of the America that was being put forth by the Reagan-era Republicans. They basically tried to co-opt every image that was American, including me."

In the 1988 campaign George Bush latched onto a popular song of the day called "Don't Worry, Be Happy," written and performed by Bobby McFerrin. After learning that the number had been played at Bush campaign events, McFerrin ordered his manager to write a cease-and-desist letter—a letter the singer shared with the press: "While we are amused that the Bush campaign would find its political philosophy reflected in the song "Don't Worry, Be Happy," we do not wish to have the composition associated with any presidential candidate." McFerrin's manager poured additional salt into the wound, telling the *New York Times*, "Bush loves this song—he plays it in his limousine all the time." Bobby McFerrin's final jab came in 1993, when he sang "Don't Worry, Be Happy" at the inaugural festivities of Bush's opponent, Bill Clinton.

The elder George Bush, like his son a few years later, had a special talent for raising the dander of the entertainment community. Actress Debra Winger, at a Dukakis election-night event in Boston in 1988, compared the newly elected president to "bad acting." Winger's prediction for the incoming administration: "It's gonna be like four years of being inside the worst B movie you ever saw."

Show business opposition has grown even more pointed against George Bush the younger. Well before the onset of war in Iraq Hollywood critics found cause for alarm in Bush's environmental policy. The most prominent and credible of the naysayers is Robert Redford, a celebrity who has been careful to ration his political cachet. Redford grants few interviews, and when he does have something to say, he tends to choose prestigious outlets like the *New York Times*. In May 2001 Redford wrote an op-ed column for the *Times* that chastised Bush in firm but restrained tones. The most biting condemnation came in the concluding line: "If he does not make environmental concerns central to his energy policy, President Bush may well leave the next generation with nothing but ashes to stand in." A year and a half later Redford was back in the *Times*, this time with a Sunday magazine interview in which the rhetoric had sharpened: "From the moment Bush stepped into office," the actor said, "he's been leading a sly and extremely disciplined campaign to destroy, dismantle, unravel, undo thirty years of environmental-regulations development."

Though Redford's warning may ultimately have effected no change, this particular message from this particular entertainer carried more weight than most such appeals. When Robert Redford challenged the White House, he did so from a position of moral authority: three decades of grassroots involvement in the conservation movement. Running parallel to this experience—and inseparable from it—is Redford's movie-derived image as a westerner and outdoorsman. Any politician who takes on Redford takes on the Sundance Kid, Jeremiah Johnson, and the Electric Horseman—which perhaps explains why George W. Bush offered no public response.

✳✳✳✳

As an internal dynamic in the relationship between presidents and entertainers, moral patronization can cut both ways: just as performers seek advantage in criticizing elected officials so do elected officials seek advantage in criticizing performers. In each case the outcome is likely to be worse for the politician than for the entertainer. When it comes to taking a stand against the practitioners of show business, presidents and vice presidents, candidates and spouses skate on the thinnest of ice. By definition major entertainment stars command large constituencies, psychically if not politically; the critic who casts moral stones at a particular performer may unwittingly target that performer's fans. Although this risk might appear obvious, for occupants and seekers of the nation's highest office the lesson remains remarkably unheeded.

The most famous—and ultimately the silliest—instance of tilting at showbiz windmills involved Vice President Dan Quayle, whose excoriation of the television comedy series *Murphy Brown* constitutes a pivotal moment in White House–Hollywood relations. Quayle had never seen the program, but that did not stop him from using *Murphy Brown* as a springboard to publicly lament what he described as a "poverty of values" in modern American life. During a 1992 speech in San Francisco, the vice president cited the recently aired season finale, in which the lead character—a successful, unmarried network journalist played by Candice Bergen—gives birth to a baby and decides to raise the child on her own. "It doesn't help matters," Quayle said, "when prime time TV has Murphy Brown—a character who supposedly epitomizes today's intelligent, highly paid, professional woman—mocking the importance of fathers by bearing a child alone and calling it just another 'lifestyle choice.'"

Media reaction to Quayle's speech struck like a sonic boom. The next morning the *New York Daily News* ran a page-one story under the headline "Quayle to Murphy Brown: You Tramp!" That evening's network newscasts led with the flap, highlighting follow-up remarks by the vice president as he intensified his attack. "Hollywood thinks it's cute to glamorize illegitimacy," Quayle told a quote-hungry pack of reporters in Los Angeles. "Hollywood doesn't get it."

Back in Washington the Bush White House seemed unsure how to handle Quayle's bombshell. The day after the speech, in response to journalists' questions, press secretary Marlin Fitzwater first endorsed the remarks, then reversed course a few minutes later, and finally offered to meet with Candice Bergen, his "personal favorite." The president likewise zigged and zagged. At a news conference with Canadian Prime Minister Brian Mulroney, reporters peppered an exasperated Bush with questions about *Murphy Brown*. "I'm not going to get into the details of a very popular television show," Bush said. Though Bush declined to comment on whether he thought Murphy Brown should have had an abortion, Fitzwater applauded the character for demonstrating "pro-life values" by carrying her baby to term. Quayle offered a contrary theory: "Probably the only reason they chose to have a child rather than an abortion was because they knew the ratings would go up higher having the child." (In fact, the baby's addition to the cast proved to be a liability with viewers.)

Members of the entertainment community, particularly the producers and cast of *Murphy Brown*, were seething. Diane English, creator of the series, took Quayle to task in a statement to the press: "If the vice president thinks it's disgraceful for an unmarried woman to bear a child and if he believes that a woman cannot adequately raise a child without a father, then he'd better make sure abortion remains safe and legal." The blatantly political tone of English's message served as a preview for hostilities to come.

Over the ensuing weeks the news media kept the controversy stoked. Quayle reveled in his newfound cause, couching the matter as Us versus Them: "Talk about right and wrong and they'll try to mock us in newsrooms, sitcom studios, and faculty lounges across America," Quayle told an audience of supporters. "I wear their scorn as a badge of honor." Diane English challenged Quayle to debate "anytime, anywhere," but predicted he would not meet her. Boasted English: "I have better writers."

At the end of the summer two events took place that showed television's willingness to deploy its weapon of choice—the clever riposte. The first was the Emmy awards in late August, which turned into a full-fledged Quayle bash. The remarks ranged from the lighthearted—Candice Bergen thanking the vice president in her acceptance speech—to the deadly serious. Producer Diane English, a winner for *Murphy Brown*, thanked "all the single parents out there who, either by choice or by necessity, are raising their kids alone. Don't let anybody tell you you're not a family." Before leaving the podium English got in an extra dig: "As Murphy herself said, I couldn't possibly do a worse job raising my kid alone than the Reagans did with theirs."

At this point in the conflict it was difficult to say which side's behavior grated more. Vice President Quayle played his role as shamelessly as the Hollywood people played theirs. The day after the Emmy telecast Quayle seemed uncertain whether to shrug off the slams or get mad—so he did both. "Now Murphy Brown, listen closely, 'cause I'm only gonna say it once," Quayle told an airport rally in Alabama. "You owe me big time!" But he also lit into Diane English: "Last night they said that I believe single mothers and their children were not families. That is a lie. Winning an Emmy is not a license to lie."

Several weeks after the Emmys and less than a month and a half before the 1988 presidential election, the season premiere of *Murphy Brown* brought the sniping to a climax and the tempest in a teapot to an end. By now any remaining boundaries between fact and fiction had been obliterated. As Jeff Greenfield reported on ABC, "Last night a fictional anchorwoman attacked a real Vice President on her fictional TV news show using real single parents—while the real Vice President watched the fictional show in a room full of real single parents." Quayle, ever eager to milk the contretemps, invited photographers to record him at a TV-viewing party with a select group of single moms. He also sent Murphy's baby a letter and a gift—a stuffed toy elephant which the producers said they would send to "a homeless shelter so that a real child can enjoy it."

Quayle and his roomful of guests were among some 70 million Americans who tuned in to *Murphy Brown* that night. Adroitly weaving the vice president's comments into the story line, the program took a number of potshots at Quayle, some funny, some leaden. The ickiest part of the one-hour special was a closing sequence in which Murphy Brown addresses the camera from the set of her news show: "Perhaps it's time for the vice president to expand his definition and recognize that whether by choice or circumstance, families come in all shapes and sizes," she says, adding that families are defined by "commitment, caring, and love." Then, as the studio audience applauds, a multiracial group of real single parents joins Murphy Brown on the soundstage. As *Washington Post* TV critic Tom Shales put it, "This was not a satisfying response to Quayle. It was more of an embarrassment, sinking not only to his level, but even lower."

Neither side emerged from the *Murphy Brown* controversy unbloodied. Hollywood showed itself to be thin-skinned, sanctimonious, and self-important—an unattractive response but not a surprising one. The vice president of the United States just looked asinine. By engaging with a fictional TV character, and a popular one at that, Dan Quayle devalued his already tarnished reputation.

George Bush may have been wary of tackling Murphy Brown, but shortly after Quayle's anti-Hollywood jihad he made his own tentative venture into the realm of cultural criticism. At the height of the Murphy furor Bush said it was "sick" to produce records that glorified the murder of police officers. Though the president cited no names, his remark referred to rap singer Ice-T, whose album *Body Count* included a much reviled song called "Cop Killer." "I stand against those who use films or records or television or video games to glorify killing law enforcement officers," Bush told his audience of law enforcement officials. Skeptics pointed out that presidential ally Arnold Schwarzenegger, in his *Terminator* movies, had killed or injured dozens of policemen.

Bush found himself on even shakier ground when he took a swipe at the animated television series *The Simpsons*. In a speech about family values to the National Religious Broadcasters the president opined, "We need a nation closer to the Waltons than the Simpsons—an America that rejects the tide of incivility and the tide of intolerance." Writers for *The Simpsons* got the last laugh with an episode that showed the cartoon family watching Bush insult them on television. Bart Simpson fired back: "Hey, we're just like the Waltons. Both families spend a lot of time praying for the end of the Depression." The plotline of a subsequent installment of *The Simpsons* had a testy ex-President Bush moving across the street from the lead characters; the episode parodied the old *Dennis the Menace* series, with Bart in the role of Dennis and George Bush as the curmudgeonly Mr. Wilson.

The experience of Quayle and Bush ought to have served as a warning to other Republicans, but in the next election cycle Senator Bob Dole picked up where they left off. Accusing Hollywood's "dream factories" of turning out "nightmares of depravity," Dole reignited the skirmish. He decried the violence in Oliver Stone's *Natural Born Killers*, but not the violence in films featuring Republican stalwarts like Schwarzenegger and Bruce Willis. He railed against what he described as the "romance of heroin" depicted in such films as *Trainspotting* and *Pulp Fiction*, but admitted he had only read the reviews. Quentin Tarantino, the director of *Pulp Fiction*, retaliated: "How can a leader condemn works of art he hasn't seen?"

In 2000 Republican presidential nominee George W. Bush backed away from his party's traditional anti-Hollywood stance, perhaps because of his own vulnerability on the issue. Bush had spent ten years as a paid director of Silver Screen Management Services, a film-financing company involved in dozens of Disney movies. Though most of the productions associated with Silver Screen were rated either G (general audiences) or PG (parental guidance), twenty-one of the films had received an R (restricted) rating. Silver Screen financed Disney's first R-rated film, *Down and Out in Beverly Hills*, as well as a 1986 HBO thriller called *The Hitcher*, which showed a woman's body being torn in two. A reviewer for *Variety* described *The Hitcher* as offering a "massacre every fifteen minutes."

In the campaign of 2000 it was Lynne Cheney, spouse of the vice presidential candidate, who took up the cultural crusade. She criticized Al Gore for attending an entertainment industry–sponsored "X-rated" fund-raiser at which off-color jokes were told, and went to Capitol Hill to testify against debauched standards in the entertainment industry. The hearing took on an absurdist dimension when Cheney recited the "despicable" lyrics to a rap number by Eminem entitled "Kill You." The juxtaposition of prim Mrs. Cheney against the raw words of the song called to mind a Sunday school teacher in a frontier town shocking the parishioners with lurid tales of depraved dance hall girls. As with Bob Dole, critics noted that Cheney seemed careful to avoid targeting anyone on Hollywood's right.

Like Dan Quayle, Lynne Cheney became creative fodder for those she had vilified. Rap star Eminem resurfaced with a new album that personally attacked both Mrs. Cheney and her husband. A song called "White America" used the "F-word" to describe Eminem's feelings about Lynne Cheney. "Without Me" made sport of Dick Cheney's heart problems; the music video version even included a mock electrocution of the vice president. When Eminem took his show on tour in 2002, he opened with three large television screens that played and replayed Mrs. Cheney's Senate testimony.

However sophomoric Eminem's reaction may have been, it is Lynne Cheney who ultimately lost the tug-of-war. Audiences expect immature, over-the-top outbursts from rap stars, just as they expect Hollywood to get excessively defensive when called on the carpet. Political figures—for good reason—are held to a higher, more serious standard. When Mrs. Cheney took on the music industry she put her own dignity at risk. Performing artists can say or do virtually anything they want without regard for the consequences; political leaders must operate within a narrower range of acceptable behavior. It is never a fair fight.

Lynne Cheney might have saved herself the embarrassment had she absorbed the lessons of an earlier crusade against explicit music lyrics. In 1985 Tipper Gore and other wives of prominent Washington figures formed a monitoring organization called the Parents Music Resource Center. Just as Lynne Cheney became the nemesis of Eminem, so did Tipper Gore draw the personal wrath of performers like Frank Zappa, Dee Snider, and Wendy O. Williams. At a Senate hearing on music lyrics Zappa likened the PMRC demands to "some sinister kind of toilet training program to housebreak all composers and performers because of the lyrics of a few." Snider, from the band Twisted Sister, defended his song "Under the Blade" by charging that "the only sadomasochism, bondage, and rape in this song is in the mind of Mrs. Gore." Rapper Ice-T, in a tune called "Freedom of Speech," denounced Tipper as a "dumb bitch."

Before Al Gore began his first run for the presidency in 1988 he and his wife traveled to Los Angeles to strike an uneasy truce with the creative community. At an off-the-record lunch with music industry executives the Gores disavowed at least some of Tipper's earlier positions. Diplomacy turned to humiliation, however, when a transcript of the meeting surfaced in *Daily Variety*. Al and Tipper

Gore came off looking doubly bad: for going on the warpath against the recording industry in the first place, and then for compromising the integrity of their initial stand. When Gore ran for president in 2000, the aftertaste of the PMRC campaign had not entirely dissipated.

Even a show business professional like Ronald Reagan could seem tone-deaf to the realities of pop culture. "Kissing in the old days was very beautiful and actually the two people doing it were barely touching sometimes—in order not to push her face out of shape," Reagan told interviewer Barbara Walters in 1986. "And now you see a couple of people start chewing on each other." The Reagans let it be known during their years in the White House that they preferred to watch movies from the golden age of Hollywood—which also happened to be the Reagan age.

Whatever misgivings Reagan may have had about modern entertainment, he was savvy enough not to pick a fight with individual performers. In one instance he and Nancy played just the opposite role, leaping to the defense of the Beach Boys after they had been maligned by a member of the Reagan cabinet. In 1983 Interior Secretary James Watt banned rock musicians—including the Beach Boys—from a Fourth of July concert on the Washington Mall. Although the Beach Boys had headlined two previous Independence Day events without incident, Watt claimed that rock acts attracted "the wrong element" and arranged instead for the "patriotic, family-based entertainment" of Wayne Newton and a military band.

The secretary's decision touched off an angry reaction that traveled all the way to the White House. Michael Deaver, Reagan's deputy chief of staff, defended the Beach Boys as "an American institution." Vice President Bush said, "They're my friends and I like their music." After Nancy Reagan personally set Watt straight about the Beach Boys, the White House rescinded the ban on rock acts. To underscore his displeasure President Reagan presented the Interior secretary with a plaster trophy of a foot with a bullet hole in it, symbolizing Watt's having shot himself in the foot. Though the Beach Boys did not perform in Washington on Independence Day, having already booked another engagement, they accepted an invitation from the Reagans to appear at a White House Special Olympics fund-raiser in mid-June.

Perhaps the only time a politician has successfully taken on an entertainer—though success in this arena is a matter of perception—was Bill Clinton's 1992 scolding of a rap singer named Sister Souljah. The dressing-down took place at a luncheon gathering of Jesse Jackson's Rainbow Coalition, a boldly chosen setting that played to the Arkansas governor's flair for the dramatic. Sister Souljah, who had spoken to the coalition's youth group the night before, had recently kicked up a fuss by suggesting to an interviewer, "If black people kill black people every day, why not have a week and kill white people?"

Before a mostly African American audience, Clinton called Sister Souljah's comments "filled with the kind of hatred that you do not honor today and tonight." Reaction to the candidate's charges ran the gamut. Jesse Jackson said Clinton had exercised "bad judgment" and suggested that he owed the singer an apology. Political commentators were quick to note Clinton's "calculated challenge to a core Democratic constituency" in calling Sister Souljah's bluff.

The dustup got a second wind a few days later at a question-and-answer session on the music network MTV. The first question asked of Clinton dealt with Sister Souljah, giving the candidate a setup for his quote du jour: "What I said is why don't we take a week and have nobody kill anybody." For her part, Sister Souljah convened the obligatory outraged news conference and delivered the obligatory outraged sound bite. "Bill Clinton," she said, "you cannot assume that black people will automatically vote for you. You should stop expecting a handout and work to earn your vote." But this time the entertainer could not outmoralize the politician.

Before leaving the subject of moral outrage between performers and presidents, let us consider a potentially golden moment that never came to pass. In 1969 Richard Nixon concocted a nutty scheme: as a gesture against what he perceived to be the country's growing obsession with obscenity, he proposed going to New York to see the musical *Hair*, much in the news at that point for featuring unclothed actors. In a dramatic display of disgust, Nixon would then stalk out of the performance. When cooler heads prevailed, American history lost an unforgettable sideshow.

✵✵✵✵

Using show business personalities for political advantage presents another pitfall: a president's choice of celebrity associates hints at where he stands culturally, in ways that may work to his detriment with voters. A president might cast his lot with the wrong celebrities or interact with the right ones in the wrong way. For national leaders attempting to establish and maintain Hollywood relations, it is all too easy to make a pop culture misstep.

Black entertainers have posed a minefield for Republicans in the past half-century. At Ronald Reagan's 1981 inaugural gala, performances by Ben Vereen and Charley Pride prompted criticism for their racial undertones. In the case of Pride, a rare African American country-western singer, the issue was whether his remarks evoked the toadying of plantation life. "It's a privilege and an honor to be here—a guy from the Delta of Mississippi," Pride told the audience at the Capital Centre. "I thank you, Miz Nancy, for inviting me."

Vereen's situation involved the song-and-dance routine he chose for the gala: a tribute to vaudevillian Bert Williams, who performed in blackface makeup even though he was black himself. The act had long been a staple in Vereen's nightclub repertoire; four years earlier he had performed it at a White House dinner given by Gerald Ford for the prime minister of Ireland. But in the context of a Reagan inaugural, the imagery took on added layers of social subtext. In the view of critic Tom Shales, Vereen "seemed unfortunately shuffly and Uncle Tom-ish—especially considering the fact that the Reagan administration has already been criticized for insensitivity to racial realities." Mike Royko of the *Chicago Sun-Times* wrote: "It's possible that this performance offended some black viewers, but it probably made many of the rich Republicans in the audience yearn for the days when you could get good domestic help."

African Americans were not the only minority group to feel queasy about the Reagans' choice of official entertainment. In November 1981 singer Robert Goulet brought his Vegas nightclub act to the White House East Room for a dinner honoring the president of Venezuela. Working the crowd as though he were back at Caesar's Palace, Goulet delivered several unseemly comments, including a joke about the difficulty of making love in a Toyota automobile. Goulet went on to tell the guests about an appearance he once made at Lake Tahoe; blinded by spotlights, he sang a love song without being able to see the audience. Only later did he realize that "it was all men—a lumberjack convention." As for the individual to whom Goulet had directed his love song, "It worked out. He's been writing every week." In Reagan's thank-you remarks after the performance, the president quipped, "I'll never forget the night you sang to me at Lake Tahoe." Several years later, at the 1987 taping of the *All-Star Gala at Ford's Theatre,* Ronald and Nancy Reagan were observed laughing heartily at a joke about San Francisco told by a comedian who affected an exaggerated effeminate lisp. When ABC televised the program, the Reagans' reaction was cut.

On occasion Reagan betrayed the extent to which his pop cultural frame of reference remained frozen in show business amber. In a 1981 speech to the Canadian parliament Reagan spun a nostalgic tale about the adventures of "little Gladys Smith" of Toronto, Ontario. "Before long," Reagan told the legislators, "little Gladys Smith was embraced by our entire nation. Gladys Smith of Toronto became Mary Pickford. And I know you'll forgive us for adopting her so thoroughly that she became known the world over as 'America's Sweetheart.'" Many in Reagan's audience had no idea what he was talking about; Pickford's fame had hit its high-water mark sixty years earlier.

George W. Bush, a president not known for his links to show business, appears similarly out of touch, as evidenced by his selection of Vegas lounge lizard Wayne Newton to entertain U.S. military personnel in the Middle East. Two months after the attacks of September 11, 2001, Bush summoned Newton to the White House to kick off an overseas USO tour. One can only puzzle over the logic behind the decision to dispatch a fifty-nine-year-old crooner to raise the spirits of American soldiers, many barely out of their teens, many of them persons of color. As humorist Bill Geist wrote, "Isn't dropping Wayne on our own troops tantamount to friendly fire?" (During the post-2000 election recount Newton had also appeared as Bush's Thanksgiving surprise to Republican workers in Florida.)

If George W. Bush has displayed too little interest in the hierarchy of show business hipness, Bill Clinton displayed too much. In his first year as president, Clinton came under steady fire for being overly chummy with entertainment figures. As Clinton's celebrity dealings mounted, so did media criticism. Press coverage begat increased press coverage, and eventually the White House, the stars, and journalists on both coasts found themselves drawn into pitched battle.

Clinton's show business affinity became evident during the 1992 campaign, when dozens of the industry's glitziest names offered their financial and moral support. Inaugural festivities in January 1993 further confirmed that Clinton's would be a presidency in which actors, comedians, and musicians could feel at home—perhaps too much at home. From every corner of the show business galaxy the stars descended on Washington to join in the transition: movie legends like Barbra Streisand, Jack Nicholson, Warren Beatty, and Lauren Bacall; music legends like Bob Dylan, Michael Jackson, Tony Bennett, Aretha Franklin, and Linda Ronstadt; comedians like Bill Cosby and Whoopi Goldberg; and specialty acts like Macauley Culkin. The sheer volume of entertainers taking part in pre-inauguration galas seemed to dilute the seriousness of the occasion, reducing the swearing-in to one star turn among many.

Like the new president himself, the 1993 inaugural was a study in excess. But anticelebrity backlash against Clinton did not reach its zenith until several months later, following a series of encounters between the White House and its newfound friends from the world of entertainment. The associations began to draw notice in mid-March. On the fifteenth of the month Paul Newman and Joanne Woodward accompanied Bill and Chelsea Clinton to dinner at a Washington restaurant called Galileo. The next night the president again met Newman and Woodward at an American Ireland Fund dinner at the Capital Hilton. Judy Collins spent the night of March 23 at the White House and went jogging with the president the next morning. Four nights later Barbra Streisand took her turn as an overnight guest of the Clintons, attending the Gridiron show with the presidential party before retiring to the mansion. Although each of these incidents was reported in the press, none generated more than cursory attention.

The first sign of trouble came at the end of March, when several Hollywood entertainment executives felt they had been mistreated by presidential aide James Carville. The Californians had flown to Washington at the invitation of the White House—and at their own expense—to present public relations ideas for communicating the president's health care reforms. But the brutally frank Carville could not curb his disdain for people he perceived as overprivileged dilettantes. Instead of deferring to their self-proclaimed expertise, he set about to berate them for being out of touch. In press accounts of the meeting one of the participants, television comedy producer Gary David Goldberg, likened Carville to "Anthony Perkins playing Fidel Castro on acid." The White House said it would not dispatch James Carville to any more brainstorming sessions with Hollywood executives.

On April 3 Bill Clinton raised eyebrows by inviting a group of entertainment personalities to his Vancouver hotel suite during a break in talks with Russian President Boris Yeltsin. The guests included Sharon Stone, Richard Gere, Cindy Crawford, and Richard Dreyfuss, all of whom were working on films in the Canadian city. Gere reportedly used the occasion to exhort the chief executive to meet with the Dalai Lama; Clinton remained noncommittal. According to the *Los Angeles Times*, Clinton's socializing "didn't go over well with some people in the entertainment field, who believe that the president may have inadvertently highlighted the role that Vancouver and Canada have played in siphoning off entertainment jobs from Southern California." More damaging was the perception of frivolousness the gathering created; here was the president of the United States on an official mission of serious import, spending his off-hours with the likes of Sharon Stone, an actress best known for flashing her genitalia in the film *Basic Instinct*.

The celebrity encounters proceeded apace. In mid-April 1993 actors Christopher Reeve, John Ritter, Lindsay Wagner, and Billy Crystal came to the White

House in connection with the Washington premiere of a film called *Earth and the American Dream*. They toured the executive mansion, exchanged greetings with Clinton and Vice President Al Gore, and received environmental briefings from top administration aides, including Interior Secretary Bruce Babbitt. On May 1 a raft of entertainers hit the capital for the White House Correspondents Association dinner: Barbra Streisand came back to town, as did Michael Douglas, Richard Dreyfuss, and a host of lesser luminaries. On May 12 the president attended a Democratic fund-raiser in New York City, where he sat at a table next to Sharon Stone and listened to Whoopi Goldberg tell him, "You're like the guys I used to go out with. You are funny. You are cute. I should've met your ass in college."

One week after the New York fund-raiser, a trip to Southern California brought Bill Clinton's celebrity problem to a boil. While parked on the runway at Los Angeles International Airport, the president received a haircut onboard Air Force One from a high-dollar Beverly Hills stylist known as Christophe. News organizations reported that runways had been idled and incoming flights detained during the procedure; the *New York Times* said it "may have been the most expensive haircut in history." Questions about the episode took center stage at the next White House press briefing, as aides scrambled to downplay the significance of the blunder. The presidential haircut became fodder for everyone from political pundits to late-night comedians. Clinton opponent Ross Perot, in an interview on public television, saw the trim as symptomatic of larger issues: "When you've got a different movie star in the White House every night, and you've got somebody up there from Hollywood pleading the case for the Dalai Lama, the average hard-working American in work clothes can't relate to that."

The following week the president defended his actions in a televised town hall meeting on CBS, terming the haircut incident a "boner" and a "blowup." "I mean look, I wear a forty dollar watch," Clinton told his audience. "I wasn't raised that way. I've never lived that way. That's not the kind of person I am." When one of the citizen questioners suggested that the administration appeared "a little infatuated with Hollywood and celebrities," Clinton strenuously denied that he had "gone Hollywood": "The answer to that is no, heck no, never no. Never. Never."

As the connections piled up between Clinton and showbiz, press coverage grew snarkier. Maureen Dowd fired the opening volley with a page-one story in the *New York Times* in which entertainment celebrities became the objects of ridicule. "The Clinton White House is extravagantly star-struck," Dowd wrote, "and Hollywood's liberal luminaries, sensing an opportunity to be taken seriously and savoring the compatible politics, are flocking to Washington." Richard Cohen followed up with an even more scathing column in the *Washington Post*, opining that "the new president's guest log is becoming hard to distinguish from a Valley Girl's autograph book." Cohen concluded with a piece of advice: "If Clinton wants to see some Hollywood stars, he could do what the rest of us do: Go to a movie."

Inevitably the entertainers struck back. In the *Los Angeles Times* Danny Goldberg, a record executive and political activist, wrote a strongly worded, well-reasoned defense of the entertainment industry. Goldberg asserted that the "central premise of the anti-Hollywood stories is false" because no one from show business was formulating White House policy. He denounced the coverage as sexist and pointed out that the same news organizations that criticized entertainers' visits to Washington had invited the stars to the correspondents dinner. "What accounts for this double standard?" Goldberg asked. "It's impossible to ignore that these criticisms are aimed at Democratic celebrities visiting a Democratic president, and for twelve years Republicans doing the same thing were ignored." In the final analysis Goldberg defined the spate of backlash stories as the product of jealousy: "Every dinner the president has with someone from Hollywood is one fewer with Washington's own media elite."

Barbra Streisand, a reliable target in the anti-Hollywood stories, gave an interview in which she accused the news media of using entertainers to discredit the new president. "We have the right as an industry, as people, as professionals to be taken as seriously as automobile executives," Streisand told the *Los Angeles Times*. She added that the coverage was "smearing the main industry in our community. It's saying there isn't a brain around." Entertainment executive Barry Diller dismissed the accounts as "typical media twaddle": "They've gotten a few photo opportunities. They had Barbra in town for a few days . . . They have now decided to create this idea that the Clinton administration is 'too cozy' with Hollywood and then they get to write all this drivel instead of doing any serious work."

As with all such media-driven firestorms, attention soon waned, and the press moved on to fresher, more fertile "scandals." For a few months Clinton backed off from his high-intensity celebrity shmoozing. In December 1993, at the end of his turbulent first year in office, Bill Clinton returned to Hollywood as the featured attraction at a star-studded fund-raiser at the headquarters of Creative Artists Agency. This time Clinton tempered his socializing with a sermon, telling the room full of producers, writers, actors, agents, and directors that violence in movies and music ought to be regarded as a potentially disruptive element in the lives of volatile young people. With this speech the president showed he had learned something from the backlash of early 1993: the value of embracing show business with one arm while holding it at arm's length with the other.

As Clinton extended his time in office, Americans got used to the idea of their president as hopelessly starstruck. Perhaps the public sensed that compared to his other vices, Bill Clinton's weakness for Hollywood was relatively benign. Clinton and his famous friends seemed to enjoy each other's company—and if actors and musicians could help relax a harried commander-in-chief, wasn't that a good thing?

But occasionally the mutual admiration society sparked some new controversy. The "Lincoln Bedroom scandal" of 1997 generated another round of criticism for President Clinton when it was revealed that campaign contributors had been rewarded with overnight stays in the White House. The guest list included sixty-seven names in the Arts and Letters category, most of them well-known show business figures like Streisand, Steven Spielberg, Richard Dreyfuss, Ted Danson and Mary Steenburgen, Judy Collins, Chevy Chase, and Neil Simon. The waning days of the Clinton administration raised the issue anew with reports that the first couple had accepted numerous last-minute farewell gifts from show business celebrities and others. Steenburgen and Danson gave china worth nearly $5,000; so did Steven Spielberg and Kate Capshaw. Jack Nicholson was good for a golf driver valued at $350. Sylvester Stallone came through with a pair of boxing gloves.

On balance, did Bill Clinton's celebrity associations hurt more than help him? Certainly the men and women of show business never stopped filling his coffers, starting with the presidential election of 1992 and continuing into the Senate career of Hillary Rodham Clinton. But entertainers demonstrated their enthusiasm in another important way: by accepting him early on as one of their own, the celebrity caste validated Clinton as a member in good standing of the aristocracy of fame. His high-profile supporters welcomed him into their circle at a time when he had not yet ascended to their heights. Well before he became president, Clinton crossed a threshold of visibility that psychologically boosted his qualification for the job.

Clinton's celebrity problem was one of degree. In his associations with performing artists President Clinton seemed indiscriminate. Too many show horses were vying for space in the corral. The star-infested inaugural of 1993 became a template for what followed over the next eight years of Bill Clinton's presidency;

every day was an inaugural gala. Clinton aides did sometimes attempt to circum-scribe the president's public associations with entertainers. When Bill and Hillary Clinton announced their intention to attend the 1996 Martha's Vine-yard wedding of Mary Steenburgen and Ted Danson, White House officials plotted to avoid photos of the Clintons posing with other well-known guests. But there was no stopping the infatuation that flowed in both directions be-tween Washington and Hollywood.

At its worst, the reciprocity came across as exclusionary. We understood what Clinton got out of the deal, and we understood what the stars got. But where did voters figure into the equation? This question, which hovers over all president-celebrity interactions, remains unanswered.

✴✴✴✴

Misbehavior by celebrity associates carries the danger of redounding to the pres-ident. The record abounds with stories of entertainers who stretched the limits of their presidential ties by disporting themselves badly: from recklessness to disloy-alty, pettiness to presumptuousness. Unfettered by the rules that keep politicians in check, performers can and do swing to a looser beat.

June Carter Cash made Richard Nixon squirm with a sexually suggestive joke during Johnny Cash's performance at the White House. Melanie Griffith wore a provocative low-cut dress to a Bush state dinner. Whoopi Goldberg used the F-word in front of the Clintons at a Democratic fund-raiser. And then there are the near misses. Less than three months before the murders of Nicole Brown Simpson and Ronald Goldman in Los Angeles, Bill Clinton went golfing with O.J. Simpson. During a San Diego vacation in March 1994 the president hit the links at the Del Mar country club with the athlete-turned-actor. Clinton told re-porters he and Simpson had talked about the film *Naked Gun 33 1/3*, which Clinton had just seen, and that O.J. had shared an "endearing" anecdote about "how he met his wife."

When Michael Jackson came to Washington in 1990 to accept an award from the Capital Children's Museum, George Bush invited the singer to the White House and sent a letter of congratulations that was read at the testimonial dinner. Jackson, Bush wrote, "is a fine role model for young people." Only a few years later Michael Jackson made international headlines for an improper rela-tionship with an underage boy. Actor Rob Lowe, an active campaigner for Michael Dukakis in 1988, kicked up a similarly lurid scandal when it came to light that he had videotaped himself having sex in a hotel room with a sixteen-year-old girl, an encounter that occurred while Lowe was in Atlanta for the Democratic National Convention. Fortunately for Dukakis, knowledge of the tape did not become public until well after the election.

Willie Nelson might have embarrassed Jimmy Carter had it become known that during an overnight stay at the White House as Carter's guest, Nelson climbed up to the roof and smoked pot.

> I let the weed cover me with a pleasing cloud, and reflected on what a long, strange trip it had been from smoking cedar bark and grapevine at the age of four or five, to getting puke-on-your-shoes drunk with my dad Ira at the age of nine, to sitting on the roof of the White House sharing a number in the warm humid night.
>
> I guess the roof of the White House is the safest place I can think of to smoke dope.

Entertainers have generated a number of uncomfortable moments for presidential candidates on the campaign trail. In 1992 actor Gerald McRaney, star of the military-themed television comedy *Major Dad,* made several appearances with George and Barbara Bush. Bush eagerly capitalized on McRaney's make-believe Marine Corps connection, telling voters in Florida he was "glad to have Major Dad on my side" and delivering an announcement about a local air force base "in honor of the Major's presence." McRaney's contribution to the rallies consisted in large part of deriding Bill Clinton for having avoided military service as a young man. "Occasionally, one of us did our duty—and most of us who didn't do our duty at least stayed loyal to our country," McRaney told a gathering of senior citizens a few weeks before the election. It soon emerged that McRaney himself had never spent time in the military, and had considered moving to Canada because of ambivalence about the Vietnam War.

Bush experienced a less direct form of embarrassment when a high-profile rap star of questionable reputation paid $1,230 to hear the president speak at an exclusive Republican fund-raiser in Washington. Singer Eric Wright, who performed under the name Eazy-E, was a member of N.W.A.—"Niggaz with Attitude," a group from Compton, California, whose hits included the controversial "Fuck the Police." Wright made no apologies for the foulness of his lyrics or for his drug-dealing street credentials, so he was surprised to receive an invitation to the closed-door luncheon, apparently by mistake. Wright decided to play along; he mailed in his check, alerted the press, and traveled to the capital for the so-called Salute to the Commander-in-Chief.

In his ball cap, black leather suit, white T-shirt, and gold-and-diamond bracelet, Eazy-E cut a striking figure among the fourteen hundred Republican luncheon guests in the ballroom of the Omni Shoreham Hotel. Press accounts of the gathering barely mention the president's speech; instead the spotlight fell on Eazy-E. "It's kind of wild, isn't it?" Wright said to a reporter after the event. "I'm not a registered Republican or Democrat. I don't even vote. I sent them the money because I was curious."

George Bush had a worse-than-average track record with celebrities. In 1992 members of the Beach Boys announced that after having previously endorsed the president they were withdrawing their affiliation with the Bush-Quayle ticket. "We like George Bush as a person and have supported him in the past," Beach Boy Mike Love told the *Los Angeles Times*, "but on the environment, we have to part ways."

Bush was hardly the first candidate to see celebrity supporters morph into celebrity turncoats. A few months after signing an anti-FDR letter Nelson Eddy performed at Roosevelt's 1941 inaugural gala. Ethel Merman, a major Eisenhower supporter, sang at Kennedy's pre-inaugural show. Helen Hayes, who had served as women's finance chairman for the National Citizens for Eisenhower and Nixon, came out foursquare for John F. Kennedy after meeting the president at the White House in 1961. "We are eating our words, with relish," Hayes announced.

The most dramatic political U-turns have been made by formerly ardent Democrats like Frank Sinatra, Sammy Davis Jr., and Charlton Heston. Sinatra and Davis, along with other members of the so-called Rat Pack, were dedicated campaigners against Richard Nixon in the election of 1960, but a decade later both became closely identified with Nixon. (According to biographer Kitty Kelley, when Nixon delayed making his election night concession to Kennedy, a furious Sinatra tried unsuccessfully to reach the vice president on the phone.)

Heston's transformation came about during the 1964 presidential campaign, in appropriately biblical fashion. While on location for a film shoot, Heston would make a daily drive past a pro–Barry Goldwater billboard that showed a portrait of Goldwater with the senator's campaign slogan: "In your heart you know he's right." Disquieted by the message, Heston deliberately avoided looking at the sign until one day when he got stuck at the intersection waiting for traffic. "As we waited," Heston wrote, "I experienced a true revelation, almost an epiphany, like St. Paul on the road to Damascus. I looked at that photograph of Goldwater and said softly, 'Son of a bitch . . . he is right!'"

Country singer Loretta Lynn, who performed at Jimmy Carter's inaugural, also became a devoted Republican. After making several visits to the Carter White House, Lynn found herself back in the executive mansion at the invitation of Ronald Reagan. "I'm a Reagan fan too," the singer told reporters. "You can love more than just one man, can't you?"

Some presidents are loved too much by their celebrity supporters. After Richard Nixon set up a golf foursome with Bob Hope, Frank Sinatra, and Vice President Spiro Agnew in Palm Springs, the question of who would ride with whom became a point of contention. As Agnew aide Vic Gold recalled, "Although diplomatic protocol establishes seating arrangements at White House dinners, no similar rules exist for golf cart placement." Agnew, as Sinatra's houseguest, might logically have been expected to share a vehicle with his host; but Nixon, eager to form an alliance with Sinatra, wanted the singer with him. When news of the seating arrangements reached Hope, all hell broke loose. Nixon associates at various levels got drawn into the crisis. Chief of staff H. R. Haldeman wrote in his diary that Hope had his "nose out of joint" over the perceived slight.

In the end neither Hope nor Sinatra rode with Nixon. Instead the seat of honor went to another entertainer, Ronald Reagan, formerly of Warner Bros. and now the governor of California. Presidential aides persuaded Reagan to move up a previously scheduled appointment with Nixon, thus resolving a thorny interpersonal conflict.

Politicians who maintain celebrity friendships soon learn that entertainers need a good deal of stroking. President Bush took time out from his 1992 presidential campaign to assuage the feelings of singer Andy Williams, unhappy over not being invited to Bush's rally in Branson, Missouri. In a memo Bush instructed an aide to phone Williams and "tell him it was a terrible oversight," and then he followed up with a handwritten note. "My regret is that I didn't take the offense and get on the phone to you," the president wrote. "Next time for sure." Though the Williams incident is of minor significance, it illustrates the extent to which chief executives get involved in smoothing the ruffled feathers of their show business supporters.

Through the years presidents and presidential candidates have endured presumptuous behavior by celebrities. Tallulah Bankhead once refused to take a phone call from Harry Truman because it interfered with her favorite television soap opera, *The Edge of Night*. "Tell him to call between five and six," Bankhead instructed her assistant. When the assistant demurred, the actress dug in her heels. "I practically elected him to the presidency with my speech in Madison Square Garden. And he should know better than to call at this hour." As instructed, Truman phoned back after the program ended.

Bankhead, whose father had served as Speaker of the United States House of Representatives, seemed singularly resistant to the niceties of political protocol. Writer Jimmy Kirkwood remembered a visit to Tallulah's New York apartment in the mid-1950s by Eleanor Roosevelt. Halfway through an intense political discussion Bankhead stood up and announced, "I've got to pee. But I don't want to miss a word of this." Making her way to a nearby bathroom, Bankhead stepped inside, and, leaving the door open, relieved herself in view of her illustrious guest.

After Mrs. Roosevelt left, Kirkwood confronted his friend: "You peed in front of Eleanor Roosevelt!"

"Oh, don't be ridiculous," Tallulah answered. "Eleanor Roosevelt has more important things on her mind than my bathroom habits. I'm sure she didn't even notice. She pees herself, you know."

At least these minor humiliations by Bankhead occurred in private. In 1976 Democratic candidate Jimmy Carter found himself the target of group condescension at a reception with entertainment celebrities in Beverly Hills—and he gave as good as he got. Though the event was closed to the press and the public, journalist Ken Reich from the *Los Angeles Times* gained access as the designated pool reporter. It is through Reich's account that we have a window on a revealing moment in the nexus between show business and presidential politics.

Carter's host for the August 24 reception was Warren Beatty, who four years earlier had played a pivotal role in the campaign of George McGovern. At this point in the campaign, a month after Carter's nomination at the Democratic National Convention but more than two months before the general election, the Georgia governor remained largely unknown. Beatty's hosting of the reception served as both a benediction and an entrée to various constellations of Hollywood stars: Diana Ross, Art Garfunkel, and Dinah Shore from the music world; Carroll O'Connor *(All in the Family)*, Peter Falk *(Columbo)*, and Louise Lasser *(Mary Hartman, Mary Hartman)* from television; Sidney Poitier, Faye Dunaway, Jon Voight, James Caan, George Segal, George Peppard, and Tony Randall from the big screen; directors Robert Altman and Alan Pakula; writers Neil Simon and Buck Henry; producer Norman Lear; and *Playboy* publisher Hugh Hefner.

In introducing the guest of honor, Warren Beatty observed that Carter's presence at the reception might allay the concerns of many in the room that he was overly religious. Quipped Carter, "If I come to Warren Beatty's party, it should wipe out the issue." Beatty proceeded to note that many in the liberal wing of the entertainment community had gotten reputations as "pinkos, leftists, and Commies." The political activists of Hollywood shared a "rising enthusiasm" for Jimmy Carter, Beatty said, and hoped he would cut $30 billion from the defense budget, free Huey Newton, aid the Chicago Seven, and "stop referring to Ronald Reagan as an actor."

"You are a far superior actor," Beatty told the nominee. "We think of an actor as someone who can illuminate the truth." Beatty described the entertainers in attendance as "a battered group with a need to win."

Carter showed no sign of being intimidated by the collection of luminaries packed into the eighth-floor suite at the Beverly Wilshire Hotel. He began by saying that Beatty had described his views "as accurately as the Republicans did at their convention," and added, "It is a real thrill to meet the famous people here tonight. I hope I don't get to know too much about you."

Hollywood being Hollywood, this was not to be. Various participants took the opportunity to engage with the candidate. Carroll O'Connor made a pitch for détente with the Soviet Union. Diana Ross asked Carter a grandiose question about his conception of the presidency. James Caan invited him to meet his Little League team, and Tony Randall pressed for government financing of a national theater and opera. When Carter noted that in all his months on the campaign trail no one else had extended such a proposal, Randall replied tartly, "You've never met with people of this level."

"That's why I won the nomination," Carter shot back.

Jimmy Carter's closing remarks gave further evidence of his ambivalence about having to make nice with a bevy of self-important Hollywood celebrities. In essence, Carter lapsed into his Sunday school mode, offering a homily about the suffering of the poor and weak at the hands of the rich and powerful: "So I say public servants . . . have a special responsibility to bypass the big shots, including you and people like you and like I was, and make a concerted effort to understand people who are poor, black, speak a foreign language, who are not well educated, who are inarticulate, who are timid . . . "

As Carter left the reception, he was once again buttonholed by Tony Randall, who warned that he was "not going to let you forget" the arts.

✷✷✷✷

Political leaders have sometimes suffered the humiliation of being outshone on the public stage by their showbiz supporters. The potential for this became apparent on January 19, 1953, when 44 million television viewers watched the birth of Ricky Ricardo Jr. on the *I Love Lucy* show. The following day only 29 million Americans tuned in for General Eisenhower's first inauguration, though in fairness, the daytime audience for the swearing-in was smaller to begin with.

The danger of being overshadowed by an entertainer seems especially pronounced on the campaign trail. In 1968 Hubert Humphrey learned that it was impossible to play anything but second fiddle to James Brown during a parking lot rally in the Watts neighborhood of Los Angeles. The gathering started off with Brown endorsing the Democratic nominee in his bid for office, then quickly evolved into a James Brown miniconcert with Humphrey singing backup—literally. As Brown launched into his hit single "I Got You (I Feel Good)," the vice president of the United States chimed in to sing the "so good" vocal chorus. At the end of the performance some two hundred members of the audience mobbed the so-called Godfather of Soul, leaving Humphrey to shake hands with only two dozen well-wishers. Arnold Schwarzenegger overwhelmed his political patron, the first George Bush, during a high-profile visit to New Hampshire before that state's 1992 primary. In their appearances together it was the president who introduced the entertainer rather than the other way around. According to political reporter David Broder, "The *Terminator* star stirred much more excitement than the liberator of Kuwait could evoke. It took me back thirty years to the days when Richard Nixon would invite a Hollywood actor named Ronald Reagan to lend some punch to his rallies in California." Broder wrote that Schwarzenegger so outdistanced Bush in personality and presence that the president was diminished as a result. "Bush normally looks and sounds like a vigorous leader, but next to Schwarzenegger he—like most mere mortals—seemed a shrimp."

How does it make a president feel to take a backseat to an actor? In January 1973 Richard Nixon got miffed when *Time* magazine featured Marlon Brando on the cover in lieu of the second Nixon inaugural. As retribution the president ordered his lieutenants not to talk to *Time* correspondent Hugh Sidey. Given the disparity in star power between popular performers and charisma-deprived politicians, one can almost understand the frustration some presidents face as they seek to maintain their hold on the public imagination. But a national leader who dares to compete on the playing field of show business finds himself on dangerous turf.

On September 16, 1968, about six weeks before being elected president, Richard Nixon made an unusual appearance on the hit comedy TV show *Laugh-In*, a lightning-paced olio of topical one-liners and irreverent blackout sketches. Nixon's participation came about through his long-time associate Paul Keyes, a sometime Nixon gagsmith who served as *Laugh-In*'s head writer. Nixon delivered one of the program's most popular catchphrases, "Sock it to me," a line the candidate read almost as a question. Producer George Schlatter recalled the taping: "It took six takes to get him to say 'Sock it to me' so he didn't look angry. He turned to that camera and would say angrily, 'Sock it to me!' 'No sir,' I said, 'could you just say *Sock it to me* kind of happy?'"

In Schlatter's opinion, Nixon served himself well by going on *Laugh-In*. "It was the first time he had been within any kind of youth-oriented vehicle or place. A lot of people said, 'Hey, wait a minute, maybe Nixon is kind of with-it and aware of today, and together.'" Others found the appearance vulgar, especially since it was juxtaposed with a Nixon campaign commercial that ran during one of the show's station breaks; the ad stressed the need for citizens to treat their president with respect. In the interest of balance *Laugh-In* producers sought to book Nixon opponent Hubert Humphrey on the program for a similar gig. Fearing that it would demean his candidacy, Humphrey declined.

Richard Nixon was not the first presidential politician to take part in a television comedy. That honor goes to Harry S. Truman, who in 1959 appeared as himself on a special edition of *The Jack Benny Program*. Truman's participation in the show offers a fascinating lesson in maintaining presidential decorum amid the inherent cheesiness of a TV sitcom.

Jack Benny had struck up a friendship with Harry Truman that went back to the 1940s; after Truman's unexpected ascension to the Oval Office Benny was among the first celebrities to wire him a telegram of support. In the years since Truman left office, the two Midwesterners had maintained a steady stream of correspondence, punctuated with occasional face-to-face meetings. They stayed in touch for the rest of their lives.

One morning while shaving Benny got the idea of inviting his friend to appear on his television program. Trembling with nerves, Benny telephoned Truman and made his pitch. Without hesitating, Truman said yes.

"The show will be dignified," Benny promised.

"Don't make it too dignified, Jack," Truman answered.

Truman's agreeability notwithstanding, arrangements between Hollywood and Independence had to be negotiated. Harry Truman had been solicited by other television stars for guest appearances—Jack Paar, for instance—and had turned them down. "They've all asked me," Truman said. "But if I started doing that, I'd do nothing else."

Like many a star in demand, ex-President Truman was given script approval for the Benny show, and he used it to delete lines that struck him as out of bounds. A draft of the teleplay in the archives of the Truman Library shows the changes Truman made. "Give 'Em Hell Harry" comes across both as a talented joke editor and a shrewd judge of presidential propriety. Truman nixed a bit in which he was asked to imitate Jack Benny's cross-armed stance; in the revision it is the entertainer who imitates the politician. The former president crossed out a corny joke referring to the famous "Dewey Beats Truman" headline in the *Chicago Tribune*, and either softened or sharpened the wording of several other lines. It is clear to see that the former president went over the teleplay with a fine-tooth comb.

When he returned the script to Benny, Truman included a cover letter which suggests that the small-town Missouri shopkeeper understood the ways of Hollywood: "Enclosed is the script your office sent me, modified, as you will see, with several page-revisions. I don't think we'll have any trouble getting along."

Filming took place at the newly opened Truman Library in Independence, Missouri. Accustomed to the perfectly calibrated setting of a television studio, Benny and his crew were frustrated by the relative chaos of working on location. Rehearsals had to be conducted while the museum was bustling with tourists. Lighting and sound equipment could not be properly installed. "The film we shot was not clear and well lighted but it was very real and so was much of the dialogue," Benny recalled.

The premise of the show has Truman taking Benny on a tour of his presidential library. Most of their dialogue is serious, but occasionally one or the other cracks a joke. When they reach a portrait of Abraham Lincoln, for instance, Truman posits that Lincoln must be a Jack Benny favorite.

"Abraham Lincoln, my favorite president? Why do you say that?"

"Well," Truman replies, "I thought that any man who would walk twelve miles to save three cents would be the kind of man you'd fall for."

The program ends in Truman's private office at the library, where the former president buzzes his secretary on the intercom and says he and Mr. Benny do not want to be disturbed. The secretary (the actress playing Truman's secretary) sneaks over to her boss's door and cracks it ajar. Through the opening come the labored sounds of Benny's violin.

Broadcast on October 18, 1959, the show drew generally favorable comment. *New York Times* critic Jack Gould wrote: "With an uncanny sense of taste, Mr. Truman was a perfect straight man for Mr. Benny and deftly handled a few prepared quips of his own. Yet the stature and dignity of the presidential office was always preserved." Others disagreed. A supporter in New York City wired Truman to say, "Lending your great name and aura of your great office to a huckstering proposition makes any sensitive American wince." A telegram from a Tucson man couched the matter in more personal terms: "How undignified can an ex-president get? One of the tragedies of history is that you could not make a living as a haberdasher."

Jack Benny penned a heartfelt thank-you note to Harry Truman in which he said, "Working with you was the greatest thrill I ever experienced in my theatrical career." So pleased was the notoriously spendthrift Benny that he sent his friend an expensive new television set, just in time for the Trumans to watch Harry's comedy debut.

Bob Hope on his first visit to the Carter White House, May 1978. (Jimmy Carter Library)

3

✳✳✳✳

Hope Springs Eternal

How Presidents Are
Good for Entertainers

IN MAY 1978 six hundred people—movie stars, members of Congress, and military brass—filled the East Room of the White House for a high-profile seventy-fifth birthday celebration. The host was the president of the United States, and the guest of honor was Bob Hope. "I figured out the other day that I've been in office for 498 days," Jimmy Carter told the gathering, "and when I spend three more weeks, I will have stayed as many nights in the White House as Bob Hope has."

No other entertainer in American history attached himself more personally, or more lastingly, to the institution of the presidency than Bob Hope. From Franklin Roosevelt to Bill Clinton, the link between Hope and the White House stood as a fact of life for several generations of Americans. As Carter's joke suggests, it sometimes seemed as if Bob Hope held a stronger claim on 1600 Pennsylvania Avenue than the short-term tenants who resided there.

Remarkably enough, the British-born jester was already past forty when he performed for his first American chief of state. Hope made his presidential debut on March 4, 1944, at a correspondents dinner at the Statler Hotel in Washington, delivering a stand-up routine before an audience that included Franklin D. Roosevelt. Although Hope had been Eleanor Roosevelt's guest at a White House tea two years earlier, this was his only appearance before FDR. The event left an indelible impression on Bob Hope, who thereafter referred to Roosevelt as "the greatest audience I ever worked for."

Waiting his turn at the microphone, Hope studied the president's weary demeanor, "all the cares of wartime written on that lined face." The comedian concluded he would never get a laugh. But FDR did laugh, beginning with Hope's very first joke: "Good evening, Mr. President. I heard you just had a conference with Winston Churchill on a battleship, about war strategy. War strategy meaning 'Where will we attack the enemy and how are we going to keep Eleanor out of the crossfire?'" As Hope recalled the moment, "Roosevelt laughed so loud, I wanted to sign him up for my studio audience."

In January 1945 Bob Hope came back to Washington for Franklin Roosevelt's final swearing-in and performed at an inaugural eve dinner attended by Eleanor Roosevelt and Vice President Harry Truman, though not FDR. Four months later—one day after the end of the official mourning period that followed Roosevelt's death—Hope played his first White House gig, entertaining President Truman with a war bond show. From that point forward, for the next fifty years, Bob Hope never ceded his status as gagmeister to the nation's chief executives.

As the decades went on, Hope carefully cultivated his ties to the highest office in the land, grafting his act onto the presidency in a way that enhanced his standing both professionally and personally. Each time he came to Washington, Bob Hope expected—and received—an appointment with whichever individual was keeping the seat warm in the Oval Office. When Hope stopped at the White House, it was like a state visit by a foreign potentate.

For the second half of the twentieth century Bob Hope made the nation's capital a regular port of call, dropping in on every president between Truman and Clinton for reasons both official and casual. Hope posed for photos with Harry Truman as part of a Red Cross publicity campaign in 1948. He did standup comedy for Dwight Eisenhower at a 1956 Washington photographers banquet, and played his first White House state dinner in 1966 for Lyndon Johnson. Ten years later Gerald Ford asked Hope back to amuse the queen of England on her bicentennial visit. Ronald Reagan invited him to sleep in the Lincoln Bedroom in 1983, and Bill Clinton took him golfing in 1995.

In a White House ceremony six weeks before his assassination John F. Kennedy presented Bob Hope with a congressional gold medal, one of a raft of presidential honors the actor collected for entertaining American troops overseas. "There is one sobering thought," Hope said in accepting the award. "I received this for going out of the country. I think they're trying to tell me something."

Hope liked to call himself a "Republocrat," and until the presidency of Richard Nixon he did not let his conservative leanings color his performing persona. To the public Hope's political philosophy was an equal-opportunity comedy agnosticism in which elected officials were all treated as punch lines. Hope's humor was respectful and benign, reducing each leader to a broad, gentle stereotype: golf jokes for Eisenhower, youth jokes for Kennedy, Texas jokes for Johnson, and so forth. The targets—and the audience—could trust that Hope's wisecracks would never cross the threshold of meanness.

But in the late 1960s Bob Hope's support for the Vietnam War and dedication to President Nixon redefined his position as a White House courtier. With national opinion sharply divided over both Nixon and the war, Hope could no longer straddle the balance beam of comedic neutrality. Particularly among the young, he began to be perceived not as a pan-political joker but as a pro-establishment, pro-military ideologue.

Personal as well as political factors propelled Bob Hope's emergence as a symbol of the right. Beyond his reflexively patriotic views he felt genuine affection for both Richard Nixon and Spiro Agnew. Agnew was a buddy, someone Hope enjoyed swapping dirty jokes with over the phone. Nixon and Hope went back to 1953, when they first bonded over a golf game and Hope referred to the youthful vice president as "Eisenhower's caddy." Throughout the 1950s and 1960s, including Nixon's years out of political office, the men kept in contact. When both received honorary degrees from Whittier College in 1965, Nixon and Hope posed for photographers in a humorous shot that highlighted their lookalike ski-jump noses.

Once in the White House Nixon booked his friend for a series of performances. In December 1969 Hope brought his USO show to the East Room before shipping out on a Christmas tour of Southeast Asia. After Hope costarred at a 1971 dinner for the nation's governors with the singing group Up With People, he and his wife spent the night as the Nixons' guests. Two years later Hope appeared at the White House party for released prisoners of war.

Bob Hope's defining moment as a Nixon booster came in 1970, when he teamed up with evangelist Billy Graham to stage a Fourth of July Honor America rally at the Lincoln Memorial. The program featured flag-waving entertainment by Republican stalwarts Pat Boone, Kate Smith, Red Skelton, Lionel Hampton, Glen Campbell, and Dinah Shore. A crowd of several hundred thousand turned out, including a sizable contingent of antiwar demonstrators. Before the event ended, thirty-four arrests had been made, tear gas had been fired, and twenty policemen had been injured; according to the *Los Angeles Times*, "hippies hooted, booed, and gave war whoops at Bob Hope's humor . . . "

Several days before the rally Hope had spoken to a network news program about the ideological composition of the show's cast. His passive-aggressive quote is priceless: "The New Left can come in if they have some entertainers. But this is not going to be political, so forget it for the New Left unless they have entertainers. Now if they want to present their entertainers, I'm judging the show as far as the entertainment is concerned. And we'd be happy to audition any of them because that's what we want." Needless to say, the slate of performers remained 100 percent red, white, and blue.

At the end of 1971 Bob Hope became briefly involved in negotiations to free American prisoners of war in Vietnam. A few days before Christmas he met with a North Vietnamese diplomat in Laos to seek passage into the POW camps; the French news agency AFP reported that Hope intended to spend $10 million of privately raised money to buy the release of some of the servicemen. Although the foreign ministry in Hanoi denied Hope's request, President Nixon expressed his gratitude: "I can only say that the efforts that he makes, that anybody makes, are deeply appreciated."

More typically, Hope's dealings with Nixon fell under the heading of fun. In 1970 the president took a helicopter to Hope's home in Toluca Lake, California, for a game of golf; Jimmy Stewart and Fred MacMurray rounded out the foursome. It required four choppers to accommodate the army of Secret Service agents, press corps, and technicians who traveled with the commander-in-chief. When the convoy touched down on Hope's six-acre estate, the host was out in the yard, unmistakable in a yellow blazer, white golf shirt, and yellow plaid trousers. "Is it all right if we park here?" Nixon asked as he stepped out of his helicopter. A week later at an awards dinner Hope turned the high-flying arrival into a gag line: "I guess the president is worrying about 1972. Why else would he be going house to house?"

In 1994 a frail Bob Hope was one of a handful of Hollywood stars—Red Skelton and Buddy Ebsen were the others—to attend the funeral of Richard Nixon in Yorba Linda, California. "He was a hell of a guy," Hope told reporters. "Playing golf, you learn a lot about a guy's character. His was a great character." Three years later Bob and Dolores Hope endowed the Pat Nixon Amphitheater on the grounds of the Nixon Library and Birthplace.

When President Nixon left the White House in 1974, Bob Hope stayed behind, taking up immediately with Gerald Ford. As with Nixon, the common bond was golf. "Of all the presidents, [Ford] is the one I can call a pal," Hope wrote in his book *Dear Prez.* "My stays at the Ford White House were more relaxed than visits with previous presidents. Dolores and I loved being in the private quarters on the second floor where we kicked off our shoes, put our feet up and just talked and laughed." Betty Ford called Hope her most enjoyable White House guest: "He was gracious and well-mannered and only tried taking over the Oval Office once."

Bob Hope's seventy-fifth birthday reception in 1978 marked the comedian's first interaction with the Carter White House, although Jimmy Carter had been in office nearly a year and a half. Standing next to the president, Hope quipped, "I used to come here quite often . . ." The edge in his voice made it clear that the chilly diplomatic relations between Washington and Toluca Lake had not gone unnoticed. After the event Hope wrote Carter a friendly note, thanking him for "loaning us the house for a few hours." But the goodwill was short-lived. When Hope sent a telegram to Carter several months later demanding that he do something to deport Iranian protesters, the White House responded with a form letter.

The election of Ronald Reagan in 1980 restored Bob Hope's accustomed access to the corridors of presidential power. Hope performed at Reagan's 1981 inaugural gala, received the Kennedy Center Honors in 1985, and hobnobbed with the first couple during their frequent visits to California. In 1983 President Reagan played supporting actor in a three-hour NBC television special celebrating the entertainer's eightieth birthday. *Happy Birthday, Bob* combined footage from a Kennedy Center tribute with an introductory sequence taped at the White House. The show opened in the Lincoln Bedroom with the president and Hope, both in shirtsleeves, holding what was supposed to be a spontaneous conversation. "You look wonderful," Reagan told his guest. "I've been in makeup for three years," replied the birthday boy. After amusing Hope with a Jimmy Stewart imitation, Reagan flashed one of his trademark Hollywood smiles and, on behalf of the entire nation, wished him a happy birthday. "Rarely, if ever, has an American president—indeed, any world leader—used popular entertainment so shrewdly and so disarmingly," observed John J. O'Connor in the *New York Times.*

Setting aside any pretense of nonpartisanship, Hope assumed an active role in the 1988 campaign of George Bush. Once again, golf provided the connective tissue. "I knew his father, Prescott, and played golf with him," Hope said. "During his eight years as Reagan's vice president, I became very close to George and I played a lot of golf with him too." Two weeks before the election Hope opened his Toluca Lake home for a Bush fund-raising reception attended by a sizable contingent of Hollywood Republicans—"most of whom looked as if they had been preserved in aspic," as one British newspaper waspishly put it. Introducing Vice President Bush to the crowd, Hope joked, "He's been with Ronald Reagan for eight years. It's time he met some real actors."

Among the real actors on hand were Robert Mitchum, Glenn Ford, Cyd Charisse, Jane Russell, Donald O'Connor, Phyllis Diller, and Pat Boone. One by one Hope called them forward, cracking a joke with each new name. Esther Williams: "Is she out of the pool yet?" Gene Autry: "If he makes it to the stage he gets decorated." According to one observer, two younger stars in the crowd, Tom Selleck and Jacqueline Smith, "looked like green shoots among the drying reeds."

Not only did Hope actively campaign for George Bush, he actively campaigned against Michael Dukakis. At a rally in California shortly after the 1988 Republican National Convention, Bob Hope warmed up the crowd with a series of anti-Dukakis jokes, many of them predicated on the Massachusetts governor's modest height. Dukakis loved campaigning, Hope said, "because he can kiss babies without lifting them up." Hope even ventured into the dangerous waters of ethnic humor. "Remember when Nancy Reagan got into the White House, she bought all of that beautiful china? If the Greeks get in, they'll break it first thing."

However stridently Republican Hope may have become, he did maintain positive relations with President Bill Clinton, at least before failing health permanently pulled Hope out of the White House orbit. The two men originally met in the late 1970s when Hope was performing at the University of Arkansas during Clinton's first term as governor. They reconnected in Little Rock a few years later. From the outset Hope recognized Clinton's potential. "Watching him work the crowd both times, this man was all showbiz," Hope wrote. "He had to be on the stage, or at least in the White House."

Though Hope campaigned against Clinton in 1992 and gave money to Bob Dole in 1996, these two pros did not let ideological differences stand between them. Early in his presidency Clinton surprised Hope by stopping at his New York hotel to wish him a happy birthday. In 1995 Clinton appeared with Bob Hope on four separate occasions. In February he joined Hope and former presidents Ford and Bush at the Bob Hope Chrysler Classic golf tournament in Palm

Springs. "With golf balls flying every which way, an outing that had been billed as historic turned out to be downright harrowing," reported the *Washington Post*. Clinton told journalists that the "best part of the day was being with Bob Hope. Presidents Ford and Bush and I see each other from time to time on the nation's business, but being with Bob Hope was special." In May Clinton invited Hope for a round of golf in Washington, Hope's last such outing with a sitting president. Bob and Dolores Hope shared the stage in Honolulu for the fiftieth anniversary of World War II in September, and a month later Clinton awarded the comedian a National Medal of the Arts in a ceremony on the South Lawn.

In 1996 Hope brought down the curtain on his career as a White House gagman with a final television special for NBC entitled *Bob Hope: Laughing with the Presidents*. Now ninety-three, the performer was showing his years. The few lines he recited were spoken with difficulty, and he remained planted in his chair in a studio replica of the Oval Office. Most of the program consisted of clips from Hope's vast presidential repertoire, supplemented by newly gathered testimonials from Bill and Hillary Clinton, George and Barbara Bush, Gerald and Betty Ford, and David and Julie Eisenhower, standing in for the Nixons. Ronald Reagan was no longer making public appearances; conspicuously absent were Jimmy and Rosalynn Carter.

The script was corny, predictable, and mild—like Hope's act. President Ford called Bob Hope "a nice guy who liked people." Bush said that when he was with Hope he never stopped feeling he was "standing with a legend," even after becoming president. Bill Clinton sounded as if he were reading a press release: "When he makes fun of me or any other president I think we know he's doing it with a genuinely good heart and a good spirit and in a way that helps us all to laugh at ourselves." Nobody had a bad word to say about Hope, of course, but no one had anything very interesting to say either.

When Bob Hope hung up his hat, he left behind no heir. Although Hope illustrates the degree to which a show business career can be built on White House access, it seems doubtful that his fifty-year run will ever be repeated. Somewhere between Franklin Roosevelt and Bill Clinton, the knives got too sharp for that.

❋❋❋❋

It is difficult to know precisely what led Elvis Presley to show up at 1600 Pennsylvania Avenue on December 21, 1970, seeking an appointment with the president. The established facts are these: the king of rock and roll (1) got in to see

Richard Nixon a few hours after dropping off a handwritten letter of introduction at a White House security gate, (2) walked out of his thirty-minute Oval Office meeting a special assistant in the Bureau of Narcotics and Dangerous Drugs, and (3) with the acquiescence of Nixon, kept the whole thing quiet for more than a year. On every level this face-to-face encounter between two American legends defies all logic. Surely its sheer bizarreness helps explain why the Nixon and Elvis tête-à-tête has loomed so prominently in the national imagination. As a signature moment in the history of presidents and entertainers, this stands squarely alongside Marilyn Monroe singing "Happy Birthday, Mr. President" to John F. Kennedy.

Presley gave two reasons for seeking an audience with Nixon, though the weight each motive carried can only be guessed at. First, as a staunch supporter of Richard Nixon, the singer thought he could serve his beleaguered president in the capacity of antidrug youth ambassador. Second, Elvis coveted a federal narcotics badge and believed Nixon could help him get it. But other, more mysterious impulses seemed to be propelling Elvis Presley toward the Oval Office. Was he throwing his celebrity weight around, showing up to see the most powerful man in the world simply because he could? Was he seeking Nixon's validation? Was he the victim of a drug-induced delusion?

On December 20 Presley rounded up a member of his entourage, Jerry Schilling, to accompany him on a red-eye flight from Los Angeles to Washington; a second friend, Sonny West, was summoned to join them from Memphis. Onboard the plane Presley struck up a conversation with a fellow passenger, California Senator George Murphy, the former song-and-dance man whose transition into elective politics presaged the similar journey of Ronald Reagan. Murphy's solidly conservative credentials were to Presley's liking, and as the jetliner flew east the two men chewed over the issues of the day.

The conversation must have gotten Elvis worked up, because afterward he returned to his seat and began composing the rambling letter, scrawled on American Airlines stationery, that he delivered to the White House a few hours hence. Presley wrote: "Sir, I can and will be of any service that I can to help the country out . . . I wish not to be given a title or an appointed position. I can and will do more good if I were made a federal Agent at Large and I will help out by doing it my way through my communications with people of all ages."

After checking into the Hotel Washington, a short stroll from the executive mansion, Elvis and Schilling made their way to the president's house. Here, at 6:30 in the morning, they dropped off the letter. Three hours later Nixon aide

Egil (Bud) Krogh, a low-level bureaucrat assigned to drug policy, telephoned the hotel to invite Presley to his office in the Old Executive Office Building, next door to the White House. Though Krogh did not make the point in so many words, the meeting would in effect serve as an audition—which Elvis did not fail. Meanwhile, the question of whether the president should see the King began traveling up the chain of command. Shortly after Elvis left Krogh's office, word came down from chief of staff H. R. (Bob) Haldeman: the meeting was on.

Elvis Presley's arrival for his 12:30 appointment with Richard Nixon presented an immediate snag. The visitor showed up with a gift for Nixon—a gun, which the Secret Service accepted on the president's behalf. Presley was disappointed that he would not be able to present the weapon in person, but he seemed to understand that not even Elvis could walk into the Oval Office packing heat. (Today the gun, a chrome-plated Colt .45 that saw action in World War II, is on display at the Nixon Library in Yorba Linda, California.)

For his rendezvous with Richard Nixon Elvis costumed himself in a purple velvet cape with matching trousers, a white shirt unbuttoned halfway down his chest, and a glittering assortment of accessories: a gold medallion necklace, metallic sunglasses with an "EP" design at the nose bridge, and an enormous gold belt buckle. His long, jet-black hair was sprayed into place like a shiny helmet.

Egil Krogh accompanied Presley into Nixon's private chamber. In his fascinating book, *The Day Elvis Met Nixon*, Krogh recounted the singer's initial reaction: "He was one of the most famous individuals in the world, someone who had entertained millions of people. I expected him to be immediately at ease on entering the Oval Office. Such was not the case." Elvis was in awe, taking in each detail of his surroundings with curious eyes. Nixon came around from behind his desk to greet Presley, and as the two shook hands, White House photographer Ollie Atkins began snapping the famous photographs that commemorated the occasion in perpetuity.

Nixon was friendly but formal, referring to his guest as "Mr. Presley" throughout their time together. Presley at first was tongue-tied, even when Krogh gave him an opening to discuss his offer to help in the president's antidrug campaign. Instead Elvis showed Nixon photographs of his wife Priscilla and daughter Lisa Marie, along with a few of the police badges from his extensive collection, spreading out the items atop the presidential desk. "I really support what our police have to do," Presley said, and the president replied, "They certainly deserve all the support we can give them. They've got tough jobs." Perhaps to compensate for the stiltedness of the small talk, Nixon suggested that they pose for more photographs, this time in front of a display of military flags.

When the picture taking ended, Elvis told his host he had been performing a lot in Las Vegas—"quite a place." Nixon smiled and replied with a non sequitur of his own: "I know very well how difficult it is to play Las Vegas." The talk turned to Elvis's possible role as a liaison to young America in the White House antidrug campaign. For someone who had written an impassioned five-page letter asking to be heard, Elvis was oddly diffident. "I do my thing just by singing, Mr. President," Presley said. "I don't make any speeches onstage. I just try to reach them in my own way." Then Presley threw a curve ball: "The Beatles, I think, are kind of anti-American. They came over here, made a lot of money, and then went back to England. And they said some anti-American stuff when they got back." Neither Nixon nor Krogh had any idea what Elvis was talking about.

The president changed the subject. "You know," Nixon confided, "those who use the drugs are the protesters. You know, the ones who get caught up in dissent and violence. They're the same group of young people." After chatting about this for a few seconds, Presley took another unexpected detour: he told the president he had been studying "Communist brainwashing for over ten years now." When Krogh again steered the conversation back to the administration's antidrug message, Elvis began to brag: "I can go right into a group of hippies and young people and be accepted. This can be real helpful." Nixon paused. "Well, that's fine. But just be sure you don't lose your credibility."

Once again Elvis caught Nixon and Krogh by surprise with a question out of left field. "Mr. President," he asked, "can you get me a badge from the Narcotics Bureau? I've been trying to get a badge from them for my collection." Baffled, Nixon turned to Krogh and asked if such a thing was possible. After briefly kicking the idea around, the president gave his order: "See that he gets one."

Elvis was thrilled. "Thank you very much, sir. This means a lot to me. Mr. President, I really do support what you're doing, and I want to help." Suddenly Elvis threw his left arm around Nixon and gave him a hug. A stunned Nixon awkwardly patted his guest on the shoulder. With time running short, Presley told Nixon about the Colt .45 he had brought, and also made a gift of the photographs of Priscilla and Lisa Marie, which he had already autographed.

Elvis had one more request: Could the president say hello to his two bodyguards who were waiting outside? Soon the others were summoned in, and the photographer began snapping more pictures. "You've got a couple of big ones here," Nixon said, as he shook hands with the men. Before everyone left, the president opened the desk drawer where he kept souvenir items for his guests. Nixon pulled out some trinkets bearing the presidential seal (tie clasps, according to Krogh; key chains, according to Jerry Schilling) and gave them to Presley and his two friends. Like a kid who has discovered a secret toy box, Elvis joined Nixon behind the desk to see what other goodies the drawer held. "Remember, Mr. President, they've got wives," Elvis said, scooping up a few presidential pins. Jerry Schilling later described the moment for a television documentary: "He had the president running around the White House . . . There's where I knew that nobody could really say no to Elvis."

With this, one of the strangest meetings in Oval Office history came to an end. After saying their good-byes to Nixon, the entourage left to have lunch in the White House mess. There was one more exchange between Richard Nixon and Elvis Presley: in September 1975 the former president called Elvis to wish him well during a hospital stay, a gesture that seemed to cheer the patient.

After Presley's death Nixon looked back on Elvis with an odd mix of pathos and denial. "He wanted to be an example for young people," Nixon said in a tape-recorded message for the Nixon Library. "And people say that because later on it was found that he had used drugs, that therefore he could not be a good example. They overlooked the fact that he never used illegal drugs. It was always drugs prescribed by his physician."

The Elvis Presley whom Nixon saw in 1970 was not the same Elvis Presley who telephoned the White House in June 1977, two months before his death from an overdose. Jimmy Carter had met Presley backstage at a concert in Atlanta in 1973, while serving as governor of Georgia. Now, in his first year as president, Carter found himself in conversation with a very stoned Elvis Presley. Presley's purpose in calling, Carter eventually realized, was to seek a presidential pardon for a friend who had been indicted by a federal grand jury. According to Carter, Elvis babbled about being shadowed by dark forces; he "didn't know what he was saying." Finally Carter got it out of Elvis that the individual had not yet gone to trial. "I said, 'Elvis, I can't consider a pardon until after a trial and sentencing and everything.' I don't think he understood that." Although Presley placed subsequent phone calls to the executive mansion, this was the last time President Carter ever spoke directly with the king of rock and roll.

When Presley died a few weeks later, White House aides debated whether to release a statement of condolence, considering Presley's well-known history of drug abuse. Ultimately the pro-statement argument prevailed, making Jimmy

Carter the first president to publicly acknowledge a rock star's death. The statement described Presley as "unique, irreplaceable and a symbol to people the world over of the rebelliousness and good humor of his country." As Carter biographer Douglas Brinkley pointed out, the decision to issue the statement was "more than good politics. Carter heard the songs and understood why people liked Elvis."

❀❀❀❀

Elvis Presley's pathetic appeals to Nixon and Carter underscore how easily a famous name opens doors at the White House, whatever the pretext. For many decades show business celebrities have not hesitated to use this access. Comedy actress Marie Dressler made so many trips to the presidential mansion in the years between Grover Cleveland and Franklin Roosevelt that she "knew perfectly well where to find the ice box." The flamboyant Dressler was a favorite with White House servants, whom she made it a point to befriend. "When she left," wrote Eleanor Roosevelt after a 1933 visit, "there was regret throughout the household and a real appreciation that a very warm and vital person had been with us."

Ronald Reagan got his first peek inside the White House in 1949, thirty-two years before moving in. The occasion was a meeting between Hollywood labor leaders and President Harry Truman to discuss employment problems in the film industry. Reagan, then head of the Screen Actors Guild, pressed his case with Truman in a session that lasted fifteen minutes; it is history's loss that no photographer was present. When Reagan ran for governor in the 1960s he used the session with President Truman to bolster his political credentials, erroneously claiming to have been the lone Hollywood representative at the meeting. "I was the only one who went to Washington and no one gave me a script," Reagan boasted. The White House apparently did not attach much importance to the event; the appointments log misidentified the visitor from California as "Mr. Roland Reagan."

Getting through the door was no problem for actress Candice Bergen, who spent several weeks at the Ford White House in 1975 on a photographic assignment for *Ladies Home Journal*. Bergen, operating under the wing of official photographer David Kennerly, enjoyed a remarkable degree of access to the first family. This was not Bergen's first political assignment. In 1968, for *Cosmopolitan* magazine, she had photographed Richard Nixon, Robert Kennedy, and Eugene McCarthy as they campaigned for the Oregon primary. "I would have been an idiot not to know it was my name and not a God-given gift for journalism that got me in the door," Bergen admitted.

Some celebrities use their access simply to spend time with a president they admire. Bette Davis visited the Warm Springs, Georgia, retreat of Franklin Roosevelt, upsetting some of the president's associates, who considered the star's presence an intrusion. Shirley Temple took her children to meet Dwight Eisenhower at the White House. Shelley Winters and her daughter got a White House tour from John F. Kennedy.

In 1965 Jack Valenti, the aide to Lyndon Johnson who later headed the Motion Picture Association of America, gave Kirk Douglas a lesson in presidential access. The actor had to come to Washington to confer with a highly placed government official, who canceled after keeping Douglas waiting for more than an hour. Douglas called Valenti, hoping to spend the time with him instead; Valenti said yes. At the White House, Valenti asked if Douglas and his wife would like to meet President Johnson. "How could I see the president when I wait an hour to see some functionary?" Douglas asked. But Valenti ushered them into Lyndon Johnson's office for a private audience. "As Kirk and Anne Douglas left, they marveled at the whimsy of Washington," Valenti wrote. "The easiest guy in town to see is the president!"

For most celebrities the mere act of meeting the president is an end unto itself. No particular business gets done; indeed much of the dialogue between these famous parties typically consists of little more than small talk. Johnny Cash and Bill Clinton compared shoe sizes—Clinton was a 12-D and Cash a 13-D. Other entertainers take advantage of their access to plead a political case. The Irish rock singer and activist Bono met with George W. Bush in 2002 to urge increased aid to poor nations; when Bush announced he would seek $5 billion in new assistance to developing countries Bono stood at his side. Barbra Streisand talked with Bill Clinton about funding for AIDS research.

Director Rob Reiner made five visits to the White House in 1993 as he prepared to shoot his film *The American President*. Reiner shadowed Clinton over two days to get a feel for the job; also along for part of the research were star Michael Douglas and writer Aaron Sorkin, who went on to create the White House–based television series *The West Wing*. "At the time we were researching the film, Whitewater was raging, the Paula Jones thing had broken, and we thought, 'My God, how do you do that job?'" Reiner said.

June Lockhart, best known for her roles in the TV series *Lassie* and *Lost in Space*, used her celebrity status to satisfy a lifelong curiosity about the news media. Although Lockhart met a number of presidents, beginning with Harry Truman, her real interest was in the White House press room. In the early 1950s presidential press secretary James Hagerty issued the actress her first White House press credentials, giving her entrée into one of Dwight Eisenhower's early news conferences. Over the next fifty years, no matter which party was in office, she would return for briefings every chance she got.

In five decades at the epicenter of American political journalism June Lockhart never wrote a word about her experiences. "It's all just been for my edification," she said. "If I wrote anything it would be exploitive, and for my own aggrandizement, which I'm not interested in at all."

✳✳✳✳

Entertainers who mingle with presidents are likely to experience as much awe as any ordinary citizen does. The White House gives even the most jaded visitors a connection to history that can be overwhelming. "The moment we walked through the doors . . . we were struck by the emotional impact of our country's history all around us," wrote actress and future Congresswoman Helen Gahagan Douglas about a overnight visit with husband Melvyn Douglas in 1939. "This building had known Jefferson and Lincoln, had echoed to the distant sound of Confederate cannon, had felt the fire of the British invasion in the War of 1812. My throat stung and I found my eyes full of tears."

In 1922 Lillian and Dorothy Gish accompanied director D. W. Griffith to the White House to screen the film *Orphans of the Storm* for President Warren Harding. "The prospect of a visit with the president of the United States was both thrilling and frightening," Gish wrote. "Poor Dorothy was sick from the moment we received the invitation." Seventy years later, singer Judy Collins described her overnight stay at the presidential mansion as "like being in a dream." Collins had never been inside the building. "All of the years I've been going to Washington," she said, "I've been shaking my fist at the person in the White House."

Katharine Hepburn may not seem like the sort of person to be intimidated by a White House visit, but when she showed up for tea with Franklin Roosevelt in the 1930s she was a bundle of nerves. Lest they be tardy for their appointment, Hepburn and her companion arrived five minutes early and sat in their car at the gate until it was time to go in. At the door of the mansion a man in a morning suit was waiting to greet them. Uncertain who he was, Hepburn approached him with her hand out. "Better friendly than formal," she thought.

"I am the usher," the man said.

"Well," replied Hepburn, too embarrassed to retract her outstretched hand. "How do you do?"

Sixteen-year-old Patty Duke became filled with emotion when she met John F. Kennedy at the White House in 1963. "The moment he walked in, I started crying," Duke recalled, "and I cried the whole time, sniffing and wiping my eyes and with a real lump in my throat. I was shaking, there was a ringing in my ears, I'm frankly surprised I didn't pass out." Hoping to assuage Duke's nervousness, Kennedy gave the young star a bracelet with a PT boat medallion on it.

President Kennedy evoked impassioned reactions from many of his visitors, especially the females. Carol Burnett met JFK a year before his assassination in an Oval Office gathering that included Judy Garland, Danny Kaye, and Broadway composer Richard Adler. Afterward Burnett told reporters that when she was introduced to the president, her vision blurred and her "ankles wouldn't hold up." "He's a beautiful man," she said.

John F. Kennedy and twenty-one-year-old singing sensation Barbra Streisand "met cute" after Streisand sang for the president at a White House Correspondents Association dinner in May 1963. Immediately after the show Streisand and the other entertainers gathered in a receiving line to greet Kennedy backstage. Producer Merv Griffin warned his cast that they were not to violate protocol by detaining Kennedy as he passed down the line. Asking for an autograph was strictly verboten.

Barbra Streisand's five-number set had been the hit of the show; one of her songs was the Roosevelt-era standard "Happy Days Are Here Again," which Streisand refashioned as a slow, soaring ballad. Kennedy appeared pleased to meet the talented newcomer, asking her how long she had been singing. "About as long as you've been president," Streisand replied. Then Barbra Streisand did what she had been warned not to do: she asked Kennedy for his autograph, saying it was for her mother in Brooklyn. Instead of being offended, the president laughed and signed her program.

Merv Griffin was less amused, and after the event he took the singer to task for her breach of propriety. When Griffin inquired if Kennedy had written a personal inscription, Streisand said he had signed the program "Fuck you—the President." Although Griffin duly reported this anecdote in his autobiography,

Streisand was kidding. The president had actually written "Best wishes—John F. Kennedy."

Entertainers who make it to the White House sometimes find themselves unable to resist the urge to place an outgoing phone call, just to prove they were there. Singer Rosemary Clooney took a break from hanging out with President Kennedy and a handful of other visitors in order to ring up her brother in Kentucky. Woody Allen, a dinner guest during the Johnson administration, phoned his girlfriend, actress Louise Lasser. "They showed me into a little private room with a phone," Allen remembered. "I wanted to say, 'Hi, I'm calling from the White House.' But she wasn't in. It was so annoying."

In 1951 Esther Williams, then at the height of her popularity as an aquatic movie star, made a semiofficial visit to the nation's capital. Asked if there was anything in particular she wanted to do during her time in Washington, Williams requested—and was granted—permission to swim in the White House pool. "When I went into one of the changing rooms, there was a bathing cap hanging on a peg," Williams wrote in her autobiography. Peeking inside, she found the name of the person who had left it behind: Eleanor Roosevelt. "With a great sense of pride, I put Mrs. Roosevelt's cap on my head and dove in to swim some laps."

Of all the historic spots in the White House, the Lincoln Bedroom elicits the strongest reactions from famous visitors. Actor Frederic March was nearly speechless when an aide escorted him to the room for a brief rest before his performance at a 1962 Kennedy dinner for Nobel Prize winners. Johnny Carson spent the night there in 1992, after receiving the Medal of Freedom from President George Bush. "I later heard that Johnny said that the Lincoln Bed (an overlong double) was the closest he had slept with anybody in years," Barbara Bush wrote. "I'm sure that other guests feel that way, but like Johnny, are so thrilled to sleep in the Lincoln Bedroom, they are willing to forgo the sleep."

Another Bush guest, country singer Larry Gatlin, did not have slumber on his mind when he and his wife stayed in the Lincoln Bedroom. Shortly after checking in Gatlin and his wife "decided to avail ourselves of the hospitality of the surroundings and try out Mr. Lincoln's bed." A knock at the door interrupted the couple at an inopportune moment. It was the White House usher, asking what they wanted for breakfast the next morning. A flustered Gatlin gave his order, closed the door, then noticed that he had left his pajamas inside out. Said Gatlin: "I'll bet the staff and 'sex police' in the basement with the high-tech listening devices had a big laugh too."

One of the first entertainment celebrities to spend the night in the Lincoln Bedroom was Sammy Davis Jr., though host Richard Nixon was out of town at the time. On an earlier occasion, after performing his one-man show for Nixon, Davis had been assigned to a different room of the mansion, just down the hall from the first family. "I wanted the pleasure of having Sammy Davis Jr. stay at the White House," the president told Davis. "No black man has slept here since 1914, when Booker T. Washington was a guest of Woodrow Wilson." After Nixon showed Sammy and his wife to their quarters, they closed the door and stared at each other in silence. Davis wrote, "I could not think of a word to say that would not have been corny or that could begin to describe what I felt. Nor could Altovise. We must have sat there for half an hour without speaking."

The weight of history resonated deeply for Sammy Davis, as it did for other African American entertainers invited to the presidential mansion. Sarah Vaughn made her White House debut in 1965 at a dinner given by Lyndon Johnson for the prime minister of Japan. "For thirty minutes," said Liz Carpenter, press secretary to the first lady, Vaughn "held the distinguished audience in her hand." At the end of the evening Mrs. Johnson's social secretary found Sarah Vaughn in her dressing room, sobbing. "Twenty years ago when I came to Washington, I couldn't even get a hotel room," Vaughn explained, "and tonight I sang for the president of the United States in the White House—and then, he asked me to dance with him. It is more than I can stand."

Burr Tillstrom, the man behind the Kukla, Fran, and Ollie puppet act, wrote movingly of his departure from the White House after performing at a Christmas party for the children of international diplomats in December 1975. In a thank-you letter to Betty Ford's social secretary, Tillstrom described his feelings as he watched the mansion through the limousine window:

> I came away with a sense of the White House belonging to me (which of course it does in a collective way), of almost being the host rather than the guest, and I was moved by a sudden and personal awareness of history. I felt and almost heard the thoughts and voices of the people who lived there. It was a tangible quality which dispelled the remoteness I had begun to feel about the White House as a symbol of power in government. I felt once again that deep pride of being a U.S. citizen and I believed again that anyone can be president of the United States. It is a lovely Christmas gift and still shines gold and red and crystal and white and green in my thoughts—like the White House itself at Christmastime.

✤✤✤✤

Stars who make public appearances with presidents bask in a double spotlight. For a young performer seeking headlines, proximity to the White House serves as a virtual guarantee of media attention. In 1945, egged on by her studio publicity agent, twenty-year-old starlet Lauren Bacall draped herself atop an upright piano being played by Vice President Harry Truman at the National Press Club, where both had been invited. "I felt a bit silly," Bacall said, "but I did it." Photographers captured for the ages the unlikely juxtaposition of leggy, full-lipped Lauren looming over good old Midwestern Harry in his wire-rim glasses.

By the time Truman figured out what Bacall was doing, it was too late to extricate himself from the situation. As Margaret Truman put it, "He was trapped between his instinctive politeness, which made it hard for him to hurt Miss Bacall's feelings, and his equally instinctive political awareness that he was flirting, not with Miss Bacall, but with trouble." The photo ran in hundreds of newspapers across the country. Bess Truman was especially critical of her husband, deeming the pose an undignified image during time of war. Though the Bacall-atop-the-piano incident did not hurt Truman, it did have a lasting effect: political handlers learned to be more protective of the physical space around the president, especially in the presence of headline-hungry movie stars.

Harry Truman held no grudge against Lauren Bacall. Several years later, during the campaign of 1948, the actress sat next to Truman at a dinner in Los Angeles. By this time she was the pregnant wife of Humphrey Bogart. In the course of the evening Truman and Bogart made a $20 bet on whether the child would be a boy or a girl. When Truman won, Bogart sent the president a check, which Truman returned along with a letter. "It is a rare instance when I find a man who remembers his commitments and meets them on the dot," Truman wrote Bogart.

Presidents of the United States do not normally serve as publicists for a particular entertainer, but Richard Nixon did just that in 1973 after seeing Debbie Reynolds in the musical *Irene* at the National Theater in Washington. The president, Mrs. Nixon, and their daughter Tricia attended the production as part of a family outing. Talking to reporters during intermission Nixon enthused that Reynolds—"a superstar"—looked younger than when he had first met her in the early 1960s. Asserting that audiences were "tired of that way-out stuff," he predicted that *Irene* would be "a big hit" on Broadway, "perhaps not with New Yorkers but with the out-of-towners." Nixon insisted that he did not want to "get into the business of criticizing some of the new art," but added that "it's very difficult these days to find a play or a movie you really want to take your family to."

The effect of Nixon's endorsement was an immediate boom in ticket sales. According to Reynolds, "his 'review' made every newspaper, including some in Europe, and was reported on every television news show, giving *Irene* the kind of publicity money cannot buy." After selling $1.5 million worth of tickets during its Washington tryout, the musical opened in New York with another $1.5 million in advance receipts. Debbie Reynolds got more than media hype; Nixon invited the actress to the White House for Sunday worship services, which she attended with her daughter, future movie star and author Carrie Fisher, then a performer in the *Irene* chorus.

Second-tier entertainers may have the most to gain from sharing the presidential limelight. Peter Lawford reaped enormous publicity from his position as John F. Kennedy's brother-in-law—or "brother-in-Lawford," to quote Frank Sinatra. "Virtually overnight," wrote Lawford biographer James Spada, "Peter's relationship to the president brought him an aura of importance that few Hollywood performers had ever equaled." By most accounts Lawford did not hesitate to make use of his newfound status, behaving, in Spada's words, "as though he were president." Already accustomed to the pampered existence of a movie star, Lawford now tasted the perquisites of life in the White House.

Peter Lawford and John F. Kennedy genuinely liked each other, even after the change in their relationship relegated Lawford to the role of supporting player. The two first met in the late 1940s in Hollywood at the home of Gary Cooper; in the intervening years they occasionally crossed paths in Palm Beach. Lawford's marriage to Patricia Kennedy in 1954, seven months after Jack Kennedy wed Jacqueline Bouvier, cemented the bond between them. Kennedy admired Lawford's elegance and sophistication; according to Spada, the young congressman from Boston "knew that Peter was someone he could learn from." But the connection soon turned into *A Star Is Born*, with Lawford on the wane as Kennedy began his dizzying ascent into the history books.

By the late 1950s, when John F. Kennedy had left the House of Representatives for a spot in the U.S. Senate, Peter Lawford's show business career was sputtering. The MGM matinee idol had once costarred with Elizabeth Taylor, Judy Garland, June Allyson, and Janet Leigh. Now he was reduced to playing the lead in two undistinguished and short-lived TV series: *Dear Phoebe*, featuring Lawford as an advice-to-the-lovelorn columnist, and *The Thin Man*, based on the popular William Powell–Myrna Loy films about a husband-and-wife detective team. *Dear Phoebe* lasted a single season, *The Thin Man* two.

At the end of the decade, in a dramatic reversal of fortune, Lawford's career began its unlikely second act. It happened not because of anything Peter Lawford did but because of who he knew. Suddenly Lawford found himself the member of not one but two of the country's highest-profile families—the Kennedy clan and Frank Sinatra's Rat Pack. At that moment in the cultural zeitgeist of America there was no surer ticket to white-hot celebrity.

On Election Day 1960 the British-born Peter Lawford cast his first vote as an American citizen for John F. Kennedy. JFK changed everything for Lawford. After a five-year absence he returned to the big screen. Between 1959 and 1962 Lawford appeared in three movies with Sinatra: a war story called *Never So Few*, the iconic Vegas heist picture *Oceans Eleven*, and a Rat Pack western entitled *Sergeants Three*. Lawford also took small roles in a pair of "prestige" pictures made during the Kennedy administration, *Advise and Consent* and *The Longest Day*.

Advise and Consent was a best-selling backstage Washington novel about sex and politics on Capitol Hill. As a film it boasted a top director, Otto Preminger, and an all-star cast that included Henry Fonda, Charles Laughton, Walter Pidgeon, Burgess Meredith, Franchot Tone, Don Murray, Lew Ayres, and former JFK paramour Gene Tierney. Lawford played the role of a handsome young senator with an eye for the ladies, a part some viewed as a thinly disguised version of John F. Kennedy. Asked about this by a reporter, Lawford called the charge "a lot of rubbish." Defensively, he recounted a recent visit with the president, who had been reading the novel. "He asked me in a friendly way if I had a good script. That didn't sound as though he were displeased."

Lawford was savvy enough to understand why Preminger had cast him in the film. Beyond the publicity value of having the president's brother-in-law onboard, the director hoped Lawford's access to JFK would open doors during location shooting in the capital. Preminger wanted to film inside the White House itself, an idea that was ultimately vetoed. Instead Kennedy invited the cast to have lunch with him at the mansion. By some reports Preminger took out his disappointment on Peter Lawford, making Lawford's life difficult on the set and nearly editing his character out of the final version of *Advise and Consent*.

During John F. Kennedy's presidency Lawford supplemented his film work with frequent nightclub and television appearances, acting in a sketch with Jack Benny, doing a guest shot on *The Andy Williams Show*, and making the rounds of game shows like *Password*, *I've Got a Secret*, and *What's My Line?* Lawford also turned his attention to a lucrative production company, Chrislaw Productions, which in 1963 had a hit TV program, *The Patty Duke Show.*

In the final analysis, was Lawford's Kennedy connection a boon to his career or a curse? "Being related to the president of the United States is a very great honor," Lawford said. "But it is not, and never will be, a career . . . Nobody would be insane enough to advertise 'Starring JFK's brother-in-law,' and if he did, I trust nobody would be insane enough to buy a single extra ticket." Still, few could deny that Peter Lawford enjoyed an exalted status during Kennedy's brief time in the White House. As for John F. Kennedy, the president never stopped feeling a sense of responsibility toward his show business in-law. In 1961, when White House aide Arthur Schlesinger asked for permission to continue a freelance job as a movie reviewer, JFK gave his approval—"as long as you treat Peter Lawford with respect."

✯✯✯✯

Presidential associations are not just about access and publicity. For many politically minded performing artists a link to the White House represents an opportunity to stretch themselves intellectually. As actor Alec Baldwin put it,

> Entertainers get a chance to exercise a socially conscious muscle that is no longer stimulated by their work. As films and television shows become less and less about spoken-word drama, actors (as well as musicians) must go outside of their chosen profession in order to display their passion for whatever issue. In a world where the film *On the Waterfront* would probably not get made today, actors look elsewhere for that forum.

The politicization of show business has been well under way since the 1930s, though it took the collapse of the studio system some three decades later to fully liberate film actors. Just as movie stars began freelancing in their career choices, so have they increasingly operated as individuals with strong political opinions. In a 1966 interview Paul Newman gave voice to the new attitude then taking root. "People in Hollywood come up to me and say, 'Why take a chance? Don't make enemies,'" said Newman. "My reaction is, 'Kiss off! I still have my citizenship papers. Did I lose them when I became an actor?'"

Shirley MacLaine, another early proponent of political activism, carried her convictions even further. In the early 1970s, MacLaine became heavily involved in the presidential campaign of Democrat George McGovern—as did her brother, Warren Beatty. MacLaine told the *New York Times* in 1971 that communications had become more important than politics, and mused that communicators might be "the new politicians": "If John Wayne can really influence Nixon and Kissinger on Cambodia, or if Bob Hope can really become a symbol of vote getting, then I will unabashedly use my celebrity to try to influence people. I think this is a proper use of power. I mean, what good does my turquoise swimming pool in California do anybody else?"

Entertainment figures from both ends of the ideological spectrum have seen value in forging political associations with presidents. Wayne Newton has been identified with Republican Presidents Nixon, Reagan, and both George Bushes. Early in his career the singer believed that performers should stay out of politics. "But I've changed my mind," he wrote. "A time came when my country had more meaning for me than my career did. It was because of what I felt about America and where it was going. I went to Vietnam twice; I went to Beirut and the Persian Gulf." Newton continues to draw the line at espousing his political beliefs on stage. "But I think there comes a time when being an American has to mean more to you than any personal gain or loss."

These comments illustrate the degree to which many entertainers feel a need to channel their fame toward more serious ends. It is all well and good to sing, dance, and put on a show, but ultimately these creative endeavors may not suffice. Presidential associations confer legitimacy on show business practitioners in a way their professional work cannot.

During the Clinton administration Rob Reiner gained a new set of credentials as an advocate of early childhood development. Reiner figured prominently in a one-day White House conference on the subject convened by the president in April 1997. A week later the Clintons appeared in Reiner's ABC-TV documentary *I Am Your Child*, alongside a roster of high-profile celebrities: master of ceremonies Tom Hanks, Robin Williams, Billy Crystal, Michael J. Fox, Charlton Heston, Martin Short, even future Secretary of State Colin Powell. In the program the first couple offered viewers a faux-spontaneous chat about raising their daughter Chelsea; Bill "confided" to Hillary that he feared they had not done enough for her. Reiner's work with young people resurfaced during the 2000 campaign of Al Gore, who appeared with the actor-director at a Cleveland event devoted to the problem of children without medical insurance.

If presidents offer entertainers intellectual validation, they also offer social validation. Comedian and talk show host Joan Rivers considered herself lucky to get a few minutes with Betty Ford during a private White House tour in 1975. Two administrations later Rivers was sitting at Nancy Reagan's table at a White House dinner for the king of Nepal. Commenting on the evening to reporters, Rivers wisecracked, "No scum here tonight!" Behind the joke is an undeniable truth: being invited to the executive mansion is an enormous social coup. Such things ought not to matter, but in the status-conscious world of show business presidential proximity is as reliable a career index as box office receipts or Nielsen ratings.

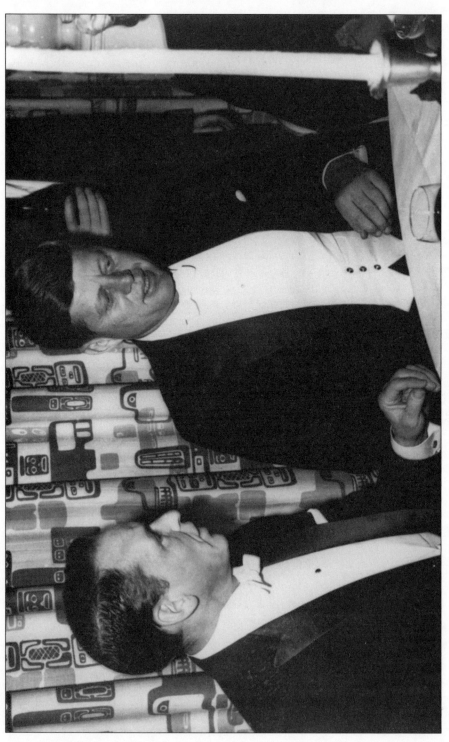

Frank Sinatra and John F. Kennedy at the Inaugural Ball, January 1961. (AP/Wide World Photos, reprinted by permission)

4

✷✷✷✷

Glad to Be Unhappy

HOW PRESIDENTS ARE
BAD FOR ENTERTAINERS

A T THE FRANK SINATRA COMPOUND in Palm Springs, California, the steady
drone of hammers, saws, and cement mixers pierced the desert silence.
Every room in the house but the owner's bedroom was in the midst of a frenzied
renovation. Guest cottages were going up by the pool. A new helipad awaited
pouring. A special telephone line had to be installed.

Frank Sinatra was as excited as a kid on Christmas Eve. For two nights beginning on March 23, 1962, the saloon singer from Hoboken, New Jersey, would
play host to the president of the United States: his pal John Fitzgerald Kennedy.
Kennedy had stayed at the desert retreat before—Sinatra commemorated the occasion by installing a "John F. Kennedy slept here" plaque on the guest room
door—but this time would be different. This time JFK was coming back as president. And Francis Albert Sinatra had helped put him there.

Sinatra took to the preparations with gusto. After the husbands of Palm
Springs went off golfing, Frank rounded up Rosalind Russell, Ruth (Mrs. Milton) Berle, and the other showbiz wives, and took them shopping for artwork
and furnishings. When it came to household decorating, the Chairman of the
Board trusted the female eye more than his own.

Kennedy was to arrive on Friday. On Wednesday the telephone rang. A nervous Peter Lawford was calling with bad news: the Secret Service had gotten cold feet about security arrangements at Sinatra's home, located in open country in the heart of the desert oasis. The president instead would occupy the estate of Bing Crosby, which backed up against a mountain. "Had the Kennedys sought deliberately to humiliate my father, they couldn't have done a better job," wrote a still bitter Tina Sinatra thirty years later. Not only was Crosby a rival singer—he was a Republican. "They might as well have stuck a poker in Dad's eye."

What caused Kennedy to change his mind? The official version, set forth by JFK aides in the book *Johnny We Hardly Knew Ye*, assigns the decision to the Secret Service. The more plausible story is that JFK decided to cut his losses because of Sinatra's persistent reputation as a mob associate. JFK was vulnerable on the Sinatra question, and he knew it. Earlier in the year FBI Director J. Edgar Hoover had warned Attorney General Robert Kennedy about the president's relationship with Judith Campbell, the Elizabeth Taylor look-alike who had been Sinatra's "gift" to Kennedy. At the time of her involvement with JFK, she was also carrying on an affair with Mafia boss Sam Giancana.

The call from Peter Lawford enraged Sinatra. According to Tina, "There was no consoling him." Tales later circulated about an infuriated Frank Sinatra taking a sledge hammer to the newly poured helipad, though the pad remained intact for many years. What was clear to one and all is that Sinatra had been treated with supreme disrespect.

The immediate target of Sinatra's wrath was Lawford, whom the singer cut out of his life with surgical precision. Though this was not the first time Sinatra had banished Peter Lawford, it was the last. Sinatra refused to accept Lawford's calls, spurned the efforts of mutual friends to mend fences, and booted Lawford off two planned Rat Pack pictures, *Four for Texas* and *Robin and the Seven Hoods*. According to Lawford's personal manager, none of Sinatra's friends would ever hire the actor again.

The only person to escape Sinatra's furor was John F. Kennedy. Like a lover spurned, Sinatra felt more sorrow than anger at his erstwhile companion. "If he would only pick up the telephone and call me and say that it was politically difficult to have me around, I would understand," Angie Dickinson heard Sinatra say. "I don't want to hurt him. But he has never called me." As Tina Sinatra saw it, JFK "enjoyed a sort of presidential immunity with my father. Dad still considered him to be his friend, and I suppose it would have hurt too much to look at the great man more clearly."

John F. Kennedy's dumping of Frank Sinatra offers an extreme illustration of the political expediency that often obtains in relationships between presidents and entertainers. Sinatra learned the hard way that a high-ranking politician will look out for himself first and his acolytes second. Because of their rarefied status presidents have the luxury of jettisoning friends without explanation, leaving the jilted party confused about why things changed. For Sinatra, the uncertainty over Kennedy's motives caused the greatest grief.

It had not started off this way. The handsome young senator from Massachusetts and the genius of song known as "Ol' Blue Eyes" met via Peter Lawford in the late 1950s. At the time Lawford and Sinatra had recently rekindled their friendship after a five-year estrangement that began when Frank accused Peter of hitting on Ava Gardner. Largely through the intercession of Patricia Lawford, JFK's sister, Sinatra had become tight with the Lawfords. When Pat and Peter's third child was born in 1958, she was christened Victoria Francis—Victoria because her Uncle Jack had won his second Senate election that day, and Francis in honor of Francis Albert Sinatra.

Did Sinatra cozy up to the Lawfords as a means of getting in with John F. Kennedy? Certainly Sinatra's affection for JFK appears genuine. Though Sinatra had been a reliable campaigner for Democrats Roosevelt, Truman, and Adlai Stevenson, Kennedy was, in the words of Tina Sinatra, "someone different, someone special—a breath of fresh air." The infatuation extended beyond politics. Sinatra and Kennedy admired each other's talents, each other's personal style. They made each other laugh. They shared a lively interest in women.

In the view of some of JFK's closest aides, Kennedy's fondness for Sinatra "was simply based on the fact that Sinatra told him a lot of inside gossip about celebrities and their romances in Hollywood." Sinatra's own adventures likewise stirred Kennedy's curiosity. According to Judith Campbell, the serial mistress of both men, JFK wanted to know everything about Sinatra's affairs. "He would say, 'Who's Frank seeing now?' or 'I heard Frank is seeing so-and-so and isn't she married?'"

Stories abounded of orgies involving Kennedy, Sinatra, and Lawford. An FBI informant reported that *Confidential* magazine was pursuing rumors of JFK's attendance at an "indiscreet party" at Sinatra's home in Palm Springs. Another FBI report quoted a prominent Las Vegas source as saying "show girls from all over town were running in and out of the Senator's suite."

Although Frank Sinatra's lifestyle posed a risky temptation for any presidential candidate, Jack Kennedy considered himself up to the challenge. On February 7, 1960, Kennedy took time off from a campaign swing through the West to catch Sinatra and the Rat Pack at the Sands Hotel in Las Vegas. The Rat Pack-ers—Sinatra, Lawford, Dean Martin, Sammy Davis Jr., and Joey Bishop—were then at the height of their performing glory, their unscripted Vegas revue a "must-see" event that entered the annals of show business history. JFK's presence in the audience that night inspired the performers. "If you get in," master of cer-emonies Joey Bishop told Kennedy, "Frank has to be ambassador to Italy and Sammy to Israel. I don't want too much for myself—just don't let me get drafted again." Like other celebrities in the house, the distinguished visitor from Massa-chusetts was asked to stand and acknowledge the crowd. As Kennedy accepted the applause, Dean Martin staggered over to Sinatra: "What did you say his name was?"

After the show the senator retired upstairs to party with the performers. Pre-viously, as an honorary member of the Rat Pack, Sinatra had given John F. Kennedy the nickname "Chicky Baby." Now, in honor of his newfound status, the candidate was "Number One." Sammy Davis recalled that sometime during the night's revels an aide suggested to Senator Kennedy that he should get some sleep before his flight to Oregon left a few hours later. "Don't worry about me," JFK replied. "I'll sleep on the plane."

As the campaign of 1960 proceeded, Sinatra's attachment to Kennedy deep-ened, and the singer became a high-visibility participant in JFK's drive for the White House. According to Tina Sinatra, Joseph P. Kennedy, the candidate's fa-ther, enlisted Sinatra in the crucial West Virginia primary—not as an entertainer but as an emissary to underworld boss Sam Giancana, whose influence was needed to put the state in Kennedy's column. Tina Sinatra's account, based on a conversation with her father near the end of his life, has the feel of a Mario Puzo novel:

> After returning from Hyannis Port, my father called Giancana and made a golf date, where they couldn't be bugged. Dad said, "I've never come to you for a favor before, Sam, but this time I have to." When he conveyed the Kennedys' request for help in West Virginia, Giancana must have been scratching his head. He went way back with Joe Sr., and he knew how the game was played. What was my father getting out of the deal?
>
> And Dad said, with wholehearted conviction, "I believe in Jack Kennedy. He's a good man."
>
> Giancana looked him in the eye and said, "It's a couple of phone calls. And tell the old man I said hello."

Sinatra's association with the Kennedys did not make his life easier. In March 1960 Sinatra found himself embroiled in controversy when he hired screenwriter Albert Maltz to write a script called *The Execution of Private Slovik*, based on a true story about an American soldier executed for desertion by the U.S. Army. Sinatra planned to produce and direct the film with Steve McQueen in the title role. Maltz was one of the Hollywood Ten, a group of screenwriters blacklisted for alleged associations with communism. Sinatra had known him since the 1940s, when Maltz wrote an antiracist film called *The House I Live In*, an Academy Award–winning short subject in which Sinatra starred. The news that Sinatra intended to violate the blacklist broke with a fury. Right-wing newspapers had a field day, joined by a chorus of conservative American voices. Among the critics was John Wayne, who wondered how "Sinatra's crony," John Kennedy, felt about the hire.

An outraged Sinatra responded with a full-page advertisement in the Hollywood trade papers: "I make movies. I do not ask the advice of Senator Kennedy on whom I should hire. Senator Kennedy does not ask me how he should vote in the Senate . . ." As the war of words escalated, the Kennedy campaign became increasingly alarmed. Joe Kennedy gave Sinatra an ultimatum: Albert Maltz or Jack Kennedy. Even on the home front the pressure mounted; daughter Tina came home from school in tears after being asked by a fifth grade classmate if she was a communist. In the end Sinatra caved, explaining his decision in a public statement: "In view of the reaction of my family, my friends, and the American public, I have instructed my attorneys to make a settlement with Albert Maltz and to inform him that he will not write the screenplay for *The Execution of Private Slovik*."

Over the next few months Frank Sinatra maintained a low profile in the campaign. But at the star-studded 1960 Democratic Convention in Los Angeles, he was back in the limelight, the biggest show business celebrity of them all, standing at the very epicenter of American entertainment. As the general election campaign intensified, Sinatra was everywhere on Kennedy's behalf: at teas in California, beachfront rallies in Hawaii, a governor's ball in New Jersey. When the new president came into office in January 1961, it was Sinatra who produced the inaugural gala.

If Sinatra expected that his efforts would be rewarded with White House access, he was mistaken. In September 1961 Sinatra was invited to the luncheon for the cast of *Advise and Consent*, but only through a fluke. A memorandum sent to the president's secretary, Evelyn Lincoln, listed the names of those who would be attending. At the bottom of the page a typed notation added this detail: "Frank Sinatra is also coming. Tish (Letitia Baldrige, Jacqueline Kennedy's social secretary) said there was no way she could keep from asking him as he was in Peter Lawford's room when she called him about the luncheon."

Around the time of the *Advise and Consent* gathering—possibly the same day, though the record is hazy—Sinatra received his only tour of the JFK White House. It is unclear whether the president spent time with him; the official log makes no mention of the famous visitor, period. We do know that Sinatra saw the private family quarters and drank Bloody Marys on the Truman Balcony with Kennedy aide Dave Powers. Powers recalled the scene on the balcony to biographer Kitty Kelley: "He turned to me and said, 'Dave, all the work I did for Jack. Sitting here like this makes it all worthwhile.'" As a souvenir of his visit Sinatra took home autographed photos of the president.

In large measure it was Jacqueline Kennedy, acting as a kind of human force field, who kept the singer out of the White House. Peter Lawford spoke about Mrs. Kennedy's antipathy with Kitty Kelley:

During one of our private dinners [the president] brought up Sinatra and said, "I really should do something for Frank." Jack was always so grateful to him for all the work he'd done in the campaign raising money. He said, "Maybe I'll ask him to the White House for dinner or lunch." I said that Frank would love that, but then Jack said, "There's only one problem. Jackie hates him and won't have him in the house. So I really don't know what to do." Here was the president of the United States in a quandary just like the rest of us who are afraid to upset our spouses. We joked for a few minutes about stuffing Frank into a body bag and dragging him around to the side door so the gardeners could bring him in like a bag of refuse and Jackie wouldn't see him. We also talked about sneaking him in in one of John-John's big diaper bundles. The president brightened up a few minutes later and said, "I'll wait until Jackie goes to Middleburg, and I'll have Eunice be the hostess." So that's what he did. When Jackie left, Evelyn Lincoln [JFK's secretary] called Frank and invited him to the White House. He flew to Washington for the day and a car drove him up to the southwest gate. Even without Jackie there, the president still wouldn't let him come in the front door. I don't think he wanted reporters to see Frank Sinatra going into the White House. That's why he never flew on Air Force One and was never invited to any of the Kennedy state dinners or taken to Camp David for any of the parties there.

After the inaugural President Kennedy was spotted in public with Frank Sinatra only once. The occasion was a family weekend on Cape Cod that immediately followed the *Advise and Consent* luncheon. Sinatra arrived in Massachusetts on a Friday night aboard the Kennedy family plane, along with fellow passengers Patricia Lawford, Ted Kennedy, Dominican playboy Porfirio Rubirosa, and Rubirosa's wife. Because of fog on the Cape, the flight had to be diverted to nearby New Bedford, where the group hired two cabs to drive them to Hyannis Port. A *Boston Globe* reporter noted that Sinatra, wearing a brown suit and felt hat, "walked down the *Caroline*'s ramp gingerly holding a glass of champagne." Sinatra had also brought along two loaves of Italian bread for Joe Kennedy, the family patriarch.

Despite the drizzly weather that extended into the next day, Sinatra joined JFK and a handful of other guests on Saturday for a three-and-a-half-hour cruise through Nantucket Sound aboard the presidential yacht, the *Marlin.* According to newspaper reports, Jacqueline Kennedy treated the passengers to a waterskiing demonstration, which was applauded by Peter Lawford. The next afternoon Sinatra again sailed on the *Marlin* with the president and his entourage, who dined on hot dogs aboard the yacht. JFK returned to Washington that evening; Sinatra remained for another night at the family compound.

Sinatra's well-publicized weekend on Cape Cod generated a wave of negative press coverage for President Kennedy. Asked about the visit by reporters, White House press secretary Pierre Salinger replied, "Mr. Sinatra went up there to confer with Ambassador Kennedy about a souvenir recording of the Inauguration gala. The record will be a money raiser for the Democratic Party." Salinger added that Sinatra had not been the guest of President and Mrs. Kennedy. Technically this was true—Frank Sinatra had stayed at the home of Joe and Rose Kennedy. A story in *U.S. News and World Report* described Kennedy's Hyannis Port neighbors as "startled" by the arrival of the "Hollywood set." The magazine quoted a Cape Cod resident: "It's about time that President Kennedy does something about those people. Although they were not strictly his guests, he could lay down the law to his relatives if he wanted to."

Six months later the president took his weekend vacation in Palm Springs, choosing Bing Crosby over Frank Sinatra. Although Sinatra never got over the slight, he also never stopped trying to win back the attentions of Jack Kennedy. In June 1962 he sent JFK a gaudy, chrysanthemum-draped rocking chair as a birthday gift. Press secretary Salinger told reporters the president never saw it. Kennedy's thank-you note to Sinatra made clear that the present had not even been kept: "I was delighted by this lovely remembrance and thought you might like to know that the youngsters over at Children's Hospital also had the opportunity of sharing, with me, your more than generous gift."

Sinatra's overtures persisted. In August 1962 he offered movie lover JFK a private screening of his new film, *The Manchurian Candidate*. "Print will be available any hour day or night for viewing by the president," Sinatra wrote in a telegram to Salinger. Occasionally Kennedy felt a pang of conscience over Sinatra, though the feeling never seemed to last long. According to Arthur Schlesinger, "For a moment in late 1963 Sinatra was on the guest list for a White House state dinner; at the last minute, on a pretext, the invitation was withdrawn."

Frank Sinatra never achieved the reconciliation with John F. Kennedy that he so desperately sought. Sinatra was shooting the film *Robin and the Seven Hoods* when word came down that the president had been shot in Dallas. As it happened, Sinatra and his company were on location at a cemetery in Burbank. After hearing the news, Sinatra walked off by himself, meandering silently among the gravestones. He came back, spoke briefly by phone with a White House staff person, then returned to the crew. "Let's shoot this thing," he said, "cause I don't want to come back here anymore." During the national period of mourning Sinatra cloistered himself in his Palm Springs home, refusing to take calls even from his family. "My father grieved alone," wrote Nancy Sinatra, "locked away in his bedroom, the only part of the house that was still the same as when his friend, the president, had visited him."

※※※※

Sinatra was not the only performer to feel betrayed by John F. Kennedy. Sammy Davis Jr., Sinatra's Rat Pack confrere, suffered humiliations of his own. Davis too saw active duty as a campaigner, appearing at numerous fund-raising events on behalf of the Massachusetts senator. But his potential for controversy became clear early on. On opening night of the Democratic National Convention in Los Angeles, when a parade of stars led by Sinatra kicked off the event with "The Star Spangled Banner," members of the Mississippi delegation booed Davis. Throughout the campaign he remained the target of racist invective—in columns, comedy routines, and cartoons. One drawing depicted Davis in two side-by-side panels: in the first, dressed as a butler serving JFK a platter of fried chicken and watermelon; in the second, dining with Kennedy at the table. The caption read: "Will it still be the White House?"

When Sammy Davis Jr. announced his intention to marry Swedish actress May Britt in October 1960, with Frank Sinatra as best man, the Kennedy forces found themselves holding a hot potato. What sort of political fallout would JFK suffer, particularly in parts of the country where interracial marriage still constituted the ultimate sexual taboo? The campaign and Sinatra were in a difficult spot: for Sinatra to cancel his gig as best man might please the racists but it would anger blacks and liberals. To go forward as planned would please blacks and liberals but cost votes in the South.

Davis had no illusions about how his marriage to a Nordic blonde would play in America's bastions of bigotry. The hate mail that poured in had made that all too clear. "Dear Nigger Bastard," read one letter, "I see Frank Sinatra is going to be best man at your abortion. Well, it's good to know the kind of people supporting Kennedy, before it's too late. [signed] An ex-Kennedy vote." Davis came to a realization: "Fair or not, my wedding was giving the Nixon people the opportunity to ridicule Kennedy and hurt him at the polls. I could imagine the pressure Frank must be under . . . "

It was Davis who ultimately proposed a face-saving solution: the wedding would be delayed until November 13, five days after the election. He instructed his publicist to make an announcement to the press: "The Sammy Davis Junior–May Britt wedding has been postponed due to a legal technicality in Miss Britt's Mexican divorce from her previous husband." As Davis put it, "That was the lie and that's how we told it." Davis kept his displeasure at the Kennedys under wraps. Said Nancy Sinatra, "Sammy loved JFK and would do anything for him, no matter how hurt he was."

According to Sammy Davis's autobiography, three days before the entertainer was scheduled to take part in Kennedy's January 1961 inaugural gala, he received a call from Evelyn Lincoln, JFK's secretary. "The president has asked me to tell you that he does not want you to be present at his inauguration. There is a situation into which he is being forced and to fight it would be counterproductive to the goals he's set. He very much hopes you will understand . . . " Fighting back his humiliation, Davis thanked her for calling. Privately he felt sick: "I could handle it from the idiot in the street who pickets or calls me a name or writes a letter. But when the president of the United States does it? To someone he knows. Someone he shook hands with and told, 'I won't forget your help'. . . My God, if he'll do this to me, then what hope have the millions of invisible people got?"

On the night his showbiz friends performed in the nation's capital for the new president and his wife, Sammy Davis Jr. played the Latin Casino in Camden, New Jersey. "Standing in the wings listening to what I used to think of as a glamorous overture, I wondered what the people would be thinking, looking at me onstage in Camden, knowing that the rest of the Rat Pack was in Washington. It hurt like a motherfucker."

John F. Kennedy had one final humiliation in store for Sammy Davis Jr. The event was a Lincoln's birthday reception at the White House in February 1963 to which some eight hundred prominent African Americans were invited, among them future Supreme Court Justice Thurgood Marshall and musician Lionel Hampton. Davis's name had reportedly been on and off the guest list several times, but in the end he showed up—with his Caucasian wife, May Britt.

"What's he doing here?" Kennedy snapped when he learned Davis was among the guests at the White House. Fearing a public backlash, JFK instructed his assistants that the Davises not be photographed together. One Kennedy aide described the panic that set in among the White House staff: "You never saw more people hiding under the table because nobody, absolutely no one, had anything to do with Sammy Davis getting invited."

The president sought the help of his wife, asking Jackie to commandeer May Britt before cameramen could capture Mr. and Mrs. Davis in a two-shot. According to JFK biographer Richard Reeve, Jacqueline Kennedy refused: "She was so angry at the suggestion she did not want to go downstairs at all, and the formal reception began without the president and his wife. He was still upstairs trying to talk her into going down." When the first lady finally did come downstairs, she stayed only long enough to pose for photographs, then excused herself, saying she did not feel well. Later, after the assassination, Jacqueline Kennedy took May Britt to lunch in New York City.

✵✵✵✵

Can we wonder that both Frank Sinatra and Sammy Davis Jr. became Republicans? Or that it took the politically astute Richard Nixon to recognize in these two battered egos an opportunity to win converts for the other side? In the case of Davis, the turn rightward was limited to Nixon. With Sinatra, the drift from liberal Democrat to conservative Republican took a deeper, longer-lasting course. By the end of Frank Sinatra's political journey the singer had completely redefined himself; once a Roosevelt liberal, he now proudly joined the ranks of Reagan conservatives.

After JFK Sinatra retained his status as a Democrat long enough to work against archenemy Bobby Kennedy in 1968. That year Sinatra supported his last

Democratic presidential candidate, Hubert Humphrey. As in the JFK campaign Sinatra faced a barrage of press scrutiny and stories about alleged ties to mobsters. In the fractious electoral battle of 1968 Sinatra found himself out of step with fellow show business liberals, who preferred candidates with more solid antiwar credentials like RFK and Eugene McCarthy.

What moved Sinatra into the Republican column was an unlikely friendship with Vice President Spiro Agnew that began after Richard Nixon's defeat of Humphrey. Agnew was a man with whom Frank Sinatra felt a strong kinship. "There was instant chemistry—personally and politically," said Peter Malatesta, an Agnew aide and Sinatra intimate who was also the nephew of Bob Hope. Among other points of agreement, both men shared a visceral hatred for the press.

The vice president began making frequent trips to Sinatra's Palm Springs home, where the guest cottage that had originally been built for JFK got a new name: "Agnew House." The Agnews attended Sinatra's highly publicized 1971 "farewell concert" in Los Angeles—as did the Ronald Reagans—then accompanied the star to Palm Springs for a retirement party. With extra time on his hands, Sinatra embarked on a mission to keep Agnew on the Republican ticket in 1972, emerging from retirement to serenade the former Maryland governor at a fund-raiser in Baltimore. Sinatra reworked the lyrics to one of his biggest hits, "The Lady Is a Tramp"; for Agnew it became "The Gentleman Is a Champ."

Friendship with the vice president offered Sinatra no immunity against ongoing allegations of criminal activity. In July 1972 Sinatra was brought before the House Select Committee on Crime to testify about his investment in a race track allegedly controlled by the Mafia. Sinatra gave a defiant performance, successfully portraying himself as the victim of hearsay and innuendo. After an hour and a half, Frank Sinatra emerged triumphant from the hearing room. He had put out the brush fire, at least for the moment.

Agnew's visits to Palm Springs stepped up in frequency. By one count Agnew made eighteen trips to the desert oasis within a year and a half, spending most of the major holidays chez Sinatra. Early in 1973 the vice president took the unusual step of publicly defending his friendship with Frank Sinatra. Speaking to a journalist from the *Christian Science Monitor*, Agnew showed a remarkable misapprehension of the criticisms that had been raised about the relationship:

Every time I see Mr. Sinatra my wife is with me . . . We live a very mundane existence in Palm Springs with respect to the ideas that are promulgated about partying and that sort of thing.

All I want to do is get out there and get some sun and some exercise, and we eat very well and we meet with some old friends that we have out there now.

It is very middle-class, lavishly middle-class in the sense that he [Sinatra] lives well. But it's not one of these what you might call big partying occasions.

I just thought that in view that everybody thinks that Frank Sinatra and I are going around raising hell together—it's not so. And I get along extremely well with him. I respect and admire him very much. He's been a very good friend. And I'm not about to let any rumors interfere with my right to select my own friends. I feel that ought to be said.

Rumors of a more substantive sort soon swirled around Agnew. Shortly after his reelection the vice president came under investigation for tax evasion, bribery, and extortion, charges stemming from his term as Maryland's governor. In October 1973 Agnew resigned from office and pleaded no lo contendere to one charge of tax evasion. Though Sinatra appeared to have once again backed the wrong horse, he remained a loyal supporter, loaning Agnew a substantial amount of money and pressuring wary friends to donate to a Spiro Agnew legal defense fund.

By now Richard Nixon had made his own play for Frank Sinatra. Nixon did what no previous president had done for Sinatra: asked him to perform at the White House. On April 17, 1973, Sinatra again stepped out of retirement long enough to sing at a state dinner for the prime minister of Italy. The appearance generated extensive press coverage and forged a bond between Nixon and Sinatra that solidified the singer's conservative leanings. Sinatra remained grateful for the legitimacy Richard Nixon conferred on him; four months after Nixon was forced from office, Sinatra called on the disgraced president at his home in San Clemente.

In some Republican circles, Sinatra continued to be viewed as political poison. In 1975 Henry Kissinger invited Gerald and Betty Ford to a dinner that would also include Frank Sinatra. When Ford aides learned of the plan they pressured Kissinger to disinvite the controversial entertainer, who at that point remained closely identified with Agnew. Instead of acceding, Kissinger drew President Ford into the dustup, pleading Sinatra's case and persuading Ford that he should attend.

"I know you don't approve," Ford told his press secretary, Ron Nessen, "but Sinatra has done nothing illegal or immoral. It probably won't play very well in the press, but I feel I have a right to have dinner with whomever I want to." In the end Kissinger circumvented the problem. According to Nessen, "with his clout reaffirmed and his ego boosted, Kissinger then did what was best for the president and told Sinatra not to come to dinner."

After being dumped by Kennedy, burned by the misbehavior of Agnew and Nixon, and avoided by Ford, it fell to Ronald Reagan to welcome Frank Sinatra back into the White House fold. Here Sinatra found the unconditional acceptance he had so long craved. As with Nixon, Sinatra had actively campaigned against Ronald Reagan, supporting incumbent Democrat Edmund (Pat) Brown in the California governor's race in 1966. According to Peter Lawford, Sinatra considered Reagan "dumb and dangerous," and threatened to move out of California if the former movie actor won.

But by the end of the 1970s Sinatra had changed his tune. Even as Sinatra basked in his role as head of Reagan's 1981 inaugural committee, the Mafia charges of old resurfaced. Asked about Sinatra's reputation a few days before the swearing-in, Reagan said, "We've heard those things about Frank for years. We just hope none of them are true." Reagan's seeming naïveté on this question characterized his attitude toward Sinatra over the next eight years. Reagan practiced a kind of "don't ask, don't tell" policy toward his Hollywood friend that allowed Sinatra to occupy a central position in the social life of the White House.

Sinatra produced entertainment for state dinners, served on a presidential arts commission, assisted Nancy with her public service campaigns, and attended family birthday gatherings for the president and first lady. In 1985 President Reagan presented Frank Sinatra with the Medal of Freedom in a ceremony that also honored Jimmy Stewart, explorer Jacques-Yves Cousteau, test pilot Chuck Yeager, and Nobel Prize winner Mother Teresa. Draping the medal around Sinatra's neck, Reagan said: "His love of country, his generosity for those less fortunate, his distinctive art, and his winning and compassionate persona make him one of our most remarkable and distinguished Americans and one who truly did it his way."

So strongly associated with Reagan was Frank Sinatra that citizens began writing to the singer in care of the White House. One woman wanted Sinatra to know how much her late father had loved his music. Another sought the president's assistance in arranging her attendance at a Sinatra concert. In 1981 residents of Love Canal, the toxic neighborhood of Niagara Falls, New York, appealed to Frank to help them resolve their crisis: "We are asking you to intercede with President Reagan on our behalf to have the Psychological Emergency rescinded so we can all go back to normal living and planning for the future."

Reagan himself was not above asking Sinatra for favors. In 1984 the president wrote his friend regarding a request from the government Austria for a benefit performance:

As reluctant as I am to ever impose on your time, if you saw your way clear to add such an event to your European schedule, you would, of course, contribute immeasurably to the good will and relations between our countries . . . Frank, let me reiterate that I am totally sympathetic to what I am sure is an onslaught of similar appeals. However, we haven't as yet found a substitute for ambassadors of good-will!—you are the greatest!"

In the end Sinatra did the concert, helping raise $200,000 for needy Austrian children.

Sinatra continued his association with the Republican Party by campaigning for George Bush in 1988. In January 1989 Sinatra performed at Bush's inaugural, as he had done for Kennedy, Nixon, and Reagan. To a generation of young Americans, Sinatra had become the personification of a Republican entertainer.

But long-time observers who watched the political transformation of Frank Sinatra remained baffled. Tina Sinatra maintained that her father never stopped holding liberal positions on gun control, capital punishment, abortion, and immigration. "Even as he took a right turn in electoral politics," she wrote, "Dad remained stubbornly left wing on many issues. Onstage and off, he moved to his own beat."

✳✳✳✳

Sammy Davis Jr.'s decision to pledge allegiance to the Republican Party brought complications that did not apply to Frank Sinatra. As with other African American performers who associate with conservative white politicians, there would be a steep price to pay. Davis's endorsement of Richard Nixon in the 1972 campaign may have made sense to Sammy, but it deeply troubled many of his admirers.

Most observers did not realize that Sammy Davis Jr. had a history with Nixon that dated back to the 1950s. In April 1954 Vice President Nixon attended a performance by the Will Mastin Trio—composed of Sammy, his father, and his uncle—at the Copacabana Club in New York, and stopped backstage to say hello. The performer and the politician later exchanged autographed photographs of the event. "Thank you for your applause," Davis wrote on his photo for Nixon, "and a night I'll always remember. Not getting 'dramatic'—but it is things like this that make me only prouder I live in a country such as the United States."

Though he campaigned against Nixon in 1960, Sammy Davis Jr.'s troubles with Jack Kennedy had given the performer reason to be wary of politicians on both sides of the aisle. But Bobby Kennedy appealed to Sammy Davis in a way that transcended politics. Some months after Davis was unceremoniously jettisoned from the inaugural gala, he received an apology from Ethel Kennedy, who told him that Bobby had been "outraged by what they did." As attorney general, RFK personally warned Davis to keep his guard up. "Whenever you plan to appear in public at anything controversial, anything to do with civil rights," Bobby told him, "be sure to call me . . . and I can have a couple of men there looking out for you." By 1968, when he campaigned vigorously for Robert Kennedy, Davis was besotted: "I heard the drums, I heard the bugles, I saw the flag flying, and I believed—as I had never before believed in any political person—that marvelous things were coming, that Robert Kennedy was going to lead America into a new age in which all Americans would be free and rich and love each other."

One election cycle later Sammy Davis Jr. had cast his lot with Richard Nixon, always an incendiary figure but never more so than in the early 1970s. To a reporter who questioned him about this sudden about-face, Davis had a quick reply: "Listen, babe, it's better to be standin' in the Oval Office than bangin' at the gates." Indeed Nixon brought Davis on board with great sensitivity, appointing him to the Council on Economic Opportunity, dispatching him as the presidential representative at the funeral of Mahalia Jackson, sending him not just to entertain American troops in Vietnam but to serve as the president's eyes and ears among them.

Following the trip to Vietnam in the spring of 1972 Nixon invited Davis to the White House for a follow-up lunch. Nixon flattered the singer by seeking his advice on a range of issues of concern to the African American community. At one point the president even requested a tutorial in racial terminology.

"It is okay to say black?" Nixon asked his guest.

"Yes, Mr. President, we say black now. Negro and colored are not in use."

According to Davis, Nixon began jotting notes on a pad of paper: "Black is preferred, colored is not."

Nixon's seduction of Sammy Davis was a complete success. Soon, to the consternation of friends and fans alike, the song-and-dance man was urging the reelection of President Nixon. Ethel Kennedy stopped returning his calls. Shirley MacLaine, a buddy from the Rat Pack days, made a special trip to Las Vegas to hear straight from Davis himself why he had thrown in with Nixon. In a conversation that lasted until the wee hours of the morning he tried to explain: "Everything I know about Richard Nixon, not what I hear, but what I know, is positive," Davis told her. "I believe deeply in what this man is doing for black people, because what could I be getting out of it that would be worth all the friends I've lost?"

Davis's signature moment as a Nixon partisan occurred at the 1972 Republican National Convention in Miami during a Young Voters for Nixon rally. At a climactic point in the proceedings, the president made a "surprise" appearance before the crowd. In thanking the rally's performers Nixon singled out Sammy Davis, recounting an incident earlier in the convention in which a reporter had asked Davis if supporting the Republican ticket meant he had sold out. "Well, let me give you the answer," Nixon said. "You aren't going to buy Sammy Davis Jr. by inviting him to the White House. You buy him by doing something for America." Deeply touched by the sentiment, Davis threw his arms around the president and gave him a spontaneous hug.

The image of Davis embracing Nixon took on a life of its own in the media, provoking particular wrath in the black community. Though Davis went on to entertain at the Nixon White House and continued to offer the president his policy suggestions, he never fully regained his standing among African Americans. His audiences got whiter and when he appeared in predominantly black contexts, Sammy Davis Jr. would be booed. Davis likened the reaction to a "body blow, a senses-stunning, throbbing pain."

Other pro-Republican black entertainers faced similar criticism in the difficult years of the Vietnam War. Like Sammy Davis, soul singer James Brown went from supporting a Democrat (Humphrey) in 1968 to a Republican (Nixon) in 1972. The move of both singers into the GOP column was engineered by Robert J. Brown, an African American businessman who had gone to work as a presidential assistant in the Nixon White House. Part of Bob Brown's mission was to bring high-profile blacks into the campaign, a task he undertook with patience and skill. James Brown's endorsement of Nixon came late in the game, about a month before the election. "I'm not a sellout artist," the "Godfather of Soul" insisted to reporters at a press conference at the headquarters of the Committee to Re-elect the President. "I'm not selling out, I'm selling in—dig it?" The backlash was immediate: less than a week after Brown's announcement, his concert in Baltimore drew demonstrators and sold only twenty five hundred tickets in a thirteen-thousand-seat arena.

Recognizing the potential for audience alienation, black performers have been cautious in their dealings with Republican administrations. Shortly before James Brown came out with his endorsement, singer Ray Charles had a brief meeting with President Nixon in the Oval Office. Making the president's acquaintance was "a gas," Charles told a black newspaper, but he quickly added, "I'm *not* for the man."

African American artists with long-term Republican affiliations seem to have suffered less disapproval, perhaps because their ideology remained consistent. Two names dominate this list: jazz vibraphonist Lionel Hampton and singer-actress Pearl Bailey. Hampton was recruited into the party in the late 1940s by Richard Nixon, then a young congressman from Southern California. Although he performed for Democratic presidents like Harry Truman and Jimmy Carter, Hampton—the so-called vibes president of the United States—felt most at home in the company of Nixon, Reagan, and Bush. "Democrats use blacks to get votes but then forget about them," Hampton said. "Republicans do good deeds for blacks without ballyhooing."

Appearing as Ronald Reagan's guest of honor at a 1981 reception, Hampton spoke disdainfully of a previous visit to the Carter White House: "At that time, they had a barbecue. Today we have caviar." Lionel Hampton was especially close to the first George Bush; he had played for the Bush family when the future president was a teenage aristocrat in Greenwich, Connecticut. As head of the Central Intelligence Agency in the 1970s Bush enlisted Hampton and his orchestra for a morale-building concert. When the bandleader died in 2002 at the age of ninety-four, George Bush delivered the eulogy.

Pearl Bailey performed a unique service for Republican presidents: she was the irrepressible good-time gal who could always be counted on to loosen up the tight-assed white folks. At a string of state dinners during the Nixon and Ford administrations, Bailey played her role to the hilt, flirting with world leaders, bantering with her hosts, and leaving laughter in her wake. In 1970 Bailey wowed the audience with a one-woman show in the White House East Room, where her threat to make off with a presidential chair became a running joke with Richard Nixon. At the end of the night he made her a gift of it.

Four years later Pearl Bailey ratcheted up the wackiness quotient at a dinner for the nation's governors. As her musical set ended, Bailey asked President Nixon a favor: Would he accompany her on the piano while she sang one last song? A few shrugs later Nixon took a seat at the keyboard and struck up an introduction: "Home on the Range." "Mister President, wait a minute," Pearl interrupted. "I wanted to sing a song, I don't want to ride a horse." Somehow they finished the number: it wasn't pretty, but it was real. Nixon's thank-you note after the event indicates how much he fun he had: "I can assure you that very few people could have persuaded me to join them in a duet of music and song— but you even managed to make my 'rusty' piano techniques add to everyone's enjoyment that evening!"

Pearl Bailey had an even closer relationship with Gerald and Betty Ford. In 1975 she gave another over-the-top White House performance, this time at a dinner for Egyptian President Anwar Sadat. During her show-stopping theme song, "Hello Dolly," Bailey dragged first Ford and then the guest of honor up to the stage with her, where she forced each man to dance with her. Though President Sadat seemed nearly paralyzed—the Egyptian ambassador later said Sadat had never danced in his life—he kept a smile on his face. The next morning's *Washington Post* noted, "If Egyptian officials were nervous about what a couple of dance steps might do to the president's image back home in Muslim country, they politely kept their feelings under wraps."

❄❄❄❄

Richard Nixon cultivated certain entertainers; others he targeted for vilification. The release of the infamous "enemies list" in the summer of 1973 revealed just how objectionable antiwar performers had become to the embattled president. Joining more than two hundred politicians, journalists, labor officials, business leaders, and academics were a handful of entertainers: Carol Channing, Jane Fonda, Dick Gregory, Shirley MacLaine, Groucho Marx, Steve McQueen, Paul Newman, Gregory Peck, Tony Randall, and Barbra Streisand. Internal memorandums showed that the Nixon White House considered "how we can use available federal machinery to screw our political enemies," a plan that included using the IRS to harass the president's opponents.

What had these performers done to incur the wrath of the president of the United States? Everything from campaigning for Nixon's opponents (Newman and Peck) to taking part in a fund-raiser for the Pentagon Papers Legal Defense Fund (Streisand). Carol Channing evidently made the list because she had serenaded Lyndon Johnson with her "Hello, Lyndon" version of "Hello, Dolly."

Most of those cited took the news as a backhanded compliment. "It was a moment of extraordinary elation," Tony Randall recalled. "The phone never stopped all day long . . . It was an honor, like winning an Academy Award." Paul Newman called the experience his "highest single honor," and noted that "all the other actors were so jealous." Newman's inclusion on the list might have been helped along by a practical joke the actor played on "Tricky Dick" Nixon in 1968 while campaigning in New Hampshire for Eugene McCarthy. A local car dealer had given Paul Newman a new Jaguar to use during a three-day swing of the state. When Newman learned the car would subsequently be driven by

Nixon, he left a note on the dashboard: "Dear Mr. Nixon: You should have no trouble driving this car at all, because it has a very tricky clutch."

Richard Nixon was not one to forget a slight. Groucho Marx supposed that he made the list because of the nasty cracks he made throughout the California politician's career. For example, after the 1960 election Nixon moved his family to Trousdale Estates, the area of Beverly Hills where Groucho lived. Asked about his new neighbor, Marx replied, "I'd rather have him here than in the White House."

During President Nixon's first term, Groucho Marx made a less amusing quip that undoubtedly piqued the president's animosity. Marx told the alternative newspaper *Berkeley Barb* that "the only hope this country has is Nixon's assassination." Groucho's comment brought the comedian under Secret Service surveillance and landed him on a second list of "potential assassins." "Later events proved that Nixon was indeed a storm trooper trampling over our personal freedoms," Marx wrote in his autobiography, "but I still shouldn't have said what I did. The language was intemperate and no better than some of Nixon's appalling statements over the course of his political career."

Characteristically, Shirley MacLaine interpreted the enemies list with a different spin, concluding that it made her "madly enthusiastic": "Of course it was an acute violation of our human and civil rights, but it proved once and for all that many of us actors, actresses, and performers were important, authentic, and influential enough to be afraid of." The actress was less forgiving of Nixon's "dirty tricksters." According to MacLaine's memoir, Republican operatives cut her telephone line and scattered garbage outside her New York City apartment.

Jane Fonda's appearance on the list surprised no one; like Groucho Marx, Fonda also made the second list of "potential assassins," along with such other would-be John Wilkes Booths as Joan Baez, Harry Belafonte, Tony Randall, and Carl Reiner. Fonda's most potent weapon, apart from the media platform her fame commanded, was an utter dedication to irritating Richard Nixon. In the late 1960s and early 1970s, the actress virtually stalked the president, taking her Vietnam War protest to the White House, the Nixon home in San Clemente, and the 1968 Republican convention.

Quite apart from the conflict in Southeast Asia, Nixon and Fonda locked each other in a fierce battle of their own. After the president announced he would send American troops into Cambodia, Jane Fonda labeled him a "warmonger." Nixon retaliated by dismissing the protesters as "just a bunch of a bums." At her next rally Fonda greeted the crowd with a hearty "Welcome, fellow bums!" The Los Angeles office of the FBI hatched a plan to send a fake letter to *Daily Variety* columnist Army Archerd, suggesting that Fonda had vowed to kill Nixon; though Washington signaled its approval, the letter was never sent. Even Pat Nixon got involved, condemning Jane Fonda's controversial radio broadcast from North Vietnam. "I think she should have been in Hanoi asking them to stop their aggression," Mrs. Nixon told reporters at a press conference.

In February 1971 Fonda teamed up with actors Donald Sutherland and Peter Boyle for an antiwar show that they hoped to perform for American soldiers. Fonda got the idea after reading an article in which servicemen complained about the kind of entertainment they were receiving at military bases. Fonda's FTA ("Fuck the Army") tour served as a counterpoint to the USO shows of Bob Hope, whom Fonda disparaged as a "superhawk who has a corner on the market on entertainers speaking to soldiers." When Nixon himself ordered that access to military bases be denied, the troupers staged their revue at an off-base coffeehouse in Fayetteville, North Carolina, hometown of the giant army post Fort Bragg. Wit took a backseat to polemics in the show, as evidenced by this excerpt from Boyle's appearance as Nixon: "I have come here to Fort Bragg to present a referendum to you as commander-in-chief of the United States Armed Forces. All those in favor of pulling out of Vietnam immediately, say 'aye.' (Loud reaction). All those in favor of staying in Vietnam say 'aye.' (No reaction). Carried by the silent majority!"

With John Lennon, another antiwar figure who rankled Richard Nixon, the White House had an arrow in its quiver that could not be used against Fonda: deportation. The British rock legend had been outspoken in his criticism of the president. "Gimme Some Truth," a song from Lennon's 1971 album *Imagine*, offered this lyric: "No short-haired, yellow-bellied son of Tricky Dicky is gonna Mother Hubbard soft soap me / With just a pocketful of hope."

In 1972 the FBI warned Nixon that Lennon was involved in a plot to disrupt that year's Republican Convention. In fact, the agency's own informant had reported that the former Beatle would attend the convention only if it was peaceful and on the condition that his participation not be publicized in advance. Using the excuse of a 1968 arrest in Britain for marijuana possession the Nixon administration sought to expel Lennon from the United States as an undesirable alien. Lennon challenged the order and, two years after Nixon resigned, won his case. In the words of Jon Wiener, the California professor who waged a sixteen-year legal fight to obtain the release of Lennon's FBI files, the episode served as "a kind of rock 'n' roll Watergate."

Rock musicians expressed their disapproval of President Nixon in a number of ways—or at least tried to. Grace Slick, lead singer of Jefferson Airplane, found herself the unlikely recipient of an invitation to a White House tea because she had briefly attended the same college as Tricia Nixon. The prospect of presidential proximity gave Slick an inspiration. Wearing go-go boots, a black leather micro-miniskirt, and a see-through fishnet top, she showed up at the mansion with her escort, political activist Abbie Hoffman. Tucked away in their pockets was a hidden cache of the psychedelic drug LSD, which they planned to slip into the liquid refreshments. "We knew we wouldn't have the pleasure of seeing Nixon tripping (LSD takes a while to kick in)," Slick said, "but the idea that he might be stumbling through the White House a little later, talking to paintings, watching walls melt, and thinking he was turning into a bulldog, was irresistible." As it happened, Slick and Hoffman did not make it past the security guards.

If Nixon's tactics against entertainers failed because of their heavy-handedness, the administration of George W. Bush found a more effective means of vengeance: letting surrogates handle the dirty work. In 2002 and 2003 celebrity critics of Bush's decision to wage war in Iraq—among them Sean Penn, Jessica Lange, Martin Sheen, Susan Sarandon, Tim Robbins, and the Dixie Chicks—came in for a wave of retaliation by right-wing media commentators and Web sites. Cast as villains in a national melodrama, performers who denounced the military action were trotted out as figures of ridicule for the audience to boo and hiss at. The Internet became especially venomous territory for antiwar celebrities, with several sites dedicated to boycotts against their films, television shows, and music.

To be sure, some in show business fed the emotionalism of the issue by personalizing the terms of their dissent. At a concert in Denver Eddie Vedder, lead singer of Pearl Jam, impaled a mask of George W. Bush on a microphone stand, then smashed it against the stage during a song called "Bushleaguer." The rap trio Beastie Boys emerged from a five-year recording hiatus with a song called "In a World Gone Mad." Its lyrics directly assailed Bush's "midlife crisis war" and exhorted the White House to "put that axis of evil bullshit on hold." At the 2003 Academy Awards ceremony, filmmaker Michael Moore, winner of the Best Documentary Oscar for *Bowling for Columbine,* used his acceptance speech to reproach the "fictitious" forty-third president in unusually strident language. "Shame on you, Mr. Bush!" Moore shouted at the end of his remarks, as music from the orchestra pit began to drown him out. "Shame on you!"

Other celebrities appeared to shrink from their convictions. A few days into the Iraq conflict Madonna withdrew a war-themed music video before its premiere on a cable television channel. The video, for a song called "American Life," featured Madonna at a fashion show in pseudo-military garb tossing a grenade into the lap of a George W. Bush look-alike. "Due to the volatile state of the world and out of sensitivity and respect to the armed forces, who I support and pray for, I do not want to risk offending anyone who might misinterpret the meaning of this video," Madonna said in a press release that sounded more like a document of surrender.

The singer's ex-husband, Sean Penn, displayed far less ambivalence in his public pronouncements. In October 2002 Penn spent $56,000 to purchase a full-page advertisement in the *Washington Post* accusing President Bush of endangering civil liberties and stifling dissent. "I beg you, help save America before yours is a legacy of shame and horror," he wrote in an open letter to Bush. Penn later traveled to Baghdad on a "fact-finding mission" designed at least in part to tweak the White House; while there the actor met with Iraq's deputy prime minister. After the war Sean Penn took out another full-page newspaper ad, this one a four-thousand-word essay in the *New York Times* defending his earlier position and terming the Iraq invasion a "grave misjudgment."

In a lawsuit against a Hollywood producer Penn claimed his activism had cost him the lead role in a motion picture, though the volley of charges and countercharges between litigants rendered the facts difficult to decipher. Martin Sheen, who played fictional President Josiah Bartlet on the TV show *The West Wing*, also considered himself a target of pro-Bush conservatives. Sheen told an audience in Los Angeles he had received an "avalanche of hate mail" and that NBC executives had "let it be known they're very uncomfortable with where I'm at on the war," an allegation the network disputed.

Two weeks before the American invasion of Iraq the Screen Actors Guild issued a preemptive statement affirming the right of its members to express their opinions: "While passionate disagreement is to be expected in such a debate, a disturbing trend has arisen in the dialogue. Some have recently suggested that well-known individuals who express 'unacceptable' views should be punished by losing their right to work . . . We deplore the idea that those in the public eye should suffer professionally for having the courage to give voice to their views. Even a hint of the blacklist must never again be tolerated in this nation."

Despite boycott bluster on both sides, the only actors to be blatantly rejected for their antiwar views were Susan Sarandon and Tim Robbins. Sarandon was canceled as guest speaker at a United Way event in Florida, and both she and Robbins were dropped from a planned Baseball Hall of Fame appearance marking the fifteenth anniversary of the film *Bull Durham*. Hall of Fame President Dale Petroskey, a former assistant White House press secretary under Ronald Reagan, wrote the couple a letter of disinvitation, saying their criticism of Bush "ultimately could put our troops in even more danger." Robbins returned fire with a letter of his own, telling Petroskey, "You belong with the cowards and ideologues in a hall of infamy and shame . . . I had been unaware that baseball was a Republican sport." In the final analysis the controversy worked to the actors' advantage by giving them the high road. Invited to speak at the National Press Club after the Hall of Fame cancellation, Robbins used his platform to tell journalists, "A chill wind is blowing in this nation. A message is being sent through the White House and its allies . . . If you oppose this administration, there can and will be ramifications."

If movie stars were difficult to intimidate on more than a piecemeal basis, musicians presented an easier target. In the spring of 2003, a new term entered the American political vocabulary: "getting Dixie-Chicked." The name sprang from the trio of female country musicians who just before the war's onset found themselves singled out for large-scale retribution. Their crime: at a concert in London lead singer Natalie Maines told the audience, "Just so you know, we're ashamed the president of the United States is from Texas."

Although the comment rated barely a mention in the British press, it arrived several days later on American shores with the force of a tsunami. Fueled by the righteous indignation of pro-war broadcasters and Web sites, Maines's remark rapidly became a cause célèbre, leading the singer to issue a written apology-cum-explanation for her "disrespectful" words: "I feel that whoever holds that office should be treated with the utmost respect. We are currently in Europe and witnessing a huge anti-American sentiment as a result of the perceived rush to war. While war may remain a viable option, as a mother, I just want to see every possible alternative exhausted before children and American soldiers' lives are lost. I love my country. I am a proud American."

For Bush supporters the apology did not suffice. The ensuing backlash took a number of forms, from Internet screeds to talk show rants. Fellow country music performer Toby Keith integrated the imbroglio into his concert show, projecting a fabricated large-screen image of Maines hugging Saddam Hussein. In Louisiana a huge tractor smashed a pile of Dixie Chicks recordings at a "destruction rally" attended by an enthusiastic crowd.

Of greatest concern to the performers were the radio boycotts. Cumulus Media, one of America's largest radio chains—and owner of the station that sponsored the Louisiana "destruction rally"—stopped playing the trio's songs at its forty-two country music outlets. Other broadcasters, yielding to the wishes of outraged fans, did the same. In a poll taken by powerhouse station KKBQ in Houston, 72 percent of the respondents said they wanted the Dixie Chicks pulled off the air. The group's number-one hit, "Travelin' Soldier," took an immediate nosedive on the charts, as did sales of its latest album.

Remarkably, through a strategy of moderating their rhetoric without ceding ground, the Dixie Chicks managed to face down their tormentors. In an interview with Diane Sawyer of ABC News Maines said, "I'm not truly embarrassed that President Bush is from my state; that's not really what I care about." But when Sawyer tried goading her into another apology, Maines replied, "Am I sorry that I asked questions and that I don't just follow? No." The Chicks followed their highly watched ABC interview with a cover story in *Entertainment Weekly*, which photographed them in the buff, their bodies stenciled with the epithets that had been used against them: "Saddam's Angels," "traitor," "opinionated," "big mouth." Bruce Springsteen also came to the women's defense, writing on his Web site, "For (the Dixie Chicks) to be banished wholesale from radio stations and even entire radio networks for speaking out is un-American."

Almost as quickly as the tempest struck, the trio regained its lost ground. Record sales picked up, and the sold-out Dixie Chicks concert tour went forward with scant protest. Playing the nation's capital, Maines got a standing ovation when she said to the crowd, "Well, what do you know—Washington, D.C. If I'm not mistaken, the president of the United States lives here." Observed Frank Rich of the *New York Times*: "From national infamy to renewed superstardom in a matter of weeks; that's the kind of story that restores your faith in an America where everything is possible."

Only six months before Maines's comment in London, actress Jessica Lange uttered an even harsher version of the same sentiment without suffering similar consequences. Speaking at a film festival in Spain, Lange said of Bush, "I despise him and his entire administration—not only because of its international policy, but also the national. It makes me feel ashamed to come from the United States—it's humiliating." Jessica Lange soon emerged as one of the most visible stars in the antiwar movement, playing a key role at a Washington rally two months before the start of the war. And though she did not escape censure, neither did Lange bear the burden imposed on the Dixie Chicks.

To some extent the double standard has to do with differences between media. Music is more immediate than film, so repercussions against its practitioners follow with greater dispatch. The audience for country music is considerably more conservative than the audience of moviegoers, who run the social and geographical gamut. Radio is a more tightly controlled medium, with a concentration of owners lording the power of the playlist over even the most popular of artists. Finally, the radio industry, regulated by the federal government, is more likely to feel beholden to the White House—and therefore less willing to pick a fight.

During a May 2003 interview with NBC newsman Tom Brokaw, George W. Bush himself weighed in on the flap. Bush's words left little doubt of his hard feelings and thin skin: "I mean, the Dixie Chicks are free to speak their mind. They can say what they want to say. And just because—they shouldn't have their feelings hurt just because some people don't want to buy their records when they speak out. You know, freedom is a two-way street."

✳✳✳✳

The retaliations of Richard Nixon and George W. Bush denote a deep-seated suspicion of entertainers. But White House paranoia about actors and musicians would appear to be misplaced. If history is any guide, presidents have less to fear from celebrities than celebrities have to fear from their own behavior vis-à-vis presidents. Anger at political leaders has repeatedly led to manifestations of hubris from the men and women of show business. Never an attractive quality in anyone, hubris can be especially annoying when it emanates from wealthy, pampered stars with seemingly little cause for complaint.

Examples proliferate of self-important pronouncements by celebrities. Stephen Stills wrote a song promoting friendship with Cuba, then sent the lyrics to Jimmy Carter in the hope of influencing the president's foreign policy. Wayne Newton told reporters he would move to Australia if Carter beat Reagan in the 1980 election. Barbra Streisand said she would "never forgive" her fellow actor Reagan for his "genocidal denial" of the existence of AIDS. Ray Charles once turned down an invitation to perform at the White House. "They called the day before the gig and I just didn't think that gave me enough time," Charles said. "I thought I deserved a little more respect than that."

The 1998 impeachment trial of Bill Clinton elicited a resoundingly negative reaction from Hollywood's entertainment elite. Clinton defenders took vigorously to fund-raising dinners, talk shows, and the streets in an effort to add their voices to the public debate. The most publicized event was a Los Angeles rally that featured appearances by Streisand, Jack Nicholson, Ted Danson, Mary Steenburgen, Elisabeth Shue, and producer Norman Lear. "Who could have imagined that we would be living in a time when those we elected to office would turn their backs on the public and ignore the voices of the American people?" Streisand asked. Steenburgen, a long-time personal friend of Bill and Hillary Clinton, directly challenged the president's Republican accusers: "We are watching, and we will remember." Nicholson seemed more bemused than outraged. "We're kind of a strange country," he said. "We're Puritan-formed about sexuality."

Speaking to an audience in Paris, Woody Allen also sprang to Clinton's defense. "We have a good president persecuted for having an affair between two consenting adults that his wife accepts," Allen said. "The political atmosphere is silly and sad." Allen could hardly be viewed as a neutral observer: a few years earlier he had made headlines for his own consenting relationship with the daughter of Mia Farrow, his former companion.

Tom Hanks, another "friend of Bill," got drawn into the battle after telling the *New Yorker* magazine that he regretted donating to Clinton's defense fund in view of the president's admission of an inappropriate relationship with Monica Lewinsky. *New York Times* columnist Maureen Dowd saw in Hanks's comment "a striking reversal." "Before, it was politicians who lectured Hollywood about setting a bad moral example. Now an actor renowned as a decent guy and cozy family man was lecturing Washington." Questioned about his *New Yorker* statement, Hanks equivocated. "Do I regret giving money to the president's legal defense fund? No, I don't," he told a reporter. "I regret having to give money to the president's legal defense fund. I'm not trying to split hairs here."

The actor who took the most heat for his impeachment comments was Alec Baldwin. In December 1998 the self-described "hope-to-die, carry-me-out-in-a-box Democrat" appeared on NBC's *Late Night with Conan O'Brien* talk show. Baldwin offered what was supposed to be a comedic rant against House Judiciary Committee Chairman Henry Hyde: "If we were in other countries, we would be all right now, all of us together would go down to Washington and we would stone Henry Hyde to death . . . We would go to their homes and we'd kill their wives and their children! We would kill their families!" The appearance provoked a strongly negative reaction. NBC announced that it would not rebroadcast the program, and Baldwin ended up writing Hyde a letter of apology. "In the current supercharged climate," he said, "there's no room for this kind of glibness."

Show business critics of President Clinton, sensing that they were out of step with public opinion, tended to keep quiet. But four years after the Lewinsky scandal comedian Rosie O'Donnell had not yet forgiven the man his transgressions. In the summer of 2002 both O'Donnell and Clinton were among a group of celebrities hired to take part in the grand opening of the Mohegan Sun casino in Connecticut. O'Donnell, making her first standup comedy appearance in six years, told the audience she had refused to speak with Clinton at an event the night before. "He disgusts me," O'Donnell sniffed. "And I know I'm not supposed to say this because I'm a good Democrat, but I didn't want to [talk] to him because he lied to me when he said, 'I did not have sexual relations with that woman,' and then put the scarlet-letter blow job on her for the rest of her life. . . . I still hate you!"

Of course entertainers have as much right to express their viewpoint as anyone else, and in both the Vietnam War and the Clinton impeachment they had not only popular opinion but also good sense on their side. Too often, however, actors and musicians forget that audiences respect them in spite of their politics, not because of them. Performers demand—and rightly so—that they be treated as artists and evaluated on the basis of their work, not their personal lives. But with that acceptance comes the entertainer's responsibility to maintain a sense of professional distance from the audience. It is possible to love Frank Sinatra's music and hate his politics, but wouldn't it be better for paying customers not to have to think about Frank Sinatra's politics at all?

In a media climate that overvalues fame, it is easy to understand why politically motivated performers avail themselves of the platform they are granted. But the platform is not extended without a certain amount of hostility. Daniel Day-Lewis, an unusually cerebral movie star, hit the nail on the head when asked by a reporter in early 2003 what he thought about the threatened boycott of antiwar actors. Refusing to be drawn in, Day-Lewis said, "The media are sick and tired of people in my profession giving their opinion, and yet you're asking me my opinion. And when I give it you'll say, 'Why doesn't he shut up?'"

In a 2002 interview with the *Boston Globe*, Jodie Foster expressed a similar modesty of approach, one that other entertainers might see fit to emulate. "Even though I have huge opinions about all those (political) things, I just feel like it's not my place," Foster said. "It's not an actor's place to go spouting off and try to guide people in their political decisions. I do feel pressured sometimes to say something. But I've been really careful not to." Jodie Foster, a graduate of Yale University and one of the best-educated and most intelligent stars in Hollywood, has yet to be accused of hubris.

Gerald Ford campaigns with John Wayne in California, October 1976. (Gerald R. Ford Library)

5

✳✳✳✳

Running Time

ENTERTAINERS
ON THE CAMPAIGN TRAIL

THE SLEEPY MIDWESTERN CITY of Marion, Ohio, had never seen such excitement. On an August morning in 1920, a delegation of fifty Broadway actors and actresses chugged into town on a chartered overnight train from New York. Vaudeville star Al Jolson headed the group, bringing with him such household names of the day as Blanche Ring, Leo Carrillo, Zena Keefe, and Lew Cody. A brass band met the troupers at the station and marched them the short distance to the Marion Club for breakfast. Newly fortified, the parade hit the road again, ending up at a house on Mount Vernon Avenue.

Waiting on the porch were homeowners Warren and Florence Harding. Harding, a little-known Ohio senator, had recently won the Republican nomination for the White House. Now, in a precedent-setting event, members of the theatrical community were staging a campaign rally in the front yard of the country's next president, a handsome man who once dreamed of being an actor himself. Newspaper accounts estimated that half the population of Marion turned out to watch the performers entertain Harding and his wife with two hours' worth of musical numbers, dramatic recitations, and comedy routines.

Jolson serenaded the senator with a song he had written especially for the campaign:

We think the country's ready
For another man like Teddy.
We need another Lincoln
To do the country's thinkin'.
Mister Harding, you're the man for us!

As the program continued, some of the show folks discreetly sipped from the silver flasks they had brought along. Townspeople recalled master of ceremonies Al Jolson as among the most enthusiastic of the imbibers; according to one local woman, by the end of the festivities, "They had to pour him into the train."

The Harding rally in 1920 marks the first significant instance of entertainers organizing themselves to campaign for a presidential nominee. After winning office in a landslide, Warren Harding died two years into his presidency, and in 1924 Al Jolson returned to the hustings on behalf of Harding's vice president and successor, Calvin Coolidge. This time Jolson brought his troupe to the White House, where they joined the first couple for a hearty New England breakfast of pancakes and sausage. At the end of the meal Jolson remarked that he had eaten everything but the sausage.

"Does that include the doilies?" Mrs. Coolidge teased.

"No," replied Jolson, "I have them in my pocket."

Following breakfast the entire group adjourned to the South Lawn, where the thirty entertainers treated the Coolidges to a talent show. Jolson sang another of his eminently forgettable campaign songs, "Keep Coolidge," and assured the president that the theatrical profession supported his candidacy "almost 100 percent—those who are not for you are those who are not working, and there are very few of us in that category."

As they left the mansion Al Jolson asked the first lady if he would be able to find his coat. "Yes," said Mrs. Coolidge. "If I can get my doilies."

✳✳✳✳

It is curious that the two opening chapters in the long-running story of entertainers as presidential campaigners involve Republican candidates. In the years to follow, beginning with Franklin D. Roosevelt, performing artists have tilted heavily and consistently toward the Democrats. Today the conquest of show business stands as one of the Democratic party's unqualified success stories.

The bond between professional entertainers and Democratic presidential candidates can be traced to a September night in 1932, when Hollywood studio moguls feted party nominee Roosevelt with an enormous, star-studded Motion Picture Electrical Parade and Sport Pageant at Olympic Stadium in Los Angeles. Sitting in a flag-draped box, the future president was greeted by some of the brightest lights of the silver screen: Charles Chaplin, Stan Laurel and Oliver Hardy, Clark Gable, Claudette Colbert, Irene Dunne, Loretta Young, William Powell, Wallace Beery, Marion Davies, Boris Karloff, Tom Mix, and a dozen others. Movie stars, horse brigades, marching bands, and floats with names like Aladdin's Paradise and Illuminated Jewel Box passed through the stadium for the seventy-five thousand spectators to admire. In the words of master of ceremonies Will Rogers, it was "the most people who ever paid to see a politician."

In two key ways the 1932 rally differed from political rallies as they later developed. First, the revenues raised went to industry charities—the Motion Picture Relief Fund and the Marion Davies Foundation for Crippled Children—not Roosevelt's campaign war chest. Second, Roosevelt gave no political speech. Instead, in his brief remarks to the crowd, he commended the charities and joked that he too had been in pictures for the past three months—newsreels. Members of the audience might never have known that a presidential election would happen in six weeks.

A similar sense of restraint characterized Roosevelt's 1936 campaign. Not until 1940, eight years into his presidency, did entertainers systematically organize themselves for FDR's reelection. By then FDR had become a reliable Hollywood favorite, not just for his progressive politics or his status as a national icon, but because the show business community felt personally connected to him. Dozens of top stars had participated in the annual birthday ball events; others met the peripatetic president and first lady on the road. From here it was but a short step into active campaigning.

On September 20, 1940, a collection of actors, producers, directors, and writers gathered at the Beverly Wilshire Hotel to form the Hollywood for Roosevelt Committee. They elected Pat O'Brien chairman and Joan Bennett vice chair; among the two hundred members were Katharine Hepburn, Henry Fonda, Betty Grable, Humphrey Bogart, James Cagney, Rosalind Russell, and Dorothy Lamour. The committee set up a speakers bureau that dispatched celebrities around the country to drum up support for the president's reelection. John Garfield went to Arizona. Claude Rains traveled up and down California. Edward G. Robinson opened his home for a fund-raiser.

Several days before the election the committee spent sixteen hundred dollars for a full-page advertisement in the *New York Times*. Under the headline "Why We of Hollywood Will Vote for Roosevelt," some two hundred of the film colony's elite listed their reasons for supporting FDR. The group also paid for a series of "deluxe illuminated billboards" at strategic Los Angeles locations that displayed the enlarged autographs of twenty-five stars.

On radio, performers like Bogart, Fonda, Lucille Ball, and Groucho Marx took part in a *Salute to Roosevelt* broadcast from Hollywood's Columbia Playhouse on Halloween 1940. Master of ceremonies Walter Huston set the stage: "Hollywood wants to tell you that Hollywood is for Roosevelt in the best way Hollywood knows how—by entertaining you." A few nights later, on Election Eve, a second radio broadcast followed, featuring two hours of music, comedy, and politicking from four locations around the country. Bill "Bojangles" Robinson did a tap dance. Irving Berlin led the studio audience in a rendition of "God Bless America." Benny Goodman and Count Basie teamed up for a jazzy little number they dedicated to FDR opponent Wendell Willkie. Its title: "Gone with What Wind?"

Although these radio shows provided more razzle-dazzle than propaganda, the pro-Roosevelt message came through loud and clear. "Ladies and gentlemen," actress Joan Bennett intoned, "this is the first speech I've ever made in my life and I'm glad it's not political. I wouldn't dare stand here and tell you for whom to vote. All I can say is that, like millions of American women I'm going to the polls tomorrow and vote . . . ." Bennett's "apolitical" speech then segued into a ringing endorsement of FDR.

The successful integration of celebrities in the 1940 campaign begat a trend that drew more stars into the fold four years later. Among the new recruits in 1944 was twenty-nine-year-old Hollywood wunderkind Orson Welles, who stumped tirelessly for Roosevelt at rallies and banquets and, most effectively, on radio. So gifted a campaigner was the silver-tongued Welles that he soon began to be mentioned as a potential candidate himself. By October, with only two weeks remaining before the 1944 election, the young star had pushed himself to the limit. After collapsing from exhaustion, Welles was sent home to rest. "I hope much you will follow your doctor's orders and take care of yourself," FDR wired Welles in a telegram. "The most important thing is for you to get well and be around for the last days of the campaign." Welles responded a few days later: "This illness was the blackest of misfortunes for me because it stole away so many days from the campaign . . . I promise to take your good advice but I still hope to be back on the road by next week."

Singing idol Frank Sinatra, one year younger than Orson Welles, also got pulled into Roosevelt's gravitational field. On September 28, 1944, Sinatra, comedian Rags Ragland, and New York restaurateur Toots Shor were among a select group invited by the chairman of the Democratic National Committee to take tea at the White House with FDR. As the guests emerged from the mansion, Sinatra, wearing a gray suit and bow tie, described the meeting to reporters. "I told the president how well he looked," Sinatra said. "He kidded me about making the girls faint." Ragland jumped in with a contradictory account: Roosevelt, he said, had left the singer "absolutely speechless." According to Ragland, "Frank swooned himself. We had to pick him off the floor twice."

This first interaction between Frank Sinatra and an American president foreshadowed the perils that lay ahead for Sinatra in his dealings with the White House. The next day Republican politicians publicly denounced Roosevelt for welcoming a "crooner" whose draft-exempt status struck them as dubious in time of war. During a concert at New York's Paramount Theater two weeks later Sinatra retaliated by altering the lyrics to one of his hit songs, "Everything Happens to Me":

They asked me down to Washington
To have a cup of tea
The Republicans started squawking
They're mad as they can be,
And all I did was say "hello" to a
Man named Franklin D.
Everything happens to me.

Hollywood stars fanned out across the country in 1944 to make their pleas for Franklin Roosevelt. But it was the radio airwaves that best displayed the talents of FDR's show business partisans. An Election Eve program emceed by Humphrey Bogart skillfully paired the gods and goddesses of cinema with a cast of ordinary Americans, all of them bound by a shared enthusiasm for the president's reelection. Judy Garland opened the show with a sprightly song called "You Gotta Get Out and Vote." Endorsements from citizens then alternated with political pitches, comedy routines, and music.

Toward the end of the broadcast an orchestra and vocal chorus simulated the rhythm of a train moving down the tracks as Bogart invited listeners to join "the millions and millions of people riding on the Roosevelt Special." Then, in rapid succession, a long line of celebrities took quick turns at the microphone, offering eight-to-ten-word testimonials: Tallulah Bankhead, Milton Berle, Irving Berlin, Charles Boyer, Claudette Colbert, John Garfield, Rita Hayworth, George Jessel, Danny Kaye, Gene Kelly, Groucho Marx, Edward G. Robinson, Frank Sinatra, Franchot Tone, Lana Turner, and Jane Wyman. The brevity of their remarks against the locomotion of the musical background gave the appeals a hypnotic urgency.

Despite the heavy involvement of entertainers in the Roosevelt campaigns of 1940 and 1944, the candidate continued to maintain a physical separation from his famous supporters. On November 4, 1944, in the final rally of his long political career, Franklin Roosevelt shared the marquee with Frank Sinatra and Orson Welles. But he did not share the stage. Sinatra and Welles, two of the century's seminal talents, were there as warm-up acts.

Forty thousand spectators filled the stands at Boston's Fenway Park on a night that was warm for early November; thousands more who could not get in listened on loudspeakers outside the park. Sinatra opened the program, pouring his golden voice into the national anthem. When female fans started to squeal, older members of the audience shushed them. Then Welles delivered a fiery denunciation of FDR's opponent, Thomas Dewey, comparing the New York governor to Adolf Hitler. At the end of Welles's speech President Roosevelt made a superstar's entrance, arriving before the cheering throng in an open convertible that motored in from center field. Speaking for forty-five minutes from the automobile, the old pol held the last campaign crowd of his life spellbound. When it was all over, FDR's convertible circled the floodlit field for ten minutes as the crowd boomed: "We Want Roosevelt! We Want Roosevelt!," their voices thundering clear to the Back Bay.

Frank Sinatra, standing in the shadows, gazed out on the president with admiration. "What a guy," Sinatra said. "And boy, does he pack 'em in."

✶✶✶✶

Not every star stood behind FDR. W.C. Fields made no secret of his contempt, referring to the disabled president as "Gumlegs" and Mrs. Roosevelt as "Tornpocket." In 1940 Fields wired Wendell Willkie his suggestion for a campaign slogan: "Vote for Willkie or the Roosevelt Family." Willkie responded with a polite, noncommittal thank-you.

A more serious anti-Roosevelt effort was waged that year by a committee of conservative stars under the leadership of actor Robert Montgomery, a popular leading man who went on to serve as a performance adviser to President Eisenhower. After the Hollywood for Roosevelt Committee took out its "Why Hollywood Supports Roosevelt" ad, Montgomery's forces responded with a *New York Times* ad of their own. Headlined "The Truth About Hollywood," the text asserted that thousands of workers at the movie studios supported Republican Wendell Willkie. Among the signatories were the industry's most reliably right-wing celebrities—Gary Cooper, Walt Disney, Irene Dunne, W.C. Fields, Hedda Hopper, Adolphe Menjou, George Murphy, Mary Pickford, Zasu Pitts, Dick Powell, and Ginger Rogers—along with less predictable names like Eve Arden, Fred Astaire, Bing Crosby, Hattie McDaniel, and Zeppo Marx. Many of these Republican stalwarts returned in 1944 and 1948 to support Thomas Dewey.

Already some in Hollywood were grumbling about the town's pro-Democratic bias. Comic actor Eddie Bracken, a screen favorite in the 1940s, told audiences at Republican rallies in 1944 that he risked his future in motion pictures by campaigning for Governor Dewey. The charge did not sit well with industry leaders. Interestingly, much of the criticism of Bracken came from other Republicans like Cecil B. DeMille. According to the trade paper *Weekly Variety*, "Fellow actors accused (Bracken) of showing marked lack of respect and regard for those in the industry regardless of which way they voted."

Ronald Reagan, not yet a Republican, campaigned alongside Harry Truman in September 1948 when the Democratic president held a rally at Gilmore Field in Los Angeles. Reagan joined other liberal celebrities like Humphrey Bogart and Lauren Bacall, Lucille Ball and Desi Arnaz, Eddie "Rochester" Anderson, and George Jessel, who introduced Truman to the crowd. Jessel had agreed to emcee against his better judgment, as a personal favor to Harry Truman. "I did not see how he could win against the Dewey-Republican machine," Jessel later confessed, echoing the conventional wisdom of the time.

Truman's staunchest supporter in the theatrical community was Tallulah Bankhead. While other Democrats ran for cover, the Broadway star gave a much publicized radio appeal on the president's behalf two weeks before the election. The outspoken Bankhead penned a stridently anti-Dewey speech in which she contrasted "Harry Truman the human being" with "Thomas Dewey the mechanical man." "Mister Dewey is trim and tidy," Tallulah declared, "but is he human? I have my doubts." Bankhead pitched a fit when a Truman aide asked her to delete another line, a reference to Dewey "in his cellophane wrapper, unspoiled by contacts with the likes of you and me." Tallulah laid down the law: "If that line is cut, all bets are off. Get yourself another girl." The reference stayed.

If Truman failed to create much enthusiasm among entertainers, show business Democrats took more eagerly to Adlai Stevenson in 1952 and 1956. Head cheerleader of the true believers was Lauren Bacall, whose devotion to the candidate betrayed a serious personal infatuation. Bacall and husband Humphrey Bogart stumped hard for Stevenson in 1952, making whistle-stop appearances on his campaign train, headlining a huge rally at Madison Square Garden, and even flying to Illinois to spend Election Night with him. When Stevenson lost to General Eisenhower in a landslide, studio mogul Jack L. Warner sent the Bogarts a sarcastic telegram: "Dear Baby and Bogie: Congratulations on the great service you did for General Eisenhower. Without love, Jack Warner."

Four years later, Bacall jumped back on the Stevenson bandwagon, along with fellow Democrats Bette Davis, Henry Fonda, Myrna Loy, Mercedes McCambridge, Robert Ryan, and Frank Sinatra. In late October 1956 these celebrities were among the performers at a nationally televised dinner for Stevenson and his running mate, Estes Kefauver. Two younger stars joined them: Janet Leigh and Marlon Brando, both of whom actively supported liberal candidates in the 1960s.

Another young performer in the Stevenson column was rock and roll sensation Elvis Presley. Arriving at the Los Angeles airport in August 1956, Presley was greeted by placards that said "Elvis Presley for President." When reporters questioned him about the signs, the singer replied, "I'm strictly for Stevenson. I don't dig the intellectual bit, but I'm telling you, man, he knows the most."

Dwight Eisenhower, Stevenson's two-time opponent, holds the distinction of being the most successful Republican presidential candidate of all time vis-à-vis the entertainment community. In both 1952 and 1956 Hollywood stars warmly embraced the wartime hero, providing not just endorsements and publicity but also substantial monetary gifts. With political campaigns entering the television age, the need for cash increased dramatically; then as now, show business celebrities were viewed as a ready source of funds.

Jack Warner was one of the studio executives charged with shaking Hollywood's money tree. At Warner's urging, Gary Cooper, Ronald Reagan, and Fred Astaire each donated $500 to Eisenhower in 1952. John Wayne gave $1,000, but complained to Warner that he could not be expected to cough up more: "In checking with my Business Manager, I find that I have to make about $15,000.00 in order to pay agents, taxes and alimony to my first wife—this does not include my second—in order to make this $1000.00. I can't afford any more than this in Capital dollars. I really can't afford this."

Months before Eisenhower officially declared his candidacy, an avid group of performing artists had flocked to his side. At a February 1952 rally in Madison Square Garden the famous names included Clark Gable, Irving Berlin, Mary

Martin, and Ike's number-one fan, Ethel Merman. At this point even Democrats Lauren Bacall and Humphrey Bogart backed Eisenhower, though they soon defected to Stevenson. Before Bogart switched sides, Jack Warner got him to write a $500 check to the Eisenhower campaign.

Hollywood's big moment in the 1952 Eisenhower campaign came in early October, when the candidate traveled to Los Angeles for a rally at the Pan-Pacific Auditorium. With future Senator George Murphy as master of ceremonies, the parade of stars featured June Allyson and Dick Powell, Edgar Bergen, Irene Dunne, Rosalind Russell, John Wayne, and the ubiquitous Ethel Merman. The next day Dunne and Ginger Rogers boarded Eisenhower's campaign train, where they were photographed with the man who would soon break the Democrats' twenty-year lock on the White House.

By 1956 Ike's standing among entertainers had risen higher still. "Dear Jack," wrote Bob Hope to Eisenhower finance man Jack Warner, "Here's a check to help your campaign. I like this administration. Never had it so good." Hope sent $5,000.

But the big money was harvested through a new source: television. In January 1956 the Republican party set a fund-raising record with a closed circuit television program beamed to fifty-three cities across the country. At each location Eisenhower loyalists gathered to watch the so-called *Salute to Ike* as it played on big-screen TVs. Jimmy Stewart offered a testimonial, but it was the president himself who roused the faithful with a stirring address. The next morning the donations began to pour in, eventually totaling $6 million.

Later that year Jimmy Stewart returned to the Eisenhower campaign as host of a remarkable CBS television special honoring the president's sixty-sixth birthday. *National Ike Day,* as the program was titled, aired two weeks before the 1956 election in the time slot usually reserved for *Gunsmoke.* "Ike Day is more than just a birthday celebration," announced Stewart in the opening setup. "It's a nationwide tribute to a man who has devoted almost all of his adult life to the service of his country. So for all of you out there who are watching in your homes, I know that I express your feeling when I say now, happy birthday, Mr. President."

Stewart then turned to a television monitor that showed Ike and Mamie Eisenhower in a room at the White House with their son, daughter-in-law, and two grandchildren. As the shot cut to the Eisenhowers full-screen, the president said, "Thank you very much, Jimmy."

The show proceeded as a kind of presidential *This Is Your Life,* with stars at locations around the country recounting Eisenhower's life in story and song. Kathryn Grayson and Howard Keel performed Ike and Mamie's favorite musical numbers from the Eisenhower boyhood home in Abilene, Kansas. At Washington's Statler Hotel Helen Hayes showed off a birthday cake, "baked according to Mrs. Eisenhower's own recipe." Eddie Fisher, one of Ike's favorite vocalists, offered a reprise of "Counting My Blessings," a song he had performed for the president at a recent B'nai Brith dinner. Nat King Cole, Irene Dunne, James Cagney, and the Fred Waring vocal chorus rounded out the bill. The program ended back at the White House, with the Eisenhowers eating cake and singing "Happy Birthday" to the slightly uncomfortable paterfamilias.

The decision to use the president's birthday as fodder for a network television special had been carefully calculated. Fearing that Ike's age might be seen as a negative by voters (Eisenhower had recently suffered a heart attack) campaign strategists decided to face the issue head-on and reposition the passage of another year as cause for a coast-to-coast celebration. The homey tone, the extended Eisenhower family, and reassuring performers like Jimmy Stewart all contributed to an aura of old-fashioned virtue. In its way the *National Ike Day* birthday telecast marks a radical innovation in the marketing of the presidency. As Eisenhower media scholar Craig Allen wrote, "Never before had the public seen serious national leaders associated to this extent with familiar, everyday situations; the offbeat nature of these programs found its way to the heart of middle America."

Pro-Eisenhower entertainers threw themselves wholeheartedly into the campaign of 1956. The comedy duo Abbott and Costello brought their antics to several rallies. Irene Dunne and Ward Bond toured Texas. Zasu Pitts barnstormed in Iowa. In October a busload of stars appeared with the candidate at the Hollywood Bowl. As the performers waited to go on, campaign operatives used the time to have them record twenty-second endorsements.

Many of these same celebrities loaned their services to Richard Nixon's run for the White House in 1960. Although Nixon was more personally attentive to his show business supporters than Eisenhower, he did not always know how to behave in their presence. The writer Adela Rogers St. John, a friend and supporter, attended a Republican rally at which Nixon was joined by a troupe of film stars. "You never saw such beautiful flesh," Rogers told Nixon biographer Fawn Brodie. "And he acted like a man utterly unsexed. It was as if he didn't know they were there." Not that it mattered much in 1960. How could Nixon expect much help from movie stars, when he was, in effect, running against one himself?

✶✶✶✶

According to popular mythology, John F. Kennedy campaigned for the White House with Hollywood as his running mate. The facts are more prosaic: Kennedy drew on the show business community to a slightly greater degree than Dwight Eisenhower. The difference was one of perception. Kennedy galvanized a younger, more glamorous crop of celebrity supporters. The contrast between JFK's stars and Ike's stars reflected the difference between JFK and Ike themselves: Kennedy was new Hollywood, Eisenhower was old Hollywood. A special energy surrounded the handsome young candidate and his court of glittering celebrities, and neither the media nor the public could resist the spectacle.

His matinee-idol looks and family connection to Hollywood undoubtedly heightened JFK's image as a showbiz candidate. These links became especially apparent during the 1960 Democratic National Convention, which delivered the Massachusetts senator into the belly of the showbiz beast: Los Angeles, California. The convention turned into a lovefest between Kennedy and Hollywood. Actors and actresses had taken part in previous political conventions, but never to the degree they did that year. The presence of the convention in the entertainment capital gave the town's luminaries an excuse to dabble in the drama of presidential politics; even die-hard Republicans turned out for the parties and receptions that swept L.A. during the second week of July.

The glamour kicked in the night before the convention opened, when three thousand guests paid $100 each to attend a dinner at the Beverly Hilton. Milton Berle and George Jessel shared emcee duty; Frank Sinatra and Judy Garland sang. Opening day of the Democratic conclave attracted a stellar cast to the Los Angeles Sports Arena. Sinatra, Janet Leigh, Tony Curtis, Shelley Winters, Sammy Davis, Nat King Cole, and Vincent Price all filed onto the speakers' platform to sing the national anthem. "The highlight of the opening moment," wrote a *Boston Globe* reporter, "was how beautifully-formed movie star Janet Leigh appeared to the packed gallery as she weaved to the speaker's rostrum in her lightweight backless white evening gown." Leigh and Sinatra became fixtures throughout the convention, mingling with delegates on the floor and promoting Kennedy to willing journalists. Sinatra reportedly blackened the bald spot on the back of his head so it would not be picked up by television cameras on the arena floor.

The *Hollywood Reporter,* a publication not known for its coverage of presidential politics, assigned a different celebrity each day to file a convention dispatch. Actor and former journalist Tony Franciosa compared the process to a casting call, with JFK as the romantic lead "seeking the hand of the Fair Young Maiden, Miss Nommy Nation." Frank Capra wrote: "As a film director, I look upon this scene of

'Politics USA' with envy!" Janet Leigh concluded her report by likening the week's events to the movie business: "This is definitely a major production with an 'A' budget and an all-star cast, and like many Hollywood productions, the script is being written as they go along. In November we'll find out how it plays!"

The final day of the convention started off with another big-name extravaganza: a huge variety show at the Los Angeles Coliseum, with Steve Allen as master of ceremonies and backup from Shirley MacLaine, Mercedes McCambridge, Ralph Bellamy, and Vincent Price. The celebrities took turns introducing a corny array of local talent: marching bands, drum majorettes, and a motorcycle drill team. Edward G. Robinson recited a poem by Walt Whitman—"Song of Democracy"—accompanied by four thousand choral singers and instrumentalists. Mort Sahl, lending some badly needed humor, told the told the crowd that Vice President Nixon had just sent a telegram to Joe Kennedy: "Congratulations. You have not lost a son. You have gained a country."

In the general election campaign that followed, Kennedy sharply limited his public appearances with entertainers. "There was never any feeling at all that having film celebrities appeal for him had any particular merit to it," said Kennedy aide Richard Goodwin. "The idea of making a big thing out of a Schwarzenegger-type endorsement would have horrified him." In early September Frank Sinatra, Janet Leigh, Tony Curtis, Peter Lawford, and Gene Kelly preceded Kennedy at a Los Angeles rally, and on October 26 a delegation of stars including Leigh, Henry Fonda, Shelley Winters, Melvyn Douglas, and Tallulah Bankhead joined the senator at a tumultuous rally in Manhattan's Garment District. More typical was Sinatra's Koncert for Kennedy at the Waikiki Shell in Honolulu a month later, in which the candidate did not take part.

John F. Kennedy made an unusual appearance in a campaign commercial with singer Harry Belafonte. The one-minute spot shows the men, both wearing suits and ties, seated side-by-side in what appears to be a humble big-city apartment. Belafonte begins his pitch: "I'm an artist and I'm not a politician. But like most Americans I have a great interest in the political and the economic destiny of my country." When Belafonte mentions that he is seated with Senator John Kennedy, the shot cuts briefly to JFK and then back to Belafonte, who continues his spiel "as a Negro and as an American." Throughout the spot, Kennedy does little more than listen.

African American performers gave Kennedy a major boost in the 1960 campaign. Belafonte, Nat King Cole, Lena Horne, and Cab Calloway contributed print or radio ads. A different series of audio spots, recorded by Milton Berle,

Gene Kelly, and Jeff Chandler, appealed to foreign-born citizens. Each ad opened with the star speaking a few words of a foreign language, then switching to English to tout Kennedy. The polyglot pitchmen taped commercials in Spanish, French, Chinese, Japanese, Hungarian, Polish, and Yiddish.

Henry Fonda and Myrna Loy recorded on-camera commercials for Kennedy in 1960. Loy, who campaigned extensively on JFK's behalf, came to feel underappreciated by the candidate. When a pro forma thank-you arrived from Kennedy's secretary a few weeks after the inauguration, Loy took it as a slap in the face. "I am certainly not vain enough to think that the newly elected president had nothing better to do than to thank me himself," she said, "but, God knows, those who contributed money rather than time got theirs. I never really felt that he recalled or cared about what I had done when he no longer needed me."

More striking than Kennedy's use of celebrities during the campaign were the half dozen star-laden fund-raisers held after his election: two in New York, two in Washington, and two in Los Angeles. The one the world remembers is the birthday gala at Madison Square Garden in May 1962. Though it is Marilyn Monroe singing "Happy Birthday, Mister President" that is seared into memory, the rest of the show shined almost as brightly. Three emcees kept the acts moving: Jack Benny, Shirley MacLaine, and Henry Fonda. The performers ranged from Ella Fitzgerald to Maria Callas, Jimmy Durante to Nichols and May. Kennedy himself provided some of the comedy, telling the audience that whenever his father railed against businessmen, "he always exempted show business."

A year later, at Kennedy's final birthday party, it was Audrey Hepburn who serenaded the president with "Happy Birthday." Some of the previous year's entertainers returned, accompanied by new faces like Ann-Margret, who sang "Baby Won't You Please Come Home" to an attentive JFK. The show ended with a male chorus made up of Bobby Darin, Mel Ferrer, Eddie Fisher, Henry Fonda, Van Johnson, Peter Lawford, Donald O'Connor, Robert Preston, Tony Randall, Ed Sullivan, and David Susskind singing "Together," followed by Louis Armstrong leading the entire company in a rousing version of "When the Saints Come Marching In."

Kennedy's Washington dinners, held in January 1962 and January 1963, celebrated the first two anniversaries of his inauguration. The 1962 event featured a relatively subdued program of entertainment by Danny Thomas, Rosemary Clooney, Lee Remick, and Peter Lawford. In 1963 they pulled out all the stops. Cohosted by Gene Kelly and Kirk Douglas, the dinner assembled an international omnibus of performers: Yves Montand from France, Shirley Bassey from Britain, Antonio and his Flamenco Ballet Espagnol, and Australian soprano Joan Sutherland. Americans on the bill included George Burns and Carol Channing; Diahann Carroll; Peter, Paul, and Mary; and the New York City Ballet. The night's signature performance came from Carol Burnett, whose comedy sketch about a European princess unable to hold her liquor brought down the house. At the beginning of the show Gene Kelly informed the president that dozens of other entertainers had volunteered their services to the occasion, so many they had to be turned away. "But they'll have plenty of chances later," said Kelly. "After all, you'll be here another six years."

Two days before John F. Kennedy's assassination, the president held a White House meeting to discuss plans for a third inaugural anniversary fund-raiser in January 1964. Those visiting the Oval Office included Lena Horne, Carol Lawrence, and Broadway producer and composer Richard Adler, who told reporters JFK "wants to know what's going on—and he knows show business!" Horne and Lawrence were to have been joined for the show by Jonathan Winters, Joan Baez, the New Christy Minstrels, and emcees Gregory Peck, Rock Hudson, and Gina Lollobrigida.

Kennedy's two Los Angeles fund-raisers drew an assortment of entertainment glitterati. In November 1961 Nat King Cole headlined at a $100-a-plate dinner at the Hollywood Palladium. The president returned in June 1963 for a considerably more exclusive $1,000-a-plate gala at the Beverly Hilton Hotel, where the cast of characters included Jack Benny, Marlon Brando, Cary Grant, Charlton Heston, Gene Kelly, Burt Lancaster, Peter Lawford, Dean Martin, and Jack Webb. Instead of giving a formal address, the president table-hopped among his famous admirers. When Kennedy sat down next to Rock Hudson, the talk turned to their common ancestry: Hudson's real name was Roy Fitzgerald. "You know all us Fitzgeralds are related, right?" JFK asked. "That's right, sir," answered Hudson. "And I'm sure Ella will be happy to hear about it too."

The Beverly Hilton event nearly caused a public relations headache for the White House. In order to accommodate the president's fund-raiser in the Grand Ballroom, the hotel bumped a Burbank high school that had booked the space for its prom. Learning of this, Kennedy insisted that the Democrats move to a smaller venue so the students could keep the ballroom.

After dinner with the stars JFK and Jack Benny astonished the high school prom goers by dropping in to say hello. Surveying the scene as he sauntered in, Kennedy cracked, "This is a better room than the one upstairs." His remarks to the teenagers were a combination of witty and wistful. "Next to being president—in fact, rather than being president," he said, "I would prefer being a member of this graduating class tonight. All this country is and hopes to be is in this room." Kennedy then turned to Benny and quipped, "Jack Benny will now give the address to the graduating class."

When Lyndon Johnson ran for reelection in 1964, he greatly benefited from the goodwill Kennedy had engendered in the show business community. Many of the same performers who worked for JFK now lent their names to LBJ. Some fresh faces joined the Democratic crusade as well, notably Woody Allen, who performed his stand-up routine at an Eiffel Tower rally sponsored by Americans Abroad. "Good evening, ladies and gentlemen," Allen began, "this is my first tower." Marlo Thomas and Connie Stevens helped form Youth for LBJ, a group that toured with an anti–Barry Goldwater satiric revue. "A great surge in political activity among motion picture stars has taken place," wrote Peter Bart in the *New York Times*. "Hollywood old-timers say they cannot recall any previous election in which so many performers were openly working for presidential candidates."

The 1964 race again called attention to the disparity in star power between Democrats and Republicans. Where Johnson supporters included the hottest names in show business, the Goldwater campaign made do with old-timers like Mary Pickford, Irene Dunne, Ginger Rogers, and John Wayne. In the 1968 and 1972 campaigns, Richard Nixon likewise came up short in the celebrity endorsement sweepstakes, despite his lifelong ties to Southern California. The youngest person on Nixon's 1968 list was singer Connie Francis, whose cachet as a pop icon had long since evaporated. As a means of generating a more exciting crop of Hollywood supporters, a 1971 White House memorandum suggested having Tricia and Julie Nixon and their spouses host a reception for youthful stars of the entertainment industry; the event did not come to fruition.

The "celebrity gap" between Republicans and Democrats became especially pronounced in the fractious campaigns of the Vietnam War era, when an increasingly vocal contingent of entertainers stepped into the political arena. In 1968 peace candidate Eugene McCarthy attracted Paul Newman and Joanne Woodward, Tony Randall, Leonard Nimoy, and Myrna Loy. Hubert Humphrey enlisted more traditional Democrats like Frank Sinatra, Gregory Peck, and Carol Channing. Robert Kennedy could boast Shirley MacLaine, Lauren Bacall, and Marlon Brando.

The activism of these performers coincided with a change in the campaign system that gave voters the power to choose candidates in primary elections. Ronald Brownstein described this shift in his landmark study of Hollywood's influence in national politics, *The Power and the Glitter*: "Under the old system, celebrities had no real place in the battles for the presidential nomination: glamour helped candidates little when their target audience was a handful of party leaders who responded to hard calculations of prospects and power. But the stars' value ascended once the candidates were forced to sell themselves directly through primaries to the public, whose affections were more malleable."

The 1972 race, which pitted incumbent Richard Nixon against challenger George McGovern, brought a new level of celebrity involvement in presidential campaigns. Brother and sister Warren Beatty and Shirley MacLaine put their careers on ice in order to serve as full-time volunteers for McGovern. Each sibling assumed a different area of responsibility: Shirley in front of the footlights and Warren behind the scenes. No entertainers in American history have played larger roles in a presidential campaign.

MacLaine plunged in feet forward, hopscotching around the country to meet the voters face-to-face, sometimes with the candidate and sometimes on her own. Working seven days a week, the star trundled through living rooms, banquet halls, and college campuses. "My first year campaigning with McGovern put me in touch for the first time with the soul and sweat of some real American people I would never otherwise have met," she wrote in a 1995 memoir. MacLaine's description of her efforts provides a telling analysis of the tangled motivations that draw entertainers into presidential campaigns. Politics, it would seem, accounts for only part of the appeal: "It didn't take long for me to rediscover the person I had been before Hollywood. I went back to my roots as an American who cared just like them. I too was a person just trying to love her country and make sense out of life. These wonderful people with whom I communicated were helping me simply to be myself again."

MacLaine's presence on the campaign trail sparked criticism, even derision, in the media. In May 1972 ABC news commentator Harry Reasoner lamented the conspicuousness of the MacLaine/McGovern alliance: "It seems no matter what the occasion, or who the candidate there is Shirley next to him, looking poignant or sometimes elfin." MacLaine responded with an op-ed column in the *New York Times* defending the role of artists in political campaigns. The essay comes across as a curious combination of insight and narcissism. On the one hand, MacLaine spoke perceptively of performers as "prophets of social change" owing to their involvement with "the full range of human life": "Politics that are void of the insight of art—its compassion, humor, and laughter—are doomed to sterility and abstractions." But by the end of the piece she had lapsed into grandiosity: "If we tend only to our private gardens, inhibited by those who say 'it's none of your business,' it could be that we will ultimately find ourselves standing silently by, upsetting no one, endeavoring resolutely to 'stick to acting,' while the United States of America sinks slowly into the West taking Hollywood, Broadway and skeptical journalists down with it." In other words, apolitical movie stars could hasten the demise of the Republic.

As a backstage strategist and fund-raiser Warren Beatty came in for less disparagement than his sister, though he too was an object of press fascination during the 1972 campaign. Like MacLaine, Beatty seemed to discover in politics a level of personal fulfillment that a career in show business could not supply. "I've led a fairly indulgent life," Beatty told an interviewer, "but once in a while I activate. I don't consider many things important, but the American presidency is the most important moral force in the world. If I can have a say in who fills it or doesn't, then I will." George McGovern greatly valued Beatty's advice. "He has a political maturity astounding in someone so inexperienced—the instincts of a man who has spent a lifetime in politics," McGovern said. As the years went on, Beatty did spend a lifetime in politics, most notably as an adviser to his friend Gary Hart, whose 1988 campaign for the White House collapsed after allegations of marital infidelity.

Beatty's most significant contribution to the McGovern campaign—and others after it—was a series of highly publicized rock concerts that netted more than a million dollars for the Democratic nominee. The first of these took place in Los Angeles in April 1972 and featured performances by Barbra Streisand, James Taylor, Carole King, and Quincy Jones. Celebrity ushers like Jack Nicholson, Goldie Hawn, Gene Hackman, and Julie Christie guided audience members to their seats, and at the end of the show the candidate came onstage to say a brief hello. A concert in New York two months later reunited three beloved acts— Simon and Garfunkel; Peter, Paul, and Mary; and Nichols and May—and added the voice of Dionne Warwick.

Beatty's pioneering use of fund-raising concerts caught the attention of subsequent candidates, especially in the Democratic party. In 1976 a string of performances by southern country-rock acts—the Marshall Tucker Band, the Allman Brothers, Black Oak Arkansas, Charlie Daniels, and the Atlanta Rhythm Section—kept Jimmy Carter's fledgling presidential candidacy afloat at a crucial stage in the race before the Georgia governor established himself as a credible figure among more traditional donors.

That same year Linda Ronstadt, Jackson Browne, and the Eagles helped jumpstart the campaign of California Governor Jerry Brown with four rock recitals. Although Ronstadt was dating Governor Brown at the time, she voiced reservations about the involvement of musicians in political campaigns. "This whole thing makes me extremely nervous," Ronstadt told a *Newsweek* reporter, in a refreshing expression of modesty. "Rock 'n' roll and politics ought to stay separate like church and state. I think Brown would make the best president, but I don't feel qualified to say the campaign is deserving of our putting $100,000 into his hands."

On the Republican side, entertainers were most evident at the national convention that nominated Gerald Ford. Cary Grant flew in to make a surprise introduction of first lady Betty Ford, whom he had hosted a few months earlier at a celebrity reception in Beverly Hills. Backstage, Grant was a bundle of nerves. "Talking to an audience is quite different from acting," the veteran star told Mrs. Ford's press secretary. "I don't talk to people. I talk to cameras!"

Mrs. Ford also made a strategic appearance with singer Tony Orlando at the 1976 convention that helped siphon attention away from her husband's rival for the Republican nomination, Ronald Reagan. On opening night, crowd reaction to Nancy Reagan had been boisterous, creating a sense among delegates and viewers at home that momentum on the floor was building toward Reagan. To prevent a repeat episode, Ford operatives struck back. The next night Betty Ford reached the convention hall early and took a seat in her VIP box alongside family guest Tony Orlando. When Mrs. Reagan arrived, producers of the event cued the orchestra to launch into Orlando's theme song, "Tie a Yellow Ribbon Round the Old Oak Tree," at which point Orlando took Betty by the hand and began dancing with her in the aisle. Just as the Ford handlers had planned, network cameras cut away from Nancy Reagan in order to capture the first lady's exuberant dance.

Despite his Hollywood background, Ronald Reagan relied little on celebrities in his political campaigns, preferring instead to operate as a solo act. Indeed, in Reagan's campaigns for governor of California, the more likely scenario was entertainers speaking *against* their former colleague. Gene Kelly was one of several stars to take to the airwaves in anti-Reagan television commercials in 1966. "I've played many roles before the camera," Kelly said. "I've been a soldier, a gambler and even a major league baseball player. I know I could play the role of a governor, but that I could never really sit in his chair and make decisions affecting the education of millions of children." The message could scarcely have been more blunt.

Reagan's 1980 presidential campaign coaxed a few old friends into the political fray. Frank Sinatra, who had organized concerts for Democrat Pat Brown in his gubernatorial run against Reagan, now sang for the other team. In November 1979 Sinatra and Dean Martin joined forces for a fund-raiser in Boston that added several hundred thousand dollars to Reagan's coffers. The two singers appeared with the candidate at a press conference, where Dean Martin stole the show. When a reporter asked Reagan about his fund-raising plans, Martin interrupted: "I don't think that's any of your business." Boston journalists were curious about Sinatra's switch to Reagan after having supported "the Kennedys." Sinatra responded that his allegiance had been "only to Jack." Of Senator Edward Kennedy, an undeclared candidate for the 1980 presidential race, Sinatra said, "Jack had presence and aptitude . . . I don't know if Teddy has that."

Sinatra and Martin were not Ronald Reagan's only supporters from the entertainment industry. Wayne Newton sang at seven fund-raising concerts, and Jimmy Stewart taped radio ads. But campaign strategists consciously avoided making a public association between Reagan and his movie star roots. Internal polling in 1980 showed that even after two terms as governor of California 10 percent of voters viewed the candidate primarily as an actor. Frequent appearances with entertainers could only confuse the issue.

In 1984, with nothing to lose, President Reagan stepped up his use of celebrity campaigners. Sinatra returned as the star attraction at a series of pricey cocktail receptions with Republican donors and barnstormed with Reagan in Hoboken, New Jersey, Sinatra's hometown. Courting the Southern vote, the president appeared with country singer Tammy Wynette at a Daytona Beach stock car race and at the Grand Ole Opry, where he led a birthday celebration for Roy Acuff. "This feller, Mr. Reagan, has put our country back in order where it should be," Acuff told the audience. Getting into the Nashville spirit, the president said, "The other side's promises are a little like Minnie Pearl's hat. They both have big price tags hanging from them." The real Minnie Pearl, standing with Reagan on the Opry stage, beamed.

✵✵✵✵

If the Reagan years muted celebrity participation in political campaigns, the succeeding election cycles more than made up for lost time, especially among Democrats. Massachusetts Governor Michael Dukakis lured a sizable stable of stars to his cause in 1988, chief among them his cousin, Olympia Dukakis, winner of that year's Academy Award as Best Supporting Actress for *Moonstruck*. On the night of the Oscar telecast Dukakis handlers arranged a bit of campaign legerdemain to link Olympia's win to her cousin's campaign. The original plan was to have Dukakis watch the awards show at the Grand Ticino restaurant in Greenwich Village, where much of *Moonstruck* had been set. But because Best Supporting Actress was the show's first item of business, Dukakis could not reach the restaurant in time to see it. Instead the candidate watched the moment of family triumph in a holding room on Staten Island, away from the cameras.

To maximize Olympia's triumph, campaign operatives taped the broadcast and played it back later at the Grand Ticino, with Dukakis reacting as though he were observing the event live. This time cameras recorded his response. "I felt Dukakis was definitely uncomfortable having to come up with this emotion as if he were seeing it for the first time," a campaign aide later said. "He got choked up at the right moment, of course. But he was uncomfortable with the fact that he had to get choked up."

Dozens of celebrities pitched in for the Dukakis campaign. Gene Hackman recorded voice-overs for TV commercials. Sally Field gave political talks. In New York Ron Silver, Christopher Reeve, Susan Sarandon, Blythe Danner, and Alec Baldwin formed a speaker's bureau called the Creative Coalition. Robert Redford appeared with the candidate at a spirited rally at Rutgers University. "Hello, everybody," a smiling Redford told the crowd. "I'm Dan Quayle."

A new generation of Hollywood performers also came onboard. Organized by Tom Hayden and Jane Fonda, some two dozen youthful entertainers stumped the West Coast on a bus tour called the Star-Spangled Caravan, registering voters and promoting Democratic candidates. By some accounts, their presence on the campaign trail was of mixed value. At one event TV sitcom actress Justine Bateman asked the audience, "What do you think of the eighteen- to twenty-four-year-old age group—pretty bitchin', huh?" Journalist Ron Brownstein reported that the young stars showed a tendency to mingle only with one another at public events, "protecting themselves from the assembled public with the impenetrable aura of superiority that people in the movie industry seem to perfect as soon as they acquire an agent."

George Bush had his celebrities as well in 1988 and 1992: country musicians like Loretta Lynn, the Gatlin Brothers, and the Oak Ridge Boys; he-man actors like Chuck Norris, Arnold Schwarzenegger, and Bruce Willis; and establishment stars like Bob Hope, Robert Mitchum, and Telly Savalas. As with all Republican campaigns, however, Bush's big names were no match for the army of entertainers who had signed on with the Democrats.

In 1992 Arkansas Governor Bill Clinton quickened the pulse of show business more than any candidate since John F. Kennedy. Like Kennedy, Clinton made the entertainment industry a vital component of not just his electoral strategy but also the permanent campaign that followed his election. His introduction to the show

business community came gradually, beginning in the late 1980s with informal receptions hosted by Harry Thomason and Linda Bloodworth-Thomason, the television producers who were Clinton's long-time friends. "It was hard to get people
to come," Thomason recalled. "I don't think anybody really believed us when we
said this guy's probably going to run for president someday."

After Clinton announced late in 1991, a series of modest fund-raisers increased the governor's standing in Hollywood. These events helped win him the
support of a number of the Thomasons' television colleagues, including actors
from the shows *Designing Women* and *Night Court*. By the spring of 1992 other
stars had come onboard, from film as well as TV—Chevy Chase, Richard Dreyfuss, John Ritter—along with executives like Dawn Steel, an early supporter who
gave a fund-raiser for Clinton in December 1991.

Once he clinched the Democratic nomination, Clinton had no trouble rallying
the show business community to his side. In September 1992 the entertainment
industry bestowed its formal blessing at a million-dollar fund-raiser at the Los Angeles estate of producer Ted Fields, a home that had once belonged to silent film
comedian and Nixon supporter Harold Lloyd. Four years earlier Fields had hosted
a similar event for the Dukakis campaign. But instead of showing up himself,
Michael Dukakis offended Hollywood by sending his wife Kitty. This time the
guest of honor was front and center before twelve hundred show business high
rollers. "Not since the days of JFK has such an array of stars been assembled to support a candidate," wrote veteran columnist Army Archerd in *Daily Variety*.

Ambassadors from various branches of entertainment offered their talents in
tribute. Tammy Wynette began the program with "America." Dionne Warwick
sang "Amazing Grace." Elaine May and Mike Nichols, who had once performed
for JFK, treated the audience to a rare stand-up routine. Nichols opened with a
message for the crowd: "We can drop the Republican code for cultural elite—
good evening, fellow Jews."

Some of Hollywood's most recognizable performers presented homilies:
Dustin Hoffman spoke about AIDS, Annette Bening about freedom of choice,
Michelle Pfeiffer about education and illiteracy, Rhea Perlman about child care,
and Danny DeVito about the environment. Whoopi Goldberg defended her fellow performers against Republican criticism. "We're part of the cultural elite,
and I'm thrilled to be part of the cultural elite," she said. "Hollywood is one of
the places where you can come from nowhere and be somebody. The scary thing
is, Washington is the other place."

As much as the guests enjoyed these entertainers, it was the endorsement of
two other Hollywood superstars that carried the most weight with the audience.

Warren Beatty extemporized with a heartfelt speech in which he predicted a close, nasty election. Beatty charged that the Republican party had moved so far to the right "that Richard Nixon disapproves" and added, "I haven't seen a presidential candidate with as much perseverance or as much of a plan as Bill Clinton. And this process has shown his strength of character."

The ultimate benediction of William Jefferson Clinton came from Barbra Streisand, the queen bee of Hollywood politics. "I used to be a director—now I'm a backyard singer," joked Streisand, as she proceeded to deliver a memorable performance that mixed sermon with song. At the end of her set all the entertainers, plus Bill and Hillary Clinton, joined Streisand onstage to sing "God Bless America."

In his thank-you remarks Clinton displayed his own canniness as a performing artist. Describing the audience members as "some of the most gifted, creative, and caring Americans in the country," Clinton spoke words that were music to their ears: "I want you to be a part of the administration—not just a part of the campaign." By the end of the evening, when the Clintons, Jack Nicholson, and others on the A-list repaired to Streisand's home for a postparty reception, Bill Clinton had Big Hollywood in the palm of his hand.

As the campaign of 1992 went forward, Clinton shared the platform with other celebrities—Whoopi Goldberg and the chorus of singing nuns from the film *Sister Act* at one rally—but never again was he cast as a supplicant before the deities of show business. The balance of power shifted: being a supporter of the president was seen as a privilege, a form of social validation in a community where such things are closely calibrated. In his first term alone, Bill Clinton held nine fund-raisers with entertainment industry elites, including a reception at the Creative Artists Agency, a fiftieth birthday variety show that blended live musical acts with documentary footage of the Clinton family, and parties at the homes of Steven Spielberg and movie mogul Lew Wasserman.

The Democrats' 1996 fund-raising efforts culminated with a backyard concert that starred Streisand, the Eagles, the Neville Brothers, and Chicago. A thousand supporters—among them Shirley MacLaine, Richard Dreyfuss, Tom Hanks, Carrie Fisher, and Sharon Stone—spent $4 million to take part in the exclusive event. Though journalists were not allowed inside, they did corner some of the attendees outside the gates for comment afterward. Most of the reporters' questions centered on the financial implications of the gathering, and most of the responses were evasive. One star, however, did not demur. When ABC's Brian Ross asked Barbra Streisand if any individual should be able to give as much money as she did, she responded, "If you have it, you can give it."

"How about those who don't have it?" asked Ross.

"They can't give it," Streisand said, "but they can vote. They can vote in a democracy."

Most show business celebrities happily accepted their status as secondary players in Clinton's long-running drama. But old habits die hard in Hollywood. At a 1996 campaign stop at Universal Studios Michael Douglas, star of the White House drama *An American President*, spoke of his admiration for Clinton and delighted the crowd by repeating a line that movie actors hear on a routine basis: "Mr. President, I'm a fan. I enjoy your work." Journalist Roger Simon described what happened next:

> Douglas walks back from the lectern and Clinton shakes his hand. Then Douglas turns and leaves the stage. He walks over to a waiting limousine and roars off. In Washington this would have been a terrible gaffe, bordering on deadly insult. Nobody leaves a podium before the president of the United States is finished speaking. But in Hollywood nobody gives it a second thought. Hey, Michael Douglas is a busy man. He is box office. What did Clinton's last film gross?

Although many celebrity Democrats campaigned for Al Gore in 2000, the absence of a bona fide superstar like Bill Clinton seemed to take the wind out of Hollywood's sails. Even as Streisand serenaded Gore and Bill Cosby cracked jokes at his side, there was a sense of going through the motions. As for the Republicans, George W. Bush made fewer campaign appearances with entertainers in 2000 than perhaps any other presidential candidate in modern history.

The younger Bush's most reliable Hollywood supporter was film actress Bo Derek, who had stumped for Bob Dole four years earlier. Derek turned up when Bush came to the Kentucky Derby in May and campaigned with him several months later in Michigan. The candidate never seemed fully at ease with her, perhaps because Bo Derek's sexpot image did not square with the anti-Clintonian values George W. Bush was striving to project.

Does Bush's reticence toward celebrity campaigners signal a trend away from show business involvement in presidential elections? Hardly. The record suggests that it is only a matter of time before America's entertainers find another candidate they can nuzzle up to. Like show business, politics is a process of renewal; fresh stars forever loom on the horizon. When the next one comes along, Hollywood will be as ready to jump on the bandwagon as Al Jolson was in 1920.

Pearl Bailey and Richard Nixon perform a duet of "Home on the Range" at the White House, March 1974. (Nixon Presidential Materials Staff)

6

✴✴✴✴

America's Toughest Gig

Performing for the President

On St. Patrick's Day 1973 Richard Nixon gave his wife an unusual birthday present: country singer Merle Haggard. Haggard and his band traveled to the White House and, in matching baby blue polyester suits, played a gig before the president, Pat Nixon, and a hundred guests. The setting was not exactly Haggard's normal venue. "I had a hard time with the crowd," he recalled. "No one in the place applauded until the president did. It was kinda like being in a room with the Mafia. No one does anything until the don does it first."

Haggard's comment suggests the difficulty of putting on a show when the audience includes the most powerful person on the planet. But performing for the president has become a rite of passage for the world's finest musicians, actors, dancers, and comedians. For two hundred years they have brought their talents to the White House for state dinners, musical tributes, dance recitals, dramatic readings, and outdoor concerts. And they have appeared before the chief executive in a variety of other contexts: at inaugural galas, fund-raisers, Kennedy Center awards shows, and banquets. Rare is the month that the president does not attend some sort of live performance, either at the residence or on the town.

The tradition of White House entertainment dates back to the first leader to occupy the mansion, John Adams, who hosted a New Year's Day reception in 1801 with his wife, Abigail. Guests listened to music by the newly formed U.S.

Marine Band, soon to become known as "The President's Own." Abraham Lincoln, a regular at Washington's opera houses and theaters, welcomed an off-beat array of performers to the White House, including a nine-year-old Venezuelan piano prodigy, a Native American singer dubbed the "aboriginal Jenny Lind," and a musical midget from P.T. Barnum's circus, who sang "Columbia, the Gem of the Ocean" for Lincoln and members of his cabinet. Teddy Roosevelt imported classical pianist Ignacy Jan Paderewski and cellist Pablo Casals, who some sixty years later played a return engagement for President Kennedy.

In her indispensable survey *Music at the White House*, Elise K. Kirk described the White House as "a stage like no other":

> Few edifices in the world can boast the variety and excellence of its music, yet few concert halls or opera houses have been so conditioned by changing political attitudes. No other single arts institution has been as progressive and at the same time as conservative as the great white mansion. No other aspect of White House life can define the presidential image quite like the music performed at the chief of state's residence.

As Kirk suggests, we gain insight into the personalities of the nation's presidents by considering the artists they summon to perform. Dwight Eisenhower brought in Lawrence Welk and Guy Lombardo. The Kennedy administration was known for classical artists, and Johnson favored jazz musicians like Duke Ellington and Dave Brubeck. Nixon enjoyed the clean-cut sounds of the Carpenters and Up With People but also Frank Sinatra and Johnny Cash, while Gerald Ford was partial to the Las Vegas stylings of glamour girls like Ann-Margret. Jimmy Carter welcomed a diverse assortment of country, jazz, and classical musicians; Reagan favored lounge singers; and Bush booked mainstream acts like Johnny Mathis and Gloria Estefan. Bill Clinton preferred the music of African American entertainers and the rock stars of his youth. Culturally and politically, a president's selection of performing artists sends potent signals.

Today it is commonplace for presidents to entertain foreign heads of state with elaborately staged after-dinner programs, but a fascinating prototype of this custom took place in 1939, when Franklin and Eleanor Roosevelt treated the king and queen of England to an "Evening of American Music." The entertainers represented an eclectic range of talents and genres: opera stars Lawrence Tibbett and contralto Marian Anderson; popular singer Kate Smith; two mountain acts, the Coon Creek Girls and the Soco Gap square dance team; hymns from the North Carolina Spiritual Singers; and cowboy ballads sung by Library of Congress folklorist Alan Lomax. An eleven-page printed program provided translations of words that might be unfamiliar to the royal guests: "Dogies," it explained, "are little yearling steers."

The selection of these performers reflected the Roosevelts' pride in the richness of America's musical heritage. Over the years different considerations have been taken into account in choosing entertainment for state dinners. Liz Carpenter, press secretary to Lady Bird Johnson, laid out a list of four criteria used by the Johnson White House: "(1) the preference of the Head of State, (2) the language barrier (if the guest did not speak English, we often had music or ballet), (3) the availability of a performer, and (4) whether the artist had recently insulted the United States or the President." During Lyndon Johnson's presidency, with the nation mired in an unpopular war, this last factor assumed particular significance.

Because most White House dinners are given for foreign dignitaries, planners must also choose entertainment that is culturally appropriate. When Guy Lombardo's orchestra played at an Eisenhower dinner for the king of Thailand, Lombardo had to jettison plans for a medley from the Rodgers and Hammerstein musical *The King and I*. It turned out that the play, set in the Thai royal court, was something of a sore spot with the guest of honor.

Another Rodgers and Hammerstein show, *The Sound of Music*, hit a sour note for Ronald Reagan at a 1984 state dinner honoring the president of Austria. Among the guests was Baroness Maria von Trapp, the former nun whose story had inspired the musical. In his after-dinner toast President Reagan quoted what he called a "prayer for Austria": the sentimental lyrics from the song "Edelweiss." Newspapers in Vienna scorned the reference as Americentric kitsch.

On occasion an entire performance raises questions of cultural sensitivity. In 1975 Ann-Margret brought her Las Vegas song-and-dance routine to the White House as after-dinner entertainment for the shah of Iran. Though the act started on a note of sweetness, with Ann-Margret cooing a Swedish lullaby, things quickly got saucier. The actress performed an up-tempo medley in a red, white, and blue can-can outfit; as the number reached its climax, the skirt flew off, revealing a skimpy showgirl body suit. Though some observers questioned the propriety of such entertainment for the leader of a predominantly Islamic nation, first lady Betty Ford defended the choice: "We picked her because the Shah of Iran likes pretty women. Let's face it, the Shah's got a reputation as one of the biggest swingers of the world."

In keeping with Gerald Ford's reputation for blunders, the Ford White House seemed to suffer more than its share of entertainment gaffes. A program of comedy and song for Queen Elizabeth and Prince Philip prompted another round of censure during the royal couple's bicentennial visit in 1976. Bob Hope opened with a series of infelicitous jokes, including one about spending the night as a guest of the Fords in the Lincoln Bedroom: "I hope they're not mad at me. I did make a mistake. How did I know that thing under the bed was a stovepipe hat?"

Following Hope was the musical duo the Captain and Tennille, who performed their novelty hit "Muskrat Love," a song about mating behavior between two swamp critters named Susie and Sam. The number featured not only lyrics rife with double-entendres but also synthesized sound effects meant to evoke the muskrats in copulation. After critics scolded President and Mrs. Ford for their choice of entertainers, Toni Tennille wrote the first lady to express her concern: "We offer you our deepest apologies if we caused you any embarrassment. However, in our defense please let me say that we chose 'Muskrat Love' because it has been a favorite of our concert audiences, particularly young children, for years. Whenever we sing about Sam and Susie, I picture little cartoon animals such as Walt Disney created in his films, particularly Bambi." The singer ended her note by inviting the Fords to watch the Captain and Tennille's upcoming television special on ABC.

The hapless Fords made yet another misstep that evening. Just as the president led Queen Elizabeth onto the dance floor, the Marine Band struck up the Rodgers and Hart standard "The Lady Is a Tramp," an unfortunate juxtaposition that did not go unnoted by the press. After that night the band deleted the number from its repertoire. (During the Reagan administration the band played "Send in the Clowns" as Secretary of State George Schultz came through the diplomatic entrance of the White House. And Vice President Spiro Agnew, arriving at an inaugural gala in 1969, found himself serenaded with "Who Can I Turn To?" and "Out of My Head.")

The cultural sensitivity of both the Ford and Reagan administrations came into question with two separate functions honoring Chancellors Schmidt and Kohl of Germany. In 1974 and again twelve years later, Joel Grey regaled the German leaders with selections from *Cabaret*, a musical set against the backdrop of rising Nazism in the 1930s. Although neither leader complained, German journalists voiced doubts about the appropriateness of Grey's program. The choice of Grey performing faux-Nazi songs for Germany's highest elected official does seem antagonistic—especially twice.

✵✵✵✵

Performers accustomed to looser venues do not always apprehend the constraints of playing the White House. When Johnny Cash sang for the Nixons in 1970, he introduced his wife, country musician June Carter. Carter, who had given birth to a son one month earlier, told the audience she had spent all day making herself beautiful for the event. Moving her hands down her white crepe dress she turned to Cash and quipped, "This is the top part, this is the bottom part, in case you've forgotten." Though some laughed, the Nixons did not, and June Carter quickly backtracked: "I don't believe I should have said that."

Cash's White House debut generated another minor controversy, this one over the president's request that the country singer perform the songs "Welfare Cadillac" and "Okie from Muskogee," neither of which were Cash originals. "The issue wasn't the songs' messages, which at the time were lightning rods for antihippie and antiblack sentiment," Cash said, "but the fact that I didn't know them and couldn't learn them or rehearse them with the band before we had to leave for Washington." When reporters found out that Johnny Cash had turned Nixon down, they portrayed it as an ideological conflict. Introducing Cash at the White House, Nixon made light of the misunderstanding: "One thing I've learned about Johnny Cash is that you don't tell him what to sing."

In 1971 a group of Nixon aides convened to plot strategy for selecting entertainment for state occasions. The confidential memorandum that emerged from this meeting offers a sense of the administration's political thinking: "We should concentrate on 'big' name stars—performers who will 'come out' for the president, and thereby influence a number of others to do the same. It was stressed that we concentrate on entertainers who appeal to young people, i.e., Burt Bacharach, Ali MacGraw, Flip Wilson and others." The memo goes on to suggest that entertainers not invited to perform because of "inappropriateness" should instead be considered as dinner guests; in this category are Frank Sinatra, who did eventually sing at a state dinner, and Elvis Presley, who neither performed nor received an invitation. The task force also came up with a wish list of specific stars under consideration as White House performers. Interestingly, one of the first names on this roster is Barbra Streisand, who soon found herself on another Nixon list—the enemies list.

The aides appraised each entertainer with cool calculation. Mexican comedian Cantinflas "was here during the Johnson Administration and apparently supported Kennedy in 1960. The president knows this but wants him anyway. Suggested that we wait until closer to election time. Mexican-American vote." Goldie Hawn was seen as "non-political and socially a lovely lady. She would be honored to come." Flip Wilson was "a fine gentleman . . . a very hard worker . . . is considered an Uncle Tom to some black people. He has enough reverence for the high office of president and would not want to dishonor or discredit his president."

In Nixon's second term, the job of talent procurer was assumed by Paul Keyes, a producer and writer of the television show *Laugh-In* who had been a Nixon intimate since 1960. With his longtime Hollywood ties, Keyes naturally gravitated toward showbiz stalwarts like Frank Sinatra, Johnny Mathis, Tony Martin, and the Johnny Mann Singers. "To the dismay of some observers," concluded the *Washington Post*, "the White House was becoming little more than a gold ring on the comeback carousel."

Keyes's stint as impresario of the East Room ended when the White House announced it would reassume responsibility for state dinner entertainment. But Paul Keyes was not the last Hollywood figure to wield power over which acts appeared on the nation's most exclusive stage. During the Reagan administration Frank Sinatra volunteered his services as unofficial talent coordinator, an offer the first couple gladly accepted.

Reagan aide Michael Deaver, in a 1981 thank-you note to Sinatra, wrote: "You understand the requirements better than anyone and know that these performances at the White House are an important part of the total impression of these crucial visits. We feel very fortunate to have your talent and knowledge to guide us." Even so, Deaver seemed eager to keep Sinatra on the straight and narrow. Referring to an upcoming dinner for Saudi Arabian Prince Faud, Deaver warned that "entertainment for the Prince must be scaled within his religious and ethical beliefs. We have to be careful about dancing girls and anything that might be construed as 'suggestive.'"

Frank Sinatra booked himself into the East Room twice during the Reagan presidency. For the first occasion, a dinner for the president of Italy, Sinatra teamed with Perry Como. After the performance the guest of honor, speaking Italian, invited the singers to accompany Reagan on an upcoming visit to Rome. Cracked Reagan: "President Pertini has just proclaimed you illegal aliens and he's repatriating you." Two years later Sinatra returned to entertain the president of Sri Lanka, singing "Strangers in the Night" and "Fly Me to the Moon" before an audience that included Fred MacMurray, Jane Powell, and Rich Little.

The first—and the finest—of Sinatra's three White House performances had come in 1973 at the behest of Richard Nixon. President Nixon's invitation to Sinatra was the showbiz equivalent of his diplomatic overtures to Communist China. "I am sure that many of our friends in the entertainment field would think it wrong to have a former anti-Nixon person entertain at the White House," wrote Dwight Chapin in a 1970 White House memo, three years before Sinatra's performance. "I am fairly well convinced that the publicity value alone—not to mention the development of a relationship between Sinatra and the president—would far outweigh the negatives." To heighten the stakes, Sinatra's appearance in Washington marked a comeback for the singer after two years of self-imposed retirement.

In preparation for his White House debut Frank Sinatra left nothing to chance. To get his voice back in shape the fifty-six-year-old legend subjected himself to a rigorous program of breathing exercises and vocal scales. Nixon aides, knowing of Sinatra's reputation for surliness, braced themselves for the worst. Instead they found him gracious and cooperative. "He was cordial and polite to all people with whom he worked," according to a staff postmortem. "He had high praise for members of the Marine Orchestra, the sound people, and virtually everyone else whose job it was to put on this performance." Sinatra even opened his dress rehearsal to White House employees who had not been invited to attend the evening event.

Sinatra sang about half an hour's worth of material before an audience of two hundred in the East Room, including guest of honor President Giulio Andreotti of Italy. Richard Nixon's introduction was effusive: "Frank Sinatra is to music what the Washington Monument is to our landscape. He is the top." With Nelson Riddle conducting, Sinatra performed many of his hits: "Fly Me to the Moon," "I've Got the World on a String," "One for My Baby (One More for the Road)," "Moonlight in Vermont," "The House I Live In," and "I've Got You Under My Skin." At the end of "Ol' Man River," the audience leapt to its feet with a standing ovation.

"Once in a while," Nixon said, "there is a moment when there's magic in the room—when a great performer, singer and entertainer is able to capture and move us all. Frank Sinatra has done that tonight." As the president spoke, Sinatra looked at Nixon with tears in his eyes. Several months after his White House premiere, Frank Sinatra announced he was coming out of retirement.

✵✵✵✵

As the Sinatra example shows, Richard Nixon knew how to parlay White House performances into moments of high drama. By contrast, the entertainment affairs of his predecessors were rather more sedate. Harry Truman spent much of his presidency living across the street at Blair House while the executive mansion underwent repairs; as a consequence he staged only a few evenings of classical music. One event was a recital by Metropolitan Opera soprano Helen Traubel, then the mentor of aspiring vocalist Margaret Truman. Traubel compared the experience to "an exquisite miniature of a Met opening": "I was tremendously impressed, open-mouthed most of the time and not altogether from singing."

President Eisenhower brought in several big-name orchestras, including a special favorite, Fred Waring and his chorus, the Pennsylvanians. The most innovative of the Eisenhower musicals imported nine stars from five hit shows on Broadway: *West Side Story*, *My Fair Lady*, *The Music Man*, *The Pajama Game*, and *New Girl in Town*. Though the lineup included such seasoned veterans as Thelma Ritter, Carol Lawrence, and Sally Ann Howes, it was ten-year-old Eddie Hodges from *The Music Man* who most impressed the president. "While older performers were almost giddy with the delight of being booked for a White House one-nighter," said the *Washington Post*, "the schoolboy star was poised almost to the point of nonchalance."

The Kennedy White House became known for its emphasis on high culture. "My main concern was to present the best in the arts, not necessarily what was popular at the time," said Jacqueline Kennedy. Though JFK's personal taste ran toward show tunes, only one Broadway-style evening took place during his presidency: a program of highlights from the musical *Brigadoon*, cowritten by Kennedy's prep school classmate, Alan Jay Lerner. The entertainment, presented at a dinner for King Hassan of Morocco, gave the audience a moment's uneasiness when overloaded electrical circuits plunged the East Room into sudden darkness. Fearing an assassination plot, Secret Service agents drew their weapons and immediately sealed the premises, as Kennedy assured his guest that nothing was amiss. "Your Majesty," the president whispered, "it's all part of the show."

Lyndon Johnson's presidency expanded the definition of White House entertainment by embracing jazz artists like Duke Ellington, Dave Brubeck, Charlie Byrd, and Sarah Vaughn. Two husband-and-wife acting teams—Hume Cronyn and Jessica Tandy, and George C. Scott and Colleen Dewhurst—gave dramatic readings. Cronyn and Tandy performed at an event for high-ranking U.S. government officials, and Scott and Dewhurst at a dinner for Irish President Eamon de Valera.

Perhaps the oddest entertainment offering of the Johnson years was a double bill at LBJ's first state dinner, a 1964 affair for the president of Italy. The first half featured Metropolitan Opera tenor Robert Merrill performing classical Italian opera arias; the second half took the form of a hootenanny by folksingers the New Christy Minstrels. The New Christy Minstrels returned to play for a delegation of Kuwaiti leaders at the Johnsons' final state dinner in 1968, puzzling the guests of honor. According to one observer, "President Johnson bounced up and down in his chair with enthusiasm. He looked back to try to encourage a row of silent sheiks behind him, but it was hopeless."

In 1967 Carol Channing brought an abbreviated version of her Broadway show *Hello, Dolly!* to the White House. The occasion was the president's annual dinner for the vice president, chief justice, and leaders of Congress. It also happened to be Carol Channing's birthday, and in honor of the event a giant cake was wheeled into the East Room after the performance. "Dear Mr. President, what a beautiful cake! You knew we were coming!" exclaimed Channing. She then told her host, "You have the finest recipes here. They all come from Dolley Madison." Twenty-six years later Channing was back at the White House on her birthday, and another president—Bill Clinton—led the crowd in singing "Happy Birthday."

Continuing the trend established by Lyndon Johnson, Richard Nixon further diversified the roster of White House performers. Nixon was the first president to present a comedian (Red Skelton), a rock act (the Carpenters), and country-western singers (Merle Haggard, Johnny Cash, and Glen Campbell). His most renowned cultural event was a musical birthday tribute to Duke Ellington in April 1969, with performances by a stellar lineup of fifteen American jazz musicians, including Earl "Fatha" Hines, Dave Brubeck, Clark Terry, and Gerry Mulligan. Equally impressive was the list of invited guests: Dizzy Gillespie, Cab Calloway, Billy Eckstein, Mahalia Jackson, Benny Goodman, Lou Rawls, and composers Harold Arlen and Richard Rodgers, to name a few. "In the royalty of American music no man swings more or stands higher than the Duke," declared Nixon, who presented Ellington with the Medal of Freedom and a presidential serenade on the White House Steinway. "Duke Ellington is ageless," Nixon told the audience, "but would you all stand and sing 'Happy Birthday' to him, and please in the Key of G?"

At the end of the formal ninety-minute program, Nixon asked the honoree if he would care to play. The seventy-year-old Ellington, whose father had worked as a butler in the Harding White House, took a seat at the keyboard. "I shall pick a name, and see if I can improvise on it," he said, "something very gentle and graceful—something like Pat." As the room listened breathlessly, Ellington proceeded to create a slow, serene melody. Although it was after midnight, Nixon invited everyone to stay for refreshments and a jam session that lasted another two hours. Among the late-night music makers was Vice President Spiro Agnew, who played a piano version of Ellington's "Sophisticated Lady." The *New York Times* called the occasion "the kind of evening the guests will talk about for years." Jazz critic Stanley Dance wrote: "Even those of differing political beliefs gave ungrudging credit to President Nixon for personally having done so much to ensure a relaxed, informal, and friendly atmosphere."

Another indelible entertainment during Nixon's presidency was a 1973 dinner for returned prisoners of war. The idea, first suggested by Sammy Davis Jr., so caught the president's fancy that he fired off a five-page memorandum to his chief of staff detailing how it should unfold. In the memo, Nixon cited Bob Hope's USO shows as a model, "provided we could get Bob to de-emphasize some of the girlie stuff and go for some of the more high-powered entertainers." He weighed the pros and cons of a ninety-minute program versus a two-hour program: "Possibly with the number of celebrities we would have to put it to two hours but this should pose no particular problem. After all, plays and movies are now two hours or more and people would be fascinated to sit there and see the greatest Hollywood production ever of superstars." Nixon even worried about acoustics: "As you know, the applause factor is almost totally eliminated when the show is held outside."

The White House dispatched Air Force One to Los Angeles to retrieve Bob Hope, Jimmy Stewart, Edgar Bergen, Connie Francis, and John Wayne. Sammy Davis Jr., Vic Damone, Joey Heatherton, Ricardo Montalban, and Phyllis Diller rounded out the roster of performers. Because of the large number of guests—thirteen hundred, including POWs and their wives—the show was staged on the South Lawn of the White House. The entertainers' remarks seemed designed to bolster the spirits of Richard Nixon, then deeply embroiled in the Watergate scandal, as much as honor the veterans. John Wayne got the biggest hand of the night when he told the crowd, "You and the president have a lot in common. You held in there when the going was rough; so does he. You stuck by your guns; so does he. You love your country; so does he. I'll ride into the sunset with you any time." For Richard Nixon, "this was one of the greatest nights in my life."

In addition to state dinners and honorary receptions, Nixon hosted an entertainment series called Evening at the White House. Nixon's "evenings" were essentially one-man shows starring performers the president held in high esteem. Red Skelton premiered the format in 1970 before an audience of congress members, cabinet secretaries, and pro-Nixon celebrities like Gene Autry, Lionel Hampton, and Connie Francis. The red-haired comedian, who had tickled the funny bone of President Roosevelt in 1940, repeated some of his familiar routines: the TV spokesman for an alcoholic beverage who gets drunk on the product, the newborn baby in the hospital, and, at Nixon's request, the Pledge of

Allegiance, Skelton's version of which had become a best-selling record. When it was all over, Patricia Nixon said, "I haven't laughed so hard for a long time." The president chimed in: "Oh, I really laughed."

In 1974 Richard Nixon made the unusual decision of booking the Carpenters, a soft-rock act, as after-dinner entertainment for West German Chancellor Willy Brandt. "The Carpenters," said Nixon in his introduction, "are young America at its very best." The gig proved to be a nerve-wracking experience for the brother and sister, who, like the president, hailed from Orange County, California. "We could play for tens of thousands of people, but to have to play for these statesmen in the East Room of the White House was quite mind-boggling," Richard Carpenter remembered. The elegant surroundings and intimate scale of the venue made it difficult for the band to perform with its usual gusto. "I was afraid to even breathe on the drums," Karen Carpenter said. "I was barely touching them because I didn't want to offend anybody." In his thank-you note, Nixon assured the duo "that there is no 'generation gap' when it comes to enjoying good music." Ten years later, after Karen Carpenter's death from anorexia, Richard Nixon wrote the family a heartfelt letter of condolence.

The Carpenters were not the first rock musicians to play the Nixon White House. Two earlier events transported the music of American youth to the executive mansion. When Britain's young royals, Prince Charles and Princess Anne, visited the first family in July 1970, Julie and Tricia Nixon hosted an outdoor supper dance with live music by the Guess Who and Gary Puckett and the Union Gap. More than five hundred young folks in formalwear boogied to rock and roll as President and Mrs. Nixon looked on from the Truman balcony.

Earlier in the day Nixon had left his office to drop in on Puckett's rehearsal. "I heard you from a couple of blocks away," the president joked, "so I thought I'd come over and see what was going on." Nixon asked the band leader how he liked working with the Marine Corps musicians who had been added to his group for the party. "Oh, they're great," Puckett said. "Their hair's a little too short, however."

Rock music's other ambassadors to the White House were the Turtles, who played at a party hosted by Tricia Nixon while the president and first lady were out of town. The occasion was a dance early in Nixon's presidency for the offspring of congressional members, Democrats as well as Republicans. "Not everyone was in favor of what was happening in Vietnam, and there was a lot of subversive literature being passed around," said Mark Volman, a founding member of the Turtles. "We didn't do it for any political reasons, we just figured it would be a hoot to play the White House, and it was."

As hosts, Richard and Patricia Nixon were formal with their guests but adventurous in their entertainment selections. Just the opposite held true of Gerald and Betty Ford, who threw the liveliest parties but staged some of the dreariest after-dinner performances in White House history. A low point came in June 1975 when country singer Tennessee Ernie Ford regaled the West German chancellor with excerpts from his Nashville stage show. Wearing a black jacket over blue-and-white plaid pants and a checkered shirt, Ford opened his set with the appropriately titled "We're Gonna Raise a Ruckus Tonight." The high-energy act that followed displayed considerably more corn than class.

Not much better was an amateurish program by Helen Reddy and the normally reliable Carol Burnett, who appeared before Israeli Prime Minister Yitzhak Rabin. Sample dialogue:

> Reddy: Have you ever been to Israel?
> Burnett: No, but I saw *Fiddler on the Roof* twice.

Burnett and Reddy then proceeded to warble one of the strangest medleys ever stitched together, opening with the Beatles' "Sgt. Peppers Lonely Hearts Club Band," segueing into Sonny and Cher's "The Beat Goes On," and thereafter incorporating everything from Burt Bacharach to country-western. The medley ended back at the Beatles with "Come Together."

Though the Ford presidency lasted only seventeen months, the list of dubious state dinner entertainers lengthened: Wayne Newton, Vikki Carr, Ben Vereen . . . The Fords' final such event, honoring the president of Italy, featured the vocal stylings of Tony Orlando and Dawn. As was frequently the case in the Ford White House, the party afterward outshone the main event, with Pearl Bailey singing "The Battle Hymn of the Republic," actor Peter Graves jamming on saxophone, and Gerald and Betty Ford dancing the Hustle. Several weeks after the performance the office of Tony Orlando submitted an expense reimbursement request for four first-class tickets from Los Angeles: for himself, his wife, and the two backup singers. The White House social office curtly responded that "the two Dawn girls fly tourist class, as is the usual procedure."

✳ ✳ ✳ ✳

In the final decades of the twentieth century the definition of White House entertainment broadened beyond state dinners. Building on the precedents established by LBJ and Nixon, Jimmy Carter hosted a 1978 concert on the South Lawn to mark the twenty-fifth anniversary of the Newport Jazz Festival. Some forty of the country's top jazz musicians took part—among them Clark Terry, Sonny Rollins, Herbie Hancock, Ornette Coleman, Lionel Hampton, and Stan Getz—before an audience that included Charles Mingus, Gerry Mulligan, Harry Belafonte, Bill Cosby, Lena Horne, Quincy Jones, Flip Wilson, Greg Allman, and Johnny Carson. Ninety-five-year-old Eubie Blake, making his White House debut, performed two original compositions. "I'm playing all my ASCAP numbers," Blake announced. "That way I get paid royalties for it." Carter asked Dizzy Gillespie for a rendition of "Salt Peanuts"; the president himself chanted the "salt peanuts!" refrain. Shortly into Lionel Hampton's "Flying Home" Pearl Bailey unexpectedly stormed the stage and began to sing something completely different: "In the Good Old Summertime." The nearsighted Hampton later said he had mistaken her for a white person.

Although the Carters presented a number of popular performers like Willie Nelson, Chuck Berry, and the Statler Brothers, some 75 percent of their musical programs fell into the classical category. The Carter White House also inaugurated two long-lasting innovations: the Kennedy Center Honors, held each December, and the PBS television series *In Performance at the White House*. During the Carter presidency *In Performance* presented five hour-long recitals by classical artists Leontyne Price, Andres Segovia, Mstilav Rostropovich, Mikhail Baryshnikov, and Vladimir Horowitz; Horowitz brought his own piano.

Ronald and Nancy Reagan continued the series in 1981, though the orientation gradually shifted away from classical repertoire and into the mainstream. The 1981–1982 season of *In Performance* ended with a country music concert at a California ranch, a setting that gave the Reagans an excuse to costume themselves in western wear and PBS set designers an opportunity to find new uses for bales of hay. The show's star was Merle Haggard, who ten years earlier had received a pardon from Governor Reagan for a string of minor crimes that included theft and jailbreaking.

During Reagan's second term the *In Performance* concerts took shape as tributes to American theater composers. The programs featured some of the country's best-known musical comedy stars and singers—Mary Martin, Liza Minnelli, Bea Arthur, Jennifer Holliday, Shirley Jones, Sarah Vaughn, Bobby Short, and Vic Damone—and also allowed Nancy Reagan to indulge in show business fantasies of her own. The first event, highlighting the work of George and Ira Gershwin, served as a preview of coming attractions. For the grand finale, "Our Love Is Here to Stay," the first lady joined the cast onstage; crooning the lyric "Oh my dear / Our love is here to stay," Mrs. Reagan walked to her husband in the front row and pulled him into the spotlight. For the Cole Porter tribute, Nancy sang backup on "You're the Top." At the final program, a salute to Broadway choreography, she danced in the chorus line.

George and Barbara Bush sponsored only three *In Performance* programs before canceling the series altogether. Each of the Bush shows revolved around a different secular holiday—the Fourth of July, Columbus Day, Presidents Day—and offered an odd grab bag of performers, from opera singers Simon Estes and Teresa Stratas to pop mediocrities John Denver and Ray Price. In 1990 the Bush White House yanked *In Performance* from its founding producers, station WETA in Washington, and awarded the franchise to a PBS affiliate in Rochester, where it went into hibernation. Bush's media adviser reportedly made the change because the head of WETA, Sharon Rockefeller, was a prominent Democrat.

Five months into his presidency Bill Clinton revived *In Performance at the White House* (once again under the aegis of WETA) with a fortieth-anniversary commemoration of the Newport Jazz Festival; in the all-star jam session that followed Clinton played saxophone. During Clinton's eight years in office the *In Performance* headliners reflected the wide-ranging tastes of the president: Aretha Franklin and Lou Rawls; Gladys Knight; Linda Ronstadt and Aaron Neville; cabaret singers Dixie Carter and Bobby Short; country artists Kathy Mattea, Alison Krauss, and Suzy Bogguss; and dancer Savion Glover.

Beyond *In Performance*, Clinton played host to a number of other musical events at the White House, many with a rock, country, or rhythm and blues slant. Twelve hundred guests gathered for a rainy South Lawn champagne-and-truffles party in 1994, where Lyle Lovett, Patti Austin, Michael Bolton, the Pointer Sisters, Booker T and the MGs, John Hendricks, Ruth Brown, and Ashford and Simpson provided entertainment. Bolton delivered the closing remarks, expressing gratitude for a White House "that appreciates music."

In 1998 Clinton became the first president to bring hip-hop to the executive mansion when Run-D.M.C. joined a lineup of performers at a Special Olympics party. Also on the bill were rockers Jon Bon Jovi and Eric Clapton. Clapton returned nearly a year later for the Save the Music Concert of the Century, a benefit for public school music programs sponsored by the cable network VH1. This multidimensional musical featured performances by rock artists John Fogerty and John Mellencamp; country singers Garth Brooks and Melissa Etheridge; soul man Al Green; plus Lenny Kravitz, Sheryl Crow, Gloria Estefan, and 'N

Sync, all backed by the Paul Shaffer Band. A different Hollywood star introduced each act: Angela Bassett, Robert De Niro, Calista Flockhart, Gwyneth
Paltrow, Sarah Jessica Parker, Keri Russell, Kevin Spacey, and Meryl Streep. In
thanking the musicians, President Clinton spoke of his respect for their talent. "I
respect them so much I left my saxophone in the White House," he said.

The Clinton White House also deemed rock and roll to be suitable entertainment for state dinners. The transatlantic duo of Stevie Wonder and Elton John
brought their high-energy brand of music to a gala evening for British Prime Minister Tony Blair and his wife, Cherie, in 1998. In back-to-back miniconcerts John
and Wonder revisited their repertoire of hits, joining forces at the end for a rousing
rendition of "Money, Money." Despite the vivacity of the performers, the stately
setting seemed to mute audience response. Elton John called the experience "a bit
like playing a wedding reception." Wonder begged the crowd to "snap your fingers, shake your head, do something! You guys sound like a library meeting!"

The George W. Bush White House has seen only a handful of entertainment
performances, a paucity that can be attributed both to the somber atmosphere that
followed the terrorist attacks of September 11, 2001, and to Bush's own profound
lack of interest in the performing arts. Exceptions to the rule were Bush buddy
Larry Gatlin, who appeared with Nell Carter, Toby Keith, and Gerald McRaney in
a salute to the United States Marine Band for *In Performance at the White House.*
Country singer Lee Ann Womack played a governors dinner, and soprano Dawn
Upshaw sang at the state dinner for Mexico held a week before the World Trade
Center and Pentagon incidents. A month later, as part of a Columbus Day attempt
at normalcy, Liza Minnelli came to the White House to belt out "New York, New
York." Minnelli's between-numbers banter included a reference to her hairdo: "Do
you like my hair? I've got big Texas hair! I did it for the president."

✳✳✳✳

Entertainers not summoned to perform at the White House may find themselves
on the guest list, where the pressure is considerably less acute. Most of the great
names of the American stage, screen, and concert hall have attended at least one
state dinner, arts festival, or awards ceremony at the invitation of the president.
Rare is the celebrity who turns down an invitation to the executive mansion.

In Franklin Roosevelt's day actors and musicians often found themselves seated
at the family dinner table with whatever other fascinating personalities the president or his wife had brought home. Helen Hayes recounted her embarrassment at

one such occasion. After the first lady announced that the gathering would adjourn to a sitting room for coffee, two burly attendants materialized, hoisting FDR out of his seat and into a wheelchair. According to Hayes, the intimacy of the moment "was so startling that I bolted from my place and was halfway across the room before I could collect myself. Then I noticed that no one else had moved: to them what had happened must have seemed routine. I felt mortified."

Regulars at the Roosevelt White House learned to dread the cuisine. Actress Joan Fontaine had an allergic reaction to an oyster served by the Roosevelts and was violently ill for three days. George Jessel once teased Eleanor Roosevelt at a banquet by remembering a meal of chicken salad she had served him. "Never in my life have I seen so much lettuce surrounding so little chicken," said Jessel. When it was Mrs. Roosevelt's turn to speak, she was ready with a comeback: "I am sure Georgie is mistaken—I don't remember putting any chicken in the chicken salad."

The practice of inviting entertainers to state dinners began on a modest scale during the Kennedy administration. Among JFK's illustrious guests were Myrna Loy, Helen Hayes, and Joan Fontaine. Fontaine used the occasion to tell the president that his father had once offered to set her up as his mistress. Kennedy listened to the story with a smile on his face. "Let's see," he said, "how old would he have been then? Sixty-five? Hope I'm the same way when I'm his age."

The presence of movie stars at state dinners increased markedly during Lyndon Johnson's administration. Kirk Douglas, Harry Belafonte, Mexican comic Cantinflas, and Jim Backus—the voice of the animated character Mister Magoo—all made their way to the White House as dinner guests of the Johnsons. An especially memorable visitor was Hollywood diva Joan Crawford, who attended a fete for top Washington officials in 1967. The White House made the faux pas of inviting to the same event Crawford's former husband, Douglas Fairbanks Jr. Despite the presence of the new Mrs. Fairbanks, Crawford spent much of the evening flirting with her ex via a series of notes delivered by a White House butler.

Seated next to Crawford at dinner was Cathleen Douglas, the young, blonde, fourth wife of Supreme Court Justice William O. Douglas. During the meal Crawford stunned her tablemates by discussing the younger woman as though she were not present. At one point the star took it upon herself to instruct Mrs. Douglas in the etiquette of finger bowl removal. "This is the way you do it, darling!" Crawford purred, as those nearby looked on in horror. "The story was trumpeted in New York and Washington," wrote Liz Carpenter, the first lady's press secretary, "and I began getting calls to confirm or deny. Miss Crawford told me, in a somewhat tearful call from the West Coast, that it couldn't possibly have occurred. I went holier-than-thou and told the press: 'The White House certainly will not discuss the dinner table conversation of its guests.'"

Woody Allen was a White House dinner guest in 1965, a few months after performing at LBJ's inaugural gala. Not wanting to spend the night in Washington, Allen flew in from New York on the Eastern shuttle and changed into his tuxedo in a bathroom at National Airport. Allen described the event to biographer Eric Lax:

> When Johnson came down for dinner—they served filet mignon but I was surprised, it tasted like institution food—there was a small military band playing "Hail to the Chief" or some such thing. I thought, "That's amazing that this guy gets played to through his meal every night." It was a wonderful evening. You had a feeling it was right out of *Gone with the Wind*, because here we were slightly South, and because it was a warm night they had opened the garden and hung it with lanterns for dancing.

The Johnson women took a particular shine to Woody Allen. "We all thought you wore a wig," the first lady confided to the tousle-haired comedian. (After seeing Allen at the inaugural gala, Lady Bird Johnson had said of his appearance, "You want to give him a blood transfusion.") One of the president's daughters complimented Allen on a joke he had made to the press about his invitation to dinner at the White House: "Maybe I should bring some cake or something."

Woody Allen offers a good example of the way in which White House invitations are doled out as political rewards to performers. He campaigned for LBJ; he played at LBJ's inaugural; he got asked to dinner. At least in Woody Allen's case, the personality, prominence, and magnetism of the entertainer in question rendered him worthy of an evening with the president. More dubious are the B-celebrities who get invited only because they offered support on the campaign trail.

Presidents sometimes reach across political boundaries in selecting guests. It took George Bush to invite Democrat Angie Dickinson to her first state dinner in 1992, something her friend and purported lover JFK did not do during his time in the White House. Nixon asked Kirk Douglas, who was closely identified with Lyndon Johnson and the Kennedys. In 1975 Warren Beatty, who three years earlier had campaigned full-time for George McGovern, attended a dinner at the Ford White House for British Prime Minister Harold Wilson; Beatty brought as his date Michelle Phillips of the Mamas and the Papas.

Like many evenings with Gerald and Betty Ford, the Wilson gala glittered with stars, including Cary Grant, Kirk Douglas, Danny Kaye, Beverly Sills, and

Van Cliburn. The seventy-one-year-old Grant told reporters he was seldom invited to White House soirees. "You must remember," he said, "I live in California. If you can arrange for more invitations I'll come." Grant returned for one of Ronald and Nancy Reagan's most exclusive parties, a private dinner for Prince Charles in 1981 with around thirty guests, one of whom was Grant's *Charade* costar Audrey Hepburn.

State dinners with President and Mrs. Ford were as cherished for their post-party merriment as for the events themselves. After the shah bid everyone good night, the rest of the guests frolicked into the wee hours, led by the indomitable Pearl Bailey. Pearl pulled everyone she could onto the dance floor: the president and first lady, Ann-Margret, Bob Hope, Douglas Fairbanks Jr. After that she grabbed a microphone and started singing, dragging up Dionne Warwick for a duet of "On the Street Where You Live" and ending with the inevitable "Hello, Dolly!" According to the *Washington Post*, by the time Pearl reached the refrain, the president "was jumping up and down and doing the bunny hop, hanging on to her for dear life while Betty Ford stood and clapped delightedly . . . "

It was Betty Ford's dancing that captivated onlookers at a gathering in 1976. Again, the honoree, President Tolbert of Liberia, had gone home for the night, leaving the rest of the guests to let down their hair. As the Marine Band played, the first lady and comedian Marty Allen launched into what the *Washington Star* described as "a show-stopping ten-minute solo dance performance" to Carole King's "I Feel the Earth Move." "All the other dancers moved to the sidelines to watch them, as they danced what Allen later said was 'free style rock,'" wrote *Star* society reporter Isabelle Shelton. When the couple stepped off the dance floor, President Ford said, "That was great, Marty."

Mrs. Ford had invited Marty Allen to the dinner with therapy in mind. Allen's wife had recently died of cancer, and Mrs. Ford hoped to draw the grieving widower out of his self-imposed isolation. "She felt he would not refuse a White House invitation," said Mrs. Ford's social secretary, Maria Downs, "and that it might help to ease his sorrow." Although Allen accepted, at the last minute he backed out. Mrs. Ford invited him again and the second time he came. After the party Marty Allen told Maria Downs that dancing wildly with the first lady for ten minutes had released the pressures and pent-up emotions of the previous months.

Betty Ford never got a chance to go cheek to cheek with her dream partner, Fred Astaire, despite his presence at a Ford White House dinner. "I begged him to dance, but he said he wasn't a ballroom dancer, that he had to have a routine,"

Mrs. Ford wrote in her memoir. Ginger Rogers had a similar effect on the men of the nation's capital. In 1981 Vice President George Bush got a chance to strut his stuff with Ginger at a Washington society dance. As they waltzed to Burt Bacharach's "What the World Needs Now," an excited Bush called over a reporter. "Ginger has something to tell you," he said. Ginger spoke her piece: "He holds a girl just like Fred Astaire—and if I can dance more than four steps with him, I'll tell you if he dances like him, too."

The Hollywood glamour conjured by Astaire and Rogers was much in evidence at the Reagan White House, where state dinners sometimes had the feel of *That's Entertainment*, the compendium of classic musicals from Metro-Goldwyn-Mayer in which familiar faces whiz by from one clip to the next. Dinner guests included Reagan's former costars—Olivia de Havilland, Patricia Neal, and Shirley Temple—and old friends from the coast like Jimmy and Gloria Stewart, Robert and Rosemary Stack, Fred MacMurray and June Haver. Claudette Colbert and Loretta Young came, as did Cyd Charisse, Jane Powell, and Esther Williams. Frank Sinatra, Buddy Ebsen, Ricardo Montalban, Charlton Heston, and Jerry Lewis represented the men of Hollywood. Rock Hudson visited the mansion in May 1984, a year and a half before his death from AIDS. Tony Randall, a liberal who had been on Nixon's enemies list, also rated an invitation.

One of the most celebrity-studded dinners of the Reagan presidency happened not at the White House but on Stage Nine of the Twentieth Century Fox Studios in Hollywood. The occasion, a 1983 party for Queen Elizabeth, boasted a mind-boggling concentration of film and TV legends: Astaire and Rogers, Bette Davis, James Stewart, Irene Dunne, Gene Kelly, Lucille Ball, June Allyson, Greer Garson, James Mason, and Loretta Young. The entertainment program, produced by Frank Sinatra, featured Sinatra reprising his White House performance with Perry Como. Rounding out the bill were Dionne Warwick and eighty-seven-year-old George Burns, who told a series of off-color jokes that many in the audience deemed inappropriate for the occasion. Example: "If a director wants me to cry, I think of my sex life. If he wants me to laugh, I think of my sex life."

A far more exclusive event during the queen's visit to the West Coast took place the following night onboard the royal yacht *Brittania,* where the Royal Couple welcomed a select group of Californians to dinner. When Frank Sinatra learned he had not been invited, he telephoned the White House and threatened to pull out of the party at Twentieth Century Fox. Only the intercession of the American ambassador to London resolved the diplomatic crisis; reluctantly Buckingham Palace allowed Sinatra to come aboard.

Beyond the classic names of Hollywood, Reagan guest lists showed a weakness for television stars, contemporary and otherwise. How else to explain the presence of both Gomer Pyle (Jim Nabors) and the Fonz (Henry Winkler) at a 1984 dinner for the grand duke of Luxembourg? Prime-time soap operas, a hugely popular television genre of the 1980s, generated a substantial number of Reagan dinner guests. From *Dallas* came Larry Hagman and from *Dynasty* Joan Collins; even the lesser soaps like *Knot's Landing* and *The Colbys* sent representatives.

To their credit the Reagans expanded the show business guest list beyond the predictable big donors or campaign volunteers. Occasionally they would invite a young performer whom they had seen and admired. Michael J. Fox, whose character on the television comedy *Family Ties* was said to embody Reagan-era capitalism, went to the White House in 1985. Several years earlier President Reagan had seen Fox's hit movie *Back to the Future* while recovering from an assassination attempt. The film includes a mildly disparaging joke at Reagan's expense: after time-traveling from the 1980s to the 1950s Fox's character tells another character that in the future Ronald Reagan will become president. "And who's vice president—Jerry Lewis?" comes back the retort. At the White House dinner Fox told Nancy Reagan he had not intended to be disrespectful; the first lady assured him that both she and the president liked the picture.

Attending the same party as Michael J. Fox was Sylvester Stallone, whose recent film *Rambo* Reagan had also seen. "It's always flattering to have the highest person in the land admire your work," Stallone told reporters as he arrived at the mansion with his date and future wife, Danish model Brigitte Nielsen. Stallone was asked if he had any advice for the president in dealing with the previous day's hijacking of an Italian cruise ship in the Mediterranean that carried American passengers. "Let's put it this way," he replied. "I'm an action actor so I'd like to have a little action."

Six years later Stallone returned to the mansion, this time with a new woman on his arm and a new president in residence. Not surprisingly, George and Barbara Bush attracted a less glamorous roster of show business emissaries than the Reagans. Without the long-standing connections of their predecessors, the Bushes tended to favor second- and third-tier entertainers who had supported them during the campaign, like Chuck Norris and Cheryl Ladd.

Among their more interesting show business guests were the three stars of *Driving Miss Daisy*—Jessica Tandy, Hume Cronyn, and Morgan Freeman—who attended a 1990 dinner for Mikhail Gorbachev. Melanie Griffith, with husband Don Johnson, made a memorable appearance at a function in 1991 for Denmark's Queen Margrethe, wearing a skimpy gold dress that barely covered her body. Several weeks later Barbara Bush received a thank-you note from the actress, who said her mother had always told her she might one day grow up and be invited to the president's house. In a postscript Griffith added: "I just wish my mother had told me what to wear when I went to the White House."

The Bushes frequently found room for comedians at their state dinners. Joan Rivers came, and so did Dom DeLuise. Don Rickles, attending an event for the leader of Tunisia, was asked if he planned to insult anyone. "I can't afford it," he answered. "The president could get moody and I could end up in Tunis." The Bushes' most inspired show business dinner guest was actor Leslie Nielsen, star of the *Naked Gun* police comedies. The newest film in the series, *Naked Gun 1 1/2*, had opened with a slapstick parody of a White House state dinner in which Nielsen's character knocks a Barbara Bush lookalike in the head with an enormous lobster claw. "I had the feeling that our president and first lady would think it funny," Nielsen said. "And they did." At the real-life state dinner Nielsen commanded a seat of honor next to Barbara Bush.

A noteworthy encounter occurred between the Bushes and legendary actress Katharine Hepburn at the 1990 Kennedy Center Honors ceremony. Hepburn showed up for the formal event in a black turtleneck, black pants, black coat, black sneakers, and white scarf. "She seemed feisty," wrote Barbara Bush, "and immediately tweaked George on his antiabortion position. She allowed as how she wondered why she had come." Hepburn mellowed as the ceremony progressed, though the Bushes were in for one more surprise: returning to her seat after intermission, the actress entered the wrong box. "Instead of going back out into the hallway to come through the right door," said Mrs. Bush, "she just climbed over the railing."

Although Bill and Hillary Clinton held considerably fewer state dinners than their predecessors, their guest lists found room for many show business personalities, including Gregory Peck, Jane Fonda, Michael Douglas, Nicolas Cage, Martin Scorsese, and Candice Bergen. At a fete for the president of Italy Sophia Loren commanded a seat of honor at President Clinton's table. "We talked about family, values, our children, and the future of our children," Loren said as she left the White House. "If you have the chance to sit beside the president, you just keep asking questions. You don't eat much. You just keep observing. As a matter of fact, I'm starving."

The most glittering of the Clinton dinners, honoring Tony and Cherie Blair in 1998, had the aura of a post–Academy Awards VIP bash. Barbra Streisand

and James Brolin, Kate Capshaw and Steven Spielberg, John F. Kennedy Jr. and Carolyn Bessette, Harrison Ford, Tom Hanks, and Carol Channing were among the 240 guests, along with top executives from Hollywood's film and television industry. Also attending was Tina Brown, British-born editor of the *New Yorker*. Brown's wide-eyed description of the evening invited readers to see Clinton as his guests did:

> . . . a man in a dinner jacket with more heat than any star in the room (or, for that matter, at the multiplex). As the president of the United States walks with Hillary and the Blairs into the State Dining Room, his height, his sleekness, his newly cropped, iron-filing hair, and the intensity of his blue eyes project a kind of avid inclusiveness that encircles every jaded celebrity he passes. He is vividly in the present tense and dares you to join him there.

In the view of columnist Maureen Dowd, Brown "sounded like a Tom Jones groupie ready to throw her room key onto the stage."

❄❄❄❄

Presidential inaugurations provide another window into the intersection of show business and the White House. The involvement of stars as inaugural performers has grown enormously since 1905, when future film star Tom Mix traveled with a troupe of cowboys from South Dakota to Washington to march in the parade for Theodore Roosevelt. Twenty-eight years later, for the inaugural of a second Roosevelt, Mix was back in town, this time a full-fledged hero of the silver screen. Mix and his equine costar, King, journeyed to Washington in style, arriving with a trainload of stars from Hollywood aboard Warner Brothers' *42nd Street Special*. The studio had arranged to send some of its brightest assets on a national publicity tour—and what better place for publicity than the inauguration of the nation's new leader? Onboard the seven-car Pullman train were Joe E. Brown, Leo Carrillo, Glenda Farrell, Laura LaPlante, Lyle Talbot, and a twenty-four-year-old starlet named Bette Davis. Davis, a studio newcomer with only two years' experience in the business, soon became one of FDR's biggest boosters and one of the movies' biggest stars.

Though celebrity-studded to an unprecedented degree, the festivities of 1933 did not offer the entertainers a formalized role in the inaugural process. The Warner Brothers stars, as well as other performers in town like the lead actors from radio's *Amos 'n' Andy*, came more as observers than participants. That changed at Roosevelt's third inaugural in 1941, when the big names who journeyed to Washington did so in order to work.

The evening before FDR's swearing-in, a host of artists appeared at a gala in Constitution Hall attended by most of the Roosevelt family, though not the president himself. The entertainers displayed a diversity of talent. Ethel Barrymore read a poem and Nelson Eddy sang. Raymond Massey presented an excerpt from *Abe Lincoln in Illinois*. Mickey Rooney played an original composition and did crowd-pleasing imitations of movie stars. Irving Berlin performed "God Bless America." The program climaxed with Charles Chaplin delivering the closing monologue from his new film *The Great Dictator*, words that offered a ringing endorsement of liberty. A reporter for the *Washington Post* wrote that just at the dramatic height of his speech Chaplin stopped himself and asked for a glass of water to wet his parched throat. "No one but a Chaplin could have picked up where he left off and scored so overwhelming a personal triumph," the journalist enthused.

The celebrity contingent at Roosevelt's 1945 inaugural included Orson Welles, Edward G. Robinson, Bob Hope, and George Jessel. Frank Sinatra, who was supposed to perform, did not make it to Washington because of wartime restrictions on civilian travel. Welles and Jessel joined Eleanor Roosevelt at an Inauguration Day dinner for individuals who had donated $1,000 or more to FDR's campaign; Welles read some of Roosevelt's speeches. Jessel and Robinson also attended a huge luncheon at the White House, where the seventeen hundred guests included Helen Keller. But unlike the inaugural of 1941, there was no public event that showcased the stars who had converged on Washington for the president's final swearing-in.

The modern era of inaugural galas began in 1949 with Harry Truman. Instead of shying away from the men and women of show business, Truman embraced them, and in so doing created a template for packing galas with celebrities that has prevailed ever since. Fifty-three hundred spectators filled the District National Guard Armory on January 19, 1949, to watch performances by Benny Goodman, Guy Lombardo, Xavier Cugat, Alice Faye, Jane Powell, and Kay Starr—plus Lena Horne and Lionel Hampton, the first African American entertainers to play a presidential inaugural gala. Among the emcees were Gene Kelly and George Jessel. Specialty acts on the bill included Abbott and Costello, Edgar Bergen with puppets Charlie McCarthy and Mortimer Snerd, and child star Margaret O'Brien.

In 1953 and 1957 song-and-dance man George Murphy, later a U.S. senator, served as "entertainment director" for Dwight Eisenhower's two inaugurals. In addition to movie stars and stage performers, the new medium of television contributed some of its favorites to the festivities, including Sid Caesar and Imogene Coca in 1953 and Phil Silvers four years later. The roster of Eisenhower's inaugural talent tended to overlap with the list of his celebrity campaigners. Ike rewarded a number of his show business supporters—Irene Dunne, Ethel Merman, Adolphe Menjou, and John Wayne—with prominent roles in the gala.

This trend continued with the inaugural of John F. Kennedy in 1961, produced by Frank Sinatra and starring many of the performers who had stumped for JFK around the country. The Kennedy event dispensed with the cornier acts that George Murphy had booked for Eisenhower. Instead, Sinatra's goal as producer was to entertain the sophisticated young president with the best talent the nation had to offer. The show embraced a wide spectrum of artists: comedians Jimmy Durante, Milton Berle, and Bob Hope; serious actors Laurence Olivier, Bette Davis, Frederic March, and Anthony Quinn; glamorous movie stars Janet Leigh and Tony Curtis; classical musicians Helen Traubel and Leonard Bernstein; Broadway belter Ethel Merman; nightclub singers Keely Smith and Louis Prima; and dancer Juliet Prowse, Sinatra's future fiancée. A stellar complement of African American entertainers also performed: Ella Fitzgerald, Nat King Cole, Harry Belafonte, Sidney Poitier, and Mahalia Jackson, who sang the national anthem. So many stars came in from California that an airplane had to be chartered; the New York actors flew in on JFK's campaign plane, the *Caroline*.

Around noon on January 19, 1961, the day of the gala, it began to snow. Soon the snow turned into a blizzard, and by evening the city of Washington lay paralyzed under a blanket of white. Some of the stars had difficulty reaching the National Guard Armory. Bette Davis started walking from her hotel, until the White House dispatched a limousine to take her the rest of the way. Ethel Merman, unable to return to her hotel for her gown, ended up singing "Everything's Coming Up Roses" in the wool suit she wore at rehearsal.

With the audience only half full, the show began an hour and forty minutes behind schedule. "I hope no one will think it presumptuous for some of us in the entertainment industry to have come here to pay tribute to the president-elect," Sinatra announced, and on that oddly defensive note the program of music, dance, comedy, and drama commenced. As the three-hour entertainment drew to a close, Kennedy approached the stage to the strains of "Anchors Aweigh." JFK told the crowd that America's "happy relationship between the arts and politics" had culminated that evening, adding: "I know we're all indebted to a great friend—Frank Sinatra." When the receipts were counted, the gala had raised $1 million for the Democratic party.

Lyndon Johnson's 1965 inaugural entertainment featured Woody Allen, Ann-Margret, Julie Andrews, Carol Burnett, Johnny Carson, Mitzi Gaynor, Harry Belafonte, Mike Nichols and Elaine May, and Barbra Streisand. Streisand, still in her early twenties, stole the show; columnist Dorothy Kilgallen wrote that the young vocal sensation "made 'People' sound like the most important song next to the national anthem." A witty addition to the cast was film director Alfred Hitchcock, who acknowledged the presence in the audience of the president's wife and daughter: "You remember I warned you in a movie not too far back that the birds were coming. Well, the Birds are here."

Richard Nixon's two inaugurals attracted a less impressive list of stars. The Nixons did not attend the 1969 gala, apparently for security reasons. They missed performances by Tony Bennett, Johnny Carson, Buddy Ebsen, Connie Francis, Buddy Hackett, Lionel Hampton, Dinah Shore, and the dance act Hines Hines and Dad. Joel Grey and the company of *George M!* delivered a spirited medley of patriotic George M. Cohan tunes, and soul singer James Brown, who had campaigned for Nixon's opponent, Hubert Humphrey, energized the crowd with "Up Tight" and "Black and Proud."

The celebrity quotient increased at Nixon's 1973 inaugural, and this time the first couple put in the requisite personal appearances. But it was the backstage antics of Frank Sinatra that created the juiciest preinaugural spectacle. A few hours before "Salute to the States," the first of three concerts honoring the president, Sinatra abruptly withdrew from his role as emcee. When the Secret Service would not allow one of the singer's comedian friends to perform in the show because he had not been cleared for security, the irate Sinatra refused to go on, leaving Hugh O'Brian to step in as a last-minute replacement.

Several hours later, during a party at a D.C. hotel, Sinatra threw an even nastier tantrum when he encountered Maxine Cheshire, a *Washington Post* reporter who several months earlier had questioned him about his alleged mob ties. "Get away from me, you scum!" he screamed at her. "Go home and take a bath. Print that, Miss Cheshire. Get away from me. I don't want to talk to you. I'm getting out of here to get rid of your stench." But the tirade was not over. Addressing the startled bystanders, Sinatra pressed on. "You know Miss Cheshire, don't you? That stench you smell is coming from her." Then, to Cheshire: "You're nothing but a two-dollar cunt. C-U-N-T. You know what that means, don't you? You've been laying down for two dollars all your life." Sinatra pulled two one-dollar bills from his pocket and crammed them into Cheshire's glass. "Here, baby," he said before storming off, "that's what you're used to." The widely publicized incident reportedly infuriated Nixon, who had already invited Sinatra to sing at the White House. Maxine Cheshire remained philosophical: "If I had not been there, someone else would have been his victim."

In 1977 Jimmy Carter's so-called People's Inaugural attracted another army of top-flight stars to the nation's capital, demonstrating anew that Democratic presidents draw a higher grade of talent than their Republican counterparts. On the stage at the Kennedy Center Opera House the evening before Carter's swearing-in were singers Aretha Franklin, Linda Ronstadt, Paul Simon, and Loretta Lynn; comedians Mike Nichols and Elaine May; movie stars Warren Beatty, Bette Davis, Shirley MacLaine, Paul Newman, Jack Nicholson, and John Wayne; and television actors Redd Foxx, Jean Stapleton, Jack Albertson, Dan Aykroyd, and Chevy Chase. Twenty-two-year-old Freddie Prinze, star of the TV comedy *Chico and the Man*, was the youngest of the headline performers; ten days after the gala he shot himself to death in Hollywood. Even the audience at the Kennedy Center was star-studded. John Lennon and Yoko Ono were there, plus Lauren Bacall. Young marrieds Greg Allman and Cher arrived halfway through the program.

Four years later Frank Sinatra returned to Washington to produce the inaugural show for Ronald Reagan, just as he had for John F. Kennedy. Sinatra not only organized the gala, he also served as commercial pitchman for a line of inauguration mementos. "Hi, I'm Frank Sinatra," the singer said in one television spot. "I know that I want something to remember all of this by, and I'm putting myself down for the beautiful inaugural medals, the handsome hardcover book, and maybe a set of commemorative license plates."

As he had done twenty years earlier, Sinatra personally recruited the performers who came to Washington to honor the new president, though this time the names had lost some of their luster. Bob Hope and Ethel Merman were back, along with Jimmy Stewart, Charlton Heston, Donnie and Marie Osmond, Mel Tillis, Debby Boone, Charley Pride, and Ben Vereen, with Johnny Carson as master of ceremonies. With a straight face Sinatra called it "the greatest collection of talent America could offer to any audience."

Also slated to perform was Dean Martin. But during dress rehearsal a few hours before the live event Martin had begun to show signs of inebriation. In the middle of Charley Pride's afternoon run-through Martin wandered onto the stage with a drink in his hand; Sinatra good-naturedly ordered him off. After Martin practiced his own number, Johnny Carson joked that "Debby Boone could get a contact high from this microphone." Hours later, as cast members changed into their formalwear, Charlton Heston observed the singer "swaying in shirt and socks, fumbling with his dress tie. I tried to knot it for him, but he sank into a chair. Clearly, he couldn't get out of the dressing room, let alone sing." Heston alerted Sinatra, who promptly cut Dean Martin from the program. Oddly, Martin instead turned up in the audience.

The gala seemed dedicated as much to the redemption of Frank Sinatra as the swearing-in of Ronald Reagan. Crediting himself as "Producer/Director and Director of Entertainment," Sinatra made several prominent appearances during the show, escorting first the vice president-elect and then the Reagans as they entered the Capitol Arena in Landover, Maryland. Near the end of the program Sinatra sang a number of his old hits; "Nancy with the Laughing Face" he awkwardly reworked as "Nancy with the Reagan Face."

In 1985 Sinatra reprised his role as inaugural producer, and found himself in another contretemps with the press. Upset over a *Washington Post* feature story that dredged up memories of the Rat Pack, the inaugural producer vented his anger at a reporter who had tried to ask him a question. Turning on her, Sinatra exploded: "You're all dead, every one of you—you're all dead!" The outburst made the evening newscasts just hours before the Inaugural Eve gala got under way.

At the tribute to President Reagan Sinatra shared cohosting duties with Pearl Bailey, Tom Selleck, and human action figure Mr. T. Dean Martin got a chance to atone for his sins of 1981, this time remaining sober enough to perform a pseudo-drunken comedy routine with Sinatra. Don Rickles told a string of mildly insulting ethnic jokes, and Jimmy Stewart served up a nostalgic salute to Hollywood, describing it as "a place where concepts like patriotism and family were extolled." Stewart added: "It was also a place where a man could be playing second banana to a chimpanzee on one day and become president of the United States on another day. I'm glad it didn't happen in reverse order."

Frank Sinatra returned once more for the presidential swearing-in of George Bush in 1989. This time he functioned not as a producer but as a performer. With a shaky but heartfelt rendition of "You'll Never Walk Alone," Frank Sinatra presented his final inaugural serenade. "That's what I wish for you, Mr. President," Sinatra said with a bow at the end of the number. "Tonight, George—tonight is the last time I will call you that. From tomorrow morning on I'll call you Mr. President and be happy to do it and proud to do it."

For television audiences Republican inaugurals often feel second-rate, and Bush's was no different. Apart from Sinatra the biggest names were Arnold Schwarzenegger, Julio Iglesias, Mikhail Baryshnikov, and the Mormon Tabernacle Choir. Eight years later the second George Bush faced similar difficulty recruiting performers from the entertainment A-list. The inaugural performers of 2001 were of historically low wattage: Delta Burke, Gerald McRaney, Drew Carey, Bo Derek, Wayne Newton, Marie Osmond, Larry Gatlin, Kelsey Grammer, George Strait, Loretta Lynn, Ricky Martin, and Destiny's Child. After the Bush inaugural committee proudly announced that it had booked Irish singer Van Morrison, Morrison's publicist informed journalists the rock legend had no intention of appearing.

In fairness to George W. Bush, it would be difficult for any incoming chief executive to match the celebrity connections of President Bill Clinton, Hollywood's most successful political seducer. If anything, Clinton was *too* popular among entertainers. In January 1993 the president-elect discovered that along with top-level entertainers come top-level egos. At least some of the famous names who made their way to the capital to honor Clinton brought with them a strongly held sense of entitlement. A source identified as a "prominent inaugural planner" described the situation to the *New York Times*: "Look, there are two stars here, Bill Clinton and Al Gore. Some of these people believe they should be holding the Bible. You have no idea."

With so many top names sharing the spotlight a certain amount of tension was inevitable. Representatives of Michael Jackson, unhappy at the singer's slot in the performing lineup, threatened a last-minute boycott, but according to inaugural producer Harry Thomason, Jackson himself overruled them. "He's my president, and I'll be there—put me anywhere you want," Jackson told Thomason.

A staggering array of entertainers participated in Clinton's transition into the presidency. "Everybody from Hollywood wanted to be involved," said Harry Thomason. "There was nobody we wanted that we couldn't get." Spread over several days, the events included a huge musical show at the Lincoln Memorial produced by Quincy Jones; a children's concert with performers suggested by Chelsea Clinton; and a traditional Inaugural Eve gala that climaxed in a show-stopping vocal set by Barbra Streisand. Virtually every genre and era of American music was represented; it would almost be easier to catalogue the performers who did not perform at Clinton's 1993 inaugural events than to list those who did. As *Time* magazine said, "The stars came out in constellations," even those not normally associated with politicians, like Bob Dylan and Jack Nicholson.

And right in the thick of it was the president-elect. To a far greater degree than any of his predecessors, Bill Clinton cast himself as a player in the inaugural festivities, cheering on the entertainers, misting up at all the right moments, clapping and swaying with the music. Lewis Lapham in *Harper's* was one of several critics to note Clinton's conspicuousness: "At the television gala presented in his honor the night before the inauguration, he couldn't prevent himself from mouthing the lyrics while Barbra Streisand sang 'Evergreen.' The cameras drifted away from Streisand—as Mr. Clinton knew they must—and found the tear-stained face of the new president, devouring the words as if they were made of sugar or chocolate." At the parties that followed his swearing-in Clinton did more than observe—he played the saxophone.

The euphoria Bill Clinton induced in the men and women of show business manifested itself in the heady whirl of Clinton's first inauguration. To some degree the feeling stemmed from the sense of possibility that Clinton evoked, especially at that inchoate moment when his presidency remained a blank slate. "I believe this president is more tuned in emotionally, philosophically and generationally," Jack Valenti told *Variety* columnist Army Archerd. "I don't think he'll sit by and let us down." Actor Christopher Reeve put it another way: "For the past twelve years, those in the arts were forced to take up the battle lines and defend our existence. With the Clinton-Gore ticket, the life of the artist is not something to be ashamed of anymore."

Reeve's remark raises an interesting point about presidential transitions: when Democrats retake the White House after a long period out of office, the inaugural turnout among celebrities increases—in number and intensity. This was the case with Franklin Roosevelt in 1933, John F. Kennedy in 1961, Jimmy Carter in 1977, and—to a greater than ever degree—Bill Clinton in 1993. In 1997, with Democrats retaining control of the executive branch, Clinton's second inaugural played out on a far more modest scale. The next Democrat who takes office can almost certainly count on another outpouring of pent-up energy from the blue-chip practitioners of show business.

Lauren Bacall, in Washington for Clinton's 1993 swearing-in, explained the appeal: "There is this mutual attraction between Washington and the entertainment world. We're doing what they can't do—we can sing and dance and act. They're doing what we can't do—they have access to power, real power. I guess we all have fantasies about the other."

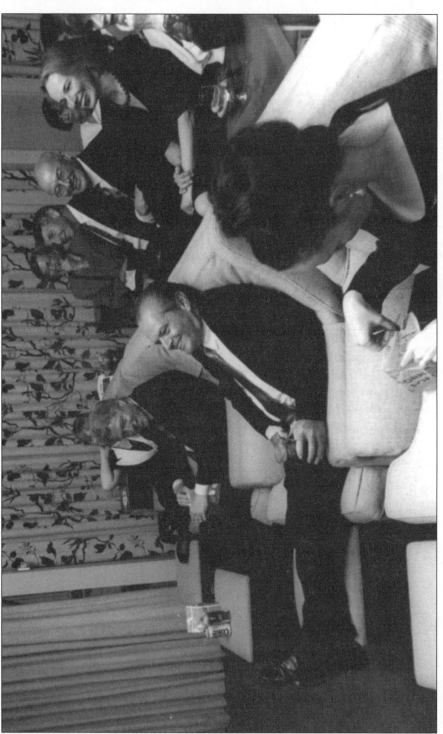

Bill Clinton and Jack Nicholson at the White House screening of *Wolf*, June 1994. (Clinton Presidential Materials Project)

7

✴✴✴✴

Groupies, Aficionados, and Philistines

PRESIDENTS AS FANS

THE ONE-HOUR SPECIAL was called *Rock 'n' Roll President*, and in June 1997 it showed American audiences something they had never seen: their highest elected official in the role of pop culture groupie. The documentary, produced and aired by cable television network VH1, led viewers through Bill Clinton's record collection, his White House music room, and his memories. "Every time I hear the Mamas and the Papas," Clinton said, a wistful smile on his face, "I think about Georgetown, I think about college, I think about 'Monday, Monday' and all those old, great songs."

Though the program had the squishy feel of a soft-focus vanity production, it nonetheless provided fascinating insights into the forty-second president of the United States. In a thirty-five-minute interview taped in the Oval Office Clinton held forth on the musical influences that had shaped his life, from gospel and the Beatles to Elvis Presley. He recalled a live performance he had seen by newcomer Cass Elliott and another by veteran Mahalia Jackson, cheered by her fans at London's Royal Albert Hall "like she was a young rock star."

Clinton spoke of his love of the saxophone: "It suits me emotionally and intellectually, and I always liked it." He rated his prospects as a professional musician: "I never stopped loving music, but I knew I couldn't be a musician. I didn't think I would be truly great at it." Supplementing the interview were archival clips of teenage Bill Clinton dancing, prepresidential Bill Clinton playing sax on the *Tonight* show and *Arsenio Hall,* and testimonials from performers Ray Charles, Judy Collins, and Carly Simon, the program's narrator. British rock singer Joe Cocker, who appeared on the same 1988 episode of *Tonight* as the then governor of Arkansas, spoke of Clinton as having "a bit of soul."

Bill Clinton's voracity as a fan of the national popular culture places him in a distinct category: the aficionado president. Only two other chief executives— Franklin Roosevelt and John F. Kennedy—share the classification, and neither can approach Clinton's dedication to the music and movies of his times. His love of the performing arts had been established long before he became president. During the 1992 campaign the candidate told *Rolling Stone* magazine that his favorite album was Judy Collins's *Colors of the Day;* asked whom he would invite to perform at his inauguration, Clinton named Collins. Judy Collins did sing at Bill Clinton's inaugural in 1993, standing close enough to make direct eye contact. "Clinton listens with his whole body, his whole being," she wrote. "All those hours of practicing and a natural gift gave him the ability to appreciate the music of others. That night I looked right into his eyes, singing with a deep sense of joy and celebration."

Clinton's preferences spanned various genres of contemporary music. In the late 1970s, as attorney general of Arkansas, Clinton kept a poster of a bikini-clad Dolly Parton in his office bathroom, though this may not qualify as evidence of a strictly musical preference. During the 1992 campaign, John Morthland, author of *The Best of Country Music,* told the *New York Times*: "I'm pretty certain there has never been a presidential candidate that seems to spring more clearly from the world of country music than Bill Clinton." Indeed Clinton's life reflects the hard-living, big-haired, emotionally untidy ethos of C&W, especially when compared with the rarefied milieu of George Bush, the incumbent leader who self-consciously lashed himself to the genre for political gain.

As a son of the South, Clinton ably bridged the worlds of country-western and African American music. "I suppose no singer ever had a bigger impact on my musical life than Ray Charles," the president said at a White House arts ceremony honoring Charles. Describing a concert he attended at Constitution Hall in 1967, Clinton recalled, "I was notable for being one of a few members of my race in the audience. Ray Charles electrified that crowd so much that night I literally could not go to sleep until five in the morning. I went out and ran three miles to get the energy out."

As his 1992 campaign theme song Clinton had hoped to use James Brown's rhythm and blues hit "I Feel Good," until concerns over Brown's criminal record dissuaded wary aides. Instead the 1977 Fleetwood Mac number "Don't Stop (Thinkin' About Tomorrow)" became the anthem of choice, played at key moments like the Democratic National Convention and the election night victory rally. "For me personally and certainly for the rest of the band it was very flattering," said Mick Fleetwood, drummer and founding member of Fleetwood Mac. When it came time for Clinton's inaugural, the band reunited to serenade the new president with the by now overly familiar "Don't Stop."

The eclecticism of Clinton's taste manifested itself in a variety of ways. After injuring his knee during a golf game, President Clinton was asked by a physician what music he wanted to hear during surgery: Lyle Lovett and Jimmy Buffett were the vocalists of choice. For a Washington fund-raiser in 2000 Clinton personally called Lenny Kravitz and invited him to participate, then danced onstage during one of Kravitz's songs. Among the gifts Bill Clinton gave to Monica Lewinsky was a compact disc by British singer Annie Lennox.

Clinton's most noted music hero was, of course, Elvis Presley, a singer idolized by Virginia Kelley, the president's mother. The connections ran deep: "He was from Mississippi, he was a poor white kid, he sang with a lot of soul—he was my roots," Clinton said in the VH1 documentary. As a boy Clinton memorized the lyrics to Presley's songs. It was an Elvis number—"Heartbreak Hotel"—that Clinton played on the *Arsenio Hall* show. Though Elvis and the future president never met, there were coincidences on Presley's side as well. Elvis got his own postage stamp the same month Bill Clinton moved in to the White House. The first on-screen character the singer ever portrayed, in the film *Love Me Tender*, was named Clinton.

In 1977, when Elvis Presley died at his home in Memphis from a drug overdose, the young attorney general of Arkansas closely followed the outpouring of media coverage. An aide who was traveling with Clinton told biographer David Maraniss that on the day of Presley's death her boss could speak of little else: "All the way home on the plane he talked about it. He talked about the passing of an era. His youth. What a wasted life. It moved him deeply." Late in 1999 journalist Katie Couric asked President Clinton to name his "entertainer of the century." Clinton replied, "For me in my lifetime . . . the early Elvis would be the best." As his favorite Presley song, Clinton picked "I Want You, I Need You, I Love You."

The link between Elvis and Clinton seeped into the national consciousness during the 1992 campaign. In a TV interview in April Clinton performed a raspy-voiced imitation of Elvis singing "Don't Be Cruel." Press materials distributed several months later listed "Elvis Aron Presley" as "Entertainment Coordinator" of the Democratic National Convention. Al Gore, in his vice presidential acceptance speech, joked that he had been dreaming since childhood of appearing at Madison Square Garden as "the warm-up act for Elvis."

Clinton's opponent, President George Bush, stoked the mythology by conflating Clinton and Presley, sometimes bizarrely, on the campaign trail. In his acceptance speech at the Republican convention Bush declared that the Democratic candidate's platform represented "Elvis economics" and warned, "America will be checking into the 'Heartbreak Hotel.'" Later Bush said, "I finally figured out why he compares himself to Elvis," although Clinton had drawn no such parallel. "The minute he has to take a stand on something, he starts wiggling." Clinton's response: "Bush is always comparing me to Elvis in sort of unflattering ways. Well, I don't think Bush would have liked Elvis very much, and that's just another thing that's wrong with him."

As the consummate aficionado president, Bill Clinton loved not only the music of his generation but also the motion pictures and television shows. Clinton, the first president to grow up with TV, absorbed a set of cultural references that placed him squarely within the post–World War II baby boom zeitgeist. "Before John F. Kennedy rode into the picture, Hopalong Cassidy was Bill's hero," his mother wrote in her memoir, citing a popular television character of the 1950s. "I treasure a photograph I took of him standing on the sidewalk in front of the house wearing a black cowboy hat, boots, and a black, short-jacketed cowboy suit with Hoppy's picture on it."

Like FDR and JFK, Clinton was an inveterate moviegoer, "almost to the point of compulsion," he once said. In 2000 the president told film critic Roger Ebert, "I saw every movie that came my way when I was a child, and they fired my imagination—they inspired me." Boyhood friends in Arkansas remembered that young Bill would collect the ten bottle caps required as admission to a Saturday movie matinee sponsored by a soda pop company.

When candidate Clinton began courting Hollywood, this long-standing fascination with show business served him well. "I have always aspired to be in the cultural elite that others condemn," he told a gathering of big-name Hollywood celebrities at a 1992 fund-raiser. Though the remark was intended as a jab at Republicans, it also rang true. Among the dozens of stars at that event was Whoopi Goldberg. Singling her out, Clinton asked the audience if they had seen Goldberg in *Sister Act*, a comedy in which she sings with a chorus of nuns. "I wanted to be in that choir so bad I could spit," he declared, and no one could doubt the man's sincerity.

As president, Clinton regularly rubbed shoulders with the leading actors of his era. At a White House dinner he joked to Harrison Ford, star of *Air Force One,* that

President Harrison Ford had a better plane in the movie than President Bill Clinton did in real life. Clinton told Mel Brooks at a party in Los Angeles that he rewatched *Blazing Saddles* every six months. On a trip to Italy the president of the United States got a warm reception from actor Roberto Benigni, who shocked Secret Service agents by running across the room and hurling himself into Clinton's arms.

One of the most coveted invitations of the Clinton presidency was to a screening in the White House movie theater. During Bill Clinton's eight years in office a parade of stars accompanied their films to the mansion. Tom Hanks saw *Philadelphia* with the Clintons and actress Mary Steenburgen. Denzel Washington brought *Hurricane*, along with its inspiration, boxer Rubin "Hurricane" Carter. Jack Nicholson and director Mike Nichols showed the thriller *Wolf*, an event to which CNN journalist Wolf Blitzer was also invited.

Clinton's passion for moviegoing followed him to Camp David. Harry Thomason, the television producer who was the president's longtime friend, recalled a Thanksgiving weekend at the Maryland retreat when the screenings started at seven in the evening and lasted until three in the morning. Among the pictures Thomason watched with Clinton were *Midnight in the Garden of Good and Evil*, *Shine*, *Shakespeare in Love*, *Billy Elliott*, and *Space Jam*.

The week the Monica Lewinsky story broke, Robert Duvall showed his film *The Apostle* at the White House. Some observers noted a potentially uncomfortable correlation between the Lewinsky matter and the adulterous character played by Duvall. "I didn't look over at (the Clintons) while the film was running," Duvall said. "They were kind of sunk back in their chairs, but someone told me they were holding hands and moving their feet in rhythm with the music." After the screening the president told Robert Duvall that he "really responded" to the film's gospel singing.

Like any dedicated movie fan, Clinton was quick to offer his opinions on the films he had seen, though the commentary was almost uniformly positive. According to Harry Thomason, "The president has never seen a film he didn't absolutely love." Clinton praised *Boyz N the Hood* for its insights into urban violence. *Schindler's List* and *Shadowlands* were his favorite pictures of 1993. *American Beauty* was "an amazing film," and "Kevin Spacey was amazing, Annette Bening was great, the kids were just great." Bill Clinton enjoyed *Mrs. Doubtfire* and described its star, Robin Williams, as "a comic genius." He "loved" *Three Kings* and said "(George) Clooney's unbelievable—the screen loves him." The 1996 film *Sling Blade*, by fellow Arkansan Billy Bob Thornton, was "brilliant"; Clinton expressed disappointment that it failed to secure a best picture nomination from the motion picture academy. "When we were there in December (1996)," reported one White House guest, "he had just seen private screenings of *Jerry McGuire*, *The English Patient*, *Scream*, and *My Fellow Americans*, and he gave a detailed critique of all of them."

In a 1997 interview with film critic Gene Siskel Bill Clinton picked Tom Hanks as the actor he would most like to have portray him. "We don't look alike, and we're not the same size or shape or anything. But I know him and I respect him as a person and as an actor," the president said. Clinton appeared to have given the matter some thought, for he went on to add, "If someone were trying to play me, and actually go through this job in the kind of roller-coaster way that life takes you, I would want someone with a lot of range and a lot of human feeling." For Hillary Rodham Clinton, the president chose Meryl Streep. "She's a phenomenally gifted actress," he said. "She's extraordinary."

In the same interview Clinton told Siskel that his all-time favorite film was *High Noon*, starring Gary Cooper. "He was the most realistic of all heroes. He doesn't have to say a word," observed the loquacious Clinton.

✵ ✵ ✵ ✵

Like Bill Clinton, John F. Kennedy became infatuated with movies at an early age. Just as Clinton got duded up in his Hopalong Cassidy outfit, young Jack enjoyed dressing like cowboy Tom Mix. The difference is that Jack Kennedy's costume came directly from Hollywood, where his father was the actor's boss. Nor did Bill Clinton, or any other president for that matter, grow up in a house with its own movie theater, like the Kennedy home in Hyannis Port. According to Rose Kennedy, the family enjoyed "an inexhaustible supply of home entertainment" thanks to the Hollywood connections of Joseph P. Kennedy. Ever the moral arbiter, Rose made sure the choices qualified as suitable family fare; if by mistake something "lurid" slipped through her safety net, the projector was unceremoniously shut off and the audience dismissed. "Our summers at Hyannis Port took on something of the character of a modern movie festival, with a different film shown three or four evenings a week," Rose Kennedy recalled. "Everyone in the house, including the staff, was invited, and almost always the children would have some of their friends over too, so there was always a large, appreciative audience." For a budding cineaste like Jack Kennedy, it must have been heaven.

Throughout his life Kennedy saw films whenever he had the chance. Touring France as a college student, JFK was amused to observe Gary Cooper in a western speaking fluent French, a sight he considered "worth the price of admission."

As a diversion on Election Day Kennedy would relax at a cinema while waiting for the returns to be counted. He took his grandfather to the movies the night of his first primary in Massachusetts in 1946. On the evening of the 1960 West Virginia primary JFK inadvertently ended up at an adult theater in downtown Washington watching a soft-core smut movie entitled *Private Property* because the picture he wanted to see—*Suddenly Last Summer*—had a policy of not admitting anyone once the feature began.

In the 1940s and 1950s, Congressman Kennedy was known to sneak off to the theater while his fellow legislators remained at work on the Capitol floor. Evelyn Lincoln, JFK's secretary, once had to page him at a local cinema so he could return to the Senate for an important vote. Kennedy might take in a favorite picture like *Red River* two or three times. A staff aide who sometimes double-dated with his boss recalled an instance when Kennedy's date announced she had already seen the film they planned to attend. JFK told her, "Why don't you take this money and go see another picture and I'll meet you afterwards."

As president, John F. Kennedy kept up his lifelong moviegoing habit, screening films in the White House theater, at the family home on Cape Cod, and, surprisingly, on the town. According to biographer William Manchester, during his first months in office JFK continued to see one or two films a week, though the rate later dropped to two or three a month. As time became more precious, Kennedy's tastes grew more discriminating. "Before the inaugural he would sit through almost any flop," Manchester wrote. "No more: if he becomes bored he may order that the last reel be shown, so he can see how everything turned out, or leave without a word." Manchester cited three films President Kennedy had walked out on: the Berlin-based comedy *One, Two, Three* by writer-director Billy Wilder; *Butterfield 8* with Elizabeth Taylor; and—interestingly—*The Misfits*, starring Marilyn Monroe and Clark Gable.

Part of Kennedy's impatience stemmed from the physical pain brought on by his bad back; he could not stay comfortably seated for long stretches of time. According to Charles Spalding, a close Kennedy friend, "it had to be a pretty good movie to keep the president in his chair." Journalist and Kennedy confidante Ben Bradlee remembered a 1962 White House screening of the Kirk Douglas western *Lonely Are the Brave*, a film JFK had selected over his guests' objections. "Kennedy watched, lying down on a bed placed in the front row, his head propped up on pillows," Bradlee said.

A little more than a year into his White House tenure the president and another old friend, Red Fay, slipped away to a Washington movie theater for the three-hour epic *Spartacus*. It is from Fay that we get the most detailed description of Kennedy the filmgoer:

> The president was an attentive viewer. His conversation while the film was being shown was limited to an occasional brief remark such as "Look at that guy," or "Amazing acting."
>
> Because of his back injuries, Jack assumed some strange sitting positions while watching films. Sometimes he would put his knee up against the seat in front of him. But I was conscious of his total absorption despite the occasional nervous gestures. Sometimes he tapped his teeth lightly with his index finger, or brushed the hair off his forehead with the full palm of his hand. But always those heavy-lidded eyes were intent on the film.

Seeing *Spartacus* at a public movie house on a Friday night became something of a production in itself. With Secret Service agents in tow, Kennedy and Fay arrived a few minutes after the start time of the film in order to avoid causing a scene. But once inside the darkened theater they realized that the movie had not yet commenced—and that the audience was growing impatient. Before long the crowd expressed its unhappiness at the delay with a slow, rhythmic, clapping sound. When at last the movie began they released a collective cheer. "Several days later," Fay said, "I found out that the film had actually started a minute or so before we got there, and had been stopped when the president stepped from his car. It was then rewound and shown from the beginning for the president." According to Red Fay, Kennedy "thoroughly enjoyed" *Spartacus*: "His intimate knowledge of the history of the period and his comments on various leaders of that time made the characters in the film come alive almost as contemporaries."

As a celebrity himself, JFK routinely ran into the big names of show business, and when he did he was always eager to talk shop. During the 1961 inaugural festivities Kennedy told Tony Curtis that he and his father had just watched *The Great Imposter* in Palm Beach. "When you pulled that guy's tooth out, we just collapsed," the president said. "I had to tell you that." Charlton Heston reported a similar encounter with Kennedy while taking a private tour of the White House. "I wasn't scheduled to see him," Heston said, "so he can't have been briefed, but he had appropriate comments on my work, even referring to an article on the historical background of El Cid in some magazine. That's awesome."

Standing in line at a buffet dinner in Washington, Kirk Douglas heard a familiar voice asking him if he intended to make a movie out of the popular 1962 novel *Seven Days in May*. The voice belonged to President Kennedy, and when Douglas responded that he did plan to film the book, Kennedy replied, "Good." According to Douglas, "He spent the next twenty minutes, while our dinner got cold, telling me that he thought it would make an excellent movie." JFK allowed director John Frankenheimer and his assistants to scout the White House so that they would be able to recreate key locations like the Oval Office and the private living quarters. When it came time to film *Seven Days in May*, Frankenheimer got permission to shoot exteriors at the presidential mansion, including a scene involving a clash between two groups of protesters. "Ironically, the demonstration was filmed two days after the initialing of the 1963 Nuclear Test Ban Treaty in Moscow, and real pickets had to be moved aside for the fictional riot," wrote film historian Lawrence H. Suid.

Having an actor in the family gave John F. Kennedy a direct conduit into the entertainment industry. In an oral history for the Kennedy Library, Peter Lawford spoke of a phone call he received from his brother-in-law shortly after Kennedy moved in to the White House. The president peppered him with questions about the box office receipts for *Oceans Eleven*, the heist picture Lawford made with Frank Sinatra and other members of the Rat Pack. Kennedy noted its strong showing in Boston and wanted to know how much the movie had grossed in England. "Now perhaps he was interested in that particular picture because I was involved in it," Lawford said. "But he did have a tremendous grasp of my business, which impressed me—which impressed every actor he came in contact with."

In Lawford's opinion, Kennedy "always had such good constructive criticism. When *Oceans Eleven* came out, he picked all the things that were wrong with it, just bang, and he was right." Lawford was particularly struck by his brother-in-law's habit of following the Hollywood trade papers: "He used to read *Variety* like I read *Variety*."

Kennedy's obsession with movies did not extend to the other popular arts. His musical tastes ran toward show tunes and standards; Jacqueline Kennedy used to joke that her husband's favorite song was "Hail to the Chief." (Officially, President Kennedy's favorite was the folk melody "Greensleeves.") It was Jackie, twelve years younger than JFK, who introduced him to the musical crazes of the early 1960s, among them bossa nova, Chubby Checker's "The Twist," and the piano novelty number "The Alley Cat Song."

Unlike their fellow Americans, the Kennedys watched little television, though JFK reportedly enjoyed *The Judy Garland Show*, *The Jack Benny Program*, and *Maverick*. The Kennedys were latecomers to the TV mania that swept the nation. The president had to persuade his wife to allow a television into the West Sitting Hall so he could monitor breaking news. As late as 1960 the family's summer home on Cape Cod lacked a TV set; in order to watch the first Kennedy-Nixon debate, Jacqueline Kennedy had to rent one.

If the first lady was out of step with the rest of the country vis-à-vis television, her cinematic preferences fell even further outside the mainstream. A devotee of Federico Fellini, Mrs. Kennedy took her husband to see *La Strada* and named *La Dolce Vita* as one of her favorite releases of 1961. Her affinity for European films included such classics as *Jules et Jim, Breathless,* and *Last Year in Marienbad*—hardly the typical choices of American audiences in the early 1960s.

One of the last films John F. Kennedy saw, on October 23, 1963, was the James Bond picture *Dr. No.* According to Ben Bradlee, who accompanied the president to the showing at a local Washington theater, "Kennedy seemed to enjoy the cool and the sex and the brutality." This comes as no surprise; Kennedy was also partial to the James Bond novels by Ian Fleming that inspired the films. After the Bay of Pigs crisis, President Kennedy asked, "Why couldn't this have happened to James Bond?"

✳✳✳✳

Franklin Roosevelt, the prototype of an aficionado president, shared Kennedy's boyish enthusiasm for the silver screen. A 1937 story in the *New York Times* dubbed FDR the nation's "number one movie fan." "It is nothing for the Chief Executive to see four and five movies a week, a figure calculated to stop the casual moviegoer in his tracks and leave even the dyed-in-the-wool fan checking up on his laurels," the *Times* said. Like Kennedy, Roosevelt watched motion pictures wherever he happened to be. For a five-week goodwill tour of South America in 1936, FDR packed twenty-six feature films and managed to screen all but a few.

Although President Roosevelt did not venture into the movie houses of Washington the way JFK did, he liked to see a newsreel and a cartoon before the main feature, as was customary at the neighborhood cinema. According to Eleanor Roosevelt, "He always had a Mickey Mouse, which amused him greatly." Roosevelt housekeeper Henrietta Nesbitt remembered a presidential preference for Donald Duck: "No matter how bad things were with the world, he could always be heard laughing over Donald Duck." FDR saw *Snow White and the Seven Dwarfs* twice. In 1940 an appreciative Walt Disney sent the president an original drawing of Mickey Mouse for his birthday.

Like millions of his countrymen in the difficult years of the Depression and World War II, Roosevelt used movies as a form of escape. In the words of his wife, "They helped him to forget temporarily the cares of his office." According to FDR's secretary, Grace Tully, "For out and out relaxation, he preferred unadulterated slapstick comedy. He was not a bit squeamish about the number of custard pies thrown." Sophisticated comedies also appealed to him. In 1941, as after-dinner entertainment for the grand duchess of Luxembourg, the Roosevelts showed *The Philadelphia Story*. Among the guests were a young Texas congressman and his wife, Lyndon and Lady Bird Johnson.

Roosevelt's moviegoing carried two proscriptions, according to Eleanor: "He hated a picture to be too long, and it must not be sad." Because *Gone with the Wind* violated both caveats, FDR never saw the most popular film of his presidency. One evening, when Franklin Roosevelt Jr. screened the Civil War drama in the family quarters after his father had gone to bed, the noise of fighting on the film's soundtrack woke up the president. "The next morning," the first lady said, "he announced decidedly that he did not understand how anyone could want to see that kind of picture." Roosevelt did not restrict himself to light entertainment. In January 1940 FDR held a White House screening of *Abe Lincoln in Illinois* attended by its star, Raymond Massey, and author, Robert Sherwood. "He was in jovial spirits and seemed to enjoy the picture," Massey said. "He mouthed, 'He wrote those speeches himself!'"

President Roosevelt's absolute favorite movie star was Myrna Loy, a choice that on every level hits the bull's-eye. According to Grace Tully, "He plied Hollywood visitors with questions about her, wanted very much to meet her, and to his great regret, when she at last came to the White House for a March of Dimes celebration, he was out of the country at an overseas conference. 'Well,' he asked when he returned, 'what was she like?'"

Loy reciprocated the president's ardor. "I absolutely idolized Franklin Delano Roosevelt," she said. "We carried on a correspondence all during the war. I'd send him telegrams whenever I approved of something he did, which was often, while he kept trying to get me down there for bond rallies or other fund-raising events." Although the two never met, Myrna Loy later developed a close friendship with Eleanor Roosevelt.

Throughout Roosevelt's tenure the moguls of Hollywood kept the president supplied with the latest movie releases, a custom that persists at the White House to this day. Jack Warner, for one, took a personal interest in feeding the presidential motion picture habit. In 1941 Warner sent a telegram to White House aide

Stephen Early: "Knowing how busy the president is I seek your good office to tell my good friend President Roosevelt if he can find the time to run a movie in the near future he will do me a great favor and I know he and his family and friends will secure a lot of enjoyment by running *Sergeant York*. Please wire me and I will arrange to have a print delivered to you at the White House." Early replied, "President much too occupied day and night to take time out for such enjoyment. As soon as conditions change, will ask you to make print available." A year later Warner was pushing another studio film, *Arsenic and Old Lace*. Roosevelt's response: "Will you tell Jack Warner there isn't a prayer of my going to the movies until 1945!?"

Like all serious movie lovers, Franklin Roosevelt functioned as both fan and critic. "I am very glad to see that you took my advice in regard to your leading lady," he wrote Will Rogers in 1934 after watching the comedian's latest film, *Judge Priest*. "This time you have one (Anita Louise) who is good to look at and who can also act." When Katharine Hepburn came to the White House in the mid-1930s, the president used the occasion to bemoan the many inferior films he had suffered through. "Invariably, he would suggest some favorite story of his which he thought ought to be filmed," Grace Tully wrote. With Hepburn it was Rudyard Kipling's *The Brushwood Boy*. "He was astounded when Miss Hepburn admitted she had never heard of it," Tully said.

Roosevelt's fascination with show business ran deep. Before becoming president, FDR had even tried his hand at screenwriting. In 1921, while recuperating from polio, Roosevelt wrote a treatment for a film about John Paul Jones, the naval hero of the American Revolution famous for his war cry, "I have not yet begun to fight!" The treatment ended up at Paramount Pictures in 1923, where it was promptly ignored. When Hollywood released a different movie about Jones shortly thereafter, Roosevelt took notice. According to his secretary, "FDR always claimed they had cribbed some of his material. In any case, he didn't get paid for it." The John Paul Jones project resurfaced briefly during the early years of Roosevelt's presidency. In an informal White House meeting FDR discussed the idea with Eugene Zukor, son of Paramount's founder, Adolph Zukor. "It's in limbo," Zukor told Roosevelt, in a phrase familiar to generations of frustrated screenwriters. "Paramount hasn't rejected it but they haven't decided anything on it yet. It's still hanging."

Though his John Paul Jones film never came to fruition, FDR received screen credit for another picture, the 1936 Republic release *The President's Mystery*, starring Henry Wilcoxon and Betty Furness. (Furness later served as a White House aide to Lyndon Johnson.) The production, a forgettable tale about a newly wealthy man who goes underground to escape the pressures of his affluence, had originally appeared in serial form in *Liberty* magazine. The film credited eight writers, including the novelist Nathanael West; a separate credit read "Story Conceived by Franklin D. Roosevelt." Reviews were lukewarm, and the picture vanished as quickly as its protagonist.

Today, directly across Route 9 from FDR's family estate in Hyde Park, New York, stand two film theaters: the Roosevelt, a modest multiscreen auditorium, and the Hyde Park, a drive-in that has been in operation since 1950. Though Franklin Roosevelt might be distressed to see the strip-malling of his Hudson River hometown, it seems likely he would approve of the pair of movie houses on the other side of the road.

✴ ✴ ✴ ✴

Beyond the aficionados, presidents can be divided into two groups: casual fans and nonfans. Most American presidents, at least those whose terms of office have coincided with the era of mass entertainment, fall into the first category. Only a handful of the country's modern leaders could be considered nonfans.

Early in the twentieth century, as a result of the very first movie screened at the White House, Woodrow Wilson received a lesson in the dangers of popular culture. The film was D.W. Griffith's *The Birth of a Nation*, and the story of how Wilson got sucked into its emotional undertow forms an early cautionary tale for any politician asked to put his imprimatur on an entertainment enterprise. Wilson agreed to watch the picture as a favor to an old college friend, Thomas Dixon, whose novel *The Clansman* had inspired Griffith's production. Dixon, a clever promoter with a racist agenda, wrote President Wilson urging him to see the film, "not because it was the greatest ever produced or because his classmate had written the story . . . but because this picture made clear for the first time that a new universal language had been invented." This high-minded appeal notwithstanding, Dixon hoped Wilson's endorsement would validate the movie's segregationist sympathies.

Still in mourning for his late wife, Wilson did not feel comfortable appearing in public at a motion picture house, so Dixon arranged to have projection equipment delivered to the executive mansion for a private screening. On February 18, 1915, President Woodrow Wilson and members of his cabinet and staff became, apparently, the first audience to see a movie at the White House. Wilson's reaction to the movie was the stuff of publicists' dreams: "It is like writing history with Lightning. And my only regret is that it is all so terribly true." As this unprecedented presidential blurb made its way into national circulation, a growing backlash against the film by blacks and liberal whites forced the White House to retrench. Although Wilson himself made no further public pronouncements on *Birth of a Nation*, his close aide Joseph P. Tumulty repudiated the president's words. Wilson, Tumulty said, "has at no time expressed his approbation of [the film]. Its exhibition at the White House was a courtesy extended to an old acquaintance."

In the final year of his presidency, incapacitated by a stroke, Woodrow Wilson reportedly sought refuge in the fantasyland of motion pictures. According to press accounts in the mid-1920s, a Washington cinema manager named Robert E. Long trekked to the White House six times a week to run movies for the ailing president. The custom began on Christmas night 1919 with the film *In Old Kentucky*, projected onto a white sheet that hung in the East Room. "Amusement and relaxation were an absolute necessity," Long said in a lengthy feature story in the tabloid *New York Graphic* after Wilson's death, "and I with my moving picture machine was the means by which this amusement and relaxation were obtained through many weary months." Wilson called Long his "movie doctor," and looked forward to his daily fix of celluloid with the eagerness of a child. "In those long months Woodrow Wilson became as enthusiastic a movie fan as any romantic boy or girl," Long said. The screenings continued right up until Wilson's final day in the White House. According to Long, "We would have been there on inauguration day if the inauguration could have been delayed until afternoon."

Calvin Coolidge, despite a reputation for dourness, was another devoted fan of the silver screen who regularly screened the latest pictures at the White House. For a 1926 vacation in the Adirondacks the Vermont-born president brought along his projectionist, who showed the Coolidges three movies a week. In those pre–Air Force One days Coolidge also liked to watch films on his yacht, the *Mayflower,* and onboard the presidential train. Returning to the capital from Florida in 1929, the president kept a welcome delegation waiting twenty minutes at Union Station while he finished a western in his private railroad car.

When the Fox Theater opened as Washington's first deluxe movie house in September 1927, the Coolidges appeared as guests of honor at the opening night festivities. Occupying a flag-draped box, the president and his party watched a forgettable film with the provocative title *Paid to Love*. Preceding the feature, a newsreel showed scenes of Calvin and Grace Coolidge at the presidential man-

Eleanor Roosevelt and Shirley Temple, probably taken at Hyde Park, July 1938.
(FDR Library)

Lauren Bacall and Vice President Harry Truman at the National
Press Club, February 1945.
(Stock Montage, reprinted by permission)

Peter Lawford and brother-in-law John F. Kennedy share a smoke and a sail, 1962. (JFK Library)

President and Mrs. Kennedy with White House visitors Prince Rainier and Princess Grace, May 1961. (JFK Library)

Lady Bird Johnson welcomes Lassie to the White House for a photo-op, May 1967. (LBJ Library)

Republican convert Sammy Davis Jr. with Richard Nixon in the Oval Office, March 1973. (Nixon Presidential Materials Staff)

Richard Nixon with Karen and Richard Carpenter at the White House, August 1972. (Nixon Presidential Materials Staff)

George Harrison checks out Gerald Ford's new lapel button, December 1974. (Gerald R. Ford Library)

Willie Nelson and Emmylou Harris call on Jimmy Carter at the White House, September 1977. (Jimmy Carter Library)

President Reagan cuts in as Frank Sinatra dances with Nancy at the White House, February 1981. (Ronald Reagan Library)

Michael Jackson receives a traffic safety award from the Reagans, May 1984. (Ronald Reagan Library)

Nancy Reagan's Christmas present for Mr. T, December 1983. (Ronald Reagan Library)

Rock Hudson with the Reagans at a White House dinner, May 1984.
(Ronald Reagan Library)

President Bush and Arnold Schwarzenegger at the "Great American Workout,"
May 1990. (George Bush Library)

Dana Carvey impersonates George Bush at the White House staff Christmas party, December 1992. (George Bush Library)

James Brolin and Barbra Streisand with Bill Clinton at the White House, December 2000. (Clinton Presidential Materials Project)

sion. According to a reporter who covered the premiere, "The audience seemed highly amused at the idea, and clapped vigorously as the executive couple strolled about the White House lawn."

Presidents tend to prefer either motion pictures or music, but rarely both. Although he made frequent use of the White House screening room, Jimmy Carter's true métier was music, specifically classical music. As a midshipman at Annapolis, Carter spent much of his income on classical records. One of his joys at moving in to the White House was discovering the collection of two thousand record albums that Richard Nixon had amassed. Carter culled the fifty or so classical titles and had them piped into his study eight to ten hours a day.

Harry Truman shared Carter's love of classical music. A talented pianist, Truman often relaxed at the keyboard of the White House Steinway, sometimes playing for an hour at a time. One song President Truman did not care for was the "Missouri Waltz," a number much performed during his presidency. "I don't give a damn about it," Truman confided to bandleader Guy Lombardo. "But I can't say that out loud, because it's the song of Missouri. It's as bad as 'The Star-Spangled Banner' so far as music is concerned."

In his younger days Truman had been an ardent fan of vaudeville; in order to catch the shows for free he took a job ushering at Kansas City's Grand Theater. Among his favorites were comedy acts like the Marx Brothers and Charles Chaplin. Though he later became friendly with the Marxes, Truman developed mixed feelings about Chaplin. "In my opinion, he is one of the greatest comedians the movies ever had," Truman wrote in a 1957 letter, "and I am very sorry that he has assumed such an attitude toward the country that recognized his talent and gave him success." The former president expressed disapproval of Chaplin's personal morality: "I think very little of any man who cannot remain loyal to the woman who shared his early, unsuccessful years." The letter ended with a handwritten postscript from Harry Truman, film critic: "When a good comedian tries to turn tragedian he usually ends in the ditch!"

Like Truman, Richard Nixon was a music president, not a movie president. Also like Truman, Nixon played piano. Nixon considered the piano a means of expression "even more fulfilling than writing or speaking," and lauded his childhood musical training as valuable preparation for the public stage. Nixon's two great ambitions, he wrote in his memoirs, were to conduct a symphony orchestra and play organ in a cathedral.

For someone with such strongly professed urges, Richard Nixon's musical tastes were decidedly middlebrow. A list of songs he wanted performed at his funeral included "California, Here I Come"—"played softly and slowly." The day after Nixon won election to the White House in 1968 he listened to a recording of Richard Rodgers's "Victory at Sea." "I put it on and turned the volume up high," he said. "My thoughts meshed with the music. The battle had been long and arduous. We had suffered reverses and won victories. The struggle had been hard fought. But now we had won the final victory. The music captured the moment for me better than anything I could say or think or write." Four years later, on Election Day 1972, President Nixon repeated the ritual.

Although he grew up in the shadow of Hollywood and personally knew many of the great film stars of his day, Nixon displayed a distinct ambivalence toward the movies. His public pronouncements were glowingly positive. "Our whole family has always loved theatre, movies, and music," he wrote in his memoirs. "Our favorite relaxation after dinner at Camp David or in Florida or California was to watch a movie. Sometimes we would experiment with films we had never heard of; sometimes we would choose current hits; and sometimes old family favorites." In 1972 Nixon told an audience of actors that the White House screening room was one of the reasons he had decided to run for reelection.

But Hollywood's creative output seemed to perturb Nixon as much as please him. The president reserved special contempt for the TV comedy *All in the Family,* which became an American phenomenon after its 1971 debut. In a tape-recorded conversation with his top White House aides, President Nixon railed against the series, claiming that the son-in-law, played by Rob Reiner, was bisexual and that another character was "obviously queer" because he wore an ascot. "You know what happened to the Greeks," Nixon warned. "Homosexuality destroyed them."

Nixon's preferred film fare was of the patently macho variety. After seeing the John Wayne picture *Chisum* in 1970, Nixon mused to reporters about the enduring appeal of westerns: "Perhaps one of the reasons—and this may be a square observation—the good guys come out ahead in the westerns, the bad guys lose." Another John Wayne film, *True Grit,* prompted Nixon to write the star a fan letter.

It was the World War II epic *Patton,* with George C. Scott in the title role, that truly spoke to Richard Nixon. He first saw the film on April Fool's Day 1970, then watched it again on April 25, five days before sending American troops into Cambodia. There were other screenings as well, sometimes with aides and sometimes alone. Although Nixon denied that *Patton* affected his military decisionmaking, those around him got used to hearing the president draw parallels between scenes in the film and the situation in Vietnam.

✷✷✷✷

The remaining casual fans on the list displayed varying degrees of enthusiasm for American pop culture. Like Jimmy Carter, military man Dwight Eisenhower spent much of his life in settings devoid of the ready entertainments of civilian life. Shortly after Eisenhower took office, the conductor of the National Symphony asked the new president what kind of music he enjoyed. "Do you know anything by Lawrence Welk?" Eisenhower responded, then added that he also liked "a good bass voice." One of the General's favorite songs was "Beer Barrel Polka"; he was also "very much touched" by Eddie Fisher's rendition of "Counting Your Blessings."

Once in office, Eisenhower gained more exposure to show business than he ever had during his military career. Like virtually all their fellow Americans, Ike and Mamie Eisenhower got caught up in the TV craze of the 1950s. "I soon discovered that the new vogue for television dictated certain aspects of life in the Eisenhower White House," wrote J. B. West in his memoir of his life as chief White House usher. The Eisenhowers enjoyed a number of the popular shows of the era, including *I Love Lucy*, Arthur Godfrey's *Talent Scouts*, and *The Fred Waring Show*. The couple would watch the evening news while eating dinner on TV trays, sometimes with Mamie's mother as company.

Like most first families, the Eisenhowers held regular movie screenings at the White House. The president's favorites were westerns, not a surprising choice for this son of the prairie. "Providing Mr. Eisenhower with enough Westerns became a major task for the Usher's office," said J.B. West, "because he'd seen them all, perhaps three or four times." When Nikita Khrushchev came to America in 1959, Eisenhower told the Soviet leader of his affection for the genre: "I know they don't have any substance to them and don't require any thought to appreciate, but they always have a lot of fancy tricks. Also, I like the horses."

Like Presidents Truman and Nixon, the first George Bush exhibited a stronger affinity for music than movies. His country-western fixation notwithstanding, Bush seemed most at home with Broadway show tunes and light classical music. Bush's father, Senator Prescott Bush of Connecticut, had been a talented vocalist who performed with the Yale Glee Club and the Whiffenpoofs, and he encouraged his sons to sing harmony together. One of George Bush's brothers, Jonathan, had a brief career on the musical comedy stage; in 1962 *Variety* ran a story about Jonathan Bush's plan to mount a revival of the blackface minstrel shows of the vaudeville era, a production that never materialized.

As president, George Bush became wildly enamored of an off-Broadway musical revue called *Forever Plaid*, a spoof of the squeaky-clean, ultra-preppy male quartets of the 1950s. After seeing the show at Ford's Theater in Washington in 1991, George and Barbara Bush invited the cast to the White House to perform in the East Room for cabinet members and their spouses. A few weeks later the Bushes brought the singers to their summer home in Kennebunkport, Maine, to entertain British Prime Minister John Major, an event for which the quartet custom-prepared a harmonic rendition of "God Save the Queen." All told, President Bush took in *Forever Plaid* five times. "Bush was much sharper and hipper than I expected," said Stuart Ross, who wrote and directed the revue. "He got all the jokes in the show."

After seeing an advertisement on CNN, George Bush once ordered a collection of Anne Murray songs by dialing the toll-free number. When Murray learned of this, she sent Bush more of her albums ("the ones he couldn't get on CNN") and invited him to a concert she was giving in Washington. Bush attended and met the singer backstage at intermission. But as Barbara Bush confessed to a reporter, the White House was as likely to be filled with the voice of Leontyne Price as the country-pop sounds of Anne Murray.

It goes without saying that Bush's predecessor, Ronald Reagan, was a movie president in every sense of the term. So why does Reagan belong in the ranks of presidents who were casual fans? As someone who spent much of his adult life working at film studios he had no cause to romanticize movies the way aficionados like Roosevelt, Kennedy, and Clinton did. For him motion pictures and their stars were facts of life, not something to moon over. Reagan did not even bother to keep up with the latest celebrities. According to Nancy Reagan, her husband failed to recognize the already world-famous Marilyn Monroe at Chasen's one night in the 1950s. "Who was that beautiful girl everyone was fussing over?" he asked Nancy on the drive home.

As a boy, "Dutch" Reagan had immersed himself in the limited entertainments of his provincial Midwestern world, including the amateur theatricals that were a family specialty. The first two decades of Ronald Reagan's life coincided with the short-lived era of silent film, and, like Jack Kennedy, young Reagan enjoyed the pretalkie westerns of Tom Mix. In his autobiography, *Where's the Rest of Me?*, Reagan wrote that his father had refused to let his sons see *Birth of a Nation* when it played in their Illinois hometown because of its racism. Considering that little "Dutch" would have been all of four years old at the time of the film's release, this claim seems dubious.

When Reagan entered politics as a conservative in the 1960s, he positioned himself as an opponent of changing mores in Hollywood films. "What writing does it take to simply have two people undress and get into bed?" he complained to a *Los Angeles Times* interviewer in 1969. "Call me a square if you want to, but I think the business has degenerated." Asked which recent films he had seen, Reagan named *Camelot, Oliver!, True Grit*, and *Gone with the Wind*—defiantly retrogressive choices at a moment of great creative ferment among Hollywood filmmakers.

After the Reagans got to the White House they were as likely to view vintage films as the latest releases. Still, during their first year in Washington they took in such newer titles as *Chariots of Fire, Gallipoli, Breaker Morant, The French Lieutenant's Woman,* and *Continental Divide.* Asked whether she had any interest in screening *Mommie Dearest,* based on the best-selling memoir by Joan Crawford's daughter, Nancy replied, "No, I don't want to see that one."

Other contemporary pictures the Reagans watched at either Camp David or the White House included *The Flamingo Kid, Places in the Heart, The Purple Rose of Cairo,* and *Witness.* One movie the Reagans did not finish was *Kiss of the Spider Woman,* recommended by media adviser Michael Deaver. The film, which dealt with the relationship between a political radical and a transvestite who share a jail cell, had drawn critical praise and won a Best Actor Oscar for William Hurt. Deaver recounted Mrs. Reagan's reaction:

"Mike," she almost gasped, "how could you recommend that film? It was dreadful. We turned it off halfway through the reel." "Once you get past the subject," I said, "it was an incredible picture." She shuddered slightly. "How can you get past that?" she asked.

One of the most unlikely White House screenings of the Reagan presidency occurred in December 1981 when Warren Beatty showed *Reds,* his biographical film about the life of John Reed, an American journalist inspired by the Russian Revolution. Included in the party were Beatty's costar Diane Keaton and a decidedly nonradical array of Reagan friends from California: Cary Grant, Douglas Fairbanks Jr., Audrey Meadows, Bonita Granville Wrather, and two dozen others. The famously anti-Soviet president joked that he was not showing *Reds*—"I look at it as showing *up* the Reds."

Apart from movies, the Reagans occasionally enjoyed television, most notably the Sunday night series *Sixty Minutes* and *Murder She Wrote.* In 1983, the night before an international economic summit in Colonial Williamsburg, White House Chief of Staff James Baker gave the president a briefing book to study in order to prepare for the next day's meetings. In the morning Baker found the material exactly where he left it, unopened. When he asked his boss why the book had not been cracked, Reagan gave a straightforward answer: "Well, Jim, *The Sound of Music* was on last night."

✣✣✣✣

What of the nonfans among presidents? On the list of modern chief executives this description applies to three men: Lyndon Johnson, Gerald Ford, and George W. Bush. Though Johnson enjoyed dancing, he was known to either talk or fall asleep during movie screenings at the White House. Watching *Guess Who's Coming to Dinner*, the 1967 drama about an interracial romance, LBJ joked that the love scenes between Sidney Poitier and Katharine Houghton were causing his brother, Sam Houston, to squirm "just like Spencer Tracy." Johnson's film preferences ran toward John Wayne pictures; the experimental movies of the late 1960s baffled him. Shortly after leaving office LBJ saw *The Graduate* with assistant and future historian Doris Kearns. "How in the hell can that creepy guy (Dustin Hoffman) be a hero to you?" Johnson asked. "If that's an example of what love seems like to your generation, then we're all in big trouble."

Two other anecdotes demonstrate Johnson's lack of fervor for sitting in the audience. After the inaugural gala for John F. Kennedy in 1961, with its roster of legends like Sinatra, Ella Fitzgerald, Nat King Cole, and Laurence Olivier, television host Jack Paar asked LBJ if he had enjoyed the show. Johnson's chilly reply: "It was too long." Several years later, in a conversation with an old friend from Texas, LBJ allowed as how he did not want to attend the Gridiron revue, the annual production staged by the Washington press corps in honor of the president. "I don't like shows," Johnson said. "I don't even like Bob Hope. I went out to hear him the other night. I wanted to go to bed . . . "

Gerald Ford did not display the outright antipathy of Lyndon Johnson toward the performing arts, but neither did he have much appreciation of them. "I've known Jerry Ford since 1946," the longtime music critic at Ford's hometown newspaper said in 1975. "Based on my observation, I think he's shown less interest in the arts than any person of similar stature that I've ever known." Ford recognized his tin ear for entertainment, joking that "Betty says I can't even listen on key."

What Ford did enjoy was dancing, specifically to the big band music of his youth. Despite a reputation as a world-class klutz, the former athlete had no difficulty circumnavigating a dance floor—as long as the music was right. Betty Ford recalled a state dinner at which her husband grew frustrated at the orchestra's selections. "If they won't play some music I can dance to, I'm just not gonna come to these things any more," the president fumed, much to Betty's amusement. Still sulking at the end of the evening, Ford raised the subject again: "Now listen—I'm the president of the United States, and I should be able to have some music I can dance to."

The final nonfan on the list, George W. Bush, is perhaps the least culturally attuned chief executive in modern history. As a presidential candidate Bush had never heard of Leonardo diCaprio, whose 1997 film *Titanic* made the young actor one of the best-known celebrities on the planet. Asked about *Sex in the City*, the hit television show about single women in New York City, Bush bristled, misunderstanding the nature of the question. He dismissed a reporter's query about Madonna, saying, "I'm not into pop music." As his favorite musicians, Bush cited the Everly Brothers and Buddy Holly, acts from forty years prior.

Bush has displayed more interest in comedy. In his first week at the White House he watched—and reportedly enjoyed—the Fox TV special *Stupid Behavior Caught on Tape*. And he is an enthusiastic fan of the Austin Powers films, lines from which he has quoted when talking to reporters.

White House screenings during the George W. Bush administration have been relatively sparse. Bush invited members of the Kennedy family to watch *Thirteen Days*, a film about the Cuban missile crisis, and Mel Gibson showed his Vietnam War movie *We Were Soldiers* to an audience that included the president and top aides. Bush, a former owner of the Texas Rangers baseball team, also saw *The Rookie*, a Disney picture about a middle-aged high school teacher who becomes a major league pitcher, and the 2003 racehorse film *Seabiscuit*.

Apart from obligatory appearances at events like the Kennedy Center Honors, Bush has shown little inclination to partake of the cultural life of Washington, D.C. A rare exception was a "presidential gala" at Ford's Theater in March 2002, where the featured performer was the blind singer Stevie Wonder. As Wonder took a seat at the keyboard, the smiling Bush started waving at him from his front-row seat. Wonder, needless to say, did not wave back, and when Bush realized his faux pas, he slowly returned his hand to his lap.

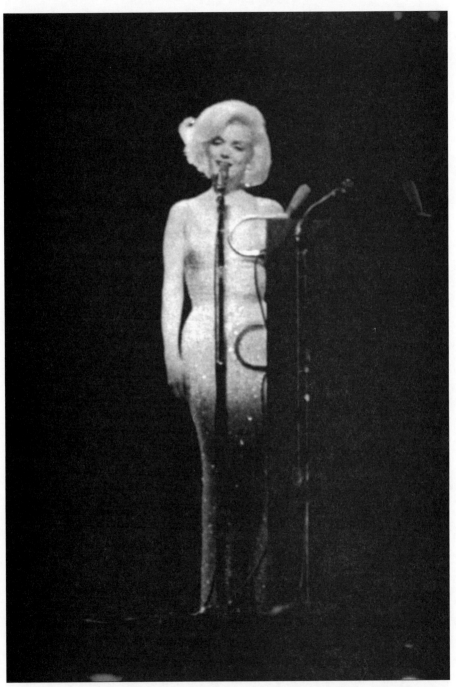

Marilyn Monroe serenades JFK at Madison Square Garden, May 1962.
(JFK Library)

8

✼✼✼✼

"Happy Birthday, Mr. President"

ENTERTAINERS
AS FRIENDS AND LOVERS

H E WAS A CIVILIAN, not a movie star, but instinctively the Hollywood pros
recognized him as one of their own. When screen siren Gene Tierney first
glimpsed twenty-nine-year-old John F. Kennedy on a soundstage at Twentieth
Century Fox, she found herself "staring into what I thought were the most perfect blue eyes I had ever seen on a man." The scene played like something from
one of Tierney's movies: the glamorous actress, hard at work on the set of her
new picture, and the handsome visitor to the set, just back from the war, still
wearing the uniform of his country. "My reaction was right out of a ladies' romance novel," Tierney recalled in her memoir. "Literally, my heart skipped."

The meeting between JFK and Gene Tierney turned out to be the one memorable thing about *Dragonwyck*, a 1946 gothic thriller about strange doings
among the Dutch patroons of the Hudson River. Tierney stands as Jack
Kennedy's most intriguing—though hardly his only—Hollywood romance, even
if she is not remembered as such. In the pantheon of twentieth-century celebrity
it is Kennedy and Marilyn Monroe who are forever linked. But the more substantial affair was with the green-eyed goddess who played the mysterious murder victim in *Laura* and the jealous enchantress in *Leave Her to Heaven*, a
performance that earned Tierney an Oscar nomination. Unlike Monroe, Gene

Tierney came from Kennedy's social class. Raised in New York and educated in Switzerland, she lived a life that in many ways paralleled that of Jack Kennedy and his siblings. Both families were well-to-do, sophisticated, and Irish Catholic. One key difference separated them: the Tierneys were Republican.

After their initial encounter at the studio Kennedy and Tierney next connected at a party at the home of Sonja Henie, the Norwegian skating star with whom JFK also had a fling. Though Tierney had arrived with a date, Kennedy talked her onto the dance floor and into his arms. "I could dance like this the rest of my life," Tierney reported him as saying. If the quote is accurate, it illustrates the degree to which Jack Kennedy had internalized the dialogue of motion pictures. Taken aback by his brashness, the twenty-five-year-old actress was nonetheless beguiled. "He had the kind of bantering, unforced Irish charm that women so often find fatal," Tierney remembered. "He asked questions about my work, the kind that revealed how well he already knew the subject."

By the time *Dragonwyck* wrapped production, the movie star and the navy lieutenant had shared a couple of dinner dates. After JFK returned east to launch his political career, he rendezvoused with Gene in New York and Washington, and the relationship grew closer. Tierney made a trip to the Capitol to watch newly elected Congressman Kennedy in action during a legislative session. When a reporter asked what she was doing in the visitors' gallery, she concocted a story about researching a part. Just at that moment Kennedy picked her out from the House floor and waved, exposing the fib.

The Hollywood beauty spent a week with Jack on Cape Cod, though she stayed with friends of her mother's and not at the Kennedy family compound. Back in California, before leaving for the Cape, she had begun a flirtation with fellow film idol Tyrone Power. "Ty was warm and considerate," Tierney said. "He had a beautiful face. But I could not fall in love with Ty Power, having met Jack Kennedy." However ardent, the romance between actress and politician was not to be. Gene Tierney was in the process of divorcing her husband, designer Oleg Cassini, and JFK's career plans precluded a serious relationship with a divorcée. When Kennedy told Tierney he could never marry her, she swallowed her pride and moved on.

After several years they ran into each other at Maxim's in Paris. Jack asked her if they should start dating again; Gene, "too crazy about him to risk renewing something that could only end by hurting us both," demurred. Six months later he wed Jacqueline Bouvier. The one-time lovers had their last meeting in September 1961, when President Kennedy invited the cast of the film *Advise and Consent* to lunch at the White House. Tierney sat next to the host, her boyfriend of fifteen years earlier; elsewhere in the room sat her new husband, a Texas oilman. She presumably did not tell Kennedy that she had cast her ballot for Richard Nixon.

JFK's romance with Gene Tierney was not his first show business affair, and it would not be his last. From Kennedy's initial trip to Los Angeles as an adolescent through the last months of his life, he was irresistibly drawn by the allure of Southern California's female flesh. "I've met this extra in Hollywood that is the best looking thing I have ever seen," the teenage Jack wrote a friend in 1936. "Will show you her picture when I get in." He signed his letter: "The extra's delight or how I got my tail in Hollywood."

In 1940 Kennedy made his second excursion to L.A., this time as a minor celebrity. The twenty-three-year-old son of America's ambassador to Great Britain, Kennedy was also the best-selling author of *Why England Slept*, and his social standing in the movie colony rose accordingly. He now hobnobbed with Spencer Tracy, "who I was very much at ease with," and Clark Gable, with whom "there were several long silent periods" in the conversation.

During this extended visit to Los Angeles Kennedy became friendly with Robert Stack, the male ingenue best known at that point for giving Deanna Durbin her first screen kiss. Stack and his friends shared a hideaway in the Hollywood Hills where the featured attraction was the Flag Room, a closet-sized space containing a bed and flags from around the world affixed to the walls and ceiling. The objective was to bring an attractive young woman to the room and require her to memorize the flags and their countries—or pay a penalty. "Since she was already in a horizontal position," Stack said, "paying the penalty was usually no problem." Jack Kennedy became a regular visitor and, according to Stack, "found occasion to further his geopolitical studies and gain future constituents at our little pad."

At the end of World War II JFK returned to Hollywood, intent on "knocking a name," as the young naval hero told a friend. His success was mixed. When Kennedy met Olivia de Havilland at a party, he pounced. "He leaned toward her and fixed her with a stare and he was working just as hard as he could, really boring in," said Chuck Spalding, a longtime JFK friend who attended the party with him. But de Havilland had another date lined up and would not change her plans. When the defeated Kennedy turned to take his leave, he opened the wrong door; instead of the exit he walked straight into a hall closet, bringing tennis rackets and balls crashing down on his head.

JFK had better luck with Sonja Henie. In 1946 Kennedy bragged to a friend that he had gone to bed with the ice-skating blonde, who was five years his senior. There were other actresses in Kennedy's life. Around the time he was seeing Gene Tierney, gossip columnists linked the future president to British starlet Peggy Cummins. Angela Greene, who played Tess Trueheart in the short-lived TV series *Dick Tracy*, was another Kennedy girlfriend in the 1940s. June Allyson, at that point a low-level contract player for MGM, also briefly dated JFK, though at first she did not know who he was. "My impression was that he was under contract to Metro or wanted to be," she said. "We had seen each other around the studio and one day he asked me to dinner and took me to a nice place. It wasn't even Dutch treat."

Other female celebrities claimed connections to Kennedy in the late 1940s and early 1950s, including Zsa Zsa Gabor and Hedy Lamarr. Lamarr wrote in her autobiography that she went out with Kennedy in Paris after the war, and that he surprised her with a bag of oranges, then in short supply. Gabor described her relationship with Congressman JFK as nonsexual. "He slept with almost all my girlfriends, but with me he had some respect," Gabor said. "I was his favorite date—he never once asked to sleep with me."

After his marriage in 1953 John F. Kennedy became more circumspect toward the glamour girls of Hollywood, though he never fully relinquished his bachelor habits. "Jack would ask me endless questions about the 'availability' of this or that star, availability not in the emotional but the logistical sense," said Gore Vidal, who shared a stepfather with Jacqueline Kennedy. "Since my own approach to sex was not unlike Jack's, I have never been as shocked as people still appear to be by his promiscuity."

Kennedy's chief source of playmates in the movie business was Peter Lawford. Patricia Seaton Lawford, the actor's last wife, called her husband "the procurer of women for his brother-in-law." Lawford, she said, saw it as "a duty he felt someone had to fulfill." Lawford provided cover for JFK; as a professional entertainer, he could be seen in the company of beautiful stars without raising suspicions. According to Sammy Davis Jr., when Kennedy visited the Lawfords at their home in Santa Monica it was not unusual to find "three or four chicks running around" waiting for the president to arrive. "Did I see them humping?" Davis asked. "No, I did not. Did I see them kissing on the lips? No, I did not. But I also know they ain't there to play shuffleboard."

During his years in the White House a number of prominent actresses were said to be involved with the president. Angie Dickinson is widely assumed to have had an affair with JFK, although she has never publicly confirmed it. Dickinson met Kennedy around 1960 and attended his 1961 inaugural as the "date" of his navy buddy Red Fay. According to JFK biographer Richard Reeves, Kennedy and Dickinson "slipped away to private rooms a couple of times during the ceremonies." In the 1980s the actress signed a contract to write her memoirs but ended up backing out of the deal. Dickinson and her publisher reportedly disagreed over how she would approach her relationship with the president. "They'll say (the affair) happened forever, no matter what I say," Dickinson told a journalist in 1989. "But whether I had an affair with him or not, I wouldn't say it then, and I certainly wouldn't wait twenty-five years to say it. I have too much respect for the Kennedy family."

Blonde bombshell Jayne Mansfield was also on the list of rumored presidential paramours. Raymond Strait, Mansfield's confidante and biographer, said he had personal knowledge of two assignations between the president and the actress in the early 1960s. "She told me that it had been no big affair," Strait said. "She had liked and respected him, and they just happened to have shared a mutual physical attraction." Stripper Tempest Storm likewise claimed to have had sexual relations with JFK.

One of the more astonishing tales of Kennedy and the women of show business involves Marlene Dietrich, whom the adolescent JFK first met during a family vacation in the South of France in the late 1930s. Dietrich described to British writer Kenneth Tynan a quick physical encounter with the president one year before his assassination. Invited to the White House for drinks, the German star soon found herself in Kennedy's boudoir. In his *Diaries* Tynan quotes Dietrich's account of what happened:

> I remembered about his bad back—that wartime injury. I looked at him and he was already undressing. He was unwinding rolls of bandage from around his middle—he looked like Laocoon and that snake, you know? Now I'm an old lady, and I said to myself, I'd like to sleep with the president, sure, but I'll be goddammed if I'm going to be on top!
>
> But it seems everything was OK; J.F.K. took the superior position; and it was all over sweetly and very soon.
>
> Before Marlene Dietrich left, Kennedy had a final question for her: "Did you ever make it with my father?" When she responded in the negative, he seemed pleased: "Well, that's one place I'm in first."

At the time of this alleged encounter Kennedy was forty-five years old and Dietrich in her early sixties.

Any discussion of John F. Kennedy and his celebrity conquests must also take note of the women he unsuccessfully attempted to seduce. In the late 1950s, during the filming in Washington of the romantic comedy *Houseboat*, Senator Kennedy hit on Sophia Loren at an Italian embassy party. Loren, then secretly married to producer Carlo Ponti, brushed him aside. Kennedy similarly struck out with British brunette Jean Simmons, who around 1957 was shooting on location in Boston. According to Simmons's husband, actor Stewart Granger, JFK "wooed her with flowers and eventually ended up practically breaking down her bedroom door." Simmons teased her husband that "he was so attractive and had such a lovely smile I nearly let him in." In 1963 singer Edie Adams performed for President Kennedy at the White House correspondents dinner in Washington. After the show one of the event's organizers, a leading Washington journalist, informed Adams that Kennedy wanted to meet her for a private drink. "In Hollywood we'd heard all the rumors, so it took me only a little while to figure out what he meant," Adams said. "I may be the only shapely blond female then between the ages of fifteen and forty-five who said no to JFK, but it wasn't because I wasn't asked."

President Kennedy did not make a pass at Ann-Margret after she sang at his birthday gala in New York in 1963. At a postshow party at Ambassador Kennedy's apartment in the Carlyle Hotel, JFK impressed the young star with his knowledge of her career and background, as he had impressed so many other entertainers. The president and his brother Bobby persuaded Ann-Margret to lead the room in a round of "Bye, Bye, Blackbird," which she agreed to perform only if everyone else would sing along. Just as the party was going strong, Ann-Margret excused herself; she had to catch an early flight to Los Angeles the next day, and business was business. "He was nothing but correct to me," she said of her meeting with Kennedy. "And very charming!"

Eddie Fisher, then involved with Ann-Margret and fully aware of JFK's reputation, had forbidden his girlfriend to attend the party. "If you go, we're through," he told her, then relented when he realized the ridiculousness of the demand—how could anyone turn down an invitation from the president? "But I insisted on taking her to the hotel in my limousine and waiting for her to come out," Fisher wrote in his autobiography.

Another star Kennedy apparently did not pursue was Grace Kelly, though their paths crossed on various occasions. Their initial encounter took place under circumstances straight out of a French farce: when Jack was in a New York hospital with back problems, Jacqueline Kennedy and her sister, Lee, talked the actress into visiting his hospital room disguised as the new night nurse. "I was terribly embarrassed," Princess Grace recalled in an oral history for the Kennedy Library. "Eventually I was sort of pushed into the room by the two girls. I introduced myself, but he had recognized me at once and couldn't have been sweeter or more quick to put me at ease."

According to Gore Vidal, when Jack and Jackie saw press photos from Grace Kelly's wedding to Prince Rainier, Kennedy made his wife cry by commenting, "*I* could have married her!" Indeed Jacqueline Kennedy seemed touchy on the subject of Princess Grace. When Grace and Rainier visited Washington in May 1961 the first lady demoted them from a White House dinner dance to a brief, informal luncheon. Social secretary Letitia Baldrige wrote that Princess Grace "stood close to the president and gazed at him with adoring eyes. She looked like a teenybopper up close to her favorite rock star."

✳✳✳✳

What, beyond pure conjecture, can be said about John F. Kennedy and Marilyn Monroe? The facts seem scarcely to matter at this point; instead it is the myth that prevails, fueled by a glorious few minutes of film footage in which the sexy star serenades the sexy president with the most erotic rendition of "Happy Birthday" ever delivered. The transcendence of the moment defies rational analysis. Together JFK and Marilyn—two comets hurtling toward a premature flameout—form a potent image of sex and death and glamour that has seared itself into the American psyche.

Part of what keeps the myth alive is that its details remain forever unknowable. In a culture in which the intimate behavior of celebrities is trumpeted throughout the land, the inside scoop on Jack and Marilyn stays tantalizingly out of reach. It is difficult even to arrive at a general chronology of their meetings. Joan and Clay Blair, who probed the early life of John F. Kennedy for their book *In Search of JFK*, believe the two were introduced by Charles Feldman, a high-powered Hollywood agent who sometimes played host to Kennedy on his trips to Los Angeles in the 1950s. James Spada, a biographer of Peter Lawford, dates the introduction to the summer of 1954 at a party at Feldman's attended by both Jack and Jackie Kennedy and Marilyn and her husband, Joe DiMaggio. It seems probable that Kennedy would have met

Marilyn Monroe through the Lawfords on additional occasions before he reached the White House, though no specific documentation of such meetings is known to exist.

As president, JFK had only four recorded face-to-face encounters with Monroe, all within the space of a year and a half. The first was a party in Kennedy's honor at the Lawford home in Santa Monica in October 1961, an event at which Monroe's competition included Angie Dickinson, Janet Leigh, and Kim Novak. The second was a dinner party in New York City in February 1962 given by socialite Fifi Fell. The third meeting took place at the Palm Springs home of Bing Crosby, where on the night of Saturday, March 24, 1962, both Jack and Marilyn were overnight guests. Marilyn is said to have placed a phone call to a friend from the bedroom she and the president shared.

The couple's last public appearance together was at the Madison Square Garden birthday show in May 1962. Defying the wishes of her studio, Marilyn Monroe left the picture she was shooting—*Something's Gotta Give*, costarring Dean Martin—and flew to New York with Peter Lawford. Ever the loyal supporter, Monroe purchased a $1,000 ticket for the fund-raiser, despite her status as a participant. The prospect of performing left Monroe a nervous wreck; as a film actress she had little experience in front of live audiences, and even for seasoned stage performers an appearance before the president was a high-stress gig. The evening before the show, Marilyn spent several hours practicing with the event's producer, Broadway composer Richard Adler, singing "Happy Birthday" over and over in her New York apartment.

Onstage at Madison Square Garden Peter Lawford introduced Monroe three times before she actually walked out—"the late Marilyn Monroe," as Lawford joked. In a dress famously described by Adlai Stevenson as "skin and beads," Monroe tremulously delivered her song. *Time* magazine reporter Hugh Sidey, covering the event for the press pool, studied the president's face as Marilyn sang. "It was quite a sight to behold," Sidey said, "and if I ever saw an appreciation of feminine beauty in the eyes of a man, it was in John F. Kennedy's eyes at that moment." When it came time to thank the performers, the guest of honor had his quip ready: "I can now retire after having had 'Happy Birthday' sung to me in such a sweet, wholesome way."

A reception followed the gala at the home of film producer Arthur Krim. Kennedy showed up, as did Marilyn and other performers from the show, including Maria Callas, Jimmy Durante, Shirley MacLaine, and Diahann Carroll.

One person not present at either event was the first lady of the United States. "This was just the sort of vulgar display that Jackie detested, and she refused to attend," her cousin, John H. Davis, said in his biography of the Kennedys. Instead Jacqueline Kennedy spent the day competing in a horse show in the Virginia hunt country. She won a third-place prize.

Two and a half months later, Marilyn Monroe died of a drug overdose in Los Angeles. She was thirty-six years old.

✳✳✳✳

JFK's prodigious record of romantic liaisons with entertainers stands in a class by itself. Today's increased levels of media scrutiny would make it impossible for any modern president to get away with what Kennedy did, as the example of Bill Clinton all too clearly demonstrates. Even an unmarried chief executive, like the one played by Michael Douglas in the 1995 film *An American President*, would be hard-pressed to date a celebrity. As Douglas's character learned, dating a noncelebrity was challenge enough.

Presidential candidates, on the other hand, have been more likely than presidents to form romantic attachments to professional entertainers. In the 1950s Adlai Stevenson cast a magnetic spell on the liberal ladies of Hollywood, who vied with one another for his attention. Lauren Bacall led the pack, becoming so attached to him that she began to fantasize about being his surrogate wife. Though happily married to Humphrey Bogart and the mother of two small children, Bacall was smitten with Stevenson's intelligence. "He offered me a mentality that encompassed not just his world or my world, but all the world," she wrote. "That had never been offered before."

Stevenson held similar appeal for other glamour gals of show business. As Bacall put it, "This man was not anyone's notion of a Don Juan, no sex symbol, not a seducer, yet he was capable of dangling so many ladies, keeping them interested, grateful for his time, and each thinking that she was the One." Visiting Bacall on a film set, Marlene Dietrich lamented that Stevenson had not telephoned and asked if Bacall would intercede on her behalf. "Of course," Bacall replied, intending no such action.

Myrna Loy's crush was equally profound. "To me he was the sun, moon, and stars," Loy said, though she also considered him "a great tease." While serving as Kennedy's ambassador to the United Nations, Adlai Stevenson dated actress Joan

Fontaine, but ended the relationship by telling her he could never marry an actress. "It's just as well," the offended Fontaine replied. "My family would hardly approve of my marrying a politician."

One Hollywood female who did not fall for Stevenson was Shirley Temple. They met on a train traveling west from Washington after the 1949 inaugural of Harry Truman. Stevenson, then governor of Illinois, learned that the twenty-year-old Temple was onboard and invited her into his private rail car. According to Shirley, the governor started to grill her "like a prosecuting attorney," demanding that she tell him everything she knew about the movie industry in one minute. As she sipped on a bourbon and cola, the former child star did her best to discourse on the effect of television on the feature film business. When Stevenson's wife tried to change the subject, he snapped at her: "This is the first time I have met Shirley. I can look at you anytime."

Republican presidential candidate Thomas Dewey had a serious relationship with singer-actress Kitty Carlisle, to whom he unsuccessfully proposed marriage. Despite their closeness the couple did not share a common politics. "He never asked me if I had voted for him—which I hadn't—but once in a while, when I looked at him, the thought intrigued me that this man had come within a whisker of being president of the United States," Carlisle said.

In more recent decades presidential candidates Jerry Brown and Bob Kerrey both dated entertainment celebrities, placing them squarely under the media microscope. Brown, the one-time governor of California, took a highly publicized African vacation with Linda Ronstadt in 1979. Kerrey, then governor of Nebraska, met Debra Winger when she came to Lincoln to shoot the film *Terms of Endearment* in the early 1980s. Polls taken at the time found that 76 percent of Nebraska voters did not object to the actress's overnight stays at the governor's mansion; another 12 percent said it was nobody's business. The Kerrey-Winger relationship endured off and on for several years, and the couple have since maintained a close friendship.

Brown and Kerrey were single when they dated entertainers. Lyndon Johnson, by contrast, had an extramarital affair with Helen Gahagan Douglas, the California actress-turned-legislator, when both served as members of Congress in the 1940s. Douglas, married to MGM leading man Melvyn Douglas, remained friendly with LBJ for the next two decades, and in 1964 traveled to Africa as the president's representative at a hundredth-anniversary observation of U.S.-Liberian relations. Johnson gave Helen only four days' notice for the trip, teasing her in a phone call that that was "four days more notice than I usually give you." As the war in Vietnam dragged on, both Helen and Melvyn Douglas fell out with President Johnson; the last time Helen saw LBJ he refused to speak to her.

Ronald Reagan is another president with romantic ties to entertainers, albeit in his pre-presidential incarnation as a film star. As a Hollywood newcomer Reagan went on a studio-arranged date with eighteen-year-old Lana Turner, escorting her to the premiere of the Warner Bros. film *Jezebel*. "She was very young and very beautiful and we were both very scared—she in a gown borrowed from wardrobe, and I in a dinner jacket from the same place," Reagan remembered. Too nervous to drive the new Nash convertible he had bought after signing with the studio, the actor took his date to the premiere in a taxi.

Reagan's 1940 marriage to fellow Warners player Jane Wyman provided ample fodder for the movie magazines, which invariably depicted the newlyweds as a wholesome, all-American family. A Warner Bros. press release from 1941 quoted Reagan on his home life: "We do the same foolish things that other couples do, have the same scraps, about as much fun, typical problems, and the most wonderful baby in the world." But wedded bliss gave way to Hollywood reality: one partner's career took off while the other's stagnated.

By late 1947, amid reports that the couple had separated, Reagan angrily defended his marriage to gossip columnist Hedda Hopper: "We had a tiff. That's right. But we've had tiffs before, as what couple married eight years hasn't? But I expect when Jane gets back from New York we'll get back together all right." Reagan told Hopper that "the bad part of Hollywood is that you have to live your life in a goldfish bowl—and what you see in a goldfish bowl is too often distorted." Distorted or not, Reagan and Wyman soon called it quits. When Jane Wyman won an Academy Award as Best Actress for the film *Johnny Belinda* in 1948, she took as her date costar Lew Ayres; Reagan attended the ceremony alone. Discussing the divorce with Hedda Hopper, Ronald Reagan quipped, "I think I'll name Johnny Belinda as the co-respondent." But behind the joke lay genuine sadness.

After his divorce Reagan embarked on a series of casual relationships before settling down with Nancy Davis, the starlet who became his second wife in 1952. Among Reagan's girlfriends between marriages was Doris Day, his costar in the 1950 film *Storm Warning* (she played his wife in the 1952 baseball movie *The Winning Team*). "There were two things about Ronnie that impressed me," Day said, "how much he liked to dance and how much he liked to talk." Doris, whose left-of-center politics synchronized with Reagan's at that point, told him he should go on a lecture tour around the country, something he eventually did, preaching a far more conservative message than he had with Day.

Once Reagan married Nancy no one ever accused him of flirting with other women. A more reliable presidential tease was Gerald Ford. In November 1974, at a White House photo op for the Christmas Seals campaign, Ford made the acquaintance of honorary chairwoman Vikki Carr, the histrionic Mexican American chanteuse who enjoyed a string of hits in the late 1960s. Apparently she charmed him, because six days later the president brought her back to entertain the chancellor of Austria at a state dinner. Dressed in a chiffon gown with a neckline described by the first lady as "nonexistent," Vikki Carr kicked off her set with the provocative number "One Hell of a Woman." At the end of the evening, within earshot of reporters, the singer invited Ford to her home in Los Angeles for a home-cooked, south-of-the-border meal. "What's your favorite Mexican dish?" she asked. "You!" replied Ford, to which Carr rejoined, "Is that a la carte?" In his memoir Ford recalled the moment: "Betty overheard the exchange, and needless to say, she wasn't wild about it." According to press secretary Ron Nessen, Mrs. Ford later vowed, "That woman will never get into the White House again. She was too familiar with my husband."

By all accounts Ford had a well-developed eye for beautiful women. Former Miss America Phyllis George, then a CBS sportscaster, used her feminine wiles to wangle an interview with the president about his days as a football player. Before George and her crew arrived for the taping, Ford excitedly confessed to an aide that "she's awfully attractive." When Elke Sommer attended a state dinner President Ford danced several times with the sexy star, ignoring the first lady's efforts to get him on the dance floor herself. Zsa Zsa Gabor claimed that during a dance with Ford, he whispered to her, "If I weren't married, the two women I'd want to go to bed with are you and Ann-Margret." As the evening went on and Ford devoted additional attention to Gabor, Betty Ford interrupted them: "I want to remind you, Mr. President, that there are other guests in the White House, not only Zsa Zsa."

The Fords enjoyed chiding each other about their celebrity crushes. According to White House social secretary Maria Downs, "The only time (Betty Ford) became a bit miffed with me was when I told the president she had suggested Burt Reynolds' name for a guest list. He teased her unmercifully."

Even nonflirtatious presidents have their celebrity crushes. Some ten years after leaving the White House Jimmy Carter presented an award to Audrey Hepburn for her work with the United Nations children's organization UNICEF. In making the presentation, Carter confided to the audience that as a young man he did not dream of being Thomas Jefferson or Andrew Jackson. "I wanted to be Humphrey Bogart or Fred Astaire or Cary Grant, I was so filled with envy of them having kissed Audrey Hepburn." Amused by Carter's confession, Hepburn said, "I'll fix that," and rewarded him with a smooch.

✳ ✳ ✳ ✳

Friendships between presidents and celebrities are more common than romances, though equally difficult to gauge. Is the relationship based on genuine admiration or the desire for mutual advantage? Does it exist in private, apart from the glare of the press, or is it primarily a media construct? Is the attraction between individuals or complementary ideologies?

One way to consider a president/entertainer friendship is to ask whether it began before one or both parties became well-known. Celebrities typically have two sets of friends: the ones they knew before crossing the border into fame and the ones they met after. Among national leaders, the purest example of a prefame relationship exists between former Vice President Al Gore and actor Tommy Lee Jones, who were roommates at Harvard and have remained lifelong friends. The determination is less easily made for presidents who became famous relatively early in life, like Kennedy and Reagan, both of whom were nationally known figures in their twenties and had decades of direct exposure to Hollywood. Then there are the semifamous, or gradually famous, like Bill Clinton, known within political circles from a young age but neither a household nor a Hollywood name until he ran for the White House. Throughout their careers politicians who ascend to the presidency cross paths with the celebrated personalities of show business; only occasionally does the initial meeting evolve into a more serious friendship.

Franklin Roosevelt managed to maintain good relations among the performing arts community in general without becoming socially intimate with any particular entertainer. Some were closer than others—Eddie Cantor, Douglas Fairbanks Jr., and Orson Welles, for example—but most relationships between FDR and show business professionals fell under the heading of "celebrity friendships" fueled by the common denominator of fame. To some extent Roosevelt's iconic status offered the illusion of friendship more than the reality, even to individuals who held iconic status of their own.

Because he seemed so accessible, stars did not hesitate to communicate directly with FDR. Three days after the Japanese attack on Pearl Harbor Clark Gable and Carole Lombard sent a telegram to the president, whom they had met in Washington earlier in 1941. "Please know if there is anything we can do to be of any help or assistance to you that we are at your service," they wrote. A week later Roosevelt responded: "For the present, at least, I think you can both render the very highest service to the nation by continuing your professional activities. In contributing your superb talents to the production of inspirational and patriotic pictures you will help maintain the spirit and morale of the nation."

When Lombard died in a plane crash one month later, Franklin Roosevelt sent Gable a heartfelt telegram of condolence: "Mrs. Roosevelt and I are deeply distressed. Carole was our friend—our guest in happier days. She brought great joy to all who knew her and to the millions who knew her only as a great artist. She gave unselfishly of her time and talents to serve her government in peace and in war. She loved her country. She is and always will be a star—one we shall never forget nor cease to be grateful to."

Roosevelt's own death in April 1945 generated an enormous outpouring of emotion from the entertainment community, as it did from the entire nation. "To the show folks, the president was 'one of us'—not only a leader to respect but a friend to depend upon," said *Daily Variety*, expressing the general sentiment of Hollywood. News of the president's passing spread quickly through the movie studios, which sent their employees home early. In an unprecedented move the country's sixteen thousand cinemas went dark on the Saturday of Roosevelt's funeral. The radio networks paused for a full minute of silence.

Dozens of film and radio stars took to the airwaves to help Americans through their grief. Orson Welles delivered a stirring eulogy. Bing Crosby sang "Faith of Our Fathers" and "Brahms' Lullaby," and even the comedians did their part. "You know, friends, in show business we speak of a great entertainer as being a hard act to follow," said Jimmy Durante, who had performed for FDR three weeks earlier. "Mr. Roosevelt is a mighty tough act to follow."

The act that did follow, Harry Truman, lacked the psychic connection to show business of his predecessor, but in the end he developed far deeper ties to individual performers. Truman had a particular fondness for comedians, forging lasting friendships with Durante, Eddie Cantor, George Jessel, the Marx Brothers, and Jack Benny. Benny met Truman in Washington in 1945, shortly before he took office. "We sized each other up and immediately felt the flow of friendship," Benny wrote. "We had a lot in common: the same Midwestern background, the same moral values, the same small-town childhood and a similar sense of humor. We talked the same language." Truman and Benny did not stand on ceremony in their relationship and were comfortable calling each other by their first names. "I felt as though he was a guy I had grown up with," Benny said. As the years went on the two friends remembered each other on birthdays and holidays.

Truman maintained sporadic correspondence over several decades with both Groucho and Harpo Marx. In 1950 president Truman had a chance encounter with Harpo at an air base in California, where the comedian was entertaining soldiers wounded in the Korean War. Truman, on his way to Wake Island to meet General Douglas MacArthur, posed for a photograph with the silent Marx brother. Several years later, after Truman had left office, Harpo Marx mailed two copies of the picture to the ex-president, one for him to autograph and the second bearing Harpo's own inscription: "I'm just wild about Harry." In his cover letter Harpo wrote, "There's an opening for a harp and piano duet. How are you in the key of D-Flat?"

Groucho's correspondence with Truman ranged from the serious to the comedic. After *Newsweek* magazine attributed an anti-Truman one-liner to Groucho—"We wouldn't have this mess if Truman was alive"—Marx wrote the president to assure him he hadn't said it. Truman replied that he knew the crack could not have come from Groucho: "You can make much better ones than that, as I have heard you on many an occasion." In 1954, when Truman was recuperating from surgery, Groucho wished him a rapid recovery. "I think that one of these days you ought to pay a visit to the Coast," Marx wrote. "If you want to come I can put you up. I have a swimming pool and a pool table. I shoot very badly and if you are any good with the cue, you could possibly win enough to pay your expenses." In 1967 Groucho sent Truman a copy of his new book, *The Groucho Letters*. "I have been flipping through the book with a great deal of amusement," Truman said in his reply, "and plan to read it at the first opportunity." Groucho wrote back: "You said that you have been flipping through the pages with a great deal of amusement. Read it, Harry. It's full of wisdom and if you can't stand the heat in the kitchen, read it in the living room."

Dwight Eisenhower had less use for entertainers as companions, though he did play golf and bridge with Freeman Gosden, the *Amos 'n' Andy* radio star who had once performed for President Hoover. After the Eisenhowers retired to Palm Springs, Gosden took an active role in helping them relocate. Another family friend was Helen Hayes. "I felt I could unbend and forget about protocol with them," Hayes said, though she sensed a "subtle shift" in the relationship after Ike won election to the White House. A few weeks before his first inauguration Hayes paid a call on Eisenhower in Denver. "When I arrived, Ike jumped up and grabbed me in a bear hug," she said. "Instinctively I stiffened, though he had often greeted me that way in the past. He was an old and devoted friend . . . but now he was president-elect, and the old welcome seemed somehow inappropriate. He pulled back too, as if to say, 'Oops, I can't do that anymore.'"

Eisenhower took a generally dim view of show people, though he kept this sentiment under wraps. A diary entry from 1953 provides a sense of his antipathy. Decrying the high cost of motion pictures, the president blamed the extravagant salaries of "so-called stars whose qualifications were normally nothing more (in the case of women) than platinum hair and shapely legs, or men with good profiles and vibrating voices." Eisenhower added another, more scathing dig: "I have personally met a number of these people; those with whom it is a pleasure to talk informally constitute a very small portion of the whole. I think one out of ten would be an exaggeration."

Jack Kennedy held almost the opposite opinion: any star was worth talking to. But like Roosevelt, JFK extended the illusion of friendship more than the genuine article, as Frank Sinatra and Sammy Davis Jr. discovered the hard way. Kennedy enjoyed the company of entertainers, but only to a certain point. He seemed to study as much as befriend them, observing their charms and their flaws with the practiced eye of a novelist. Through a mutual friend JFK went to dinner at Gary Cooper's house in 1945 and found the actor unbelievably dull. "That's about a three-word dinner we had," Kennedy commented to his friend afterward. "Nobody said anything, and if they did, Gary said zero!"

Thanks to his father, Kennedy grew up with show people, and many of them continued to surface in later stages of Jack's life. Marion Davies, the Ziegfeld Follies chorine, film comedienne, and mistress of William Randolph Hearst, was one such celebrity. Davies attended the wedding of John F. Kennedy and Jacqueline Bouvier, and she lent the couple her home in Los Angeles for part of their honeymoon in September 1953.

During their stay at the Davies mansion, the young bride sent her hostess a thank-you note, handwritten and punctuated with an abundance of dashes: "We have just had the most perfect four days imaginable at your house—how can the rest of our lives help but be a tragic anticlimax—" The new Mrs. Kennedy told Davies that a technician from the Fox film studio had come to the house to show the visitors a newsreel of their wedding—"which Jack had him run through 4 times!"—along with a Marion Davies picture, the 1933 comedy *Going Holly-wood*. At the end of the letter JFK appended a postscript: "The house is *sensa-tional*—as we say here on the Coast. Many many thanks. Am anxious to see you when we get back as I want you to show me how to do the dance you did in *Going Hollywood*. It will insure my social success in Washington!"

In May 1963 Jacqueline Kennedy organized a surprise birthday party for her husband, and as a special treat invited British actor David Niven. The party, which took place onboard the presidential yacht *Sequoia*, was primarily a family affair, though a three-member musical combo also accompanied the revelers. When Kennedy arrived for what he thought would be a private dinner with Jacqueline, the band struck up "Happy Birthday" and the party began. "We cruised up and down the river, followed by a Secret Service launch," Niven said. "We gave presents and in the early hours of the morning played some fairly strenuous Kennedy games." As the yacht plied the waters of the Potomac, the guest of honor made several requests for the band to play Chubby Checker's "The Twist." The next morning the president showed Niven the Oval Office and let the actor try out his desk. Niven and his wife spent the rest of the weekend with the Kennedys at Camp David, where they hiked, golfed, shot skeet, and swam. Niven had neglected to bring swim trunks; according to Ben Bradlee, who was also a guest, JFK gave Niven his trunks and swam in his underwear.

John F. Kennedy's most poignant show business friendship was with Judy Garland. Their first meeting, arranged by Peter Lawford, occurred in 1954 at the postpremiere party in New York for Garland's film *A Star Is Born*. Also present were Tennessee Williams and Italian actress Anna Magnani, who played piano while Judy sang. In 1960, at the candidates' banquet the night before the Democratic National Convention in Los Angeles, Garland occupied a seat of honor between JFK and Adlai Stevenson. Because the actress was in Europe for most of the electoral season, she did not join other pro-Kennedy performers on the campaign trail, though a few weeks before the balloting she entertained American military troops at a JFK rally in Wiesbaden, Germany. On Election Day Garland attended a party in London given by the American ambassador, an Eisenhower appointee. To tweak her Republican host, Judy pinned a large Kennedy button to her dress.

Garland grew closer to JFK after the election. In April 1961 she and her husband, Sid Luft, had a private meeting with the president in the Oval Office. Garland told interviewer Jack Paar she had broken down and sobbed with pride at seeing her old friend in the White House. "It was my biggest moment, my best scene, and I blew it," she said. That summer Garland rented a beach house on Cape Cod, just down the road from the Kennedy compound. "There were so many Kennedys, they just seemed to multiply as you watched," recalled Garland's daughter, Lorna Luft. Eight-year-old Lorna was particularly intrigued by the president's hair: "He had more hair than any man I'd ever seen, and I used to stare at it and marvel at how thick it was."

Garland and Kennedy kept in regular touch throughout his presidency. She made another visit to the White House in November 1962 to discuss plans for an upcoming Democratic fund-raiser, and a week later the president and members of his family joined Garland and Burt Lancaster for a screening of their film *A Child Is Waiting*. The picture dealt with mental retardation, a subject of personal interest to the Kennedys, and its Washington premiere raised money for the family's charitable foundation.

In the summer of 1963 Garland began production on a television series for CBS, a variety program designed to showcase her formidable talents. By this point in her career the star's erratic work habits had become legendary, and the set of her TV show soon degenerated into a battlefield. When the politics grew unbearable, Garland decided to consult an expert—the president of the United States. According to Lorna Luft, "None of this seemed unusual to her. That's simply what you did when you were Judy Garland." Garland would call Kennedy at the White House and, after a brief commiseration, end the conversation by fulfilling a presidential request for a few bars of "Over the Rainbow." When *The Judy Garland Show* debuted in September, JFK sent his friend a telegram, which she proudly displayed: "Congratulations on a wonderful show last night. Know it will be a big hit in the coming season."

The assassination of John F. Kennedy two months later came as a severe blow to Judy Garland. Frantic at the news, she rushed to the home of Patricia and Peter Lawford in Santa Monica. When she left an hour later, reporters besieged her with questions. All she could say was, "It's too much, it's just too much." Garland returned home to watch TV coverage of the assassination with her children. "Every television in the house was on; even if you went into another room, you saw it," Lorna Luft recalled. CBS would not give its star time off to attend Kennedy's funeral in Washington; instead she viewed the services on television.

The network then fought her proposal to perform an hour of classic American songs in tribute to the slain president. Defying the executives, Judy Garland ended her December 13, 1963, show with a powerful rendition of "Battle Hymn of the Republic," though CBS cut the singer's dedication: "This is for you, Jack."

According to Mel Torme, Garland's music director, the performance reduced everyone in the studio to tears, even hard-bitten members of the crew. "Garland had touched a responsive chord in every man and woman in the audience that night," Torme said. "Now they rose in a body and gave her the most genuine standing ovation I have ever witnessed." At Judy Garland's funeral six years later, her own children sang "The Battle Hymn of the Republic."

Kennedy's assassination, like the death of Franklin Roosevelt, resonated deeply in the show business community. Ann-Margret, who had performed for the president at his birthday celebration six months earlier, spent hours huddled in front of the television set with Elvis Presley. "Elvis and I clung to each other, tried futilely to make sense of what had happened, and prayed for the future," she said. Veteran Hollywood journalist Army Archerd found himself at MGM studio when news broke of the shooting in Dallas. In a fascinating account in *Daily Variety*, Archerd catalogued the first reactions of some of the stars on the lot. Connie Stevens "wept openly" and received assistance from a studio doctor. Keenan Wynn worried that the killer, unknown at that point, might turn out to be an actor. Debbie Reynolds launched into an emotional tirade. "What can you expect," she asked, "with so many slutty books, dirty movies and pornographic material going through the mail? The country's morals are at a new low."

"There was something special about the movie industry's grief," wrote Murray Schumach in the *New York Times*. "In President Kennedy, the men and women of the cinema and video factories thought they had a partisan, even a friend. He seemed by his youth and temperament, to have a particular fondness for show business and a special sympathy for the problems of those who try to make a living by entertaining others." As the nation mourned its leader, the lights of Broadway, the soundstages of Hollywood, and the country's thousands of movie screens went dark. At the White House arrangements were quietly scrubbed for a December 10 luncheon that President Kennedy had been planning to host. Its theme: a tribute to the motion picture industry.

✳✳✳✳

For obvious reasons the celebrity friendships of Ronald and Nancy Reagan outpaced those of all other presidents. Both Reagans brought a coterie of famous friends to the marriage, his from a fifteen-year Hollywood career and hers through long-standing family connections. Nancy Davis was the daughter of a one-time actress named Edith Luckett. After Luckett left the stage to marry a

Chicago neurosurgeon, she remained faithful to her theatrical friends, who ranged from Katharine Hepburn and Spencer Tracy to Walter Huston and Mary Martin. Nancy's godmother was silent screen star Alla Nazimova, Rudolph Valentino's costar in the 1921 film *Camille*.

Although Ronald Reagan did not form friendships easily, in his early Hollywood days he drew close to several fellow performers, including Dick Powell, Jimmy Cagney, and Pat O'Brien; O'Brien also became buddies with Reagan's father. One of Ronald Reagan's first contacts in the movie business was singing cowboy Gene Autry, who met the young Midwesterner when he was still a play-by-play baseball announcer from Iowa. Visiting the set of an Autry picture that was filming on Catalina Island, Reagan told the star that "just from watching, it sure looks interesting, making pictures. I think I might like to get into that business." Autry counseled him to stick with sportscasting, a piece of advice they would laugh about after they became Hollywood peers.

The longer Reagan worked in motion pictures the wider his social circle became. Reagan's marriage to Jane Wyman placed him in a group of young marrieds that included Dick Powell and June Allyson. According to Allyson, Wyman resented having a husband so intent on talking politics. Wyman warned her, "Don't ask Ronnie what time it is because he will tell you how a watch is made."

On March 4, 1952, Reagan married Nancy Davis at the home of William and Ardis Holden; Holden did the honors as Reagan's best man. When Patti Davis Reagan was born seven months later, the couple chose silent film star Colleen Moore as her godmother and Holden as her godfather. But Patti met Holden only once as a child, and when he died in 1981 the White House aide who gave Reagan the news said the president "didn't show any real emotion over Holden's death." According to Patti Davis, "There was something transitory about many people in my parents' lives. Friends were discussed as though they had a place in our lives, but they were rarely present." In her view, Ronald and Nancy Reagan led "a rather isolated existence in which the two of them were there for each other."

Matinee idol Robert Taylor and his wife, Ursula, were probably the couple's closest Hollywood friends. When Reagan traded acting for politics in the mid-1960s, Taylor replaced him as host of the television anthology series *Death Valley Days*. In 1969 it fell to Governor Reagan to deliver the eulogy at Robert Taylor's funeral, a duty he also performed for Dick Powell and Edgar Bergen. Reagan's voice quivered with emotion as he called the MGM leading man "a star among stars . . . of all the gods and goddesses on Mount Olympus, the most handsome." Longtime Reagan handler Michael Deaver said he had never seen his boss more broken up. It was Taylor's death from lung cancer that inspired Reagan to quit smoking and take up jellybeans.

The Reagans socialized with many of their Hollywood contemporaries on a casual basis. Lucille Ball described a dinner at William Holden's at which Ron and Nancy arrived nearly an hour late, breathless with excitement. The Reagans told the rest of the group that on the drive over they had stopped to check out an incredible sight: an unidentified flying object. "After he was elected president, I kept thinking about that night, and wondered if he'd have still won if he told everybody that he'd seen a flying saucer," Ball told a friend.

Ronald and Nancy Reagan continued to draw on their show business contacts after they moved to Sacramento. Each year the governor and his wife would import a famous Hollywood performer to entertain at an outdoor party for state legislators; Jack Benny, Danny Thomas, and Red Skelton all played poolside gigs in the couple's backyard. Various friends from Los Angeles also took part in Reagan's gubernatorial inaugural events, including Irene Dunne and Shirley Temple Black in 1967 and Frank Sinatra, Dean Martin, Sammy Davis Jr., and John Wayne four years later. At the end of the 1971 gala John Wayne got into a shouting match with a crowd of several hundred antiwar demonstrators outside the auditorium.

The Reagans' professional contacts came in handy in other ways as well. When son Ron Reagan announced his plans to study ballet, the elder Reagan called Gene Kelly for advice on local dance schools. According to Michael Reagan, Kelly offered a recommendation and an assurance that not all male ballet dancers were homosexual. The news, Michael said, "obviously pleased Dad."

Once they got to the White House the Reagans remained intimate with a select group of their associates from Hollywood, most notably Frank Sinatra and Jimmy Stewart. The two actors were among the hundred-plus guests at a surprise party for the newly installed president two weeks after his 1981 inauguration. In 1985 Reagan awarded both Sinatra and Stewart the National Medal of Freedom, repeating the oft quoted remark that studio chief Jack Warner made on learning that Reagan was running for governor: "No—Jimmy Stewart for governor. Ronald Reagan for best friend."

Not all of Reagan's Hollywood colleagues recalled him with unbridled affection. Bette Davis, his costar in the 1939 classic *Dark Victory*, never stopped referring to him as "Little Ronnie," her less than endearing nickname from their Warner Bros. days. When interviewer Hadleigh Boze asked Davis if she ever had an inkling Ronald Reagan would become a star, she answered tartly, "Reagan didn't become a star." Boze pointed out that he had been the leading man in a number of films. "B movies," Davis shot back, then added, "Hopalong Cassidy also starred in films, for that matter." In 1987 Bette Davis set aside her aversion long enough to accept a Kennedy Center Honors medal from Reagan. Waiting in line to be presented to the president, the actress was instructed by an aide to give her name to an usher so she could be properly introduced. "My dear," she responded, "I don't need to be introduced to the president! I've known him for *years.*"

Kirk Douglas got acquainted with the Reagans when their sons attended the same school in Los Angeles. One day when young Eric Douglas went to his friend's house to play, he made a mildly derogatory remark about the Goldwater bumper sticker affixed to the Reagans' car. Nancy Reagan immediately phoned the boy's parents and demanded that they take him home. On another occasion, while Kirk Douglas was dancing with Mrs. Reagan, he mentioned that although he was a registered Democrat, he might support the right Republican—Nelson Rockefeller, for instance. "She turned on her heel and walked away," Douglas said. "I was stunned. I knew how Eric felt." But in 1981, after the attempt on President Reagan's life, Douglas sent a note of condolence to the first lady. "More than stunned," Douglas wrote, "I was angry. I had not voted for President Reagan but he is my president. Please extend our best wishes to the president, and tell him I try to endure the loss of the best dancing partner in town."

The Reagans' friendship with Rock Hudson helped shape Ronald Reagan's thinking on the issue of AIDS. Early in 1985 Hudson attended a White House state dinner, looking gaunt and ill. Hudson brushed away concerns over his appearance, telling Nancy he had "picked up a bug in Israel." A few months later, when the star underwent treatment in a Paris hospital, President Reagan telephoned Hudson to wish him well. Shortly before Hudson's death in October 1985 Reagan made his first public pronouncement about AIDS, a statement that was read by Burt Reynolds at a Los Angeles charity event. When Reynolds delivered a line about the "remarkable progress" made by the U.S. Public Health Service, some in the audience started hissing. Reynolds stopped reading. "I don't care what your political persuasion is," he said. "If you don't want the telegram read, then go outside." Reynolds then finished the statement.

An interview with the president's former physician several years later revealed that until Rock Hudson's illness became publicized Reagan did not regard AIDS as a serious matter. "He accepted (AIDS) like it was measles and would go away," the doctor, Brigadier General John Hutton, told a Seattle newspaper. When the news emerged about Hudson's condition, Dr. Hutton briefed Reagan on the disease, and only at that point—five years after AIDS had first been identified—did the administration begin paying heed.

✳✳✳✳

Apart from Ronald Reagan, Bill Clinton is the president with the most obvious personal ties to show business performers. His entertainer friends range from those he first met in Arkansas to the ones he got to know as a presidential candidate and in the White House. To some extent Clinton's showbiz friendships stemmed from political expediency: performing artists gave extravagantly of their money and talent to his campaigns, and they continue to support his wife. But the connections ran deeper, and even after leaving office, Clinton cultivated his personal relationships in the entertainment community.

Actress Mary Steenburgen was Bill Clinton's first well-known Hollywood friend. The North Little Rock native made Clinton's acquaintance in the late 1970s when he was governor of her home state and she was just beginning to create a name for herself in movies. In the 1992 campaign Steenburgen defended Clinton after a *60 Minutes* interview in which the governor was grilled about his relationship with nightclub singer Gennifer Flowers. "Bill is very capable of being a friend to a woman," Steenburgen said, "and not every man can do that."

Mary Steenburgen lamented what she saw as the distortion of Clinton's image in the national press. "It was painful to watch somebody that I know as a whole person being picked apart and have people take really isolated moments or aspects in his life and construct a character out of them," she told the *Los Angeles Times* in 1994. As Clinton's presidency unfolded, Steenburgen receded into the background, balancing her public support with private reticence. "It's a little bit like that thing the Indians say: If you photograph someone too much, you'll steal their soul," she explained. "I think if you talk about something too much, it's not yours anymore."

One of Clinton's favorite Hollywood friends is actor Kevin Spacey. "Getting to be friends with Kevin has been one of the best perks of being president," Clinton said a few months before leaving office. At a New York fund-raiser, the president quoted Franklin Roosevelt as saying that America's chief executive also needed to be its best actor. "Well, I'm the second best actor," Clinton continued. "Kevin is the best actor." (Clinton echoed FDR more than he may have realized;

Roosevelt used to tell Orson Welles, "We're the two best actors in the world.") The Clinton-Spacey relationship has lasted beyond the White House. In October 2002 the actor accompanied his friend on a trip to England for Clinton's address to the British Labor Party's annual conference. At the end of the speech, Clinton and Spacey left the auditorium together for a late-night run to the local McDonald's.

Other presidents have been less inclined to strike up personal relationships with entertainers, although even chief executives with little interest in pop culture have had their Hollywood pals. Lyndon Johnson developed a friendship with Gregory Peck after Peck narrated a biographical film about LBJ for the U.S. Information Agency, and soon the actor became a White House regular. Late one evening in October 1965 Lady Bird Johnson, fresh from a swim in the White House pool, walked in on her naked husband getting a rubdown on a massage table in front of Peck, actor Hugh O'Brian, Vice President Humphrey, and about ten aides. "I shrieked and backed out," she wrote in her diary. According to Jack Valenti, who was also in the room, Johnson engaged his guests in a conversation about the Vietnam War as the masseur went about his work. At one point LBJ scooped up some documents marked "top secret" from a nearby table and pressed them on Peck and O'Brian, who hesitated to read them despite the president's insistence.

In 1968 Peck and his French-born wife, Veronique, spent three days as guests at the Johnson Ranch in south Texas. Film of the visit shows President Johnson collecting the couple at the airstrip, where they arrived in a private jet. The president, wearing a khaki safari outfit and a goofy tam-o'-shanter, drives them to the ranch in a white Lincoln convertible. Later we see Johnson and the Pecks reclining in a field of wildflowers, the wind blowing through their hair as though they are models in a shampoo commercial.

At a farewell party at the end of Johnson's presidency the president escorted Veronique Peck onto the dance floor. "You know, Veronique," he said as they danced, "we both have something in common. We both love Gregory." LBJ told her that in a second Johnson administration Peck would have been his choice as ambassador to Ireland. Instead, on his final day in office, Lyndon Johnson awarded Gregory Peck the Medal of Freedom.

Richard Nixon had few intimate personal connections with entertainers, although he lived among them in both California and New York. When the Nixons returned to Los Angeles after the 1960 presidential race, they moved into a section of Beverly Hills packed with such show business celebrities as Fred MacMurray, Joe E. Brown, Cesar Romero, and Groucho Marx. Marx said he did not expect to associate with his new neighbors "unless there's a bomb, and we all meet in the same hole in the ground." Later the Nixons had a famous neighbor in San Clemente: James Arness, who played Marshall Dillon on the television show *Gunsmoke*.

After Nixon's presidency, when the couple moved to New York City, they lived behind actress Mary Tyler Moore. The balcony of Moore's house on East 64th Street afforded a view of the Nixons' backyard on East 65th. One Fourth of July, when the temperature topped one hundred degrees, Moore watched Nixon as he filled a plastic wading pool for his grandchild. Despite the heat, the former president was wearing a dark blue suit and tie; his wife, who watched the procedure in silence, appeared costumed for a fancy tea party. "I never saw either of them out of their strangely formal attire all summer," Moore said, "but I was pleased to see how often the little ones visited and the ready smile on the face of the man who was 'not a crook.'"

Nixon's successor, Gerald Ford, became friendly with sports announcer and TV pitchman Joe Garagiola when the two made campaign commercials together during the 1976 presidential race. The "Jerry and Joe Show" was a series of soft-edged half-hour interviews between Garagiola and the president that aired as paid political announcements on network television. The night before the election, in the last of the Ford commercials, Garagiola introduced another friend of the president, Pearl Bailey, who ad-libbed a remarkably unpolished endorsement of her candidate. "Oh, he's made some mistakes, honey," Bailey said. "You better believe he has. I wouldn't sit here and try to say he even didn't." She then began a litany of Ford's good qualities, damning him with faint praise by citing his "simplicity" and "get-up-and-go." When Bailey's blatherings finally came to a halt, Garagiola returned and said, "That's a real lady. She gives you a lump in your throat. She's talkin' about my kind of guy. And I think he's your kind of guy, too." The next night both Bailey and Garagiola watched election returns with Gerald and Betty Ford at the White House.

The first George Bush maintained a handful of show business friendships, though class barriers separated the blue-blooded president from most actors and musicians. The Bushes played host to only a few famous overnight guests at the White House, including Johnny Carson and Bush impersonator Dana Carvey. Arnold Schwarzenegger and his family spent two weekends with George and

Barbara Bush at Camp David, and Bruce Willis and Demi Moore came once. On the last weekend of the Bush presidency, country musician George Strait was a guest at the Maryland retreat.

The Bushes' closest friends in Hollywood were not performers but film producer Jerry Weintraub and his wife, singer Jane Morgan, who owned a home near the Bush family retreat in Kennebunkport, Maine. In 1991 the Weintraubs threw the president and first lady a dinner that Bush described as "the name dropping party to end all name dropping parties." The gathering at the Weintraub's Malibu estate proved to be the biggest celebrity event of the Bush presidency, attended by some 250 stars. There were entertainers representing every point on the political compass. Stalwart Bush supporters like Bruce Willis and Tony Danza mingled with liberal Democrats like Warren Beatty and Richard Dreyfuss, who sported a button that said "Now Let's Have a Domestic Desert Storm." The guest list spanned several generations of show business, from Jimmy Stewart to Jon Bon Jovi.

"It was a most glamorous night," Barbara Bush wrote in her diary, "and to top it all off I danced with a very bright Sylvester Stallone and a very attractive John Travolta." Addressing the crowd, the first lady confided, "I've fallen in love tonight. I'm not going to tell you with whom. But I want him to know I'm safe . . . I'm taken."

The president's tablemates included Clint Eastwood and Goldie Hawn, whom Bush described in his diary as "cute, full of fun and very nice to sit next to." Back in Washington Bush wrote Hawn a note, thanking her for being "a fantastic dinner partner." Bush said that when he discovered he had been placed with Goldie Hawn he was "a little worried" because "sometimes I'm not too hot of a dinner partner." Bush ended his note, "Thanks for being so darn nice!!"

The day after the event Chevy Chase wrote Bush a four-page letter. "Even if I do get out for the 'Dems' in '92, it wouldn't hurt me a bit to know you were still there," Chase told him. (As threatened, Chevy Chase actively campaigned against Bush on behalf of Bill Clinton.) Bush replied, "The fact that you understand that there are values that transcend issues shows both Barbara and me a lot about the Chevy Chase whose name we are now freely 'dropping' (even though he is a damned Democrat!)"

At the Weintraub party, Chevy Chase offered a more comedic take on the evening to a camera crew that recorded the event for posterity. Chase's on-the-scene description of his interaction with the president appropriately characterizes the shallowness that pervades most dealings between entertainers and chief executives: "He said hello, it was good to see me . . . We shook hands briefly, I asked him how his tennis was, he said it was good, Barbara said his tennis was good. I said that my tennis was fair, and then we just sort of looked at each other and wondered why are we talking about tennis, and he went on to the next guy."

Dwight Eisenhower and Robert Montgomery at the White House, April 1954. (Time Life Pictures, reprinted by permission)

9

✳✳✳✳

Secrets of the Stars

ENTERTAINERS

AS PROFESSIONAL ASSOCIATES

FOR SEVERAL YEARS IN THE 1950S actor Robert Montgomery led two professional lives—one in show business and one at the White House. For most of
the week the veteran leading man worked in New York, producing and hosting
the popular NBC television anthology series *Robert Montgomery Presents*. But on
Tuesday, the day after the broadcast, he would board a plane for Washington,
head to his office at 1600 Pennsylvania Avenue, and work to make the president
of the United States look good on camera.

Time has largely forgotten the relationship between Dwight Eisenhower and
Robert Montgomery, perhaps because journalists of the day—the ones writing
the first draft of history—deemed it too trivial to record. Today the media would
hardly ignore a Hollywood actor coming to the White House to serve as the
president's TV coach, but between 1953 and 1958 that is exactly what happened. Working without pay, Montgomery made suggestions on lighting, camera angles, wardrobe, and vocal delivery—everything but content. Ike, grateful
for the assistance and respectful of his teacher, eagerly complied. Occasional stories would surface in the press—a photo layout in *Life* magazine, for example,
that showed the former MGM star behind the scenes with his illustrious pupil—

but for the most part Eisenhower and Montgomery went about their business devoid of public scrutiny.

By the time he reached the White House, Montgomery had enjoyed a long and successful career in Hollywood. Handsome, well-bred, and intelligent, Montgomery rose to prominence at the dawn of talking pictures. Montgomery was still in his early twenties when he signed with MGM, which remained his home studio for most of the next two decades. Twice nominated for an Academy Award, the actor specialized in playing upper-crust sophisticates opposite the likes of Joan Crawford and Norma Shearer.

But there was a serious side to Montgomery that his frothy film roles belied. In the 1930s this son of a New York business executive helped organize the Screen Actors Guild; like Ronald Reagan, he served several terms as its president. After interrupting his career for World War II, Montgomery returned to Hollywood to star in the 1945 film *They Were Expendable*, a story that closely paralleled his own experience as commander of a PT boat. Montgomery next tried directing, but his 1946 Philip Marlowe mystery *The Lady in the Lake* proved disappointing. Substituting the lens of a camera for the leading man, Montgomery shot the film entirely from the protagonist's point of view. For audiences and critics alike, the result was more mystifying than satisfying, though Montgomery deserves credit for his willingness to challenge visual orthodoxy.

In 1950 Montgomery became one of the first Hollywood stars to make the transition into television. His *Robert Montgomery Presents* ranked among the many live dramatic series to originate from New York during the so-called golden age of television. The program gave early employment to a number of young actors, including James Dean, Joanne Woodward, Gena Rowlands, and Elizabeth Montgomery, the actor's daughter, who in the 1960s starred in the sitcom *Bewitched*.

Throughout his years in show business Robert Montgomery remained a staunch Republican in a town dominated by Democrats. He was a conservative radio commentator, a founding member of the Hollywood Republican Club, and a reliable campaigner for his party's presidential standard-bearer. In 1952 Montgomery played an active role in the Republican campaign for the White House, just as he had done in 1940, 1944, and 1948. This time his candidate won.

During the campaign Montgomery impressed top members of Eisenhower's circle by suggesting improvements in the general's television presentation, and in 1954 Montgomery became the first official media consultant in White House history. As Eisenhower's TV coach, Montgomery's first order of business was to shatter his student's preconceptions. "People had told him a good many horror stories about what he could or could not do with television, and most of them were untrue," Montgomery wrote in his 1968 polemic *Open Letter from a Television Viewer.* "The television education of the president began as soon as I got to the White House, and for an hour and a half I listened to his remembrances of what he had been told by a great variety of people in and out of the medium, including Winston Churchill." Eisenhower believed, for instance, that he needed to plant himself behind a desk in order to avoid distracting the audience with too much motion. Montgomery quickly dispelled this and other myths.

One of Montgomery's first moves was to liberate Eisenhower from the TelePrompTer, a device the president intensely disliked. For a television address in April 1954 Montgomery urged Ike not to read but to extemporize from cue cards. He also encouraged him to rise out of his chair and perch casually on the edge of his desk as he spoke. When *Life* magazine applauded the telecast as Eisenhower's "most professional TV performance to date," the president was pleased. "That's what I've been telling you boys for a long time," he explained to his aides. "Just let me get up and talk to the people. I can get through to them that way. I don't feel I do when I have to read a speech or use that damn teleprompter. It's not me and I feel uncomfortable."

Montgomery stage-managed every aspect of Eisenhower's on-air appearances. "He accepted my advice without reservation," the actor said. "As far as television was concerned, no authority was to supersede mine." At Montgomery's suggestion a vacant kitchen in the basement of the White House was converted into a TV studio. Though the president made frequent use of this facility, Montgomery preferred that live addresses originate from the Oval Office, where lighting equipment could be positioned at a high angle. The low ceilings in the basement studio offered no such possibility, resulting in a lighting setup that drew attention to Ike's bald head.

Montgomery helped coordinate the president's wardrobe, opting for the dark suits and light blue shirts that came across most favorably on camera. The actor recommended that Eisenhower avoid wearing eyeglasses on television; when Ike did use glasses Montgomery chose the pair. Montgomery employed stand-ins for Eisenhower to test various combinations of clothing, makeup, and lighting. Although this became standard procedure for subsequent presidents, in the 1950s it represented a radical break from convention.

Montgomery's control was total, extending even to the terminology used to describe the presidential broadcasts. He insisted that they be referred to as "programs" and not "shows," a word he thought "was used against us" in some of the press commentary after Eisenhower's early telecasts. "This criticism was unjustified," Montgomery wrote in a 1953 memorandum, "but we might help avoid it in the future if everyone connected with the president's appearances forgets 'show' and makes exclusive use of the quite accurate, descriptive and professionally accepted word, 'program.'"

Because Dwight Eisenhower was not a natural performer, Montgomery had his work cut out for him, especially at the beginning of their partnership. Eisenhower found it difficult to acclimate himself to the hubbub of technical activity that attended televised addresses; in order to minimize the distractions Montgomery hung a black drape between the technicians and the president, cutting holes in the cloth for the camera lenses. Like any good director, Montgomery was sensitive to the moods of his star, sometimes playing practical jokes on Eisenhower just before a live broadcast in order to loosen him up.

Most observers agreed that Montgomery reaped positive results. "Those who have watched the president's appearances on television have noted distinct intimations of his distinguished coach," said the *New York Times*. Eisenhower regularly expressed his own gratitude to Montgomery, as in this note that followed a 1954 speech:

> My friends (and even Mamie, who is my most severe critic) tell me that from a technical standpoint, at least, the television show last evening was my most successful "appearance." If this is true, the credit—all of it—goes squarely to you.
>
> I want you to know of my sincere and genuine appreciation of your patience and skill in trying to improve a difficult and, I am afraid, stubborn subject. I am tremendously grateful.

In 1957, after a steady decline in viewership, NBC canceled *Robert Montgomery Presents*. A year later the actor moved back to California to resume his career in motion pictures, though he continued to consult informally with the White House. One of the first film projects Montgomery pursued in Hollywood was a feature-length biographical film of Dwight Eisenhower; it never got off the ground.

In the summer of 1960 President Eisenhower learned that his vice president, Richard Nixon, had agreed to a series of debates with John F. Kennedy, a move Eisenhower had counseled against. As a friendly gesture Ike offered Nixon the services of Robert Montgomery; this too was ignored. Eisenhower considered Nixon's refusal a major blunder, telling an aide, "Montgomery would never have let him look as he did in that first television debate . . ." Montgomery's own take was less anti-Nixon than antidebate. "I believe this to be the really dangerous aspect of television in its relation to politics. It obscures, if it does not actually overwhelm, the facts about the issues in any campaign by giving the candidate who makes the best visual impact on the voters a powerful advantage." Given Montgomery's work with Eisenhower, this criticism would seem to be at least somewhat self-directed.

✻✻✻✻

After fifty years Robert Montgomery remains the most influential show business adviser any American chief of state has ever had. Most such relationships have been conducted on a less official basis. The only other president with his own full-time entertainment consultant in the White House, briefly and improbably, was Gerald Ford, who for a few months during the campaign of 1976 placed himself in the hands of a court jester–cum–media guru named Don Penny.

Penny was a forty-three-year-old actor, comedy writer, and producer whose most visible Hollywood credits had come in TV sitcoms. On *That Girl* he played Marlo Thomas's agent; on *The Wackiest Ship in the Army* he played a cook. He once made a guest appearance on *Bewitched*, opposite Robert Montgomery's daughter. A committed Republican, Penny came to Washington early in 1976 to shoot campaign commercials for President Ford. Here he got to know David Kennerly, Ford's friend and official White House photographer, who decided Penny's brand of irreverence was just the tonic Ford needed as he girded for reelection.

Penny first came to the attention of his presidential patron on the day Ford delivered his 1976 State of the Union address on Capitol Hill. Assessing the frenzied atmosphere in the Oval Office in the hours before the speech, the diminutive Penny decided levity was in order. He maneuvered his way through the huddle of aides surrounding the president, leaned into Ford's ear, and whispered, "Boss, don't worry. If you play your cards right, I think I can break you out of here." Ford laughed, the tension broke, and several weeks later Penny had a new job as a consultant in the speechwriters office, at the rate of $150 a day.

A profile of Penny in the *Chicago Tribune* shortly after his arrival captured the novelty of the arrangement and the resentment the comedian's sudden appearance engendered:

> Nobody is quite sure what Don Penny does at the White House, including Penny himself, but he has been seeing a lot of the president in recent days, and that has people upset.
>
> "He's broken more china in the last three weeks than anybody I've ever seen," said a veteran White House official. "Nobody quite knows what his responsibility is and he keeps cutting across other people's turf."

Penny's happy-go-lucky style, so at odds with the formal atmosphere of the executive mansion, alienated him from many of the president's aides. Penny did not seem to mind. "There is no defense against a guy like me around here," he told a reporter. "I seep through the cracks like a piece of Silly Putty." What particularly galled the staff was Penny's unfettered criticism of Ford's performance. "Half the time he sounds like a Florsheim shoe salesman," Penny complained in a page-one interview in the *Washington Post*. Penny told another newspaper, "The president has a lot of talents, but they just don't include doing a dog and pony show."

Penny's public comments showed a remarkable disregard for the other members of Ford's campaign team. "The president does more speaking than any major film star or stand-up comic in America," he said in the *Washington Star*. "He's got advisers for everything, but nobody seemed to realize that he needed some coaching in his speeches."

Describing himself as a "director-coach," Penny wasted no time attempting to goose Ford's notoriously plodding oratorical style. Penny's influence was felt almost immediately when the president turned in a better-than-average comedic performance at the 1976 White House correspondents dinner, matching wits with Chevy Chase. Penny began accompanying Ford on the campaign trail, where he undertook to streamline the candidate's message and simplify his language. As an example of the presidential tendency to speak in bureaucratese, Penny cited Ford's use of the term "private sector": "What is he talking about—somebody's unmentionables here, or what? What I'd like to do is help him get rid of all that jargon, all that political rhetoric, until he's completely naked, until you see the real man." For Ford's acceptance speech at the Republican Convention, Penny held two videotaped dress rehearsals, then critiqued the tapes afterward with the president at his side. The result for Ford, according to the *Post*, was "the best speech of his life."

However leery others in the White House may have been, Gerald Ford saw only the positive side of Don Penny. "He called me 'Big Red,'" Ford wrote in his memoir, "and we hit it off extremely well." Ford appreciated Penny's ceaseless attempts to cheer him up, a mission that sometimes involved other members of the Ford family. The president recalled that Penny would visit the Oval Office with first daughter Susan Ford and announce that the two of them had decided to get married. According to Ford, "I would smile and say something like 'Get out of here, you two,' but they would have succeeded in brightening my day."

What is striking about Don Penny is the ambiguity of his role. A media adviser on the one hand, he was also in charge of providing the boss with comic relief. It is difficult to say which function mattered more. No other administration combined these tasks into a job description or put on its payroll an individual whose chief credential appeared to be an ability to make the president laugh.

Other entertainers have lent their professional services to the White House, most notably during campaigns. In the presidential race of 1944 Orson Welles served as an informal media consultant to Franklin Roosevelt. "He liked to be directed," Welles said of the president. "He was a pure actor. You couldn't direct Churchill, but you could him."

Welles claimed partial authorship of one of FDR's most celebrated rhetorical triumphs, the so-called Fala speech of September 1944. Political opponents had falsely accused the president of spending taxpayer dollars to retrieve his Scottish terrier, Fala, from the Aleutian Islands in Alaska, where the dog had inadvertently been left behind. Welles told biographer Barbara Leaming that it had been his idea to turn the allegations into a joke, a suggestion Roosevelt put to use in a speech before a labor union. With mock ire FDR charged that the Republicans had libeled the defenseless animal, and that Fala's "Scotch soul was furious" at the accusation of wasted dollars. Fala, the president said, "has not been the same dog since" the story broke.

After delivering the address the president telephoned Welles, eager for his professional assessment. "He asked me afterwards, 'How did I do? Was my timing right?'" Welles said. "Just like an actor!"

The next high-profile performer to lend his comedy writing talents to a Democratic presidential campaign was political satirist Mort Sahl, who in 1960 concocted one-liners for John F. Kennedy. On the surface Kennedy had little use for the services of a gagman, as funny as he naturally was. But even he could not be expected to crank out the endless repartee demanded on the campaign trail. Ambassador Joseph Kennedy approached Sahl, who agreed to contribute jokes as long as he did not have to endorse the candidate. In choosing Sahl, the Kennedys were going for the best. Then thirty-three years old, the comedian was at the top of his game, having recently broken out as the freshest voice of his generation. A story in *Time* magazine in August 1960 called Sahl "the first notable American political satirist since Will Rogers"; *Time* ran Sahl's portrait on its cover, juxtaposed alongside the images of JFK and Nixon.

Mort Sahl's contributions to the campaign were modest, consisting largely of self-deprecating *bon mots* and digs on President Eisenhower, few of which JFK actually used. Like other show business notables, Sahl eventually came to feel betrayed by Kennedy. He watched from the sidelines as Frank Sinatra and other celebrity campaigners participated in the inaugural gala. "They all went to Washington," Sahl said. "Nobody ever said thank-you to me." Once JFK took office, Sahl's relationship with the new president quickly frayed. As a satirist, Mort Sahl expected to continue drawing on the White House for material, even with Kennedy as its occupant. "All the people around him were telling me not to joke about him like I did about other presidents," Sahl recalled. "They wanted me to be reverent." When he failed to be reverent, Sahl got called on the carpet by friends like Peter Lawford. He even claimed that the Kennedy family pressured film producers and nightclub owners not to hire him.

The experience, which left Mort Sahl deeply bitter, illustrates the dangers of trying to work both sides of the comedy fence. Sahl had tried to warn JFK what would happen, telling him after the election, "You're the new sheriff, but I'm still a bank robber by vocation." Word soon got back that the White House was not pleased with Sahl's relentless targeting of the president. "People don't understand," Sahl lamented. "I'm not on the left side; I'm not on the right side. I'm on the outside."

✶✶✶✶

Since Kennedy's day, presidential administrations have taken a more systematic approach to joke writing, just as they have heightened their attention to wardrobe and makeup. The Lyndon Johnson White House had its own "Humor Group" headed by Liz Carpenter, the wisecracking Texan who served as Lady

Bird's press secretary. Every Monday at the end of the workday five or six of LBJ's funniest aides would gather to craft one-liners for the president's use. "The meetings were well attended because I served drinks," Carpenter said. "There is nothing about producing humor that gin doesn't improve." When members of the Humor Group found themselves blocked, Carpenter would telephone a Hollywood friend named Larry Markes, who wrote for the Sally Field TV sitcom *The Flying Nun*.

Bob Hope also contributed gagwriters to Lyndon Johnson, after LBJ asked the veteran comic for lines to use against Barry Goldwater. "I always suspected that you could do my job," President Johnson told Hope in a thank-you letter, "but after seeing the quality of jokes that you must constantly produce, I know that I can never do yours." Hope was not altogether satisfied with the transaction: "He may have thanked me for the jokes, but I'll be damned if I ever heard him use any."

Joke contributors are more likely to come from the ranks of screenwriters and producers than performers. Gary Ross, author of the presidential film comedy *Dave*, is one of several Hollywood writers to offer their services to the Democrats. Ross got his political start crafting sound bites for Michael Dukakis, then went on to perform similar duty for Bill Clinton. "A lot of people can write funny lines," said Dee Dee Myers, President Clinton's first press secretary. "But Gary can write a joke which also incorporates the candidate's message, and that's fairly unique."

Another member of Clinton's comedy brain trust was Al Franken, the actor and *Saturday Night Live* alumnus who became a social friend of Bill and Hillary Clinton during their years in the White House. In addition to furnishing gags, Franken directed a well-received comedy video for the 1995 Gridiron show that starred Hillary as a Washington version of *Forrest Gump*, an idea that originated with *Tonight Show* host Jay Leno. Affecting a southern accent, the first lady delivered lines that spoofed those of Tom Hanks in the film: "My mama always told me the White House is like a box of chocolates. It's pretty on the outside, but inside there's lots of nuts." The president took part in Mrs. Clinton's comedy debut with a cameo appearance, five years before his own video with Kevin Spacey. When Hillary offered her husband a chocolate, he grabbed the whole box and asked if she had any French fries to go with it. At the video's Gridiron premiere, the audience gave Mrs. Clinton a standing ovation.

The most significant of Bill Clinton's Hollywood connections predated his presidency by many years. Television producer Harry Thomason first got to know Clinton in the late 1960s in Arkansas. Clinton had grown close to Thomason's brother, a high school biology teacher who told Harry, "I want you to meet this guy because he's going to be president some day." Over the years, as both Bill and Harry made their way up in the world, they maintained a steady friendship. While Clinton's path led back to Arkansas and a career in politics, Thomason's took him to Hollywood, where after years of paying dues on low-budget horror films and TV movies he found his niche as a producer and director of series television. When Thomason married Linda Bloodworth, a comedy writer from Missouri with roots in Arkansas, the friendship with Bill Clinton expanded to include their wives.

In 1986 the Thomasons got their big break with *Designing Women*, a well-regarded comedy series for CBS that gave the couple autonomy over their own work. The Thomasons' success with *Designing Women* roughly coincided with the rise of Bill Clinton as a national political figure, and in 1988, the professional interests of these longtime friends began to merge. After the Arkansas governor delivered a disastrous nominating speech at the Democratic convention in Atlanta, the Thomasons summoned their show business savvy and industry connections to help rehabilitate his image. Their solution: to book Clinton on the *Tonight Show*.

Thomason set the wheels in motion the morning after the speech, even before checking with the governor. At first, producer Fred De Cordoba turned down the offer, citing the program's long-standing prohibition on politicians. Undeterred, Thomason upped the ante: What if Clinton came on as a musician? De Cordoba remained dubious but promised to take up the matter with Johnny Carson. Ten minutes later Thomason heard back from Fred De Cordoba: Clinton was booked for the following week.

When Thomason called the governor's mansion in Little Rock to report the news, the governor was out jogging. A couple of hours later Clinton returned the call.

"You're on the *Tonight Show* Tuesday night," Thomason informed him, "but you've got to play the saxophone so you'd better start practicing."

Bill Clinton was unfazed. "You know," he said, "while I was out running I was thinking what I really need to do is be on something like the *Tonight Show*."

In the days leading up to the appearance Johnny Carson joked relentlessly in his monologue about Clinton's long-windedness, and when Clinton walked onto the set for his interview, Carson reinforced the point by whipping out an hourglass. (The Thomasons, struck by the same inspiration, had armed Clinton with an hourglass of his own to bring on the set. Backstage before the show De Cordoba insisted that Clinton forgo the hourglass gag, without explaining why.) As his musical selection Bill Clinton played a semiprofessional saxophone rendition of the Gershwin classic "Summertime," but it was the aw-shucks charm of the attractive young governor that won over Carson and the television audience. More viewers saw Clinton on *Tonight* than had caught his speech at the convention, and among political insiders the maneuver reestablished Bill Clinton as a player on the national stage.

The years between the *Tonight Show* and the 1992 campaign brought continued professional connections between the Clintons and the Thomasons, albeit on a less consequential scale. Exteriors of the Arkansas governor's mansion, where the Clintons were living, appeared on *Designing Women* as the home of one of the show's characters. Hillary came up with the title of the Thomasons' second series, *Evening Shade*, naming it after a town in Arkansas. When the Clintons visited California, their friends introduced them to potential political supporters in the television industry. The first such gathering followed the governor's 1988 guest shot on the *Tonight Show*; the Thomasons decorated the party room with a banner that said "Clinton for President in 1996."

In October 1991, when Bill Clinton announced his intention to run for the presidency at a Little Rock rally, it was Harry Thomason who introduced him to the crowd. Over the next thirteen months, Harry and Linda devoted themselves to their friend's election, making production suggestions, contributing one-liners to the candidate's speeches, and, in Harry's case, helping stage events like political infomercials. No task was too small: a Clinton campaign operative recalled watching Thomason on his hands and knees, installing carpet on a debate stage in New Hampshire.

The Thomasons brought to the campaign a valuable show business know-how that gave Clinton a different perspective from the advice he received from the professional handlers. Drawing on their contacts in Hollywood, the couple put the Clintons in touch with experts on hair, clothing, and makeup. The hairdresser Christophe, he of the headline-provoking presidential trim at Los Angeles International Airport, first met Hillary through actress Markie Post and Linda Bloodworth-Thomason. The Clintons signed Christophe to a personal services contract, and imported him for major events during the campaign. A costume designer and makeup artist from the Thomasons' television programs also traveled as necessary with the candidate and his wife.

The behind-the-scenes endeavors of Harry and Linda Thomason sailed into view at the 1992 Democratic National Convention that officially nominated Clinton as the party's standard-bearer. Linda wrote and produced the campaign biopic *The Man from Hope*, a video paean to the governor that generated a good deal of buzz in the press. The film's money shot is a brief piece of footage that shows sixteen-year-old Bill Clinton shaking the hand of John F. Kennedy in the White House Rose Garden in 1963. Locating the clip at the National Archives had been a stroke of good fortune for Bloodworth-Thomason. Knowing that Clinton possessed still photos of the event, she hoped motion picture cameras might also have recorded the moment, as indeed they had. The footage amounted to a coronation, a palpable link between two handsome, charismatic, movie-loving presidents whom fate had brought together for one symbolic exchange. As an example of political theater, *The Man from Hope* succeeded on a grand scale, largely on the basis of that signature clip.

For his part, Harry Thomason came up with the staging of Bill Clinton's "rock star" walk to the convention floor the night before his formal nomination, a bit of campaign choreography that further highlighted the role of the couple from Hollywood. Trailed by handheld cameras, Clinton made his way from the basement of Macy's, where a party had been staged for his benefit, through a stretch of the Manhattan streetscape and into the bowels of Madison Square Garden. As the candidate emerged onstage, the convention hall audience, which had been watching the approach on giant video monitors, hit a crescendo of enthusiasm. At the podium Clinton delivered a line that had been a last-minute contribution from Linda Bloodworth-Thomason: "Tomorrow night, I will be the Comeback Kid."

Six weeks before the nation went to the polls, the *Los Angeles Times* wrote that "the intensity of the Thomasons' volunteer effort in the Clinton campaign is considered a nearly unprecedented combination of politics and show business." Although accurate in one sense, the analysis overlooked the fundamental nature of the connection, which had more to do with friendship than a professional alliance. As Clinton later told a group of friends at a surprise birthday party for Thomason, "Harry was there when I got sick and I was under siege and I got so fat I could hardly walk. Everyone else was making fun of me, but Harry just went out and bought me bigger suits."

In January 1993 Thomason took the reins as executive producer of the Clinton inaugural festivities, a position that subjected him to criticism in the press when the scope of the plans became known. Thomason described himself as "shocked at the resentment" expressed in the news stories. "It appeared to us that the insiders in Washington had had this little event to themselves so long that we were sort of sullying it up by bringing a lot of people along," he said.

The carping prefigured the troubles ahead. Several months into the Clinton presidency, when the media launched its backlash against the president's ties to Hollywood, Harry and Linda Thomason found themselves caught in the cross fire. Much of the reporting about them was erroneous; for example, stories that the couple had leased a beach house in California for use by the Clintons as a vacation home, and that Harry Thomason had been given his own office at the White House. Nonetheless, Thomason's naïveté about the ways of Washington did not serve him well. When he came to town to discuss media strategy for the Clinton health plan with administration aides, or misguidedly took it on himself to restructure the White House travel office, the press piled on.

In May 1993 reporters questioned the president, who was out for a jog, about his relationship with the adviser from Hollywood. "He has no official role," Clinton said. "He's just our friend." The statement was true; the Thomasons, with three network series on the air, had neither the time nor the inclination to assume major tasks at the White House. But the news media interpreted them differently, reading their motives through the lens of Washington. Unsure what to make of the Thomasons, and oblivious to the twenty-five-year history between Bill Clinton and Harry, capital pundits depicted the couple not as old friends eager to lend their expertise but as the vanguard of an invading Hollywood army bent on taking over the White House. At the height of the media's anti–show business backlash Linda Bloodworth-Thomason astutely assessed the coverage in an interview with *USA Today*. "The Washington press corps practices central casting in every administration," she said. "There has always got to be a Lady Macbeth, a big fool relative, an unscrupulous businessman, and sleazy immoral people from Hollywood. In Harry's and my case, they've decided to assign us the last two categories."

✿✿✿✿

One of the most fascinating links between an entertainer and a would-be president never came to fruition. In September 1968 Alabama Governor George Wallace, then making a White House run on the segregationist American party ticket, invited John Wayne to be his vice presidential running mate. The choice seems counterintuitive: Wayne was a Nixon man, so strong in his support that a few weeks earlier he had endorsed Nixon in a patriotic speech at the Republican convention in Miami. John Wayne had even braved the crowds at Miami International Airport to welcome the nominee to town.

But a month after the convention George Wallace phoned the tough-talking actor to invite him onto his ticket. "You and I think the same way about what's happening to this country," Wallace said to him. Wayne listened politely, then turned the governor down. "I explained that I was working for the other Wallis—Hal Wallis—the producer of *True Grit*, and that I'd been a Nixon man," Wayne later told an interviewer. A few days after Wayne declined the offer, Wallace announced retired Air Force General Curtis LeMay as his running mate.

Wallace's "you and I think the same way" comment was more an expression of wishful thinking than a correct reading of Wayne's politics. Although steadfastly conservative, Wayne did not hold racist views. After getting off the phone with Wallace, Wayne told his secretary, "If blacks had been allowed to vote all along we wouldn't have all this horseshit (civil rights unrest) going on. George Wallace is part of the goddam problem, not the solution." Wayne later vehemently denied press reports that he contributed $30,000 to Wallace's campaign.

Political partnerships between presidents and performers typically take place well below the level of running mate. Over the years many professional performers have served as presidential appointees, usually in a ceremonial capacity, though sometimes with more substantive responsibilities. In 1941 Franklin Roosevelt dispatched actor Douglas Fairbanks Jr. on a combination goodwill and fact-finding mission to South America. According to a White House press release from the time, Fairbanks's job was to "ascertain the views and suggestions of the Governments and peoples in these countries with respect to improving the role of the theatrical arts as a possible vehicle for bringing about improved inter-American understanding."

Beneath this high-blown language lay a more pragmatic reason for Fairbanks's trip: Roosevelt officials hoped the charming young film star would make inroads with pro-German sympathizers in the Latin American capitals. Undersecretary of State Sumner Welles expounded on this goal in a memorandum to FDR urging approval of the trip: "As you know, there has been a somewhat marked pro-fascist tendency on the part of the younger generation of the well-to-do groups in Brazil and in Argentina . . . and I think that Fairbanks could probably do a pretty effective job in combating this trend. Both his moving picture celebrity as well as his personality would appeal to the elements I have mentioned." Roosevelt returned the memo with a handwritten notation—"Very good"—and allocated $5,000 for travel expenses.

As a member of one of America's most famous theatrical families, Douglas Fairbanks Jr. had long-standing connections to the Roosevelts. FDR first met Fairbanks's father during the 1918 war bond drive, and the two men had kept in touch. Douglas Jr. was a childhood playmate of Franklin Roosevelt Jr., who introduced Fairbanks to his father in the late 1930s. After Fairbanks threw himself into Roosevelt's 1940 reelection campaign, the actor and his wife received invitations to Hyde Park and the White House. Both Eleanor and Franklin enjoyed the company of the aristocratic young man with the celebrated name.

Fairbanks approached his assignment to South America with great seriousness. Before shipping out, he enrolled in a crash course in Spanish and Portuguese at the Berlitz language school in New York. Among the other students in class was a "toothy, rather polite young fellow" in his early twenties who, Fairbanks said, was quite impressed to be "in a language class with a movie star." Twenty years later, the student, now President John F. Kennedy, recalled the connection and, in a conversation at the White House, asked Fairbanks if he still spoke Spanish and Portuguese.

Between April and June 1941 Fairbanks visited five countries, cabling Washington with frequent and detailed updates from the road. Some of his reports were insightful, others bordered on sycophancy. "I don't think it possible for you to realize what a world symbol you have become to people outside of this country," Fairbanks wrote the president. "Everywhere I went, because I was representing you, I was cheered to the echo by chanted repetitions of your name." Fairbanks tactfully omitted the news that his own name was also the subject of enthusiastic chants in film-crazed Latin America, where Douglas Fairbanks Sr. had been an audience favorite for many years.

The formation of the United Nations at the end of World War II gave American presidents a fresh source of rewards to dish out to their show business supporters. In 1950 Harry Truman named loyal Democrat Myrna Loy as an adviser to the U.S. delegation to UNESCO, the United Nations Educational, Scientific, and Cultural Organization. President Eisenhower appointed Irene Dunne in 1957 and Marian Anderson a year later to the U.S. delegation to the General Assembly; Dunne had been a tireless campaigner for Ike.

Shirley Temple Black made international headlines in 1969 when Richard Nixon nominated her as one of five General Assembly delegates from the United States. Vowing that her days as an actress were over, the former child star told an

ABC News reporter that she had first gotten interested in politics as a military wife in Washington in the 1950s. "I was privileged to know many of the leaders at that time in our government and I felt maybe this is a place where I belonged, where I could help more than being in the entertainment business," Black said. True to her word, Shirley Temple Black went on to a respectable diplomatic career, serving as American ambassador to Ghana under Gerald Ford and to Czechoslovakia under the first President Bush.

In the 1970s Gerald Ford named Pearl Bailey as a delegate to the United Nations, a position to which she was reappointed by Ronald Reagan. Bailey was no fan of the United Nations, complaining that the delegates lied, failed to listen to one another, and read their speeches "like a broken record." The lack of spontaneity in the General Assembly seemed to bother her the most. "My theory is that all of us here should get up and talk with their hearts, instead of their heads," Bailey told a reporter. On the plus side, she said, the work was "very easy." In 1978 Jimmy Carter named Paul Newman, a longtime Democratic activist, as one of five American representatives to a U.N. session on disarmament. "I'm not trying to be cynical," an anonymous European diplomat commented to the *Washington Post*, "but I just don't see much merit in this practice of bringing in actors and actresses to U.N. meetings."

The question of entertainers' appropriateness as diplomats resurfaced in 1981, when Ronald Reagan chose actor John Gavin, a political supporter, as his ambassador to Mexico. "Mexico Dismayed That Actor Might Be U.S. Envoy," read the headline in the *New York Times*, which quoted a Mexican official as saying, only half in jest, "Perhaps we should name Cantinflas to Washington." Reaction from south of the border ranged from humor to outrage. "If you're going to send us an actor, I would have preferred Wonder Woman," joked one newspaper editor. A top labor leader said, "Mexicans have nothing against actors. We just don't like bad actors like Reagan."

The selection of John Gavin was not totally without logic. The son of a Mexican national, he grew up speaking Spanish and was well acquainted with the country to which he had been nominated. Gavin held a degree in Latin American economic history from Stanford University and had spent several years as an adviser to the secretary-general of the Organization of American States. Like Reagan and Robert Montgomery, Gavin's political experience included a stint as president of the Screen Actors Guild.

At the time of his nomination John Gavin was best known in Mexico as the spokesman in a long-running television commercial for Bacardi rum. The advertisement's tag line—"Have you tried the test of maturity?"—inspired widespread sarcasm in the Mexican press. In testimony before the Senate Foreign Relations Committee Gavin was asked whether the commercial was still on the air and whether it would affect his ability to execute the duties of ambassador. The actor gave a terse response: "The answer to both those questions is no, sir." Regarding the suitability of an actor in the role of ambassador, the nominee offered a Reaganesque one-liner. Gavin's record of forty motion pictures, he said, "prove that I'm no actor." He had a point: his career in films was based more on good looks than artistic talent.

After a controversial five-year term John Gavin resigned from the ambassadorship and returned to California. According to a tale that circulated around Mexico City, the American ambassador held a farewell dinner shortly before his departure for high-ranking local politicos. Gavin made a gracious speech, thanking the Mexicans and summarizing his experience at the embassy. After the remarks an awkward silence ensued; none of the officials in the room saw fit to deliver the reply that protocol required. At last someone stood up: Cantinflas, the comedian who had been jokingly touted as ambassador to the United States. The subtext could not have been plainer. To the power brokers of Mexico, Gavin remained what he was when he got there: an entertainer.

✶ ✶ ✶ ✶

Another reward presidents have doled out to friendly entertainers is a seat on the board of the John F. Kennedy Center for the Performing Arts. During the Reagan administration Charlton Heston held this post, as did Bonita Granville Wrather, who played Nancy Drew in the juvenile film mystery series of the late 1930s. In 2002 George W. Bush named Bo Derek as a Kennedy Center trustee. Although her dramatic career consisted of little more than B movies and softcore porn, she had been one of the few entertainers to campaign for Bush in the presidential race of 2000.

Because they carry no real responsibility, ceremonial appointments of this sort rarely generate controversy. President Eisenhower faced a rare moment of embarrassment in 1957 when he nominated Jimmy Stewart for a loftier honor—a brigadier generalship in the United States Air Force Reserve. In view of Stewart's distinguished service as a pilot in World War II, confirmation seemed a sure thing. But opposition arose from Senator Margaret Chase Smith of Maine, who complained that Stewart lacked the necessary hours of active duty since his discharge from the Army Air Corps in 1945. By a vote of eleven to two the Senate Armed Service Committee rejected the promotion, and only after Eisenhower renominated the actor for a lesser post did the confirmation go through, two years behind schedule.

It is rare for presidents to grant entertainers positions of genuine responsibility. A notable exception is Betty Furness, the actress-turned-commercial spokeswoman whom Lyndon Johnson named as his "special assistant to the president for consumer affairs" in 1967. Furness achieved national prominence in the 1950s as the TV pitchwoman for Westinghouse appliances, delivering the memorable tag line "You can be sure if it's Westinghouse." When Westinghouse sponsored television coverage of the 1952 political conventions, Furness appeared in every advertisement, clocking more time on camera than either Eisenhower or Stevenson. As the Johnson administration's consumer advocate, Furness had to overcome opposition from groups skeptical of her commercial background. But through hard work she won over her critics. After leaving the White House in 1969 Furness parlayed her experience into a new career as the nation's first TV consumer reporter, most prominently on NBC's *Today* show.

If George McGovern had been elected president in 1972, Shirley MacLaine expected to be rewarded with a White House job. "I would probably have asked to be a part of something to do with the issue of overpopulation in the world," she wrote. A McGovern administration, she believed, would have given equal weight to men and women in decisionmaking roles. During the campaign McGovern appointed MacLaine to cochair his "women's advisory committee," a position she shared with former congresswoman Bella Abzug.

Several years later MacLaine played unofficial diplomatic courier between Cuban leader Fidel Castro and the Jimmy Carter White House. The actress had been in Havana for a screening of her film *The Turning Point*, and before she left the country Castro gave her a box of Cuban cigars to take to Carter and his aides. As a gift for national security adviser Zbigniew Brzezinski, Fidel sent a pipe, telling MacLaine, "I would like to smoke the pipe of peace with him."

When Shirley MacLaine showed up at the White House with the items, Brzezinski was horrified. "You have a present from that murderer with you and you got past security?" he asked. Brzezinski said he thought the box might contain a bomb, to which MacLaine sensibly replied that a bomb hand-carried all the way from Havana could not possibly know when to go off. Gingerly, as Brzezinski and other high-level Carter officials looked on, she unwrapped the packages. Though the cigars were a big hit with the president's assistants, Brzezinski scorned his peace pipe, tossing it onto the desk. "I'll smoke this thing with him when every last Cuban soldier is out of Angola and not a minute before!" he vowed.

Perhaps because it appeals to their instinct for drama, a number of entertainers have volunteered for special diplomatic assignments over the years. In the late 1940s Douglas Fairbanks Jr. approached President Truman with just such a task, hoping for an ambassadorship or a post in civilian intelligence; though Truman spoke encouragingly, no appointment followed. Two decades later Gregory Peck tendered his services to Lyndon Johnson: "If there is ever an occasion when the president wants to reach out for someone who has no political ambitions or an axe to grind; someone who would be glad to use his capabilities on a diplomatic errand, a special mission, or a chore of any description, I would be proud to serve," Peck wrote LBJ aide Jack Valenti.

In 1976 Frank Sinatra personally offered his assistance to Central Intelligence Agency Director George Bush, though it is unclear what sort of espionage Sinatra had in mind. Sinatra made his pitch during a gathering at the Manhattan apartment of Jonathan Bush, George's brother. Jonathan Bush described the exchange a few weeks later to a *Boston Globe* reporter: "Sinatra said he was always flying around the world, and meeting with people like the Shah of Iran and the Royal Family of Great Britain. He emphasized time and again that his services were available and that he wanted to do his part for his country."

Despite the sincerity of Sinatra's offer, George Bush remained understandably noncommittal. At one point in the conversation Bush joked about the singer's well-publicized tribulations during an Australian tour some years earlier. "There is some special work you can do for us," Bush told Sinatra—"in Australia." According to Jonathan Bush, after Sinatra left, the others present "felt like applauding." "We had a big laugh about it," Bush said, "and then we all got smashed."

Like other stars with close personal ties to the White House, Sinatra did not hesitate to proffer the occasional political suggestion. In 1987 "Ol' Blue Eyes" wrote his friend Ronald Reagan with an idea he had been mulling over, one that could be "a pretty good positive move politically": House leader Tip O'Neill as ambassador to Ireland. "I've never spoken to him about it, nor he to me, but I get a feeling that he can taste it," Sinatra said. "It's just a thought; if not throw it in the basket." The president responded with a handwritten letter thanking "Francis Albert" for the advice, but explaining that he already had a perfectly suitable ambassador in place. Reagan took the opportunity to vent his spleen about O'Neill: "Tip has joined that chorus back here that's bent on a lynching, with me in the noose. He's been saying some pretty harsh things publicly."

The archives of America's presidential libraries abound with examples of unsolicited counsel from show business performers. John Wayne was an inveterate White House correspondent, no matter who held office. In 1971 he wrote Nixon to denounce his trip to China, a "real shocker" in Wayne's opinion. More surprisingly Wayne went to bat a few years later for convicted heiress Patricia Hearst. In a 1978 telegram to Jimmy Carter Wayne urged clemency: "In the spirit of Christ respectfully suggest a full pardon for brainwashed Miss Patricia Hearst." Robert Redford wrote Carter to express his displeasure over an appointee to the Nuclear Regulatory Commission. Cary Grant sent Vice President Walter Mondale his thoughts about the U.S. boycott of the Moscow Olympic games.

Advice from entertainers extends beyond public policy. Rudy Vallee informed Richard Nixon that he had mispronounced the word "Venezuela" in a speech. "Knowing your facility with Spanish," wrote Vallee, "I of course felt that you know that the U in ZUELA merges with the Z and the two become in effect, SWAY not ZOO-AY . . . It was probably a slip, but I like all of my pupils to speak correctly!!!!!"

The first Bush White House once received an unusual phone call from Buffalo Bob Smith, host of the 1950s children's television show *Howdy Doody*. Marlin Fitzwater, President Bush's press secretary, talked with Smith, who passed along this brainstorm: "I have one word for you to use—to put in all the president's speeches—and it will magically make things right." The word: "Cowabunga!"

For sheer nuttiness it would be difficult to surpass a letter actor Lionel Barrymore wrote President Roosevelt during World War II. Concerned over the fate of dogs left behind by soldiers leaving for military service, Barrymore decided to express his feelings to the man in the White House. But instead of Lionel Barrymore writing Franklin Roosevelt, the letter took the form of a note from Barrymore's Scottish terrier, Johnnie, to FDR's Scottie, Fala:

Dear Fala:

I have been thinking about the sad plight of the thousands of dogs left at home by soldiers now away fighting for our country. Some of these dogs are having a terrible time, being very lonesome for the boys that belong to them, and many of them are hungry and starving. Now, this man that belongs to me is in some respects a very nice man, but I have looked into the matter and discover that he has no influence.

This man that belongs to you, though, has got a lot of pull. I thought perhaps you might take up with him this matter of the poor dogs who have sent their men away and are now in trouble.

It might be that you would come out this way sometime. If you do, please look me up. I have a long line of trees and posts. Yesterday I bit the postman. He is a Republican.

Respectfully yours,
Johnnie

Neither Barrymore nor his canine alter ego received a reply.

Nancy Reagan and Gary Coleman on the set of *Diff'rent Strokes*,
March 1983. (Ronald Reagan Library)

10

✳✳✳✳

Leading Ladies, Supporting Cast

FIRST FAMILIES
IN THE SHOWBIZ PRESIDENCY

IN THE SPRING OF 1982, after a yearlong onslaught of negative press, the first lady of the United States dusted off a career that had been in mothballs since the late 1950s. Over the next year and a half Nancy Reagan performed a song-and-dance number onstage at the Gridiron dinner, taped a public service announcement for the Super Bowl, read poetry with the National Symphony Orchestra, sang a duet with Frank Sinatra, cohosted a morning television talk show, appeared in a popular TV sitcom, and narrated two docudramas. It took the White House to do what Hollywood could not: make a star out of Nancy Reagan.

The reemergence of Nancy Reagan, entertainer, provides a valuable case study in the uses of show business to retool a battered political image. The experience and ego of the prima donna in question lent themselves particularly well to this brand of makeover, and like the dutiful actress she had been at Metro-Goldwyn-Mayer, Nancy Reagan listened closely to her directors. The result was a success story whose proportions were impressive even by the standards of Washington, where image management is the coin of the realm. Nancy Reagan utilized performance techniques as a means to reinvent herself, and in the process pulled the disparate worlds of Hollywood and the White House as close as they have ever been. If the presidency for Ronald Reagan was "the role of a lifetime," as biographer Lou Cannon put it, for Nancy it was even better: a role that combined the weight of history with the razzle-dazzle of showbiz.

During her first year in the White House the new first lady was roundly condemned for her imperious ways. Mrs. Reagan showed a knack in those initial months for generating one miniscandal after another: extravagant decorating schemes, expensive new china, haute couture and jewelry "borrowed" from New York designers. A highly visible circle of society friends reinforced the aura of country club privilege and snobbery that surrounded Nancy Reagan. Two popular postcards from the time illustrate the first lady's image problems: one depicted her as "Queen Nancy," wearing a crown and wielding a scepter, and the other as "Nancita," an American version of Evita Peron. By early 1982 Mrs. Reagan's approval rating had plummeted to 50 percent, an unusually negative number for someone occupying the country's most beloved ceremonial position.

The rehabilitation of the first lady began that March before an audience of high-powered Washington journalists at the annual Gridiron Club dinner. Mrs. Reagan performed a self-parodying version of the song "Second Hand Rose," with lyrics that turned the criticism on its head. Nancy ended the number by smashing a plate, a playful reference to the controversy over the costly new china she had acquired for the White House. In her memoir, Nancy Reagan wrote that she never dreamed her Gridiron appearance would wield so much influence: "This one song, together with my willingness to sing it, served as a signal to opinion-makers that maybe I wasn't the terrible, humorless woman they thought I was—regal, distant, disdainful. From that night on, my image began to change in Washington."

Mrs. Reagan followed her Gridiron triumph by aggressively taking up a pair of pet causes: drug abuse, which she was against, and foster grandparents, which she was for. Both campaigns called on the first lady to tap into her roots as a performer, a challenge to which she gladly rose. The most notable of these efforts was a March 1983 appearance on the NBC television comedy *Diff'rent Strokes*, a gig that brought Nancy Reagan back to the soundstages of Hollywood for the first time since 1957, when she and her husband costarred in *Hellcats of the Navy*. The taping drew extensive press coverage, and though the first lady's "acting" consisted of little more than playing herself in a few quick scenes, the message came through loud and clear: Nancy Reagan cared about the millions of young people who tuned in to *Diff'rent Strokes*. When the program aired, both Reagans posed for photographs as they watched from a couch in the family quarters of the White House. In each shot the president wears the same expression: an exaggerated laugh that makes Nancy's episode of *Diff'rent Strokes* look like the funniest program in the annals of television.

Mrs. Reagan's "Just Say No" antidrug campaign cast her in a range of roles that smudged the lines between politics and show business: comedy actress, talk show interviewer, public television documentary presenter, chanteuse. In 1985 she joined a group of young people to make a public service music video, singing a number called "Stop the Madness." A year later she and her husband gave one of the strangest performances in White House history, a live telecast from the third-floor residence in which the two former thespians appealed to the public for a "national crusade" against drugs. Sitting hand in hand on a sofa, the Reagans took turns addressing the camera. "I've asked someone very special to join me," the president began, establishing that it was Nancy's show as much as his. In form, if not content, the joint appearance closely paralleled the couple's work on *General Electric Theater*, the 1950s TV series that featured the Reagans showing off their new home and its amazing electrical appliances. This time, instead of refrigerators and washing machines, they were peddling a drug-free America.

Mrs. Reagan's second project, the foster grandparents program, entailed a more modest public relations effort. Nancy Reagan was credited as the author of *To Love a Child*, a book that profiled foster grandparents around the country. In honor of its publication in October 1982 several hundred program volunteers were invited to a party on the White House lawn, where the star attraction was Frank Sinatra. Sinatra and the first lady, backed by a children's chorus, entertained the crowd with a newly written song, also called "To Love a Child," with lyrics by Hal David and music by *Sesame Street* composer Joe Raposo. "She hit an off-note or two singing," reported Bruce Morton on CBS News. "So, come to that, did Sinatra." Indeed Sinatra, who had skipped the previous day's rehearsal, turned in a decidedly halfhearted performance. Reporters noted that the first lady spent more time with Frank than she did with her guests.

Nancy Reagan's relationship with Frank Sinatra, much remarked on during the Reagan presidency, supplies an interesting sidebar to the lives of these long-time celebrities. Through Nancy, Sinatra finally gained the White House access he had been craving since 1960. Through Sinatra, Nancy shored up her standing as a member of Hollywood royalty. But the friendship was far more than a transaction between two inveterate social climbers; they genuinely enjoyed each other's company and talked on the phone for hours on end. A friend of the first lady told the *Washington Post* that Nancy had had a childhood crush on Sinatra. "She twinkles when he arrives," the friend said. "They're real cute together."

Frank Sinatra proved to be a loyal companion. Hearing of the assassination attempt on President Reagan in March 1981, Sinatra immediately caught a plane to Washington to be with Nancy. "He shut down his show and just came," the first lady told Nancy Sinatra Jr. "The next thing I knew, he was in Washington to be of support and help to me." Two months after the shooting Sinatra surprised Nancy Reagan on her birthday by popping up unannounced at a Congressional Club luncheon where she was being honored. Introduced as a "gift" for Mrs. Reagan, Sinatra joked, "I've been called a lot of things, but never a gift." For half an hour he serenaded the spellbound guest of honor with a selection of his hits, joking that it was the earliest he had sung since he was an altar boy.

Throughout the Reagan presidency Frank Sinatra made regular White House visits. He came to the mansion for state dinners, awards ceremonies, birthday parties, private lunches with Nancy, and in his capacity as presidential entertainment consultant. When Sinatra performed a concert in Washington in 1983, the Reagans were in the audience. When Nancy got an award in Los Angeles for her work against drug abuse, Sinatra made the presentation.

Inevitably the chumminess between Frank and Nancy led to hard feelings on the part of Sinatra's wife, Barbara. At the Congressional Club luncheon in 1981, before Frank surprised Mrs. Reagan, Barbara Sinatra had hidden behind a centerpiece lest her presence at the event give the secret away. Metaphorically this is where she remained in the relationship between her husband and the first lady. "Even when the Sinatras were invited to a White House state dinner, Mrs. Reagan always wanted Frank seated next to her, and Barbara . . . well, we had to seat Barbara in outer Mongolia," a White House staff person told Kitty Kelley.

According to Tina Sinatra, at a stressful point in her father's marriage, when Frank and Barbara had temporarily separated, Nancy counseled Sinatra in a series of nightly phone calls. Tina quoted Mrs. Reagan as telling him, "Francis, this woman is not for you. She's not going to make you happy. You've got one foot out the door—keep going!" Sinatra ignored the advice and reconciled with his wife. When he died in 1998, Barbara informed her stepdaughter that Mrs. Reagan need not be invited to the funeral. At the insistence of family members, Nancy Reagan did attend, exiting the church just behind the Sinatra family.

✳✳✳✳

Like her husband, Nancy Reagan brought Hollywood with her when she moved into the White House. Mrs. Reagan faced the performance demands of her position with the aplomb of someone who had spent her entire adult life in front of cameras. No photo opportunity exceeded her grasp, as evidenced by one of the most sublimely silly moments of the Reagan presidency: the 1983 pre-Christmas visit to the

White House of television action hero Mr. T—a short, muscular African American actor known for his Mohawk haircut and twenty-plus pounds of gold chains. He showed up in a sleeveless Santa Claus outfit at a party for diplomats' children, toting a bag and ringing a bell. The slightly sinister Kris Kringle entered with a question and a growl: "Who been good and who been bad?" Nancy had the perfect antidote to a scene stealer like Mr. T: she sat on his lap and gave the top of his bald head a peck. The shot appeared in virtually every newspaper and newscast in America.

In addition to preparing her for the technical demands of being first lady, Mrs. Reagan's experience in Hollywood attuned her to the realities of fame. From the time Nancy Davis was a child, this daughter of a retired actress mingled with some of the biggest names in show business. As a stagestruck fifteen-year-old she got to meet Jimmy Stewart, developing an "instant crush" on him. When Nancy declared her intention to work in the theater, her mother's friend Katharine Hepburn sent the budding thespian a long letter warning of the difficulties of the profession. After Nancy moved to New York in 1946 to launch her career, she regularly visited Hepburn's home.

Mrs. Reagan wrote in her memoir that in the late 1960s Katharine Hepburn suddenly and unceremoniously dropped her as a friend. Though Nancy considered the cause of Hepburn's about-face a mystery, the reasoning seemed straightforward enough. According to Nancy's memoir, "Once, when I called her on the phone, she said, 'I'm terribly busy, and besides, I don't know what we'd have to talk about. After all, you're a staunch Republican and I'm a staunch Democrat . . . '"

As a fledgling actress Nancy Davis led a charmed life. She dated Clark Gable and appeared on Broadway opposite Mary Martin; her MGM screen test was directed by George Cukor. In each of these cases she directly benefited from the connections of her mother. Mary Martin was a close friend of Mrs. Davis. George Cukor came about via Spencer Tracy, another family friend. And it was through Tracy that Clark Gable got Nancy Davis's phone number in New York. Gable and Nancy saw each other every day for a week, attending baseball games in the afternoon and plays at night. It was Nancy's first exposure to celebrity at that scale, and she found the experience both fascinating and unsettling. She wrote, "Clark was sexy, handsome, and affectionate, but I found him less the seducer he was reputed to be than a kind, romantic, and fun-loving man. He sent me flowers and we held hands, but I think that in his case the lover image had been so built up that it was a relief for him to be with someone like me, who made no demands on him."

Like the vast majority of actors, Nancy Davis never achieved the superstar status to which she aspired. Most of the dozen or so films she made are likely to be remembered only for her appearance in them. Just one—*East Side, West Side*, starring Ava Gardner, Cyd Charisse, Van Heflin, James Mason, and Barbara Stanwyck—could be classified an A picture. Nancy's last shot at movie stardom came in 1995, when she reluctantly turned down the title role in the Albert Brooks comedy *Mother*; the part instead went to Debbie Reynolds. Essentially, after 1952 Ronald Reagan became Nancy's career, and she devoted herself to it with unbridled tenacity. "I think if left to his own devices, he might have ended up hosting *Unsolved Mysteries* on TV or something," son Ron Reagan once told a *60 Minutes* interviewer. Jimmy Stewart put it a different way: "If Ronald Reagan had married Nancy the first time, she could've got him an Academy Award." His consolation prize—and hers—was the White House.

It is interesting to note that Nancy Reagan was not the first president's wife with a Hollywood track record. In the mid-1930s, Patricia Nixon—then Patricia Ryan—fleetingly appeared in several studio pictures, including two that surpassed in quality any of Nancy Davis's films: *Becky Sharp*, Hollywood's first full-length Technicolor production, and *The Great Ziegfeld*, winner of the 1936 Academy Award as best picture. In neither did Pat Ryan receive screen credit; her single line in *Becky Sharp* landed on the cutting-room floor, though she is momentarily visible in a ballroom scene behind Miriam Hopkins. Her only real role was a walk-on in *Small Town Girl*, a 1936 romantic comedy with Janet Gaynor and Robert Taylor, whom Patricia considered the handsomest man she had ever seen. More typically, Pat would be cast in crowd scenes, teaming up with friends from the University of Southern California to earn $6.50 a day as extras.

Although the future first lady enjoyed the costumes and makeup, the utter boredom of moviemaking left her cold. "An entire day would go by," she told her daughter, "and the director would take and retake just one scene." Another Hollywood reality also turned off Patricia Ryan: the casting couch. According to Julie Nixon's biography of her mother, Pat had "several brushes" with presumptuous studio employees. During the filming of *Becky Sharp* an assistant director showed up drunk at the Ryans' apartment one night and demanded to see Pat; her brothers slammed the door in his face.

Another of Patricia Ryan's jobs before she married was at Bullock's Wilshire, the posh Los Angeles department store frequented by the famous names of the movie colony. When Walter Pidgeon treated his teenage daughter to a shopping spree at Bullock's, Pat modeled the clothing. Marlene Dietrich made frequent visits to the store, disappointing the staff because she usually hid her legendary legs under slacks. Pat Ryan once caught a glimpse of another celebrated Bullock's customer, Greta Garbo.

Despite her early exposure to Hollywood, Patricia Ryan Nixon showed little inclination for the spotlight. As her husband's career flourished, Mrs. Nixon played the dutiful political wife to the degree required, but never did the role seem a comfortable fit; as a performer her shyness was palpable. After she left the White House it came as no surprise that Patricia Nixon withdrew from public life.

The first modern first lady to feel completely at home in the media was Eleanor Roosevelt, who became as ubiquitous in the national consciousness as any goddess of the silver screen. Eleanor assumed full partnership in the public relations enterprise that was the Roosevelt White House, writing a popular syndicated newspaper column, hosting her own radio program, and making regular appearances in motion picture newsreels, the TV newscasts of their day. These involvements brought Mrs. Roosevelt into direct contact with most of the major entertainment figures of the 1930s and 1940s, to an extent far greater than the celebrity interactions of her husband. Eleanor Roosevelt was FDR's ambassador to show business; she did more to bridge the gap between Hollywood and Washington than any White House figure before her.

As first lady Eleanor made three excursions to the movie capital: she dropped in on Shirley Temple at Twentieth Century Fox in 1937, visited the Goldwyn studio (where her son, James, worked as a producer) in 1939, and in 1941 received a tour from Walt Disney of his animation facility. During the second trip Mrs. Roosevelt attended a private screening of *Wuthering Heights* and had dinner with its star, Merle Oberon. The first lady wrote in her column, "What magnificent gamblers the people in this business are! Mr. Goldwyn told me that millions of people would have to see this picture for it really to pay. No wonder that at a dinner before the preview, Merle Oberon . . . and even Mr. Goldwyn, who has been in the business so many years, were excited and anxious to know the verdict of the public."

Just as Eleanor came to Hollywood, so did Hollywood come to Eleanor. In addition to the annual FDR birthday ball events, movie stars made their way to Washington to promote other causes, and when they did it fell to the first lady to play hostess. One of the largest such celebrity contingents called at the executive mansion in April 1942 as part of a nationwide Victory Caravan war relief tour. Thirty stars and starlets arrived in the capital aboard a train called the *Star-Spangled Special*—among them, Desi Arnaz, Joan Bennett, Joan Blondell, Charles Boyer, James Cagney, Claudette Colbert, Bing Crosby, Olivia de Havilland, Cary Grant, Bob Hope, Bert Lahr, Laurel and Hardy, Groucho Marx, Merle Oberon, Pat O'Brien, and Eleanor Powell. Before their evening performance at the Capitol Theater, the entertainers accepted an invitation for tea at the White House with Eleanor Roosevelt.

Groucho Marx used the opportunity to test the first lady's sense of humor, both at the White House and during the show later that evening. After tea Mrs. Roosevelt led the actors on a tour of the White House. According to Bing Crosby, in the gallery housing the portraits of the country's presidents, Groucho pointed to Ulysses Grant and asked his hostess, "Did General Grant wear a Vandyke, or did Vandyke wear a General Grant?" Replied Eleanor, "I really don't know." During the performance, Marx tried out another gag on the first lady. As they watched the acrobatic dancing of Charlotte Greenwood, a musical comedy artist famous for her high kicks, Groucho turned to the proper Mrs. Roosevelt and remarked, "You know, with a little practice, you could do that too." History does not record the first lady's response.

Blessed with the gift of unflappability, Eleanor Roosevelt could hold her own in the unpredictable milieu of show business. Appearing as a guest on Gene Autry's radio show, Mrs. Roosevelt was introduced to a baby in the audience who had been christened Franklin Delano Gene Autry Johnson. With Autry standing behind her and reporters and cameramen looking on, she lifted the little boy onto her lap for a photograph. "As the flash bulbs popped," Autry recalled, "the baby tinkled all over her dress." Everyone in the room fell silent. The first lady was headed to a formal party after the show, and now the entire front of her dress was soiled. According to Autry, "Mrs. Roosevelt slowly rose, handed the baby to his mother, took a handkerchief, dabbed at her dress, and reassured everyone in that familiar, high voice with the trill in it: 'Don't mind that. Remember, I raised five babies.'"

Eleanor Roosevelt's finest moment vis-à-vis performing artists came in 1939, when she resigned her membership in the Daughters of the American Revolution after the organization denied permission for African American contralto Marian Anderson to sing at Constitution Hall. Mrs. Roosevelt explained her decision in her newspaper column: "The question is, if you belong to an organization and disapprove of an action which is typical of a policy, should you resign or is it better to work for a changed point of view within the organization?" Concluding that she could not actively work within the D.A.R., she canceled her membership. A Gallup poll found that two-thirds of the American public supported the decision, and the incident sparked a nationwide debate about segregation.

In the wake of the controversy Franklin Roosevelt gave permission for Marian Anderson to perform a free concert at the Lincoln Memorial, which she did on Easter Sunday 1939 before a crowd of seventy-five thousand. Several weeks later she sang at the White House for the king and queen of England. This was not Anderson's first such appearance; the Roosevelts had invited her to entertain at the mansion in 1936. In 1961 Anderson sang at the inauguration of John F. Kennedy, who decorated her two years later with the Presidential Medal of Freedom, the nation's highest civilian award. Marian Anderson was honored in 1978 with a seventy-fifth birthday concert at Carnegie Hall; sitting next to her in the box was first lady Rosalynn Carter.

✵✵✵✵

Unlike Nancy Reagan, Jacqueline Kennedy did not train for the job of presidential wife. Unlike Eleanor Roosevelt, she never made her peace with the spotlight. Instead, as one of the most reluctant celebrities in White House history, the glamorous Mrs. Kennedy commanded the stage almost in spite of herself. Her reticence could hardly be attributed to naïveté about the media. Before marrying JFK Jacqueline Bouvier worked as the "Inquiring Camera Girl" for the *Washington Times-Herald*. Becoming a member of the Kennedy family further exposed her to life in the public eye, beginning on the day of her wedding, when newsreel cameras turned the event into a spectacle. As a senatorial spouse she even toyed with the idea of an acting career, asking stepbrother Gore Vidal in 1956 if it was too late for her to start. "Isn't what's happening to you now a lot more interesting?" Vidal wondered. "For Jack it is," she replied. "Not for me."

Jacqueline Kennedy's early television appearances did not betoken a natural ease before the lens. In October 1953 Edward R. Murrow brought his TV program *Person to Person* to the home of Senator Kennedy and his twenty-four-year-old bride, marking the new Mrs. Kennedy's national network debut. Jacqueline did little of the talking as she sat nervously by her husband's side on a floral chintz couch, uncertain where to look. Seven years later, when *Person to Person* returned for a visit shortly before the 1960 presidential election, Jacqueline Kennedy had grown more comfortable on camera, though still not fully relaxed. Because her husband was running late, the pregnant Mrs. Kennedy had the first eight minutes of the program to herself. She showed interviewer Charles Collingwood through the couple's Georgetown home, and, in a touchingly spontaneous moment, introduced two-year-old Caroline, playing with dolls in her bedroom.

Collingwood reunited with Jacqueline Kennedy for a second, more celebrated television show that aired on Valentine's Day 1962: the first lady's historic tour of the redecorated White House. The veteran CBS newsman was greatly impressed by Jackie's lack of vanity. "Now if you're interviewing a Hollywood star or a famous international or society beauty in London or Paris, she would always be fussing with her hair, her lipstick, and her eyebrows," Collingwood said. "She would show an instant awareness of the camera angle and the lights. These affected Mrs. Kennedy not a bit."

Although CBS had anticipated a two- to-three day production schedule, shooting at the mansion took only six hours. Collingwood and the first lady did a quick walk-through of each room on the tour before the cameras rolled, but when it came time to film, Jacqueline Kennedy reeled off the appropriate information and anecdotes without benefit of a script. The chief White House usher stood just out of camera range to supply any missing details; he was never called upon. Another assistant was on hand to help with matters of grooming, repositioning a microphone at one point and touching up Mrs. Kennedy's hair. But over the course of the hour-long program only three retakes were required, none of them the first lady's fault.

Nearly 50 million Americans—a third of the country—watched Jacqueline Kennedy's White House tour. A deluge of mail followed the broadcast, eventually totaling around seventeen thousand letters; some viewers enclosed cash donations for the redecoration effort. Mrs. Kennedy taped introductions in French and Spanish, and the program was screened around the world as part of the U.S. government's cultural outreach efforts. JFK immediately apprehended the political value of the footage; according to a White House aide who watched the broadcast with him, his first reaction was to ask, "Can we show it in 1964?"

A Tour of the White House with Mrs. John F. Kennedy solidified the first lady's status as a media icon. Women across the country had already begun to emulate her clothing and hair. The most prominent homage was paid by Mary Tyler Moore on *The Dick Van Dyke Show*, which premiered the year the Kennedys moved into the White House. Though not a direct imitation, the resemblance was unmistakable: Moore's character, Laura Petrie, dressed like Jackie and wore her hair in the same bouffant flip. Mrs. Kennedy, born seven years earlier than Mary Tyler Moore, might have been Laura's older, more sophisticated sister.

The celebrification of Jacqueline Kennedy reached a turning point in June 1962 when the first lady appeared on the cover of the movie magazine *Photoplay* alongside a shot of Elizabeth Taylor. "America's 2 queens!" the headline screamed. "A comparison of their days and nights! How they raise their children! How they treat their men!" The story, published at the halfway point of the Kennedy presidency, represents a watershed in the blending of Hollywood and the White House. Not only does it equate the wife of the president with a movie star; in a brazen bit of circularity, the magazine invited film personalities to comment about the propriety of Mrs. Kennedy as a *Photoplay* cover girl. "She has had too much of the wrong kind of publicity," sniffed Connie Stevens. "I think it's all right for her to be in the news, or even in a woman's service magazine—but on the cover of *Photoplay*! It doesn't seem right to me at all." Troy Donahue took the opposite point of view: "If Jacqueline Kennedy is in public demand, then of course her picture should be shown. Why not? She's unique. She's the only person who could hold the special position she's made for herself in the world. Yes, she's just the kind of girl the new Troy Donahue would like to date!" Even Jayne Mansfield, a reputed JFK lover, weighed in, complimenting the first lady on her parenting skills and "very attractive figure."

Although Mrs. Kennedy never appeared in a single motion picture, she remained a fixture of fan magazines—and an engine of the celebrity industry in general—for the rest of her life. Ultimately her fame transcended both Hollywood and the White House. Jacqueline Kennedy occupied a higher plane of celebrity, one which, at least until the emergence of Britain's Princess Diana, she had all to herself. "This woman wrote her own script," observed *New York Times* critic Herbert Muschamp in 2001. "President Kennedy needed his family, and battalions of advisers, courtiers, historians, medical experts, and other technicians to put his identity together. Jackie created herself." In the final analysis it was this quality—this clarity of identity—that gave Jacqueline Kennedy more in common with the leading ladies of Hollywood than with the other political wives of Washington. Like Hepburn, Dietrich, and all the archetypal women of the screen, Jackie was an instantly recognizable symbol, existing on levels both visual and metaphysical.

After she moved to New York Mrs. Kennedy enjoyed tracking the elusive Greta Garbo, with whom she once dined at the White House. Through a mutual friend a meeting was set up in New York, but at the last minute Garbo backed out. Jackie, like everyone else in the city, had to make do with unexpected Garbo sightings on the streets of Manhattan. Nancy Tuckerman, Jacqueline Kennedy's close friend, described the fascination: "She was always excited to see Garbo, and to update me. 'I saw her today again! Just walking along by herself,' Jackie would say. 'She's so mysterious!'" In the end the allure of Jacqueline Kennedy had much in common with the allure of Garbo: the more they held themselves in reserve, the more irresistible they became.

✵✵✵✵

Betty Ford brought to the White House a natural affinity for show business. Trained as a classical dancer, she enjoyed the company of entertainers and felt at home in their presence. In 1976 Mrs. Ford became the first presidential wife to perform onstage at the Gridiron dinner, dancing a soft-shoe to "Once in Love with Amy." To prepare for the show Betty Ford rehearsed at the White House with a professional dance coach and a three-piece band. Converting the second-floor hallway of the mansion into a makeshift studio, the group spent a day polishing the routine until it was ready for an audience of the capital's most august figures. Just before her dance coach left the White House, Mrs. Ford had one last request: Could he teach her the Hustle, a dance that had taken the discotheques of America by storm? Within a few minutes the first lady and her coach were hustling up and down the West Hall.

Betty Ford projected a sense of fun that made her attractive to the public and to professional performers as well. In 1975 Woody Allen escorted her to a benefit for the Martha Graham dance troupe in New York City—"sort of," as Mrs. Ford put it in her memoir. Allen reached the theater a few minutes before the first lady, accompanied by his girlfriend, Diane Keaton. Instead of waiting outside for Mrs. Ford to arrive, the comedian ducked into the building and had to be coaxed out. "In the end," said Sheila Weidenfeld, Mrs. Ford's press secretary, "Woody Allen did greet Mrs. Ford, but with all the social grace of an eleven-year-old forced to go to dancing school." Betty Ford later told Weidenfeld, "He was like a little boy. Diane Keaton and I each took a hand and kind of led him in. But he was really funny. He told me why he gave up dancing—his self-consciousness in a leotard." At a brief press conference during intermission reporters asked Allen about his presence as Betty Ford's escort. Said Allen: "We're just good friends."

Betty Ford boasted a string of notable show business escorts during her husband's presidency. In March 1976 Fred Astaire accompanied Mrs. Ford to the American Film Institute award ceremony for director William Wyler. "When I was a girl I never dreamed of growing up and marrying a president," she told the audience, "but I did dream of gliding across a floor with Fred Astaire." The experience of delivering remarks at the AFI salute gave Betty Ford valuable insight into the ways of professional entertainers. "All these other women had played Mrs. Miniver or Jezebel," she said, "so I assumed they'd speak extemporaneously. I didn't know how I was going to be able to offer my salute, which I had written out on cards in my bag, without feeling like a klutz." To Mrs. Ford's relief, each of the stars who preceded her also spoke from cards. "Nobody wanted to be up there without a crutch," she said.

Three months later Sammy Davis Jr. threw an exclusive private party for Mrs. Ford at his home in Los Angeles. Initially the invitation struck press secretary Weidenfeld as a dubious proposition. "Since I think the Nixon pardon has hurt

Ford and continues to hurt Ford each time it comes up," she wrote in her diary, "I have avoided all symbols that consciously or unconsciously reinforce a Nixon-Ford relationship in people's minds." Davis, she felt, was just such a symbol. But Mrs. Ford insisted on going, and the best Weidenfeld could do was close the event to the news media.

The host and his wife met Betty as her car pulled into the driveway. They presented her with a huge bouquet of roses, then guided her past a sign at the door that said "Welcome, First Mama! With Love, Altovise and Sammy." Inside the house a galaxy of 1970s A-list celebrities awaited: Liza Minnelli, Marlo Thomas, Lee and Farrah Fawcett-Majors, Angie Dickinson, and Johnny Carson, all of whom were "responsive and fascinated by everything she said," according to Weidenfeld. Betty Ford was the star attraction that night, an exotic specimen among the garden variety luminaries of the entertainment world. Weidenfeld summarized the party in her diary: "A surprisingly warm and comfortable evening, much laughter, much kissing (they're very affectionate in Hollywood)."

By the time of these celebrity encounters in Los Angeles Betty Ford had already made her highly publicized television acting debut. In November 1975 the first lady put in an unprecedented appearance on the *Mary Tyler Moore Show*, playing herself in a short segment that was shot across the street from the White House at the Hay-Adams Hotel. The two-minute scene showed Mrs. Ford on the phone, having a conversation with Mary Richards, the TV news producer played by Moore. Mrs. Ford received a minimum union scale fee of $172.50 for her work, which aired in January 1976.

Though the press reported all these details, behind the scenes a more interesting story was unfolding. Before the taping Moore and her producers paid a call at the White House, where the first lady led them on a tour. According to Moore, Mrs. Ford "glided from room to room with the occasional help of a doorway or chair back, or a promptly offered arm for balance, as she described the functions of the various chambers." Her speech, Moore observed, was slurred.

The Hollywood visitors left for the Hay-Adams, where Betty Ford was to join them for the taping. But presently the guest star got cold feet. The first lady's personal secretary called Sheila Weidenfeld to ask if the shoot could be postponed. "In the background," Weidenfeld said, "I heard Mrs. Ford putting the request a bit less delicately. 'She can't make me do something I don't want to do!' she was yelling. 'She can't ruin my life!'" Eventually Weidenfeld pacified her nervous prima donna, and they made their way across the street, an hour and a half behind schedule.

According to Mary Tyler Moore, "Rehearsing was out of the question because she couldn't remember her lines. We tried several times to go through the scene, but inevitably she'd lose track, lose confidence, and be even less able the next time." Moore had an inspiration: she remembered that during the filming of *Thoroughly Modern Millie* Julie Andrews fed lines to costar Beatrice Lillie, then suffering from Alzheimer's disease. Taking a seat out of camera range, Moore spoon-fed Betty Ford her handful of dialogue until the scene was finished. "It was shocking and sad to see firsthand what had been whispered about," Moore recalled in her memoir.

Ironically, eight years later Mary Tyler Moore was a patient in the recently established Betty Ford Clinic for treatment of alcoholism. Midway through the program, Moore got fed up and left. "The next morning," she said, "I was awakened by a call from Mrs. Ford herself, asking me to come back for a talk. That phone call saved my life."

Betty Ford's position as a "patron saint of recovering partyers," in the words of writer John Strausbaugh, permanently aligned the wife of the thirty-eighth president with the men and women of show business. Since the early 1980s the Betty Ford Center in Palm Springs, California, has been synonymous with celebrities in need of detoxification. Elizabeth Taylor, Liza Minnelli, Johnny Cash, Chevy Chase, and Peter Lawford are just some of the marquee names to pass through the doors of the treatment facility bearing the former first lady's name.

Betty Ford's winning battle against addiction also entitled her to another singularly American honor: an eponymous television movie of the week, *The Betty Ford Story*, which aired in 1987. Edging out Glenn Close for the role, Gena Rowlands gave a creditable performance in a tasteful account of Mrs. Ford's descent and resurrection. Betty Ford did not have script approval, and as a consequence producers included several elements of the story over her objection. The former first lady was most concerned about the scene that reenacted the Ford family confronting her alcoholism. "That's a strong scene, and she resisted it, but I would not do the film without it," said producer David L. Wolper. "Eventually she came around." In the end, Betty Ford said, the experience of watching her life story "brought tears to my eyes."

✳✳✳✳

Presidents and first ladies are not the only White House residents with ties to show business; a number of their children made inroads into the entertainment community. In the late 1930s James Roosevelt, eldest son of FDR and Eleanor, parlayed his family connections into a studio job with Samuel Goldwyn. Roosevelt's Hollywood career was short-lived; after producing one film, the 1941 musical comedy *Pot O'Gold* with James Stewart and Paulette Goddard, he began marketing a coin-operated "movie jukebox" machine. James eventually left the entertainment business for a career in politics. John Boettiger, the husband of the Roosevelts' only daughter, Anna, also worked briefly in Hollywood in the office of Will Hays, the film industry's overseer of morality.

During World War II the Roosevelts' second son, Elliott, wooed and wed Warner Bros. starlet Faye Emerson. The story of their relationship stands as a warning to presidential offspring who wade into the treacherous waters of Hollywood. Roosevelt had been sent to Los Angeles by the War Department to make recommendations to the U.S. government about the purchase of reconnaissance aircraft. While there he was courted by Howard Hughes, the high-living film producer and defense contractor, who hoped to sell his prototype plane to the military. Hughes invited the president's son to a party at his home in the Hollywood Hills, where Faye Emerson was among the beautiful female guests. Elliott was smitten, and when he took Emerson on a romantic getaway to Catalina Island, Hughes picked up the tab. The couple next traveled to New York, with Hughes again subsidizing a portion of their expenses. In Washington Elliott Roosevelt presented a glowing report on Hughes Aircraft's reconnaissance plane, and the government awarded Hughes a multimillion dollar contract.

In November 1944, while he was home on leave from the air force, the twice-divorced Roosevelt exchanged marital vows with Emerson in an observation tower overlooking Grand Canyon National Park. Soon after the wedding the newlyweds made unwelcome headlines when it came to light that three servicemen had been bumped from an army transport flight in order to make room for Faye Emerson's bull mastiff dog. Within a few years the marriage soured, and in 1948 Emerson was back in the news following a suicide attempt at the family home in Hyde Park.

After the Roosevelts divorced in 1950, Elliott refashioned himself as his mother's agent and producer. Building on an earlier career as a radio executive, Elliott produced a forty-five-minute daily show with Eleanor as host. Other members of the family were appalled at the degree to which Elliott Roosevelt commercialized his mother's image. Elliott himself delivered the show's advertisements, telling listeners that "Mother washes" with a particular brand of detergent and "Mother eats" a particular brand of soup. *Billboard* magazine observed wryly that the program proved beyond doubt that "a boy's best friend is his mother."

Margaret Truman, the only child of Harry and Bess Truman, is the highest-profile White House resident to tackle a career in show business. For Margaret, the Truman name was both a blessing and a curse. Absent her status as the president's daughter it is doubtful that she would have found employment as a classical vocalist, but in the final analysis the publicity catapulted Margaret Truman into the limelight before she was ready. Miss Truman started big, making her professional debut in March 1947 at the age of twenty-three. Before an audience of 15 million radio listeners she sang a miniconcert of three songs with the Detroit Symphony Orchestra. Later that year she performed at the Hollywood Bowl.

Margaret soon began a period of intensive study with Metropolitan Opera star (and fellow Missourian) Helen Traubel, who overcame her initial misgivings and took the young singer under her wing. But Traubel's key piece of advice—that Margaret train for at least five years before accepting public engagements—could not hold up against the flood of offers that poured in for the president's daughter. When Margaret pressed forward with her professional career, Traubel broke off relations.

In her autobiography the Wagnerian soprano devoted a full chapter to what she called "l'affaire Margaret," claiming that her time with Miss Truman "cost me considerably in lost concert fees, an incredible amount of sweat and disappointment—and, finally, a loss in the eyes of the musical world for ever having my name connected with such a musical aspirant." The relationship, which began on a modest scale, soon became all-consuming; according to Traubel's husband, "Margaret just took us over." Helen Traubel wrote that she lacked the courage to level with Margaret: "I had never faced such a situation before. How does one tell the daughter of a United States president that she is not a good singer?"

Unfortunately for Miss Truman, questions about her talent persisted, most famously in December 1950, when she gave a concert at Washington's Constitution Hall before an audience that included her parents. The next morning *Washington Post* music critic Paul Hume offered a charitable but blunt assessment of the performance:

> Miss Truman is a unique American phenomenon with a pleasant voice of little size and fair quality. She is extremely attractive on stage. Yet Miss Truman cannot sing very well. She is flat a good deal of the time—more so last night than at any time we have heard her in past years.
>
> It is an extremely unpleasant duty to record such unhappy facts about so honestly appealing a person. But as long as Miss Truman sings as she has for three years, and does today, we seem to have no recourse unless it is to omit comment on her programs altogether.

The president reacted defensively, firing off an irate letter to Paul Hume on White House stationery and giving it to an usher to mail. "I've just read your lousy review of Margaret's concert," Truman wrote. "It seems to me that you are a frustrated old man who wishes he could have been successful . . . Some day I hope to meet you. When that happens you'll need a new nose, a lot of beefsteak for black eyes, and perhaps a supporter below . . ." Although the *Post* did not print the note, word of its existence leaked out, and soon the entire country knew. The White House received some ten thousand letters on the matter, with sentiment running two to one against the president. What the public did not realize was that at the time he wrote the note Harry Truman was under a great deal of stress. Hours before Margaret's recital, Truman's press secretary and close friend died of a heart attack in his office; Margaret was not informed until after her performance.

After he left the White House, Harry Truman patched up his differences with Paul Hume. In the aftermath of the controversy Hume had shown a good deal of class, issuing a statement that said, "A man suffering the loss of a friend and carrying the burden of the present world crisis ought to be indulged in an occasional outburst of temper." In 1958, when Hume called on the former president at his office in Independence, Missouri, the two music lovers ended up playing piano together.

For her part, Margaret Truman persevered with a career that never quite transcended the level of novelty act. In the 1950s she ranked among television's most visible guest performers, sharing the stage with some of the biggest names of the day: Milton Berle, Jimmy Durante, Groucho Marx, Tallulah Bankhead. The typical appearance involved a comedy dialogue between Margaret and her host, followed by a vocal solo from Margaret. The humor was exceedingly gentle, as in this exchange with Phil Silvers from 1950:

Phil: Where do you live?
Margaret: 1600 Pennsylvania Avenue.
Phil: Is that an apartment or a hotel?

Margaret tried her hand at a range of television positions: introducing clips with Allen Funt on *Candid Camera*; acting in a sketch with Sid Caesar and Imogene Coca on *Your Show of Shows*; appearing as the mystery guest on *What's My Line?* (Dorothy Kilgallen, a neighbor of Miss Truman, correctly guessed her identity); and essaying a dramatic role on television. Margaret Truman made her acting debut on radio in a 1950 comedy called *Jackpot* with James Stewart playing her husband. "The girl is good," Stewart told reporters. "She came through perfectly. She has a great amount of ease and that means a lot in acting."

Perhaps the most charming of Margaret's broadcast outings was a live television interview she conducted with her parents for the CBS program *Person to Person* in

May 1955. With Margaret in New York, Harry and Bess held their end of the conversation from the family residence in Missouri. The exchange was an entertaining blend of mediated awkwardness and genuine family affection. Margaret at one point asked her father what sort of manual work he did around the house.

Harry: I do an immense amount of it from my rocking chair.
Margaret: How many times have you mowed the lawn in the last few years?
Harry: Well, as I remember, I think about once.
Margaret: Is that right, Mother?
Bess: I don't remember the once.

In the late 1950s Margaret Truman set aside her girlhood dream of show business stardom and retired to raise a family. Except for a brief stint as a talk show host, she has conducted her life largely out of the public eye. Truman found success in the 1980s and 1990s as the author of the *Capital Crimes* novels, a series of Washington-based murder mysteries. Several years after Margaret Truman published her first novel, Elliott Roosevelt began writing his own White House murder series, featuring his mother as the amateur detective solving the crimes.

✶✶✶✶

During the presidency of Lyndon Johnson a different sort of Hollywood–White House connection surfaced: the romance between twenty-one-year-old Lynda Bird Johnson and twenty-six-year-old movie star George Hamilton. After meeting at a party at the Manhattan apartment of socialite Charlotte Ford, the couple began a courtship that kept reporters from both coasts on high alert throughout 1966. In March Lynda brought her beau to the family ranch in Texas—he had already been a guest at the White House—and Hamilton reciprocated by inviting Johnson to meet his family in Beverly Hills. In Los Angeles Hamilton showed the president's daughter around the MGM studio, where she met Elvis Presley and took a peek at Greta Garbo's dressing room. George Hamilton feted Lynda with two parties at Grayhall, his chateau-style home that once belonged to Douglas Fairbanks. The first drew a variety of Hollywood luminaries, including Greer Garson, Agnes Moorehead, Edward G. Robinson, Cesar Romero, Elke Sommer, Jill St. John, and Rod Taylor. The following night, on Lynda's twenty-second birthday, Hamilton threw a more exclusive dinner party, with Tony Curtis and Samantha Eggar among the dozen guests.

A month later Lynda returned to L.A. for the Academy Awards, where Hamilton served as a presenter. The appearance of the president's daughter at Hollywood's most glamorous event created a media spectacle. "Among the stars attending the thirty-eighth annual awards presentation," wrote Peter Bart in the *New York Times*, "a nonprofessional, Miss Lynda Bird Johnson, attracted perhaps the most attention." Master of ceremonies Bob Hope used the first daughter's presence to pepper his monologue with jokes. "I had a hunch Lynda Bird was here tonight," Hope said. "I was frisked twice on the way in." Seated in the audience were former actors George Murphy, now a U.S. senator from California, and first-time gubernatorial candidate Ronald Reagan. "This is a nice switch," joked Hope, "someone from Washington coming to Hollywood."

In June George Hamilton traveled to Austin for Lynda's graduation from the University of Texas, and he spent both Easter and Christmas 1966 with the Johnson family at the LBJ Ranch. Film footage from Christmas morning shows Hamilton exchanging gifts with the Johnsons; Lynda and her sister Luci are still in their robes. Amid the festivities Lady Bird cuts a holiday cake decorated with the phrase "It's good to have you in Texas."

A few days later George and Lynda left for Acapulco, Mexico, where they spent New Year's Day as the houseguests of actress Merle Oberon. During their stay Oberon invited John Wayne and his family to join the party for lunch. When Wayne's three-year-old son, Ethan, suddenly dived into the pool, Lynda panicked and jumped in after him, unaware that he knew how to swim. As luck would have it, Johnson was wearing a paper dress, a style then in vogue. By the time John Wayne pulled Lynda and Ethan out of the water, the dress had dissolved, leaving the would-be rescuer in her underwear. "Daddy," Ethan asked, "why did that crazy naked lady jump on me?"

The Hamilton-Johnson romance generated an enormous amount of publicity for George Hamilton, much of it negative. Because the relationship unfolded against the backdrop of the Vietnam War, the actor's draft status became a favorite concern of the press. Although Hamilton had been granted a deferment from the draft board as his mother's sole means of support, reporters suggested that Hamilton's White House connections brought him special treatment. In 1981 Hamilton told an interviewer that at the height of the controversy he had been strong-armed to enlist by the general in charge of the Selective Service System. "I will go if you draft me," was Hamilton's reply, "but I will not do that simply to take the pressure off the draft board."

Journalists also charged Hamilton with using Lynda Bird Johnson to enhance his professional standing in Hollywood. In a typical comment, an anonymous source told *Newsweek*, "George Hamilton would do anything to get his name on page one." But more than Hamilton, it was the news media that kept the story in the public eye. Hamilton himself displayed remarkable patience in the face of relentless speculation over the possibility of a Hamilton-Johnson marriage. "I will not use the publicity of the First Family for my career," Hamilton said in an interview. "I have more morals than that."

As it happened, the Johnson family did not feel taken advantage of. Although it was rumored that the president disapproved of George Hamilton, White House insiders insisted otherwise. According to Liz Carpenter, the first lady's press secretary, the allegations made LBJ "indignant." When Lynda announced her engagement to Chuck Robb several months after breaking up with Hamilton, President Johnson wanted the actor to know he had not lobbied against him. He directed Carpenter to call Hamilton "and tell him that I have always liked him and respected him."

The general feeling at the White House was that George Hamilton served as a positive influence for Lynda. Social secretary Bess Abell said, "I think he really came along at a marvelous time in Lynda's life. I think through George she learned that there was more to being a woman and a person than just being a good student." Lady Bird Johnson concurred. Three decades after the fact Mrs. Johnson told a biographer, "He was extremely good for her—he really brought her out as a woman." As for Lynda, when she married Chuck Robb in a December 1967 ceremony, George Hamilton was included among the wedding guests.

✵✵✵✵

The children of Ronald Reagan—Maureen, Michael, Patti, and Ron—spent much of their adult lives unsuccessfully chasing careers in show business. Attempting to break into the family business, each of them flitted from job to job, role to role, always in the public spotlight yet never fully in focus. Maureen was both actress and political activist; Michael everything from radio interviewer to game show host; Patti a novelist, actress, and musician; and Ron a commercial spokesman, television journalist, and ballet dancer. None of the incarnations ever seemed to stick. The Reagan offspring blurred into generic celebrities, more famous for being famous than for any specific accomplishment.

Having grown up in the limelight, they were better prepared than most presidential progeny for membership in the first family. "I was one of the most publicized and photographed children in all of Hollywood," wrote Maureen, the daughter of Reagan and Jane Wyman. "Studio photographers took countless posed shots—roll upon roll upon roll—of our happy little family, which then turned up in fan magazines and newspapers all across the country."

As a young girl Maureen Reagan made her screen debut in her parents' film *It's a Great Feeling*, and she never got the bright lights out of her system. Her adult career began with uncredited roles in the films *Hootenanny Hoot* and Elvis Presley's *Kissin' Cousins*. In the 1970s Maureen sang in nightclubs, did commercials for Crisco and Duncan Hines, and played small parts in television series like *The Partridge Family* and *Marcus Welby, M.D.* By the time of her father's presidency she had given up show business for politics. Here too success proved out of reach: Maureen Reagan's two runs for elective office resulted in defeat.

Maureen's brother, Michael, likewise existed on the fringes of the entertainment industry. In the 1980s he launched an ill-advised acting career that gained him roles in a Sylvester Stallone movie, a Washington-inspired soap opera called *Capitol*, and the nighttime drama *Falcon Crest*, which starred his mother, Jane Wyman. After approving his hire, Wyman warned her son not to trade on his White House connections. According to Michael's autobiography, Wyman threatened to have him fired if he mentioned the president in any interviews. "This is my show," she told him, "not Ronald Reagan's. Understand?" In 1992 Michael Reagan began his own nationally syndicated, politically conservative radio talk show. The position brought him success, if not respectability. Still trading on the family name, he hawks videotapes such as *The Greatest Speeches of Ronald Reagan* and other memorabilia relating to his father's term in office.

Patti and Ron, the children of Nancy Reagan, grew up a generation apart from their older siblings, but equally steeped in the ethos of showbiz L.A. As toddlers, they appeared with their parents in television commercials for products like Crest toothpaste and General Electric appliances. Their schoolmates were the children of movie stars; one year Judy Garland showed up for Parents Day. "It was an elite atmosphere," Patti wrote in her 1992 memoir, "but it didn't seem so to us. We just accepted celebrity as a part of life."

Like Maureen, Patti Davis (she changed her professional name in the mid-1970s) never quite found her niche as a performer. After years of struggling as a singing waitress and bit-part actress—and after affairs with an impressive roster of celebrities that included Dennis Wilson of the Beach Boys, Kris Kristofferson, Timothy Hutton, and Peter Strauss—she turned to writing. In 1986, halfway through her father's second term in the White House, Davis published her first novel, *Home Front*, a thinly disguised roman à clef about an affable but distant California governor-turned-president, his icy, social-climbing wife, and their messed-up daughter. The book quickly became a cause célèbre, especially when several national television shows canceled interviews with the budding author. The public feud grew even more public when Ronald and Nancy Reagan discussed their reaction to Patti's literary career with journalist Barbara Walters. "I didn't recognize anyone in (the book)," the president said, "and certainly the happenings never happened." The first lady told Walters, "I don't think anybody's perfect . . . there's no perfect parent, there's no perfect child."

Patti Davis spent much of her professional life settling scores with her famous parents. Her autobiography, a compulsively readable account of family dysfunction, all but charged Nancy Reagan with drug addiction. In 1994 the president's daughter took one last jab at propriety, posing nude for *Playboy*. Not only did the forty-one-year-old Davis appear in the magazine, she also performed in a *Playboy Celebrity Centerfold* videotape, swimming at the base of a waterfall, being pawed by bodybuilders, and dancing in a kickboxing arena—all in her birthday suit.

Unlike his siblings, Ronald Prescott Reagan seemed to spoof his fame as much as capitalize on it. In a 1986 ad for the American Express card, Reagan openly made fun of his status as a celebrity by association: "Every time I appear on a talk show, people ask me about my father. Every time I give an interview, people ask me about my father. Every time I pull out the American Express card, people treat me like my father. Come to think of it, that's not so bad!"

In 1986 young Reagan served as guest host on *Saturday Night Live*, where he performed a parody of *Risky Business*, the popular Tom Cruise comedy about a teenager who throws a wild party when his parents leave for vacation. In the *Saturday Night Live* version, Reagan played himself; the house was the White House. Like Cruise, Reagan danced around the living room playing air guitar in his underwear. In the same Barbara Walters interview in which they expressed their displeasure at Patti, the Reagans spoke glowingly of Ron's appearance on *Saturday Night Live*. According to Nancy, her son had shown "a presence and a warmth and a humor and a timing in something he had never done before." President Reagan offered a more cryptic assessment: "We were kind of surprised because we had never seen him do anything."

One other presidential child has fashioned a career as an actor: Steve Ford, the youngest son of Gerald and Betty Ford, whose credits include the films *When Harry Met Sally* (Ford played Meg Ryan's boyfriend), *Armageddon*, *Contact*, and *Black Hawk Down*. His entry into the profession came about by accident. An accomplished rodeo rider, Ford got hired for a 1981 western called *Cattle Annie and Little Britches*. "They needed some guys who could fall off horses," Ford said. "I was doing it for free, so the idea of someone actually paying me to fall off a horse in a western sounded like a good summer job."

During the shoot Steve formed a friendship with cast member Rod Steiger, who encouraged him to consider a career in show business. The young cowboy returned to Los Angeles, took acting classes, and soon landed a role on the television soap opera *The Young and the Restless*, where he spent the next six years. One of the show's biggest fans was the former president of the United States, who closely followed his son's progress on TV. Like other soap opera addicts, Gerald Ford developed an emotional attachment to the program. In 1987 Steve told an interviewer, "Dad's always pumping me about what's going to happen . . . "

Finally, though not an entertainer, John F. Kennedy Jr. was as much a celebrity as any actor in Hollywood. The real-life movie in which he starred kept JFK Jr. in the public eye for four decades; his "career" as a household name started around the same time as the professional careers of Barbra Streisand (whom he once escorted on a tour of Harvard University) and the Beatles. As a young man Kennedy showed a passing interest in becoming an actor, and in his early twenties he took to the stage in several amateur theatricals. But John Kennedy's single professional show business moment came during the 1995 season opener of *Murphy Brown*, in which he appeared as himself. The *Murphy* guest shot coincided with the debut of *George*, Kennedy's magazine about politics and entertainment; the episode has the real-life John giving the fictional Murphy a one-year subscription as a wedding present.

George provided Kennedy with a platform from which to examine his own experience as an icon of both media and politics, though sometimes the tail-chasing grew dizzying. In honor of Bill Clinton's fiftieth birthday the magazine ran a cover with Drew Barrymore posing as Marilyn Monroe in her "Happy Birthday, Mr. President" incarnation; JFK Jr. offered no public comment on the choice of imagery. An interview between Kennedy and Oliver Stone, the director of the controversial film *JFK*, fell through after an uncomfortable get-acquainted dinner in which Stone grilled the fledgling journalist about who he thought killed his father. More felicitously Kennedy interviewed Warren Beatty, the actor who in the early 1960s turned down the part of John Fitzgerald Kennedy in *PT 109*. During the session Beatty asked Kennedy if he had seen Oliver Stone's *JFK*.

"I didn't," the president's son responded, "though I probably should have."

"Why didn't you?" Beatty asked.

Said Kennedy, "I didn't want to."

George Bush joins Reba McEntire at the Country Music Association awards show in Nashville, October 1991. (George Bush Library)

11

✺ ✺ ✺ ✺

Is Everybody Happy?

PRESIDENTS AS ENTERTAINERS

T HEY WERE TWO HARD-DRINKING PARTY BOYS born a year and a half apart on
opposite sides of the Atlantic. One of them, Ozzy Osbourne, grew up to become the prototype of a heavy metal rocker and the improbable star of a popular
autobiographical TV reality show. The other, George W. Bush, became governor of
Texas and the improbable president of the United States. In May 2002, at the annual White House Correspondents Association dinner in Washington, D.C., Bush
and Osbourne found themselves sharing top billing in a media sideshow.

Shortly before the official after-dinner entertainment got started, Osbourne
made his way toward the head table. From a distance of about ten feet, he paid
his respects to Bush with a prayerlike gesture. Then, grabbing his unkempt
brown-and-pink hair, the rock star hollered to the politician, "You should wear
your hair like mine!" Momentarily taken aback, Bush blushed, then grinned and
fired back: "Second term, Ozzy . . ." In his remarks to the audience a few minutes later, Bush acknowledged the man who had everyone in the room buzzing:
"The thing about Ozzy is, he's made a lot of big hit recordings: 'Party with the
Animals,' 'Sabbath Bloody Sabbath,' 'Facing Hell,' 'Black Skies,' and 'Bloodbath
in Paradise.' Ozzy, Mom loves your stuff."

The juxtaposition of Ozzy Osbourne and George W. Bush offers a classic example of the sometimes bizarre nexus between show business and the White

House. And nowhere do the stars and the pols come into closer proximity—physically and psychically—than at the correspondents dinners. Once a relatively tame series of events, the gatherings in recent years have lured entertainment celebrities to Washington in droves. At the same time the role of the president at these dinners has evolved. Where the chief executive once sat benignly as a guest of honor, today's president functions as the de facto star of the show, as much a performer as any of the showbiz professionals in the room.

The press dinners, a series of three springtime events sponsored by different organizations of journalists, took root as a Washington tradition in the 1920s. John F. Kennedy was the first president to use the occasion to present his own comedy routine. In the years since, other occupants of the White House—not just presidents but also members of their families—have staged musical and comedy performances of their own. According to Marlin Fitzwater, press secretary in the first Bush White House, "No president really enjoys any of them. But it's a ritual they feel they have to go through. It's a price they feel they have to pay for goodwill from the press corps."

The dinners provide a window into the performing prowess, or lack thereof, of America's chiefs of state. Kennedy drew the pros' admiration for the speed of his ripostes. Master of ceremonies Merv Griffin kept an eye on JFK during his opening monologue at the 1963 White House correspondents dinner. "While I was doing the jokes, the president jotted down a quick retort to each one," Griffin recalled, "and when it came his turn to speak, his impromptu lines topped mine."

Presidents Reagan and Clinton took similar delight in commanding center stage before the audience of Washington's political and journalistic aristocracy. Ronald Reagan, who never sang in a Hollywood musical, performed a vocal solo at the 1983 Gridiron show, the year after his wife delivered her parody of "Second Hand Rose." Reagan's years of experience as an after-dinner speaker served him well at the press parties, though a joke from his 1985 Gridiron monologue landed the old pro in hot water. When the president quipped, "I think we should keep the grain and export the farmers," farm state politicians were not amused. Asked a few days later if he regretted the crack, Reagan exacerbated the problem by telling reporters, "Yeah, 'cause I didn't get a laugh."

Bill Clinton made his debut on the press dinner circuit playing saxophone at the 1993 Gridiron. As the years progressed Clinton gave a series of stand-up comedy performances that dazzled his audiences and laid waste to his critics. In March 1998, in the early stages of the Monica Lewinsky scandal, Clinton stepped up to the microphone at the Gridiron dinner and nonchalantly asked, "So—how was *your* week?" Continuing the theme, he added, "Please withhold the subpoenas until all the jokes have been told." It is impossible to envision the similarly beleaguered Richard Nixon delivering such lines.

Kennedy, Reagan, and Clinton had fun at press dinners because of their highly developed oratorical skills. But less verbally dexterous presidents have also risen to the occasion. In 1976 Gerald Ford boldly appeared on the dais with Chevy Chase, who had wreaked havoc on Ford's image in a celebrated series of *Saturday Night Live* sketches. Right off the bat President Ford sent up his reputation as a klutz by dropping a sheaf of papers at the podium. "Good evening," he began, "I'm Gerald Ford and you're not," reworking one of Chase's catchphrases. The president proceeded to compliment his tormentor: "Mr. Chevy Chase, you're a very, very funny suburb."

Even George Bush, a president not known for sparkling wit, tried his hand at comedy, appearing in a Gridiron sketch that parodied Johnny Carson's Karnak the Magnificent fortune-telling routine. Wearing a shimmering cape, Bush played "Tarmac the Magnificent" in a crowd-pleasing exchange of one-liners with press secretary Marlin Fitzwater. "We ended the skit, walked out the door, through the hotel to the president's limousine, and repeated our best lines all the way back to the White House," Fitzwater said.

Other presidents have resented having to take part in press dinners. Lyndon Johnson and Jimmy Carter could barely conceal their disdain; Carter eventually stopped going altogether. Richard Nixon usually attended the dinners but seethed at the perceived abuse. On the heels of the 1971 White House Correspondents Association dinner, Nixon fired off a lengthy, extraordinarily bitter memorandum to his chief of staff, H.R. Haldeman. "I'm not a bit thin-skinned," Nixon wrote, "but I do have the responsibility and everybody on my staff has the responsibility to protect the office of the Presidency from such insulting incidents . . ." Nixon felt that members of the audience "pretty much sat on their hands" during jokes about Democrats by emcee Arte Johnson. By contrast, "this disgusting group" singled out Nixon for "three hours of pure boredom and insults." At the end of the memo the president insisted he would participate in no such events in the future, a vow he soon broke.

One year earlier Nixon and Vice President Spiro Agnew had performed a controversial piano duet at the 1970 Gridiron show that deeply offended some in the audience. The routine involved Nixon playing a medley of previous presidents' favorite songs, each of which was interrupted by Agnew drowning him out with the tune "Dixie"—a not so subtle reminder of the Republicans' "southern strategy" of appealing to conservative white voters. For his half of the dialogue Agnew affected an exaggerated plantation-style accent.

Roger Wilkins, a prominent African American civic leader, was one of only two blacks in the audience. In an op-ed column for the *Washington Post* a few days after the show Wilkins decried the performance as "a depressing display of gross insensitivity and both conscious and unconscious racism." As disturbing as the sketch, in Wilkins's view, was the approbation accorded Nixon and Agnew by the Gridiron crowd. "I don't believe that I have been blanketed in and suffocated by such racism and insensitivity since I was a sophomore in college," Wilkins wrote, "when I was the only black invited to a minstrel spoof put on at a white fraternity house."

The "Dixie" number illustrates the pitfalls that lie in wait for presidents who function as entertainers. Every action a chief executive takes, official or informal, carries a political charge. Richard Nixon may have thought he was courting the press with a clever bit of innocent theatricality, and many in his target audience felt he succeeded. But another segment was needlessly insulted. Moral of the story: the president of the United States is never "just" an entertainer.

✹✹✹✹

As American presidents have increasingly mingled with show folk, they have assumed a stepped-up level of entertainment demands. Delivering the goods at the annual press dinners is only one. The roster of required performances used to be limited to official occasions—speeches, press conferences, ceremonies, and the like. Modern presidents, by contrast, find themselves thrust into roles once regarded as the domain of professional entertainers.

Consider the evolution of the televised White House tour. Although Jacqueline Kennedy's behind-the-scenes glimpse of the mansion remains the most famous example, it was Harry Truman who inaugurated the tradition in 1952, following a major renovation of the mansion. Truman led three journalists, including Walter Cronkite, through the public rooms, offering a running commentary as they went. In the East Room the president stopped to play a few chords on the piano, which, Truman said, had "one of the most wonderful tones of any piano I've ever heard." That was as close to showboating as President Truman got.

On Christmas Eve 1971 CBS aired a television special ostensibly designed to show off White House holiday decorations, with Julie Nixon Eisenhower as an informal guide. But the real attraction was an unusual group interview with the president and first lady, plus the two Nixon daughters and their husbands, all of whom were living in the residence. Against the backdrop of the family Christmas tree, and with the three family dogs barking alongside them, the extended Nixon clan reminisced about holidays past with a pair of journalists.

Relishing his role as paterfamilias, the president cut a vivid figure in a dark red paisley smoking jacket and red and white checkered tie. "I only wear this at Christmastime," Nixon confided to his interviewers, adding that a "very dear friend" had sewn the jacket especially for him. "I wear it every Christmas and never any other day of the year. It's beautiful. I must wear it another day sometime." At the end of the program the six members of the household lingered on camera decorating a tree. Despite the awkward staging, the Nixons seemed oddly natural, and viewers gained a rare and reassuring glimpse into the family dynamic.

By the end of the century the White House television special had developed into an even more intimate experience. With only a month left in his presidency, Bill Clinton led viewers on a so-called personal tour of the residence as part of a Fox television program grandly entitled *The First Family's Holiday Gift to America*. This time, the journalists were dispensed with altogether, and it was the president—with a supporting appearance by the first lady—who took the reins as host. Clinton showed Americans parts of the White House normally off-limits to visitors, including a room devoted to his collection of musical memorabilia: saxophones, a shrine to Elvis, an original music chart from Dave Brubeck, and a Yellow Submarine cookie jar that was a present from Yoko Ono. In the third-floor family quarters Chelsea Clinton appeared for a brief exchange with her father, one of the few times she was seen and heard on television in her eight years as first daughter.

Bill Clinton's preternatural ease in front of the camera allowed him to persuasively master a range of television performance modes during his career as a public servant. With equal facility he tackled the roles of talk show host, commercial pitchman, award ceremony emcee, evangelist, and comedian. That he would steep himself in the show business aspect of politics became apparent during the 1992 campaign, when Clinton popped up on TV in a series of incarnations familiar to any viewer: confessing to trouble in his marriage on *60 Minutes*; answering personal questions on MTV; matching wits with talk show tiger Phil Donahue; impersonating Elvis Presley and Marlon Brando for interviewers Larry King and Charlie Rose; playing saxophone on the Arsenio Hall show. (Among those watching the candidate's Arsenio performance was Richard Nixon, who commented to an aide, "Oh, boy! Is that desperation to be liked or what?" Nixon had perhaps forgotten his own appearance on Jack Paar's talk show thirty years earlier, when he performed an original piano composition.)

Once in office Bill Clinton expanded his television repertoire. In 1997 Clinton became the first sitting president to appear as an actor when he played himself in the CBS television movie *A Child's Wish*. The film starred Clinton supporter John Ritter as a father who loses his job when his daughter's cancer causes him to start missing work. The political subtext was less than subtle; in his first term Clinton had passed the Family and Medical Leave Act to prevent just such a catastrophe. The final segment of *A Child's Wish* shows the dying girl, portrayed by Anna Chlumsky, treated to a dream come true: an audience with the president in the Oval Office. Clinton played his seventy-five-second scene with almost papal beneficence. As Tom Shales put it, "Clinton looks presidential and projects warmth, but then he's had plenty of practice."

Clinton's final months in office brought his greatest concentration of on-camera entertainment gigs. In the spring of 2000 there was the comedy video with Kevin Spacey for the correspondents dinner. In December there was the Fox Christmas special. And in the final weeks of his presidency Clinton shot an hour-long documentary with movie director Wes Craven for future use in his presidential library in Arkansas. Craven, best known for such slasher movies as *Scream* and *Nightmare on Elm Street*, filmed the president giving a tour of public and private rooms in the White House.

Six months after leaving office, at the invitation of a graduating senior who wrote him a letter, Clinton attended the commencement exercises at the Professional Performing Arts High School in New York City. After watching the students deliver a program of sketches, songs, and dances, the former president spoke wistfully to the class about his own aspirations as a performer. His remarks offer a fascinating window into Bill Clinton the frustrated entertainer. "I had to give up singing when puberty took my voice from three octaves to three notes," he said. "I had to give up saxophone when I realized that, you know, I was real good, but I was never going to be great."

"If I went into politics," Clinton told the students, "I could stay in acting and never have to change roles."

✳✳✳✳

Ronald Reagan is the only individual in American history to hold the country's two most glamorous jobs: president and movie star. Because Hollywood came first, Reagan had the opportunity to channel the techniques he had mastered as an entertainer into a career in public service. More than any other chief executive before or since, Reagan knew the secret recipe for manufacturing myth; he had been doing it his entire professional life.

As a radio sports announcer in Iowa Ronald Reagan gained the technical skills of mass communication—he was renowned for his ability to vividly describe games he had only read about on the wires—as well as an apprehension of its power. The strapping young man with the husky voice, then in his early twenties, quickly achieved the status of local celebrity, and for the rest of his life he never stopped being famous. The folks in Iowa did not find it surprising when their hometown star journeyed to Hollywood, landed a screen test, and signed a contract with Warner Bros. How else could the story turn out?

Reagan launched his movie career in 1937 playing a radio sports announcer in *Love Is on the Air*, and though the acting assignments grew less literal as his career matured, Reagan's film persona never strayed far from its original source. Unsure how to position their new leading man, studio executives tended to cast him as a stout-hearted action hero. "I was the Errol Flynn of the Bs," Reagan wrote in his autobiography, somewhat overstating the case. "I was as brave as Errol, but in a low-budget fashion."

Interspersed among the second-tier films were A pictures like the 1939 Bette Davis drama *Dark Victory*, in which Reagan played a supporting part, and the actor's two personal favorites, *King's Row* and *Knute Rockne, All American*, in which he starred. Throughout most of the 1940s and into the early 1950s, Reagan amassed a respectable filmography without ever ascending to the elite circle of Hollywood immortals. In the view of Garry Wills, "He was in the league of Van Johnson, Peter Lawford, Rod Taylor, Gig Young—not a bad league; they were solid performers." But not up there with Cagney or Bogart or Jimmy Stewart.

By the mid-1950s Reagan was on his way to being one of the has-beens so prevalent in Hollywood—still a celebrity, but one whose luster was gradually diminishing. The parts got smaller and the work migrated from motion pictures to the less prestigious pastures of network TV. In 1952 Reagan hosted the televised arrival ceremonies of the Academy Awards, trying to look dignified amid a rare Southern California rainstorm as younger, trendier actors headed indoors for the party. In 1955 he served as one of three cohosts at the grand opening of Disneyland, a live television special on ABC notorious for its many technical mishaps. Reagan also pioneered the role of "on-camera presenter," an assignment somewhere between commercial announcer and actor, in the anthology series *General Electric Theater* and *Death Valley Days*.

In 1964 Reagan's final full-length picture cast him in a role he had never played: the heavy. *The Killers*, a remake of a 1946 Burt Lancaster film, was originally shot for television. But because NBC deemed the film too violent for broadcast—at one point Reagan slaps Angie Dickinson—it was given a theatrical release. Ronald Reagan received seventh billing, after Lee Marvin, Dickinson, John Cassavettes, Clu Galager, Claude Akins, and Norman Fell. As a coda to Reagan's acting career, *The Killers* fell far short of a victory lap.

But redemption was close at hand. To the surprise—and chagrin—of many of his fellow entertainers, the former head of the Screen Actors Guild won the governorship of California in 1966 and again four years later. Asked by a reporter what kind of governor he would make, Reagan offered a telling reply: "I don't know. I've never played a governor before."

In both Sacramento and Washington, the veteran thespian took comfort in the routines of his former profession. "Reagan thought in terms of performance," wrote biographer Lou Cannon, "and those closest to him approached his presidency as if it were a series of productions casting Reagan in the starring role." According to Cannon, White House aides soon learned that the best way to engage the president was to frame his political duties as a succession of scenes to be played, each with its script and set and costars. As Joan Didion observed, "Even that most minor of presidential idiosyncracies, the absolute adherence to the daily schedule remarked upon by virtually all Reagan's aides, the vertical line drawn through the completed task and the arrow pointing to the next task, derives from the habits of the set, where the revised shooting schedule is distributed daily."

Much noted during his presidency was Ronald Reagan's tendency to conflate movies with reality. The examples were legion. Reagan's indignant line in a 1980 New Hampshire primary debate—"I'm paying for this microphone!"—came directly from the Spencer Tracy–Katharine Hepburn film *State of the Union*. Reagan quoted Clint Eastwood—"Go ahead, make my day"—in taunting Congress to vote for a tax increase that he intended to veto. He recycled a line from *Back to the Future*—"Where we're going, we don't need roads"—in his 1986 State of the Union address. He cited Gary Cooper in *Mr. Deeds Goes to Town* and Frederic March in *The Bridges at Toko-Ri*, referenced Sylvester Stallone as Rambo, and borrowed the *Star Wars* catchphrase "May the force be with you." During a 1983 meeting with members of Congress about the MX missile, the president departed from his script for an impromptu discussion of the film *War Games*, in which Matthew Broderick plays a young computer hacker who taps into the U.S. military's command center. Reagan quoted from his own pictures as well, serving up numerous variations on the phrase "Win one for the Gipper" from *Knute Rockne*.

Asked by a Florida high school student about the Russian people's approbation of Mikhail Gorbachev, President Reagan responded, "I don't resent his popularity or anything else. Good Lord, I costarred with Errol Flynn once." When

Reagan joined Gorbachev for a 1988 state dinner in Moscow, he regaled his host with a homily about the Gary Cooper movie *Friendly Persuasion*, which dealt with a family of Quakers during the American Civil War. Reagan raised his glass "to the art of friendly persuasion, the hope of peace with freedom, the hope of holding out for a better way of settling things," and presented the Soviet leader with a copy of the film.

In a book about the Reagan White House television journalist Bob Schieffer furnished several other remarkable instances of the president's weakness for entertainment allusions. According to Schieffer, Reagan once followed up a disquisition on the internal politics of Lebanon by that country's foreign minister with this observation: "You know, your nose looks just like Danny Thomas." Schieffer also reported that Reagan told Speaker of the House Tip O'Neill that he had portrayed President Grover Cleveland in a movie; in fact, Reagan had played baseball player Grover Cleveland Alexander in the picture *The Winning Team*.

Reagan seemed especially willing to blend Hollywood's version of World War II with the real thing. A story oft repeated by the president about a dying B-17 turret gunner posthumously awarded the Congressional Medal of Honor came from the fictional 1944 war film *A Wing and a Prayer*. Even Reagan's own wartime experience was subject to soft-focus reinterpretation. Disqualified from combat because of his nearsightedness, the actor spent the war years in California making training films for the First Motion Picture Unit of the Army Air Corps. Still, he spoke publicly of his firsthand knowledge of "all the bad things that happened in that war" and erroneously told Israeli Prime Minister Yitzhak Rabin that he traveled with the unit that filmed the liberation of the concentration camps in Europe after the fall of Germany.

For the duration of his political career Ronald Reagan never quite left the soundstage behind. Like most actors, he was vain about his physical appearance. When the Secret Service insisted that he wear a bullet-proof vest, the president complained, "Everybody will think I'm getting fat." He refused to be photographed wearing glasses. He preferred moving footage to still photos because stills could isolate moments of unattractiveness in a way motion pictures could not. Reagan, who posed for publicity shots in swimming trunks as a studio newcomer, remained proud of his physique and appeared bare chested as he went for a swim in Hawaii in 1984.

Like all professional performers, Ronald Reagan never stopped craving the approval of his audience. White House speechwriter Peggy Noonan described her boss as a "compulsive entertainer":

He couldn't not do it. Before he entered a room, he would pause at the entrance and prepare. He sucked in his breath, straightened his shoulders, sucked in his stomach—he would sort of blow himself up. His upper body would get higher, and when he turned he was sort of swiveling. Then he would walk that smooth walk . . .

He would bound into a room, acknowledge the applause with a nod, and begin his remarks. He needed a joke at the top to relax him; he still had some stage fright. He would make a small speech, put the cards back into his pocket, wave and nod again, and as he left he would walk backward, edging out of the room like a vaudeville hoofer shuffling off stage right. All he needed was a cane, a straw hat, and a glove—*Is everybody happy?*

About the only presidential performing duty Reagan did not enjoy was the annual presentation of the so-called national Thanksgiving turkey. According to chief of staff Donald Regan, "the president always groaned when he saw the event on his schedule, and more than once suggested that the Vice President stand in for him." In Regan's view, Ronald Reagan had to summon "all his skill as an actor" to hide the disdain he felt for the silly photo opportunity in which the chief executive "pardons" a Thanksgiving fowl.

In the final analysis, Reagan managed to interweave Hollywood and the White House with enormous skill. In so doing he raised expectations for how a president should comport himself on the public stage. With Reagan the American people came to a new understanding of the casting requirements of the highest office in the land. The nation's leader must be more than a statesman; he must also be a welcome media presence, ready with a quip, a grin, or a few words of inspiration. Will we ever have another president who brings to the task such a munificence of theatrical experience? Or is Reagan—apprenticed on the airwaves of Iowa, buffed and polished on the soundstages of Hollywood, and crowned by history in the marble halls of Sacramento and Washington, D.C.—destined to remain a unique case?

"I was happy when I first heard Ronald Reagan was running for the presidency," Bob Hope said. "I've always thought, once you're in show business you should stay in it."

✴ ✴ ✴ ✴

Two previous performer-presidents helped pave the way for the acceptance of Ronald Reagan as a plausible chief executive: Franklin Roosevelt and John F. Kennedy. Roosevelt had the good fortune to begin his presidency at the dawn of talking pictures. Blessed with a handsome face and euphonious voice, FDR was the perfect leader for America during the so-called golden age of Hollywood. His numerous appearances in the newsreels of the day made Roosevelt as familiar in the national consciousness as the stars whose pictures followed.

A story in the *New York Times* from 1937 provides an extraordinary look into FDR's attitude toward the camera:

> The President gives every cooperation to the newsreels, is patient and understanding with delays and will keep visitors waiting at length until the cameramen have been served. He uses professional terms such as "take," "cut," "footage," "fadeout," etc. When a shot is finished he is likely to say, "How did that go? Need another take?" Or before a shot is made, "Let's keep my eyes out of the sun. Did you see the footage we made last week?"
>
> There is no personal vanity in his attitude toward the newsreel, but a sincere belief that people are entitled to see him at his best if they see him at all, and he does everything he can to achieve this end. Realizing the enjoyment he derives from seeing newsreels, he assumes a like interest on the part of the audience.
>
> Unlike professional actors, the president isn't critical of himself on the screen, greeting his appearance with roars of laughter, gay and pertinent remarks. "I looked like Scrooge in that one," he's likely to say, and once, when a slight flaw in the soundtrack brought his voice forth for a few words with undue huskiness, he called out jovially to a group of guests, "That's the Garbo in me."

FDR coolly evaluated his relationship with the audience, rationing the number of radio "fireside chats" to avoid what he described as "a constant repetition of the highest note in the scale." Media consultant J. Leonard Reinsch, who served Presidents Truman and Kennedy, once watched FDR deliver a broadcast from the White House. "He worked the microphone with the flair of a professional," Reinsch wrote. "He beamed at the mike. He grimaced. He smiled. He scowled. He was the consummate communicator." A newspaperman enthused, "He's all the Barrymores rolled into one." An actual Barrymore—Lionel, who happened to be a political opponent—offered this assessment of President Roosevelt: "If you will agree that it is the best compliment I can pay, I always considered him a superb actor."

Just as Roosevelt learned to perform in radio and newsreels, John F. Kennedy honed his art in the burgeoning medium of television. As a senator, Kennedy made several notable appearances on national TV, ranging from news and inter-view programs like *Meet the Press* and *Person to Person* to nonstandard venues like *Kraft Television Theater*, for which he introduced a dramatic segment based on a chapter of his book *Profiles in Courage*. In June 1960 candidate Kennedy turned up on the *Tonight Show*, where he followed actresses Ann Bancroft and Peggy Cass as the final guest of the evening. Asked by Jack Paar to recall an amusing ex-perience on the campaign trail, JFK said, "I was made an honorary Indian, and I now cheer for our side on TV. Otherwise, it was not very amusing."

The extent of Kennedy's performing prowess came into sharp focus during the 1960 debates with Richard Nixon. Adopting the techniques of the professional showman—extensive rehearsal, close attention to makeup and costuming, and psy-chological command of the stage—the Democratic candidate crossed the threshold of presidential acceptability before some of the largest audiences in American his-tory. Watching a tape of his TV appearances from the campaign, President Kennedy remarked, "We wouldn't have had a prayer without that gadget."

Once in office Kennedy continued his conquest of television with a cele-brated series of sixty-four live press conferences that premiered just five days into his term. Viewers and journalists alike relished the president's quick wit and air of amused detachment. Asked by a female reporter how his administration was advancing women's rights, Kennedy shot back, "Well, I'm sure we haven't done enough . . ." When another questioner cited a Republican National Committee resolution that pronounced the president "pretty much a failure," Kennedy quipped, "I'm sure it was passed unanimously." Reporters understood their role in the proceedings. "We were props in a show," said Peter Lisagor of the *Chicago Daily News*. "We should have joined Actors Equity."

Though JFK exuded an air of casualness on camera, thorough preparation undergirded his performances in the press conferences and debates. Wisely real-izing that the best actors do not wing it, Kennedy put great effort into displaying himself as advantageously as possible. No media opportunity escaped his consid-eration. White House photographers called the president "Jack the Back" for his habit of turning his back to the camera until he was composed and ready.

To some extent JFK's savvy as a performer stemmed from personal vanity. Journalist Ben Bradlee described Kennedy's "horrified" reaction to a shot taken of the two men in their swim trunks. "It shows the Fitzgerald breasts," JFK an-nounced with displeasure. "Better get rid of that." Kennedy aide Theodore Sorensen noted that his boss refused to pose in honorary Indian headdresses or marshal's hats, "and could avoid putting them on or take them off faster than most photographers could raise their cameras." Rare is the picture of John F. Kennedy with anything atop his head, despite the almost universal acceptance of hats in the early 1960s. "Singlehandedly," wrote John Strausbaugh, "he made all American men feel silly about their hats and killed a fashion habit that they'd been blithely carrying on for generations.

"That's what stars do."

Throughout his life Kennedy held a trump card whose value cannot be overestimated: sex appeal. "You're better than Elvis Presley!" screamed a group of Kentucky coeds when Senator Kennedy visited their campus in 1956. A national poll of college women in 1962 deemed the president to be sexier than Rock Hudson. Nowhere was this quality more appreciated than in Hollywood, where actors embraced JFK as a member of their fraternity. Robert Stack, who first met the future president around 1940, put it this way: "I've known many of the great Hollywood stars, and only a very few of them seemed to hold the attraction for women that JFK did, even before he entered the political arena. He'd just look at them and they'd tumble. I often felt like asking him why he wasted his time on politics when he could have made it big in an important business like motion pictures."

✵✵✵✵

Presidents who did not qualify as natural performers include Dwight Eisenhower. Though he improved considerably under the tireless tutelage of Robert Montgomery, Eisenhower at first showed little inclination for the presentational demands of big-time politics. His official campaign kickoff, broadcast nationally on live television from Abilene, Kansas, in June 1952, turned disastrous when strong winds and heavy rain struck just as the candidate began his speech. Viewers could see the rain-soaked manuscript and beads of water dripping from Eisenhower's eyeglasses as he spoke. In a televised campaign appearance a few months later the general engaged in on-air battle with an uncooperative TelePrompTer, trying to keep pace with the erratic motions of the scrolling text. At the end of the speech, a frustrated Eisenhower cried, "Turn the goddam thing off!" unaware that he was still live in millions of homes across the country.

Dwight Eisenhower deserves credit for recognizing the significance of television and striving to master its requirements. Ike was the first president to appear in a campaign commercial, the first to televise his White House press conferences (a move that brought him an Emmy Award from the National Academy of Television Arts and Sciences), and, after leaving office, the first to become a paid network commentator. In the opinion of media historian Craig Allen, "Not only did Eisenhower take advantage of the mass media at their landmark period of rapid expansion; he also acted before anybody was really ready to take note."

Lyndon Johnson, one of the cleverest politicians to occupy the White House, was also one of its worst public communicators. "Television was not his friend, it was his enemy," said Lady Bird Johnson, and few observers would disagree. With his plodding speaking style and utter lack of animation, Johnson had a soporific effect on audiences. Compounding LBJ's difficulties was the inevitable contrast with his predecessor; not only did Johnson have to follow the mediagenic John F. Kennedy, he came into office with an abruptness that did not prepare the public for so radical a stylistic change.

Attempts to make LBJ more comfortable on camera only underscored the problem, as with a 1967 news conference in which the president was fitted with a wireless microphone. Aides hoped the freedom of movement would get Johnson out from behind "Mother," the podium he stood behind as he answered reporters' questions. Instead LBJ took only a few tentative steps beyond his normal range—and remained planted there for the remainder of the press conference.

The one performing trick Lyndon Johnson had up his sleeve was the deadpan reaction. Headlining at a USO dinner in 1965, Bob Hope was surprised when the president made an unannounced appearance at the dais. Because it was too late to change his LBJ-heavy lineup of jokes, Hope went ahead as planned, painfully aware that Johnson was not so much as cracking a smile. "It took me a moment to realize Lyndon was pulling a Jack Benny, trying to help my jokes," Hope said.

Johnson's successor, Richard Nixon, enjoyed a much greater comfort level with television. As vice president in the 1950s Nixon used the medium to advantage in events like the "Checkers" speech and the "kitchen cabinet" debate with Nikita Khrushchev. But the 1960 debates and the 1962 "You won't have Nixon to kick around" press conference brought out the performer's darker side. Though more effective on TV than Presidents Johnson, Ford, and the two George Bushes, Nixon was never as adroit as he thought he was. After his 1968 convention acceptance speech, Richard Nixon bragged to an aide about how he had consciously changed his voice while declaiming about the "impossible dream." "Reagan's an actor," said Nixon, "but I'd like to see him do that."

What Nixon did possess was a clear-eyed recognition of the value of theater as a political communication tool. "You always have to make an entrance," he told speechwriter William Safire. "You have to walk right in and take charge. A lot of politicians never learn that, they mosey in or kind of poke their heads in first—that's all wrong." Nixon's interest in mechanics could border on the obsessive. In a 1969 memo to H.R. Haldeman Nixon analyzed the televised phone call he made to the Apollo astronauts: "Even the question as to whether I should have held the phone with my right hand or my left hand is quite pertinent. The president should never be without the very best professional advice before making a television appearance."

Not surprisingly, it was during Nixon's administration that the White House Television Office came into operation. To staff the office Nixon hired a pair of Los Angeles TV producers whose credits included shows like *The Newlywed Game*, *The Dating Game*, *The Soupy Sales Show*, and Pat Paulsen's *Half a Comedy Hour*. "The Television Office was a major innovation," concluded John Anthony Maltese in his history of White House news management. "For the first time, the president of the United States had the services of a full-time producer to plan his every appearance before television cameras."

For Gerald Ford the question of performing skills took on added urgency because of his reputation as a bumbler. More than any president since Eisenhower, Ford relied on coaching to get him through his public appearances. But as a student of the dramatic arts, the long-time Michigan congressman proved to be a difficult case. Aides made a few cosmetic changes—putting Ford in a vest, for instance, so his tie would not flop around—but there was little they could do to counteract his profound lack of vivacity. With Gerald Ford public relations meant playing defense. In order to avoid unflattering still photos and news footage, press secretary Ron Nessen wrote, "we cut back Ford's attendance at public events involving football and other sports, curtailed pictures of him in such cutesy activities as playing with his dogs, and even skipped press coverage of the presentation of the annual White House Thanksgiving turkey."

Jimmy Carter, on the other hand, was initially thought to be a highly gifted television performer, a sentiment no doubt enhanced by the dullness of his predecessor. Carter neither feared nor scorned television. Just three years before moving in to the White House, the Georgia governor showed his inclination to operate at the people's level by appearing as a mystery guest on the quiz show *What's My Line?* So little known was Carter that the panel could not guess his occupation.

The media side of Jimmy Carter's presidency started off with great promise. His first address to the nation, a televised "fireside chat" in which the president wore a Mister Rogers–like cardigan sweater, drew praise for its straightforwardness. After the speech Franklin Roosevelt Jr. told *Time* magazine, "President Carter fits television like my father fitted radio." One month later Carter embarked on a riskier on-air venture, a live radio call-in program with host Walter Cronkite entitled *Ask President Carter*. Giving unrehearsed answers to unforeseen questions from listeners around the country, the new leader displayed an admirable willingness to interact directly with his constituents. According to the *Washington Post*, "The president was snappy, intimate, and impressively knowledgeable." Not to mention brave.

As his administration proceeded, Jimmy Carter allowed the warm glow of these early performances to turn cold. With the passing years his informal approach gave way to an aloofness that left voters wondering what had become of the down-to-earth man they elected. In 1980, when Ronald Reagan emerged as Carter's Republican opponent, the Carter White House seriously underestimated the challenge, refusing to believe Americans would prefer an actor over an incumbent president. Writing in his diary after the single presidential debate of 1980, Jimmy Carter caustically sized up his opponent's glibness: "He has his memorized lines, and he pushes a button and they come out." Carter nonetheless understood that he had been outperformed. His postdebate diary entry contains this postscript about Reagan: "Apparently made a better impression on the TV audience than I did."

Like Truman after Roosevelt and Johnson after Kennedy, both George Bushes have suffered by comparison with the media-savvy presidents who came before them. As a performer the first George Bush came across as the anti-Reagan: tongue-tied where Reagan was eloquent, awkward where Reagan was commanding, gaffe-prone where Reagan was Teflon-coated. According to a White House speechwriter, "Bush was very conscious that he was following Reagan. He would say, 'Now Reagan would do that, but I can't.'"

Unlike Reagan, Bush resented the modern requirement that presidents stage an occasional dog and pony show. This antipathy manifested itself most glaringly in the campaign of 1992, when Bush had the misfortune of running against another Reagan-quality media maestro, Bill Clinton. In his diary President Bush wrote: "I told Larry (King) I'd like to do his show, but we've got to do it all with a certain sense of dignity, a certain sense of propriety. I don't want to get caught up, obviously, with Phil Donahue and these sensationalistic, left-handed Mary's-lost-her-cousin kind of shows . . ." Bush did go on Larry King in 1992, as well as the Nashville Network, and even MTV, where interviewer Tabitha Soren conducted an interview notable mostly for the president's grumpiness.

During his term in office Bush made a number of entertainment-style television appearances. He participated in the Country Music Association awards and an American Film Institute gala. He taped a message for broadcast during NBC's coverage of the Ryder Cup golf tournament and provided the on-camera introduction to an ABC television movie called *Heroes of Desert Storm*. But sandwiched between Ronald Reagan and Bill Clinton, the first President Bush left faint footprints as a media persona.

A more vivid image attends the younger George Bush, whose administration has coincided with enough grim news to alter the tone of the presidency's usual entertainment requirements. In the 2000 campaign and prior to the attacks of September 11, 2001, the former Texas governor seemed most at ease in comedic settings such as the *Saturday Night Live* preelection TV special, in which he mocked his knack for malapropisms. Later, especially in the aftermath of the conflict in Iraq, Bush repositioned himself as a warrior, a media makeover helped along by skillful White House producers and a pliant press.

In May 2003 the former Air National Guard pilot "starred" in a much-ballyhooed photo opportunity aboard the aircraft carrier USS *Abraham Lincoln,* arriving in an S-3B Viking warplane that made a dramatic tailhook landing on the ship's deck. Emerging from the cockpit in an olive-green flight suit and combat boots, Bush worked his way through a military receiving line with his helmet tucked under his arm, all swagger and smiles. As a number of observers noted, the entire visual exercise called to mind the Tom Cruise movie *Top Gun. New York Times* columnist Frank Rich, citing *Top Gun* producer Jerry Bruckheimer, wrote that "the White House has absorbed the Bruckheimer aesthetic so fully that its *Top Gun* was better, not to mention briefer, than the original (no obligatory Kelly McGillis love story, for starters)."

Though widely applauded in the press, the event also provoked criticism. Beyond the cost of staging such a spectacle, the White House found itself on the defensive over the rationale for the president's mode of transportation. Spokesmen who first said the ship was too far out to sea for Bush to come in by helicopter later admitted that the Viking jet was a matter of presidential choice. Indeed the *Abraham Lincoln* came so close to San Diego that efforts had to be made during the photo op to keep the carrier out of range of the downtown skyline. Most troubling, the casting of George W. Bush as a "flyboy" cynically contradicted Bush's own checkered history with the Texas Air National Guard, a record marked by preferential treatment and chronic absenteeism. As historians pointed out, none of the genuine war hero presidents like Dwight Eisenhower and John F. Kennedy ever saw fit to don a military uniform in their capacity as commander-in-chief. For George W. Bush the effect was less an evocation of Ike or JFK than a half-baked salute to Tom Cruise.

Chevy Chase and Gerald Ford at the Radio and Television
Correspondents Association dinner, March 1976. (Gerald R. Ford Library)

12

"I'm Gerald Ford, and You're Not"

Presidents as Entertainment

Little more than a year after taking office, Gerald Ford found himself at the mercy of a political force beyond his control: a new television comedy program called *Saturday Night Live*. An obscure thirty-two-year-old writer and actor named Chevy Chase, seizing his moment in the media spotlight, depicted Ford as America's first klutz in a series of sketches that redefined the country's view of its leader. A typical episode that aired in December 1975 featured Chase as Ford delivering holiday greetings to the citizenry. After spilling a stocking full of goodies, the president topples the White House Christmas tree, bringing himself down with it. "This will indeed be a wonderful Christmas for the entire nation," Chase says. "I hope."

Chevy Chase's portrayal of Gerald Ford marks a turning point in the long national tradition of packaging presidents as entertainment. This was not an imitation—Chase made no attempt to replicate Gerald Ford's voice or mannerisms—nor an affectionate, Bob Hope–style collection of one-liners. Instead Chase presented Ford as an object of outright derision. "Anybody who was so guilty about being president that he kept trying to kill himself was inherently funny," Chase told *Playboy* magazine in 1977. "It was the guilt that kept him banging his head on helicopter doors."

Gerald Ford seemed more bewildered than nettled by the antics of his chief interpreter. What particularly chafed the athletic president was Chase's relentless emphasis on his supposed physical clumsiness. Ford could handle being ridiculed, but he did not like being ridiculed on false charges. "I developed a good exterior posture," he wrote in his memoir. "The truth of the matter is that some of my favorite pipes have teeth marks in their stems that you wouldn't believe." At least in public, President Ford displayed an admirable maturity toward Chevy Chase; one can only imagine how Richard Nixon would have responded. "You cannot cry out dramatically about your outrage or your indignity," Ford wrote. "That, as sure as tomorrow's sunrise, will open a floodgate that you'll never be able to close."

The White House did not remain a passive bystander vis-à-vis *Saturday Night Live*. In March 1976 the president of the United States preemptively shared the dais with Chevy Chase at the correspondents dinner, a move that defused any perception of thin skin on Ford's part. As Chase performed his routine for the crowd—"I have asked the Secret Service to remove the salad fork embedded in my left hand"—the butt of the joke sat at the head table, smiling and placidly smoking a pipe. When it was the president's turn to rejoin, he wisely kept the humor self-deprecating.

One month later the White House overshot its counter-Chase strategy by dispatching press secretary Ron Nessen to New York City as guest host of *Saturday Night Live*. Ford himself contributed the show's opening line—"Live from New York, it's Saturday Night!"—and two other short videotaped bits. But this time the eagerness to be in on the joke backfired. By hitching the dignity of the presidency to the sophomoric humor of a TV comedy show the White House looked more desperate than hip. With Nessen playing himself, Chase-as-Ford stapled his own ear and stabbed himself with a letter opener; the juxtaposition was equal parts funny and squirm-inducing. Other sketches on the show, the ones lacking a Ford connection, pushed the boundaries of taste in different ways, as with a mock commercial for a carbonated vaginal douche called "Autumn Fizz." In the final accounting it was *SNL* that got the better of the president rather than vice versa.

Chevy Chase played Gerald Ford eleven times over the course of the show's first season and a half, culminating in the weeks leading up to the 1976 election with a series of presidential debate parodies that costarred Dan Aykroyd as Jimmy Carter. After Ford lost the race, Chase made no apologies for possibly helping bring down the president. "I didn't want him in the White House because he hadn't been elected," he told an interviewer years later. "I wanted Carter in, and I had a forum of twenty million people watching." Chase and Aykroyd both performed at Carter's inaugural.

Chevy Chase's portrayal of Gerald Ford represents the first ripple in a tidal wave of unflattering presidential depictions that has extended into the new century. The bitter trauma of Nixon's resignation sounded the death knell for the gentle barbs of Bob Hope and paved the way for less deferential modes of comedic expression. *Saturday Night Live* declared open season on the White House in the fall of 1975, and every president thereafter has been fair game for entertainers.

❋❋❋❋

The balance of power between presidents and performers has shifted dramatically since the early years of mass entertainment, when Will Rogers got the cold shoulder from Warren Harding for cracking harmless jokes about Harding's obsession with golf. Throughout the first half of the twentieth century actors and writers either avoided presidential material or approached it with extreme caution. In 1934 comedian Eddie Cantor sought Franklin Roosevelt's personal approval for a benign radio sketch in which "Dr. Roosevelt" ministers to "Mrs. America," a patient in need of mending. Needless to say, FDR had no objection to a script that contained the line, "He's got that magnetic personality—the minute he walks into a sickroom the patient feels better already."

Hollywood film studios were similarly skittish about depicting the popular president, who in spite of his enthusiasm for the movies maintained a deliberate distance from the dream factories of the West Coast. In the 1934 Shirley Temple film *Stand Up and Cheer!* Roosevelt's presence is intimated by an actor coached to speak like the president, but audiences saw only the back of his head. FDR is visualized somewhat more directly in the 1942 Jimmy Cagney classic *Yankee Doodle Dandy*, but as before he is never shown from the front, and in the closing credits the Roosevelt character is referred to only as "The President."

The actor who portrayed FDR in *Yankee Doodle Dandy*, a Canadian private investigator billed as "Captain Jack Young," enjoyed a brief run in Hollywood as a Franklin Roosevelt look-alike. Young came to California after being "discovered" at a baseball game in Washington, D.C., by fans who mistook him for the genuine article. In 1938, when FDR visited Los Angeles, the president's doppelgänger was among the dignitaries who greeted him at a welcoming reception. "I meant to tell him I was his double," a disappointed Young said afterward, "but there wasn't time."

Franklin Roosevelt was not the first sitting president to be turned into a motion picture character. In 1908 a newsreel company hired a look-alike to reenact

President Theodore Roosevelt's recent African safari. Shot in Chicago and released under the title *Big Game Hunting in Africa*, the silent movie showed the presidential double firing a gun at an aged lion as African American extras looked on. Though the production carefully avoided any direct mention of the man in the White House, the real Teddy Roosevelt was said to have been annoyed, particularly after the film's producer reaped hefty financial rewards.

More typically, early Hollywood tended to treat American presidents with almost religious veneration. Abraham Lincoln, the chief executive with the greatest number of cinematic portrayals to his name, generated a pair of back-to-back biographical classics: *Young Mr. Lincoln* (1939), starring Henry Fonda in the title role, and *Abe Lincoln in Illinois* (1940), with Raymond Massey and Ruth Gordon beautifully cast as the president and his wife, Mary Todd Lincoln. Woodrow Wilson was played by Alexander Knox in *Wilson* (1944), a successful film from World War II that is little known today. *Sunrise at Campobello* (1960) featured Ralph Bellamy as Franklin Roosevelt and an uncharacteristically buck-toothed Greer Garson as Eleanor.

When Bellamy originated the role of FDR on Broadway, the real Eleanor gave not only her blessing but also technical advice about how to physically portray her husband's disability. An earlier attempt by Hollywood to cast Lionel Barrymore as President Roosevelt had met with stiff resistance from the recently widowed first lady, who knew Barrymore to be a political opponent. Not wishing to offend Mrs. Roosevelt so soon after the president's death, MGM dropped Barrymore from the cast of *The Beginning or the End*, a 1947 docudrama that traced the development of the atom bomb. The part, more a cameo than a starring role, went to the obscure Godfrey Tearle.

Better-known FDR interpreters have included Edward Herrmann, who played Roosevelt opposite Jane Alexander in a well-executed 1970s television miniseries, and, incredibly, Charlton Heston. In 1967 Heston appeared as Franklin Roosevelt in a reading from *Sunrise at Campobello* at the White House before an audience that included LBJ and Lady Bird, FDR Jr., and Alice Roosevelt Longworth. In a merciful gesture to those present Heston did not attempt an impersonation or perform in a wheelchair. Actor Melvyn Douglas, a personal acquaintance of President Roosevelt, never portrayed FDR in a literal sense, but used the "memory of his astonishing smile" in playing the veteran politician who is Robert Redford's father in the influential political drama *The Candidate*. Katharine Hepburn credited Eleanor Roosevelt with inspiring her unforgettable performance as the missionary spinster who travels downriver with Humphrey Bogart in *The African Queen*.

President Roosevelt stacked up favorably against his fictional contemporaries in the films *Gabriel over the White House* (1933) and *The President Vanishes* (1934). The latter, a B picture that featured a very young Rosalind Russell, involves a commander-in-chief who stages his own kidnapping to prevent a fascist takeover. *Gabriel over the White House*, possibly the strangest presidential picture ever made, posits a favorable view of fascism. Released only a few weeks after Franklin Roosevelt's first inauguration, this allegorical film features Walter Huston as a corrupt chief executive who makes a political U-turn after surviving a near-fatal automobile accident. Emerging from a coma, Huston's character suspends Congress, dispatches the army to battle gangsters, and blackmails foreign governments into laying down their arms. Although *Gabriel* deserves credit for probing the psychology of its leading man, the movie's message is simplistic and antidemocratic. "Judging by *Gabriel*," wrote journalist Walter Lippmann, "I should say that the body politic is one kind of body that Hollywood has not yet learned about."

✵✵✵✵

Shortly before the end of World War II General Dwight Eisenhower was approached by several Hollywood producers who wanted to film his life story. The ensuing negotiations showed the future president to be a hard-nosed bargainer with a clear sense of the stakes involved. Eisenhower appointed his brother, Milton, to act as his agent, and in a remarkable letter in 1944 outlined his terms:

> To start with, *I could not, and would not*, touch a cent of the money offered, and the mere fact that the minimum offer to me is $150,000 has no bearing on the case at all. The following facts, however, appear somewhat pertinent.
>
> a. Sooner or later, assuming that I don't stub my toe, some movie firm will get into a project of this sort with or without my consent.
>
> b. If properly handled in a water-tight contract, the theme of the picture could take the slant of glorifying opportunities presented under the American system and tend to support initiative, effort and persistence in an average American family . . .
>
> c. Contracts could clearly establish that no publication of the picture and no publicity concerning it could take place before the end of the war.
>
> d. The funds, at least those that are intended for me, would all be paid directly to a university to be handled by that university to promote the purpose or idea that I myself would dictate.

Admirably skeptical of the ways of Hollywood, Eisenhower went on to note, "If the picture were so edited as merely to make some false and completely unnatural movie character out of myself I would not have anything to do with it, no matter what the sum offered." As the war in Europe ended and American occupation began, the transatlantic negotiations continued. Ike insisted on not only script approval but also final say over the publicity and advertising campaigns. Despite a press announcement in July 1945 that named Samuel Goldwyn as producer and Robert Sherwood as screenwriter, the picture never came to fruition, apparently because a suitable financial arrangement could not be worked out. "I feel a definite sense of relief," Eisenhower wrote his brother after the project collapsed. "As you know, I have always feared the whole thing might go sour."

Eisenhower's trepidation stemmed in part from what he recognized as Hollywood's tendency to mythologize individual achievements over group effort. Ever the good soldier, Ike did not wish to diminish the contributions of his troops. John F. Kennedy apparently felt no such compunction, as evidenced by the making of *PT 109*, the film version of the best-selling book about JFK's exploits as a naval officer in the South Pacific. The 1963 production, with Cliff Robertson in the title role, was actually the second rendering of Kennedy's wartime tale. In 1957 an ABC television anthology show called *Navy Log* devoted its half-hour season premiere to the story. Senator Kennedy was heavily involved in the production, meeting with its writer and producer in Washington and following up with suggested changes to the script. "If possible," JFK wrote producer Sam Gallu, "I would like to have a photo of the person who will play my part." The role went to a little-known twenty-nine-year-old actor named John Baer, who bore a passing resemblance to the real-life hero of the tale. Kennedy flew to San Diego for the filming and, with a fellow member of his PT 109 crew, served as a technical adviser.

The more famous 1963 effort, a big-budget Warner Bros. "prestige" picture, constituted a clear case of political opportunism, timed to refresh the voters' memory of their president's military service a year before they headed to the polls. The Kennedy White House took an active part in the production; according to JFK biographer Richard Reeves, "the casting director for *PT 109* was John F. Kennedy." Warren Beatty, then in his mid-twenties, turned down the lead role. In a 1995 interview for *George* magazine, Beatty told JFK Jr., "I was thrilled to be asked, though I didn't want to do it." Beatty said that Jacqueline Kennedy had suggested him for the role after admiring his performance in *Splendor in the Grass*.

Although Warren Beatty was criticized at the time for declining the offer, history has proven him to be prescient. *PT 109*, muzzled by the constraints of hagiography, turned out to be an unmitigated dud. A review in *Time* magazine complained that "Warner Brothers has approached the story of JFK's 1943 hero-ism with a reverence usually reserved for a New Testament spectacle"; the result was a "wide-screen campaign poster." In the role of twenty-five-year-old Commander Kennedy, thirty-eight-year-old Cliff Robertson captured none of the character's playfulness or inner glow. Instead he came across as stiff, ponderous, and boring—the very antithesis of the president-to-be. With its running time of two and a half hours, the film remains excruciatingly unwatchable.

PT 109, the first full-length biopic of a sitting president, received prominent play in the press, just as the White House had hoped. In July 1963 the movie's Los Angeles premiere occasioned a $100-a-plate fund-raiser for Kennedy family chari-ties, attended by Rose Kennedy, the Lawfords, Marlon Brando, Jack Lemmon, and actors from the cast. The president himself remained aloof from the hoopla; just as the picture opened around the country, JFK left on a ten-day trip to Europe.

The experience of *PT 109* demonstrates that Hollywood's powerful myth-making machinery cannot preordain audience approval of presidentially based entertainments. Show business depictions of national leaders succeed in ways that are impossible to foretell, as indicated by the unexpected success of another diversion from the Kennedy era, a novelty recording called *The First Family*. Re-leased in November 1962, the collection of comedy sketches by unknown actors impersonating various Kennedys became an instant national sensation. Accord-ing to the album's producer, the first pressing consisted of forty thousand copies; at least 5 million were sold.

The First Family made an overnight star of its JFK sound-alike, Vaughn Meader, much as *Saturday Night Live* launched the career of Chevy Chase in the decade that followed. The twenty-seven-year-old Meader had not set out to be-come a presidential impersonator; the Kennedy bit was just one small piece of the comedian's act. But once the record album took off, Meader found himself thrust into the big leagues, headlining in Las Vegas, guest-starring on national television, and raking in hundreds of thousands of dollars.

The White House gave *The First Family* mixed reviews. Asked by reporters if he found the album annoying, President Kennedy responded with a wisecrack: "I listened to Mr. Meader's record, but I thought it sounded more like Teddy than it did me—so *he's* annoyed." Privately JFK told journalist Ben Bradlee that he found parts of the album amusing, including a parody of the famous press conferences and a skit in which the numerous Kennedys wish each other a good night. Kennedy's favorite line, according to Bradlee, was Meader-as-JFK telling

Senate Minority Leader Everett Dirksen in a thick Boston accent, "Ev, you drive a hahd bahgain."

Jacqueline Kennedy was less amused, especially by the impersonation of young Caroline Kennedy. The first lady instructed an aide to telephone Meader "and say that Mrs. Kennedy finds it in appalling taste that he should make money out of a five-year-old child . . . Tell him I don't care what he says about us." White House press secretary Pierre Salinger wrote a letter to a Washington radio station asking that it "desist from using a recording by Mr. Meader in imitation of the president's voice plugging Station WWDC." And an internal White House memorandum expressed concern over a 1963 Steve Allen TV show in which Meader, posing as the president, phoned an elderly woman in Kansas and asked her opinion about various items of legislation. Meader himself seemed to sense he was on shaky ground; in July 1962, several months before the release of the album, he sent JFK a telegram informing him of his appearance on the CBS show *Talent Scouts*. "I impersonated you but I did it with great affection and respect," Meader wrote. "Hope it meets with your approval."

On the afternoon of November 22, 1963, Vaughn Meader stepped into a cab at the Milwaukee airport. The driver asked, "Did you hear Kennedy was shot?" "No," replied Meader, "how does it go?" Not having heard the news, he thought he was being set up for a joke.

Meader's career collapsed almost instantly. "One year," Meader told a reporter thirty-five years later. "November to November. Then boom. It was all over." In the days following the assassination the album was pulled from retail outlets, CBS canceled him as a celebrity panelist on *To Tell the Truth*, and a string of nightclub bookings evaporated. Meader began a descent into alcoholism that was punctuated by occasional attempts to reestablish himself. In 1979, when Ted Kennedy announced his intention to run for the presidency, the comedian peddled a song called "I'm Getting Ready for Teddy." But the audience that had accepted Meader as a faux John F. Kennedy now associated him with their grief. Vaughn Meader became an ancillary casualty of that dark day in Dallas.

❋ ❋ ❋ ❋

Hollywood had already imagined the assassination of an American president in a pair of films that starred none other than perennial White House booster Frank Sinatra. *Suddenly,* released in 1954, marks a daring departure for presidential movies. In this taut thriller the country's leader, referred to generically but never seen or named, is the target of snipers who stage an elaborate plan to fire on his train as it passes through a small western town. Learning of the production, the Secret Service detail assigned to Dwight Eisenhower lodged a complaint with the Motion Picture Association of America. But because *Suddenly's* producers were not members of the MPAA, the organization had no power to intervene, and the project proceeded over White House objections.

Sinatra's second assassination picture, *The Manchurian Candidate,* reached theaters in 1962 at the height of the Kennedy presidency. Based on a popular novel by Richard Condon, the story recounts a Communist plot to take over the United States through the deployment of programmed political assassins. According to Condon, who also wrote the screenplay, Sinatra sought JFK's endorsement for the production after studio executives balked at the subject matter. At Sinatra's behest Kennedy made a phone call to United Artists president Arthur Krim—also the Democratic party's national finance chairman—and made it clear he had no objections. "That's the only way that film ever got made," Condon said. After JFK's death Sinatra and the studio hastily withdrew *The Manchurian Candidate* from circulation, and for the next twenty-five years it remained off-limits to audiences.

The immediate aftermath of the Kennedy assassination brought another tonal shift in Hollywood's approach to the presidency. In 1964 the studios released five feature films with presidents as major characters: three dramas and two comedies. In each case the characterization departed from the hero worship of traditional big-screen presidencies. In *Fail-Safe* and *Seven Days in May* the commander-in-chief—Henry Fonda in the former and Fredric March in the latter—confronts a military crisis that is at least partly of his own creation. Gore Vidal's *The Best Man* takes the national party convention as its setting and pits a conniving, sexually promiscuous war hero against an Adlai Stevenson–style liberal with marital problems of his own. Fonda played the Stevenson character, while the role of the randy war hero went to Cliff Robertson, just a year after he starred as JFK in *PT 109.*

The two comedies presented moviegoers with 1964's least conventional presidents. Polly Bergen appeared as the country's first female chief executive in *Kisses for My President*; when she discovers she is pregnant, she resigns from office to pursue full-time motherhood. Far more subversive was President Merkin Muffley, one of three roles essayed by Peter Sellers in Stanley Kubrick's *Doctor Strangelove.* Muffley's leadership style combines naïveté with ineffectuality; his plea—"Gentlemen, you can't fight in here; this is the War Room!"—became one of the picture's most quoted lines. Audiences in 1964 were amazed to see a president portrayed as a figure of comic ineptitude, especially since the consequence of his bungling is nothing less than the annihilation of the planet. Even the character's name is a low-brow joke: "merkin" is an old English word for fake pubic hair, while "muffley" plays on a slang term for the real thing.

The changing mores of 1960s Hollywood coincided with the tumultuous presidencies of Lyndon Johnson and Richard Nixon. In the 1968 film *Wild in the Streets* the world's most popular rock star, played by Christopher Jones, conspires with a politician to extend voting rights to fourteen-year-olds, then uses the newly enfranchised adolescents to get himself elected president. Once in office the youthful leader drives all the old people into retirement homes and force-feeds them LSD. Though *Wild in the Streets* shamelessly played to the antiestablishment values of its target audience, it also anticipated the Reagan presidency by creating a lead character who channels his show business experience into a political career.

However unglamorous he may have been in real life, Richard Nixon has held intense fascination for the writers, directors, and actors of Hollywood. The sweeping trajectory of Nixon's career and the complexity of his character have inspired an astonishing range of interpretations, beginning in the late 1970s with a cycle of Watergate-related films. There were docu-dramatic accounts like *All the President's Men* (1976), which incorporates actual news footage of Nixon; *Blind Ambition* (1979), a TV miniseries about Nixon attorney John Dean with Rip Torn as the president and Martin Sheen as Dean; and *Born Again* (1978), about Watergate figure Charles Colson and his conversion to Christianity. Other films approached Nixon obliquely, as in the allegorical comedy *Nasty Habits* (1977), a trenchant send-up of the Watergate scandal with Glenda Jackson as a Nixonian nun who resorts to dirty tricks to ensure her election as head abbess at a Philadelphia convent. Even *Star Wars* (1977) boasts a Nixon connection; George Lucas has said he based the character of the emperor on the disgraced president.

More multidimensional depictions of Richard Nixon began to surface in the 1980s. Philip Baker Hall gave an indelible performance in Robert Altman's *Secret Honor* (1984); the film takes the form of a rambling, paranoid, Scotch-fueled monologue spoken into a tape recorder on the president's final night in the White House. Anthony Hopkins memorably played the title role in Oliver Stone's *Nixon* (1995), opposite Joan Allen, who gives a pitch-perfect reading of the first lady. Dan Hedaya portrayed Nixon for laughs in the comedy *Dick* (1999), in which a pair of ditzy Washington teenagers uncover presidential malfeasance, and Beau Bridges played the role straight in the TV movie *Kissinger and Nixon* (1995) opposite Ron Silver. Peter Riegert took the part of Richard Nixon as a young congressman in *Concealed Enemies* (1984), a retelling of the 1950 Alger Hiss case. Describing Nixon as "an actor's dream," Riegert emphasized the "physical awkwardness" of the character. "It was like blocks of wood stacked on one another," Riegert said, "a block of wood for the head, a block for the body."

In 1961 Nixon was approached to appear as an actor in the political drama *Advise and Consent*. According to a memo Nixon sent to his lawyer in Los Angeles, he had received a call from cast member Gary Merrill, who wondered if the recently defeated vice president might be willing to play the film's fictional vice president. "I took it somewhat as a gag," Nixon wrote, "but he insisted on sending the script over for me to read and when I told him that under no circumstances could I play a part he said he thought that my serving as technical director would be of great value to the Producer—Otto Preminger—and would be compensated for quite substantially." Nixon added that his cursory reading of the last few pages of the script had turned up "glaring and obvious" errors, examples of which he cited. "I only mention these two items to indicate to you that I might be able to serve a useful role if you concluded the offer is worth looking into." In the end *Advise and Consent* went forward minus the participation of Richard Nixon.

Although Ronald Reagan spent decades on the soundstages of Hollywood, the movies have been slow to accord him much screen time as a historical character. Richard Crenna played Reagan in the TV movie *The Day Reagan Was Shot* (2001), but the real star of the film was Richard Dreyfuss as power-hungry Secretary of State Alexander Haig. And in *Clear and Present Danger* (1994), the fictitious president played by Donald Moffat keeps a jar of Reaganesque jellybeans on his desk. Less literally, Johnny Depp cited "the blind optimism of Ronald Reagan" as a key influence in his 1994 characterization of cross-dressing B movie director Ed Wood. Because Reagan lacks the inner turmoil of a Richard Nixon, he has sparked little interest among Hollywood's creative artists. Instead, impersonators like Jim Morris and Phil Hartman have produced characterizations that unfold closer to the surface.

Like Reagan, George Bush lent himself more readily to impersonation than three-dimensional interpretation. The most prominent Bush mimic was *Saturday Night Live* actor Dana Carvey, who replicated the speech patterns of the forty-first president by grafting the voice of children's TV host Fred Rogers onto that of John Wayne. In 1992 Carvey performed his act at the White House staff Christmas party before an audience that included President and Barbara Bush. When Carvey appeared as the guest host of *Saturday Night Live* two years later, George Bush returned the favor by videotaping the opening setup, though the ex-president declined to deliver the signature line "Live from New York, it's *Saturday Night!*" In introducing Carvey, Bush recycled the jokes that Carvey's impersonation had popularized; in effect, George Bush was imitating Dana Carvey's imitation of George Bush. The boundary separating presidents from entertainers did not just blur, it vanished.

✳✳✳✳

To a degree experienced by no other president in American history, Bill Clinton functioned as raw material for professional entertainers while still in office. The 1990s generated an explosion in presidential comedy and a spate of presidential films unlike anything that had gone before. The larger-than-life character of the nation's first baby boomer president was pure catnip for the creative juices of show business, with results both flattering and demeaning. "Rational—and irrational—people may differ over the merits of Bill Clinton's presidency," wrote critic Frank Rich in the *New York Times*, "but few can dispute that he was without peer as our entertainer in chief. He turned the whole citizenry, regardless of ideology or demographic, into drama fiends."

The problem for writers and performers was staying ahead of the ever climactic Clinton presidency. Comedians, who operate under more immediate deadlines, had an easier time keeping pace than filmmakers, and the nightly monologues of the television talk shows remained dependably Clinton-centric. Hosting the 2000 White House Correspondents Association dinner, Jay Leno confessed that he dreaded the president's impending departure. "You bought my house!" Leno told his comedy muse. "You bought my car!"

Clinton humor reached its high-water mark in 1998, the year of the Monica Lewinsky scandal. According to a study by the Center for Media and Public Affairs, Clinton was the subject that year of 1,712 jokes by the late-night TV comedy hosts, up from 338 in 1995. "The squeamishness is long gone," said Mandy Grunwald, Bill Clinton's media adviser in the 1992 campaign. "Things have been said about him that have never been said about any president on television—some true, some not." The jokes about Clinton may have been indecorous, but no less indecorous than the reality.

Also in 1998 two highly publicized feature films put the Clinton presidency under Hollywood's microscope. The first was *Wag the Dog*, whose title soon entered the lexicon as shorthand for the most cynical application imaginable of spin control: staging a war to distract voters from a political scandal. In this black comedy the White House attacks Albania in an effort to curtail fallout from a presidential dalliance with a teenage girl. *Wag the Dog* opened in limited release on Christmas Day 1997, one month before the name Monica Lewinsky began to saturate the American airwaves.

When President Clinton ordered bombing strikes on terrorist targets in Afghanistan and Sudan in August 1998, the parallels between fact and fiction proved irresistible to media pundits. A reporter at a Pentagon news conference asked Secretary of Defense William Cohen the inevitable: "Some Americans are going to say this bears a striking resemblance to *Wag the Dog*. Two questions: Have you seen the movie? And second, how do you respond to people who think that?" Ignoring the first question, Cohen gave a steely response to the second: "The only motivation driving this action today was our absolute obligation to protect the American people from terrorist activities."

Primary Colors, released as a book in January 1996 and as a film in March 1998, gave audiences an even more direct pipeline into the persona of Bill Clinton. The best-selling roman à clef about a soulful southern presidential candidate with a hearty appetite for female flesh created enormous media buzz when its author initially declined to identify himself. Eventually it came to light that "Anonymous" was political reporter Joe Klein, who had covered Clinton's 1992 campaign for *Newsweek*. At a Beverly Hills fund-raiser in 1996, the president jokingly told master of ceremonies Tom Hanks, "Tom, you have suffered so much tonight, it's okay with me if you go and do *Primary Colors*. As a matter of fact, I'd like to see somebody make some money out of that thing using their own name."

Hanks, one of Clinton's favorite actors, turned down the part when it was offered. According to director Mike Nichols, "Tom just couldn't identify with the character's promiscuity. He didn't know how to play a man who was like that." Instead John Travolta portrayed the fictitious Clinton, giving a performance that was as thoroughly an imitation as the mimicry of presidential impersonators. "I'm really playing him," Travolta admitted to *Time* magazine. "It's false p.r. for me to do it any other way . . . unless there are some legal issues I don't know about." To prepare for the part Travolta spent hours studying footage of Bill Clinton on the campaign trail. Travolta called Clinton "the blueprint for the illusion."

Other participants in *Primary Colors* seemed less comfortable with the picture's real-life similarities. "I absolutely didn't want to do an impersonation," said Emma Thompson, cast as the candidate's wife. "My character isn't Hillary; it's a composite of various people." Billy Bob Thornton, playing a James Carville–like consultant, got a White House benediction before he agreed to act in the film; he and Clinton knew each other as fellow Arkansans. "If he'd had a problem with it, I wouldn't have done it," Thornton said. Director Nichols, a political supporter who had performed at a 1992 Clinton fund-raiser, exerted himself mightily to draw a distinction between the Travolta character and the real thing. "It's about us more than them," Nichols told a journalist. "It's not about Clinton, but about the 'Clinton thing.'"

As the first motion picture about a sitting president since *PT 109*, *Primary Colors* drew extensive press attention, much of it tied to the Lewinsky matter. But media chatter did not translate into box office traffic. *Primary Colors* never found the audience it deserved. Though not without flaws, the film does a creditable job illustrating the circus atmosphere of a national political campaign, and Travolta's performance as Clinton is one of the actor's finest. The White House refused to say if the movie-obsessed president saw the film, but at the 1998 Gridiron dinner Clinton joked, "This is not the first time John Travolta has modeled a character on me." Striking Travolta's famous disco pose from *Saturday Night Fever*, Clinton told the audience, "That's my theme song: 'Stayin' Alive.'"

Bill Clinton found himself at the center of a different sort of Hollywood hornet's nest with the release of the 1997 science fiction film *Contact*. If *Primary Colors* coopted the president's image in a figurative sense, *Contact* did so literally, intercutting two actual Clinton sound bites into a story line about extraterrestrial communication. In 1996 the president spoke about a meteorite from Mars that suggested the possibility of life on that planet. Filmmakers took the remark out of context and digitally altered the background to make it appear as though Clinton were at a news conference answering a reporter's question about radio messages from outer space. The second, more troublesome, clip came from Clinton's early reaction to the bombing of the Oklahoma City federal building. "I would warn everybody not to be influenced by suggestion beyond the known facts. We are monitoring what has actually happened," Clinton said at the time. As critic Stephen Hunter pointed out in the *Washington Post*, "In effect, Warner Brothers and *Contact* have tried to make a few bucks out of an atrocity."

The Clinton administration voiced its objections in a letter to *Contact* director Robert Zemeckis, who several years earlier had used similar digital legerdemain to insert Tom Hanks as Forrest Gump into news clips with Presidents Kennedy, Johnson, and Nixon. At a White House briefing press secretary Michael McCurry elaborated on Clinton's objection: "The President's image, which is his alone to control, is used in a way that would lead a viewer to imagine that he had said something that he didn't really say." The filmmakers countered that it was not Clinton's statements that were altered, only the context in which he had spoken them. Although the White House let the matter drop, the issue remains unresolved: To what extent should presidential words and pictures be "repurposed" as entertainment?

As a movie president, Bill Clinton had lots of competition in the 1990s. An assortment of actors tackled the role of chief executive, making the White House a steady film presence throughout Clinton's tenure in office. Playing the part for laughs were Kevin Kline in *Dave* (1993); Alan Alda in *Canadian Bacon* (1995); Jack Nicholson in *Mars Attacks* (1996); and Jack Lemmon, James Garner, and Dan Aykroyd in *My Fellow Americans* (1996). On the dramatic side were Donald Moffat in *Clear and Present Danger* (1994); Bill Pullman in *Independence Day* (1996); Harrison Ford in *Air Force One* (1997); Gene Hackman in *Absolute Power* (1997); Ronny Cox in *Murder at 1600* (1997); Sam Waterston in *The Shadow Conspiracy* (1997); Morgan Freeman in *Deep Impact* (1998); Kevin Pollak in *Deterrence* (1999); and Jeff Bridges in *The Contender* (2000). The White House became the unlikely setting of a romantic drama in *An American President* (1995), with Michael Douglas in the title role and Annette Bening as his lobbyist girlfriend. The writer of *An American President*, Aaron Sorkin, went on to produce the popular television series *The West Wing*, in which a fictional president played by Martin Sheen runs an administration whose fantasyland goodness harks back to the reverential Hollywood pictures of yore.

"I have been very interested in this huge spate of movies with the president playing a prominent role in the last few years," Bill Clinton told critic Gene Siskel in 1997. "I can't really account for it. But if it has anything to do with the energy and action that we've tried to bring to this town, then that's good."

Since Clinton's departure from office presidential depictions have dwindled. Apart from Will Ferrell's dead-on impersonations of George W. Bush on *Saturday Night Live*, the entertainment industry's most notable contemporaneous take on the forty-third president was a cable TV sitcom called *That's My Bush!* With Timothy Bottoms in the title role, the show savaged Bush, depicting him as a bumbling moron kept afloat by his wife and the White House staff. The series debuted on Comedy Central in April 2001; it was canceled four months later due to low viewership.

Ronald Reagan in a publicity still from *The Last Outpost*, 1951.
(Ronald Reagan Library)

Conclusion

✴✴✴✴

THE COMMON VOCABULARY
OF PRESIDENTS AND ENTERTAINERS

O NE MONTH BEFORE leaving office, Ronald Reagan sat down with journalist David Brinkley for a television interview about his eight years as president of the United States. Brinkley asked Reagan if anything he had learned as a Hollywood actor was helpful to him in the White House. Replied the president, "There have been times in this office when I've wondered how you could do the job if you hadn't been an actor."

Though Reagan intended the remark at least partly in jest—it was one of his stock gags—he was also articulating an unavoidable truth about the modern presidency: it functions as a combination of statecraft and stagecraft. As presidents and entertainers lock themselves into an ever tighter embrace, the common ground between politics and show business is expanding. These once disparate communities find themselves thrown together in the fraternity of fame, two branches of the same tree that for the past hundred years have been steadily intertwining.

In the view of Jack Valenti, chairman of the Motion Picture Association of America and a former assistant to Lyndon Johnson, "Politicians and movie stars spring from the same DNA. Both hope for applause, read from a script, and hope to persuade audiences." As this comment suggests, the relationship between presidents and voters finds a direct analogue in the relationship between performers and fans. In both cases the connection is fraught with mystery and contradiction. Citizens come to "know" their presidents just as fans come to "know" movie stars, though in reality the relationship never advances beyond the realm of abstraction. Critic Richard Schickel has appropriately described celebrities as "intimate strangers," figures both familiar and remote. The label applies to presidents as appositely as it applies to actors.

Dependent as they are on audience approval, both professions operate according to the intangible rules of stardom. Why do some political figures resonate with voters while others, equally qualified or perhaps even more qualified, fall flat? Why, for instance, was Reagan reelected to a second term and Jimmy Carter tossed out after one? Though many reasons apply, at least part of the answer rests with the relative charisma of the men in question. To frame the question in Hollywood terms, why was Cary Grant a bigger star than Ralph Bellamy? Success on the playing fields of both politics and entertainment involves an almost alchemical process of seducing vast numbers of human beings, individually and collectively, then keeping them on your side over the long haul. Reagan had the magic. Carter did not.

As in show business, the intensely competitive world of presidential politics makes room for only a handful of genuine superstars. Anyone who ascends to the heights of 1600 Pennsylvania Avenue breathes the same rarefied air as the elite names of Hollywood. The two groups have more in common with each other than they do with the 99.9 percent of the body politic who are not world famous.

Superstar politicians, like superstar performers, know that reaching this plateau carries a price. Alec Baldwin, among the country's most devoted actors to matters political, notes that presidents and entertainers both live lives "dramatically impacted" by the consequences of celebrity. "Once a state best described as 'stardom' is achieved," Baldwin said, "maintaining one's position becomes paramount. Creativity contracts. Risk is avoided. Fame and comfort replace artistry for the actor, and replace reform and public service for the elected official."

Both presidents and entertainers function in a splendid isolation, cut off from the day-to-day lives of the people on whose support they depend. To the celebrity—in Hollywood as in the White House—the audience becomes as much an abstraction as the celebrity is to the audience. The challenge for both types of performers is to maintain a personal link to the public without ceding the psychic aloofness that is the mark of a bona fide star.

✳✳✳✳

At the 1986 Gridiron show Ronald Reagan brought up Clint Eastwood's campaign for mayor of Carmel, California. "Can you imagine that?" the president asked. "What makes him think a middle-aged movie actor who has played with a chimp could have a future in politics?" With so much in common it is surprising that even greater numbers of professional entertainers have not sought elective office. The election of Arnold Schwarzenegger as governor of California in 2003 may encourage other performers to toss their hats into the ring, although the unusual circumstances of Schwarzenegger's victory could lack general application. More typically, top actors have declined offers to run for high-profile political positions, usually seats in Congress; the list includes such marquee attractions as Harry Belafonte, James Garner, Charlton Heston, Gregory Peck, and Christopher Reeve.

With the encouragement of President Franklin Roosevelt, cinematic boy wonder Orson Welles, barely past his thirtieth birthday, toyed with the possibility of a run for the U.S. Senate. Campaigning around the country for FDR in 1944 whetted Welles's appetite for politics, and after the election he continued speaking out as a lecturer and newspaper columnist. In 1946 Welles seriously considered pursuing a Senate seat in his home state of Wisconsin, as he recounted in a 1982 BBC interview:

> We discovered that the dairy interests, who I felt I had to fight, were so powerful that I would almost certainly be beaten unless I was the greatest campaigner ever known. But now, supposing I was the greatest campaigner ever known . . . because if I had been, there never would have been Joe McCarthy. He was the candidate who ran on the Republican ticket and got in. So I have that on my conscience. Maybe I could have run and beaten him and there never would have been a McCarthy.

Welles confessed to the BBC interviewer that his ultimate goal in politics would have been the White House, though as a presidential candidate he felt he had two strikes against him. "I didn't think anybody could get elected president who had been divorced and who had been an actor," Welles said. "I made a helluva mistake—in both directions."

The only other well-known actor to be mentioned as a potential occupant of the Oval Office is Warren Beatty, Hollywood's second-most experienced veteran of presidential politics after Ronald Reagan. In the summer of 1999 Beatty found himself at the vortex of media speculation about whether he would launch a run for the White House. Beatty did little to dispel the rumors, perhaps because his new movie—*Bulworth*, which just happened to revolve around a political campaign—was then being released around the world. Under the provocative title "Why Not Now?" he wrote an op-ed column for the *New York Times*; though borderline inscrutable, the key point of the piece was Beatty's call for a return to Democratic liberalism.

In September 1999, at the height of the hoopla, Warren Beatty accepted an award from a liberal political group in Los Angeles. The news media devoted enormous attention to the banquet, positioning the event as an opportunity for Beatty to toss his hat into the ring. Introducing the honoree at the Beverly Hilton, comedian Garry Shandling advised, "If you run, make sure you get your name above the title of the country." But the actor disappointed his supporters—and the press, which had already begun polling voters about a Beatty candidacy—by using his platform to recapitulate the arguments he had made in the *Times*.

In hindsight the Beatty-for-president hype of 1999 reads wholly as a media invention. Warren Beatty had already made the case against himself as an elected politician when he was an operative in George McGovern's 1972 campaign. Beatty told a journalist then, "I don't think I'm generous enough. I care too much about my private life and my habits." And he pointed out another obstacle: "I've never worked for anyone else in my life. I'm my own man. In politics you have to eat shit all the time. Even the candidate."

The electoral flirtations of both Orson Welles and Warren Beatty make the point that similarities notwithstanding, careers in show business and politics also require fundamentally different levels of commitment. Screenwriter Joe Ezterhas, in his take-no-prisoners polemic *American Rhapsody*, writes with characteristic bluntness about the downside of politics for individuals like Beatty who have grown accustomed to the pamperings of Hollywood:

> Bill Clinton . . . knew that a politician had to be a whore for the cameras. Cameras could invade him from a thousand different angles at any moment. He'd been invaded so often, he couldn't feel it anymore. Warren tried to give cameras only his right profile. He tried to control the lighting, the distance, and the shutter speed. To Bill Clinton, a camera meant any schmuck at any campaign appearance. To Warren, a camera meant Vilmos Zsigmond or Helmut Newton.

Another key difference separates the professions: although [ ]tion as the leading man in the national soap opera, the role is or creation of the person who plays it. Powerful outside forces—media coverage, public opinion, national tragedies—constantly subvert the performer's desired interpretation. Actors, especially movie actors, work under tightly controlled circumstances and follow a predetermined script; presidents react on the fly to situations not of their own making.

Clearly, because the stakes are so much higher, political leaders play a far more sobering game than the men and women of show business. Entertainers with aspirations to public office must therefore overcome a good deal of skepticism. This was Ronald Reagan's challenge when he first ran for governor, and it is why the policy pretensions of Hollywood stars so often grate. When entertainers err egos suffer; when presidents err the world suffers.

Showbiz and politics function best when each sticks to its own side of the street. Excessive intermingling demystifies the mutual allure. "The two communities are made for each other in terms of attraction," Robert Redford told an interviewer in 1983. "Washington has the credibility—our community is perceived as a flaky one. Washington is fascinated by Hollywood, which it finds enormously attractive. It's a marriage made in heaven." But a marriage works only if each partner honors the other's uniqueness. The classic comment about Fred Astaire and Ginger Rogers, attributed to Katharine Hepburn, was that "he gave her class, she gave him sex." In the relationship between politics and showbiz, Fred is Washington and Ginger is Hollywood—and so they probably ought to remain.

✳✳✳✳

One final episode from the intersection of politics and show business brings the discussion to an end: the attempted assassination of Ronald Reagan on March 30, 1981. In its bizarre way this incident illuminates more starkly than anything else the extent to which presidents and movie stars have coalesced in the national imagination. In a twist no Hollywood scriptwriter would have dared, the sunny leading man from Warner Bros. found himself forever linked to two of the darkest characters ever captured on film: Robert De Niro's political assassin and Jodie Foster's teenage prostitute from the 1976 Martin Scorsese picture *Taxi Driver*.

Shortly after the shooting outside the Washington Hilton, police searched the hotel room of the young man they had taken into custody, John Hinckley.

ere they discovered an unmailed letter to Foster, the child actress who had put her career on hold in order to study at Yale University. "Jodie," Hinckley had written, "I would abandon this idea of getting Reagan in a second if I could only win your heart and live out the rest of my life with you whether it be in obscurity or whatever." The headline in the next morning's *New York Post* reduced the tale to its essence: "Reagan Shot over Movie Star."

At a press conference in New Haven Foster read a statement: she had received a number of unsolicited letters from Hinckley, but none that threatened violence against the president. A reporter asked Foster about parallels drawn by the FBI between the assassination attempt and *Taxi Driver*. "As far as I was concerned, there's no message in *Taxi Driver*," Foster replied. "It is a piece of fiction."

In Los Angeles the Academy of Motion Picture Arts and Sciences announced it would delay the telecast of the fifty-third annual Academy Awards "in deference to the tragedy in Washington." When the program aired on March 31, twenty-four hours behind schedule, a groggy Ronald Reagan watched with his wife from a hospital bed. The show opened with a welcome message that the president had videotaped a week earlier at the White House. "It's surely no state secret that Nancy and I share your interest in the results of this year's balloting," the former Hollywood actor began. In his remarks Reagan unwittingly commented on his own mortality: "Film is forever," he said. "I've been trapped in some film forever myself." Then, "as a former member of the Academy," the president invited everyone to enjoy the ceremonies.

That night Robert De Niro in *Raging Bull* won the Oscar for Best Actor; four years earlier De Niro had been nominated for playing Travis Bickle, the political assassin in *Taxi Driver*. In his acceptance speech De Niro mentioned "all the terrible things that are happening," but otherwise steered clear of the elephant in the room. His agent later described De Niro as "very upset and very concerned" by the implication that *Taxi Driver* had somehow inspired the incident in Washington. The agent also reported that "special precautions" had been taken to ensure his client's security at the Academy Awards.

A cinematic sensibility permeated every aspect of the attempted assassination of Ronald Reagan. In the critical hours after the shooting the president had communicated with emergency room personnel by scrawling notes on a pad of pink paper. One message in particular caught their attention: "I'd like to do that scene again," wrote Reagan, "starting at the hotel."

NOTES

✦✦✦✦

Abbreviations—Media

ABC: ABC News
AP: Associated Press
BG: *Boston Globe*
BH: *Boston Herald*
CBS: CBS News
CSM: *Christian Science Monitor*
CST: *Chicago Sun-Times*
DV: *Daily Variety*
HC: *Houston Chronicle*
HR: *Hollywood Reporter*
LAHE: *Los Angeles Herald Examiner*
LAT: *Los Angeles Times*
NBC: NBC News
NYDN: *New York Daily News*
NYHT: *New York Herald Tribune*
NYP: *New York Post*
NYT: *New York Times*
SLPD: *St. Louis Post-Dispatch*
SPT: *St. Petersburg Times*
TNR: *The New Republic*
TNY: *The New Yorker*
TS: *Toronto Star*
UPI: United Press International
USAT: *USA Today*
WP: *Washington Post*

WS: *Washington Star*
WSJ: *Wall Street Journal*
WV: *Weekly Variety*

Abbreviations—Libraries

CCL: Calvin Coolidge Library (Northampton)
CPMP: Clinton Presidential Materials Project
DDEL: Dwight D. Eisenhower Library
FDRL: Franklin D. Roosevelt Library
GBL: George Bush Library
GRFL: Gerald R. Ford Library
HSTL: Harry S. Truman Library
JCL: Jimmy Carter Library
JFKL: John F. Kennedy Library
LBJL: Lyndon B. Johnson Library
MHL: Margaret Herrick Library, Academy of Motion Picture Arts and Sciences
NPMS: Nixon Presidential Materials Staff (College Park)
RNL: Richard Nixon Library (Yorba Linda)
RRL: Ronald Reagan Library
USC: University of Southern California Special Collections

Abbreviations–Miscellaneous

OH: Oral History
WH: White House

Introduction: The Showbiz Presidency

The account of Bill Clinton's comedy video comes from an author interview with Phil Rosenthal, 12/6/02.
"upstaged us all": DV, 5/2/00.

Chapter 1: Gilt by Association: How Entertainers Are Good for Presidents

Descriptions of the 1940 birthday ball are drawn from the *Los Angeles Daily News*, NYT, and WP, 1/31/40; *Life*, 2/12/40; and several autobiographies and biographies: Rooney, 172–173; Lamour, 92; Arthur Marx, 70.
Ginger Rogers at the 1936 birthday ball: Rogers, 155–158; Tully, 93–94.
Jean Harlow at the 1937 birthday ball: NYT, 1/31/37; DV 4/18/45; Stenn, 210.
1938 birthday ball: "The President's Birthday Magazine 1938," Vol. I, No. 3, FDRL; WP 1/30/38.
Lana Turner at the 1941 birthday ball: WP, 1/31/41; *Life*, 2/10/41; Turner, 69–70; Eleanor Roosevelt, *My Day*, 194–195.

1942 birthday ball: Gardner, 55–6; NYT, 1/31/42; WP, 1/31/42.

1945 birthday ball: Kotsilibas-Davis and Loy, 187–189; Lake, 149–150; Margaret Truman, *Souvenir*, 81; Hassett, 314; WV, 1/31/45; WP, 1/30/45.

1946 birthday ball: WV, 2/6/46.

FDR's affinity for show people: Rosalind Russell, 140; Bankhead, 276.

Lincoln's affinity for show people: Braudy, 503.

"most vigorous and magnetic": Dressler, 177.

Movie stars meet Wilson and Harding: Pickford, 238; WP, 4/17/18; Gish, 245.

Shirley Temple and the Roosevelts: Shirley Temple Black, 214–215, 233; WP, 6/24/38; Eleanor Roosevelt, *My Day*, 92.

JFK's affinity for show people: Blair, 482; WP, 2/28/61.

Nixon's 1972 celebrity reception: Various memoranda, WHCF Subject Files SO, Box 23, Folder 6/26/72–9/7/72, NPMS; LAHE, LAT, and WS, 8/28/72.

Nixon's 1973 celebrity fiesta for Brezhnev: LAT, 6/24/73; NYT, 6/25/73; Fury, 221–222; Strausbaugh, 96–97.

John Wayne and Jimmy Carter: WP, 1/20–21/77; Wills, *John Wayne's America*, 29; Correspondence, Executive File, JCL; Wayne, 264–266.

Bush's affinity for country music: SLPD, 8/22/90; WP, 10/7/90; Country Music Association awards show, CBS, 10/2/91; NYT, 8/23/92.

Bush and Arnold Schwarzenegger: *Great American Work-Out* videos, 5/1/90, 5/1/91, and 5/1/92, GBL.

Lassie and Lady Bird Johnson: Carpenter, 138–139.

George Harrison and Gerald Ford: WP, 12/14/74.

Dolly Parton and Jimmy Carter: WP, 10/3/79.

Michael Jackson at the WH: ABC, 5/14/84; WP, 5/15/84.

Clinton's affinity for show people: NYT, 5/9/93; WP, 9/17/92.

Chapter 2: Attack of the Cat Woman: How Entertainers Are Bad for Presidents

Sources for Eartha Kitt at the WH are Kitt, 228–241; NYT, 1/19/68; WP, 1/19/68; WV, 1/24/68; Claudia T. Johnson, 620–624; Carpenter, 202–203; "Women Doers Luncheon" film, LBJL.

Carole Feraci and Richard Nixon: WP, 1/29/72; LAT, 4/15/72; WP, 7/27/97; and various items of correspondence found in WHCF, Subject Files SO, Box 12, Folder 1/1/72–12/31/72 1 of 3, including Letter, Nixon to Ray Conniff, 2/2/72; Letter, Conniff to Nixon, 2/3/72; Letter, Jay Meyer to Nixon, 1/31/72; and Letter, Norman Vincent Peale to Nixon, 1/31/72, NPMS.

"But, after a while. . .": NYT, 9/14/75.

John Wayne and JFK: *Life*, 7/4/60; Roberts and Olson, 473.

Springsteen and Reagan: WP, 9/13/84; NYT, 9/20/84, 10/2/84, and 5/7/95; Marsh, 255–256, 260.

Celebrities critical of Bush: NYT, 10/14/88; Simon, *Roadshow*, 335.

Robert Redford and George W. Bush: NYT, 5/23/01 and 12/8/02.

Dan Quayle versus *Murphy Brown*: CBS, 5/20/92; BG, 5/21/92; NYT, 5/21/92; ABC, 6/10/92, 8/31/92, and 9/22/92; Quayle, 319–327.

Bush critical of violent entertainment, *The Simpsons*: NYT, 6/30/92; WP, 6/30/92; NYT 1/28/92; CST, 8/21/92.

Bob Dole critical of entertainment violence: ABC, 6/1/95; LAT, 9/18/96.

"massacre every five minutes": DV, 9/18/00.

Lynne Cheney versus Eminem: USAT, 9/14/00; NYDN, 5/14/02; *Buffalo News*, 7/19/02.

Parents Music Resource Center: Turque, 167–179; WP, 9/20/85.

"Kissing in the old days. . .": *Barbara Walters Special*, ABC, 3/24/86.

The Beach Boys and James Watt: ABC, 4/7/83; WP, 4/7/83.

Clinton versus Sister Souljah: ABC, 6/13/92; BG, 6/14/92; NYT, 6/14/92; CBS, 6/16/92.

Nixon and *Hair*: Haldeman, 43.

Ben Vereen and Charley Pride at 1981 Inaugural: WP, 1/20/81; Royko quoted in Kitty Kelley, 461.

Robert Goulet and Reagan: WP, 11/17/81; WP, 6/30/87.

"little Gladys Smith": Donaldson, 92.

"Isn't dropping Wayne on our own. . .": NYT, 11/11/01.

"Anthony Perkins playing. . .": LAT, 4/25/93.

Clinton's 1993 celebrity troubles: LAT, 4/12/93; USAT, 5/13/93; NYT, 5/21/93; *CBS This Morning*, 5/27/93.

Press coverage of Clinton's 1993 celebrity troubles: NYT, 5/9/93; WP, 5/13/93; LAT, 5/23/93; WP, 5/25/93.

O.J. Simpson and Clinton: BG, 3/31/94; USAT, 4/29/94.

Michael Jackson and Bush: BG, 4/6/90; Letter, Bush to Capital Children's Museum, 4/5/90, Subject File, General ME02, GBL.

Willie Nelson and Carter: Nelson, 195–196.

Gerald McRaney and Bush: CBS, 10/3/92; HC, 10/4/92; WP, 10/20/92.

Eazy-E, the Beach Boys, and Bush: WP, 3/19/91; LAT, 3/20/91 and 9/12/92.

"We are eating our words. . .": WP, 3/1/61.

Sinatra's attempt to reach Nixon: Kitty Kelley, 281.

Charlton Heston's conversion: Heston, 353–354.

"I'm a Reagan fan. . .": NYT, 3/23/81.

Golfing with Nixon and Agnew: Gold, 152–153; Haldeman, 378.

Andy Williams and Bush: Memorandum, Bush to Ronald F. Kaufman, 9/3/92; Letter, Bush to Andy Williams, 9/4/92, Subject File, GBL.

Tallulah Bankhead and Truman, Bankhead and Eleanor Roosevelt: Israel, 296–297, 320–321.

Jimmy Carter in Beverly Hills: Stroud, 339–341.

Viewership for 1953 inaugural: Andrews, 79.

James Brown and Hubert Humphrey: LAT, 7/30/68.

Arnold Schwarzenegger and Bush: CBS, 2/15/92; WP, 2/18/92.

Nixon miffed at *Time* magazine: Haldeman, 574.

Nixon on *Laugh-In*: NYT, 9/17/68; WP, 2/20/77.

Jack Benny and Truman: Post-Presidential Files, Name File: Barkley to Benson, Box 50, Jack Benny Folder 1; Benny, 245–247; NYT, 10/19/59.

Chapter 3: Hope Springs Eternal: How Presidents Are Good for Entertainers

Bob Hope at the Carter WH: NBC, 5/24/78.

Hope and FDR: Hope, *Don't Shoot*, 44.

"There is one sobering thought": WP, 9/12/63.

Hope's friendship with Nixon and Agnew: *NYT Magazine*, 10/4/70; Hope, *Dear Prez*, 81, 90.

Hope's "Honor America" rally: NYT, 7/5/70; LAT, 7/5/70; CBS, 6/29/70; *NYT Magazine*, 10/4/70.

"I can only say": WP, 12/25/71.

"He was a hell of a guy. . .": LAT, 9/28/94.

Hope and Ford: Hope, *Dear Prez*, 99.

Hope and Carter: ABC, 5/24/78; Letter, Hope to Carter, 5/25/78, and other items of correspondence, Executive File, JCL.

Hope and Reagan: *Happy Birthday, Bob*, NBC, 5/23/83.

Hope and Bush, Michael Dukakis: Hope, *Dear Prez*, 150; *The Guardian*, 10/29/88; *Daily Telegraph*, 10/29/88; Black and Oliphant, 191.

Hope and Clinton: Hope, *Dear Prez*, 167: WP, 2/16/95; *Laughing With the Presidents*, NBC, 11/23/96.

The account of Elvis Presley and Nixon is drawn from Egil Krogh's definitive *The Day Elvis Met Nixon*; *Elvis Memories*, syndicated television broadcast, 1981; Marcus, *Dead Elvis*, 187.

Elvis and Carter: TNY, 8/18/97; CBS, 8/17/77.

Marie Dressler at the WH: Dressler, 176–177; Eleanor Roosevelt, *This I Remember*, 111.

Reagan and Truman: WH appointment log, 4/1/45, HSTL; Chuck Connors Collection, Folder, "Reagan Political Campaign," USC.

"I would have been an idiot. . .": Bergen, 190.

Bette Davis and FDR, Shirley Temple and Eisenhower, Shelley Winters and JFK: Lippman, 13–14; Shirley Temple Black, 514; Winters, 367–368.

Kirk Douglas and LBJ: Valenti, 100.

Johnny Cash and Clinton, Bono and Bush, Streisand and Clinton: Cash, 213; NYT, 3/15/02; WSJ, 5/14/93.

Rob Reiner and Clinton: NYT, 11/12/95.

June Lockhart at the WH: Author interview with June Lockhart, 11/20/02.

"This building had known. . .": Helen Gahagan Douglas, 150.

"The prospect of a visit. . .": Gish, 245.

"like being in a dream. . .": USAT, 3/30/93.

Katharine Hepburn at the WH: Hepburn, 163–164.

"The moment he walked in. . .": Duke, 119–120.

"ankles wouldn't hold up. . .": WP, 11/29/62.

Barbra Streisand and JFK: Spada, *Streisand*, 124; Griffin, 70.

Rosemary Clooney, Woody Allen at the WH: Clooney, 191; Lax, *Woody Allen*, 211.

"With a great sense of pride. . .": Williams, 205–206.

Celebrities in the Lincoln Bedroom: Baldrige, 189–190; Barbara Bush, 506–507; Gatlin, 255–257; Sammy Davis, 269–270, 291–292.

"For thirty minutes": Carpenter, 205.

"I came away with. . .": Letter, Burr Tillstrom to Maria Downs, 1/9/76, Maria Downs Files, Box 22, Folder: "Kukla, Fran & Ollie," GRFL.

Lauren Bacall and Truman: WP, 2/10/45; Bacall, 146, 188–189; Margaret Truman, *Harry S. Truman*, 199–200.

Debbie Reynolds and Nixon: WP, 2/22/73; Reynolds, 350–351.

Peter Lawford and JFK: Spada, *Peter Lawford*, 243–244; *Good Housekeeping*, Feb. 1962; WP, 12/25/84; Memorandum, Evelyn Lincoln to Arthur Schlesinger, 9/8/61, President's Office Files, Box 62, Folder: "Staff Memoranda, E. Lincoln," JFKL.

"Entertainers get a chance. . .": Author interview with Alec Baldwin, 10/24/02.

"People in Hollywood. . .": *NYT Magazine*, 11/6/66.

"If John Wayne can really. . .": NYT, 8/8/71.

"But I've changed my mind. . .": Newton, 145.

"No scum here tonight!": WP, 12/8/83.

Chapter 4: Glad to Be Unhappy: How Presidents Are Bad for Entertainers

Sources for Frank Sinatra's Palm Springs renovations are Tina Sinatra, 77–80; Nancy Sinatra, 160.

Kennedy's decision to stay at Bing Crosby's: O'Donnell and Powers, 379; Schlesinger, 495.

Sinatra's anger at Peter Lawford: Spada, *Peter Lawford*, 294; Kitty Kelley, 302.

"If he would only pick up. . .": Schlesinger, 495.

JFK's fascination with Sinatra: O'Donnell and Powers, 18; Wills, *The Kennedy Imprisonment*, 22–23; Kuntz, 125.

The Rat Pack and JFK: Sammy Davis, 107–108; Clipping, "Off the Record" by Michael V. Kelly, Pre-Presidential Papers, Box 927, Folder "California, Frank Sinatra et al," JFKL.

Sinatra and Sam Giancana: Tina Sinatra, 71–74.

Sinatra and Albert Maltz: Kitty Kelley, 271–275; Tina Sinatra, 66–67.

Sinatra at the JFK WH: White House appointment log, September 1961, JFKL; Kitty Kelley, 292.

Sinatra on Cape Cod: BG, 9/24/61 and 9/25/61; BH, 9/24/61 and 9/25/61; *U.S. News and World Report*, 10/16/61.

"I was delighted. . .": Letter, JFK to Sinatra, 3/4/62, Name File: Sinatra, Box 2577, JFKL.

"Print will be available": Telegram, Sinatra to Pierre Salinger, 8/28/62, Name File: Sinatra, Box 2577, JFKL.

"For a moment in late 1963. . .": Schlesinger, 496.

Sinatra and the JFK assassination: Nancy Sinatra, 178.

The account of Sammy Davis Jr. in the 1960 campaign is taken from Sammy Davis, 110–111, 116–120, 129–132; and Tracey Davis, 27.

Sammy Davis at the WH: Lee White OH, 104–105, JFKL; Reeves, *President Kennedy*, 464; Tracy Davis, 50.

Sinatra and Spiro Agnew: Kitty Kelley, 402; CSM, 3/26/73.

"I know you don't approve. . .": Nessen, 99–100.

Sinatra and Reagan: Kitty Kelley, 361; NYT, 1/8/81; WP, 5/24/85.

Letters to Sinatra via Reagan: Letter, "Concerned Area Residents" to Sinatra 1/23/81, and miscellaneous letters forwarded to Sinatra from WH Social Secretary Mabel Brandon, 12/7/81, WHORM Alphabetical File: Frank Sinatra, RRL.

"As reluctant as I am. . .": Letter, Reagan to Sinatra, 2/28/84, WHORM Alphabetical File: Frank Sinatra, RRL.

"Even as he took a right turn. . .": Tina Sinatra, 143–144.

"Thank you for your applause": Autographed Photo, Sammy Davis to Nixon, 4/9/54, RNL.

Sammy Davis and Robert F. Kennedy: Sammy Davis, 144.

Sammy Davis working for Nixon: Stroud, 172; NBC, 8/23/72; Sammy Davis, 258–272.

"I'm not a sell-out artist": Brown, 229–230.

Ray Charles and Nixon: *Los Angeles Sentinel*, 9/29/72.

Lionel Hampton and Republicans: WP, 9/1/02; WP, 1/20/85.

Pearl Bailey and Nixon: ABC, 3/8/74; CBS, 3/8/74; Letter, RN to Pearl Bailey, 5/10/74, WHCF Subject Files SO, Box 14, Folder 3/1/74–3/31/74, NPMS.

Pearl Bailey and the Fords: WP, 10/29/75.

Actors on Nixon's enemies list: NYT, 6/28/73; CST, 4/25/94; *Time*, 7/8/02; Lax, *Paul Newman*, 148–149.

Groucho Marx and Nixon: Groucho Marx, 239.

Shirley MacLaine and Nixon: MacLaine, 216, 211–212.

Jane Fonda and Nixon: Andersen, 217–218, 229–230; Julie Nixon Eisenhower, 347.

Jane Fonda's antiwar show: CBS, 3/14/71.

John Lennon and Nixon: See Jon Wiener for a full discussion; also LAT 9/25/97; WP 3/19/00.

Grace Slick at the WH: Slick, 189–194.

Madonna's music video: NYT, 2/2/03.

Sean Penn and George W. Bush: WP, 10/18/02; NYT, 5/30/03.

Martin Sheen backlash: UPI, 3/14/03; LAT, 3/22/03.

Screen Actors Guild: *Ottawa Citizen*, 3/29/03.

Tim Robbins and Susan Sarandon protest the war: NYT, 4/11/03; NYDN, 4/11/03; Robbins remarks to National Press Club, 4/15/03.

Sources for the Dixie Chicks incident are HC, 3/15/03; LAT, 3/19/03; *Prime Time Thursday*, ABC, 3/24/03; NYT, 3/25/03; *Entertainment Weekly*, 5/2/03; WP, 6/27/03; NYT, 7/6/03.

"I despise him. . .": NYDN, 10/31/02.

"I mean, the Dixie Chicks. . .": NBC *Dateline*, 4/25/03.

"genocidal denial. . .": USAT, 11/20/92.

"They called the day before. . .": Charles, 290.

Clinton anti-impeachment celebrities: CBS, 12/16/98; LAT, 12/17/98; NYDN, 12/23/98.

Tom Hanks and Clinton: TNR, 12/7–14/98; NYT, 12/2/98; USAT, 12/1/98; WP, 12/17/98.

Alec Baldwin versus Henry Hyde: WP, 12/17/98.

"He disgusts me. . .": NYP, 6/25/02.

"The media are sick and tired. . .": UPI, 3/14/03.

"Even though I have huge opinions. . .": BG, 3/24/02.

Chapter 5: Running Time: Entertainers on the Campaign Trail

Al Jolson and Harding: WP, 8/25/20; Anthony, *Florence Harding*, 220.

Jolson and Coolidge: NYT, 10/18/24; WP, 10/18/24.

FDR in Los Angeles, 1932: LAT, 9/25/32; NYT, 9/25/32; WV, 9/27/32.

Hollywood for Roosevelt Committee: Committee Report, PPF, File 7024, FDRL.

"Salute to Roosevelt" radio broadcast: NBC, 11/4/40, FDRL.

Orson Welles and FDR: Telegram, FDR to Welles, 10/23/44; Telegram, Welles to FDR, 10/26/44; Letter, FDR to Welles, 11/25/44; Letter, Welles to FDR, undated but received 12/23/44, all found in PPF File 8921, FDRL.

Sinatra and FDR: WP, 9/29/44; Kitty Kelley, 92; LAT, 10/12/44.

1944 Election Eve radio show: Brownstein, 100–101.

Welles, Sinatra, and FDR at Fenway Park: BH, 11/4/44 and 11/5/44; BG, 11/5/44; *Boston Sunday Post*, 11/5/44.

W.C. Fields and Wendell Willkie: Ronald Fields, 181, 189.

"The Truth About Hollywood!": NYT, 11/4/40.

Eddie Bracken on the campaign trail: WV, 11/8/44.

"I did not know he could win. . .": Jessell, *The World I Lived In*, 164.

Tallulah Bankhead campaigning for Truman: Bankhead, 276–279; NYT, 10/22/48.

"Dear Baby and Bogie. . .": Telegram, Jack Warner to Bogart and Bacall, 11/6/52, Box 64:32, Jack Warner Collection, USC.

"I'm strictly for Stevenson. . .": NYHT, 8/18/56.

Jack Warner's fund-raising for Eisenhower: Various memoranda, "Entertainment Industry Joint Committee for Eisenhower-Nixon"; Letter, John Wayne to Warner, 10/1/52; Letter, Bob Hope to Warner, 5/4/56, all found in Folders: "Political 1 and 2" Box 64:32, Jack Warner Collection, USC.

"Salute to Ike": Video, 1/20/56, DDEL; Craig Allen, 90.

Eisenhower birthday telecast: "National Ike Day," CBS, 10/14/56, DDEL; Craig Allen, 143.

"You never saw such beautiful flesh. . .": Brodie, 237–238.

1960 Democratic National Convention: BG, 7/12/60; HR, 7/11/60, 7/12/60, and 7/13/60; NYT, 7/16/60.

"The idea of making a big thing. . .": Brownstein, 144.

JFK political ads with Harry Belafonte, other entertainers: Video reel F80, JFKL; Audio Reel DNC 60–18, JFKL.

"I am certainly not vain enough:" Kotsilibas-Davis and Loy, 300.

JFK birthday fund-raisers: NYT, 5/20/62; NYT, 5/24/63.

JFK inaugural anniversary dinners: WP, 1/20/63; WP, 11/21/63.

JFK Los Angeles fund-raisers: LAHE, 6/6/63; LAT, 6/6/63; Clark, 139.

Celebrities in 1964 campaign: Lax, *Woody Allen*, 210; NYT, 10/13/64.

WH memo regarding Tricia and Julie Nixon: Dwight L. Chapin to David N. Parker, 12/18/71, WHCF Subject Files SO, Box 12, Folder 10/1/71–12/31/71, NPMS.

"Under the old system. . .": Brownstein, 234.

Shirley MacLaine and George McGovern: MacLaine, 208–209; ABC 5/4/72; NYT, 5/18/72.

Warren Beatty and George McGovern: *Harper's Bazaar*, Nov. 1972; *Redbook*, May 1974.

"This whole thing makes me. . .": NW, 5/31/76.

"Talking to an audience. . .": Weidenfeld, 345.

"I've played many roles. . .": *Time*, 10/7/66.

1980 celebrity campaigners for Reagan: BG, 11/3/79; WP, 11/13/79; Brownstein, 277.

1984 celebrity campaigners for Reagan: NBC 9/13/84; NYT, 9/14/84.

Michael Dukakis campaign: Simon, *Roadshow*, 200–201; WP, 9/30/88.

"Star-Spangled Caravan": Brownstein, 300.

"It was hard to get people to come. . .": Author interview with Harry Thomason, 2/17/03.

1992 Clinton fund-raiser in Los Angeles: CBS, 9/17/92; NBC, 9/17/92; DV, 9/18/92; HR, 9/18/92; LAT, 9/18/92.

1996 Clinton fund-raiser in Los Angeles: ABC, 9/13/96.

Michael Douglas and Clinton: Simon, *Show Time*, 10.

Chapter 6: America's Toughest Gig: Performing for the President

"I had a hard time. . .": Haggard, 193–194.

Early WH entertainment: Kirk, 21–22, 83–85, 174, 180–181.

"Evening of American Music": NYT, 6/9/39.

Criteria of the Johnson WH: Carpenter, 200.

"We picked her because. . .": *McCall's*, Sept. 1975.

Queen Elizabeth at the Ford WH: Videotape of entertainment, 7/7/76, GRFL; WP, 7/8/76; Letter, "The Captain and Tennille" to President and Mrs. Ford, 8/8/76, Maria Downs Files, Box 22, Folder: "Bob Hope and Captain and Tennille," GRFL.

Johnny and June Carter Cash at the WH: WP, 4/18/0; Cash, 211–212.

Nixon and WH entertainers: Confidential Memo, Connie Stuart and Penny Adams to Dwight Chapin et al, 5/13/71, WHCF, Subject Files SO, Box 12, Folder 1/1/72–12/31/72, NPMS; WP, 7/27/73.

"You understand the requirements. . .": Letter, Michael K. Deaver to Sinatra, 9/25/81, WHORM Alphabetical File: Frank Sinatra, RRL.

Sinatra at the Nixon WH: ABC, 4/18/73; Memo, Dwight Chapin to Connie Stuart, 11/30/70, quoted in Kuntz, 212–213; Memo, Stephen Bull to Mary Fenton, 5/9/73, 225, quoted in Kuntz, 225.

"I was tremendously impressed. . .": Traubel, 205.

"While older performers. . .": WP, 5/9/58.

Entertainment at the JFK WH: Kirk, 287; Baldrige, 188.

Entertainment at the LBJ WH: WP, 12/12/68; WP, 1/18/67.

Duke Ellington at the Nixon WH: NBC, 4/30/69; Nixon, 540; NYT, 4/30/69; *Saturday Review*, 5/31/69.

Nixon party for POWs: Memo, Nixon to H.R. Haldeman, 3/4/73, quoted in Oudes, 580–581; WP, 5/25/73; Nixon, 867–868.

"I haven't laughed so hard. . .": WP, 1/30/70.

The Carpenters at the Nixon WH: Coleman, 143, 325; Letter, Nixon to Karen and Richard Carpenter, 5/10/73, WHCF, Subject Files SO, Box 13, Folder 5/1/73–5/30/73, NPMS.

The Turtles, Gary Puckett at the Nixon WH: NYT, 7/18/70; LAT, 4/24/97.

Entertainment at the Ford WH: Videotapes of performances by Tennessee Ernie Ford, 6/16/75, and Carol Burnett and Helen Reddy, 1/27/76, GRFL; WP, 12/7/76; Memo to Linda Baker, WH Social Office, 1/12/77, Maria Downs Files, Box 23, Folder: "Tony Orlando," GRFL.

Jazz festival at the Carter WH: WP, 6/19/78 and 9/10/81.

In Performance at the WH: WP, 6/14/93.

Entertainment at the Clinton WH: USAT, 9/23/94; WP, 10/25/99 and 2/6/98.

"Do you like my hair?": NYDN, 10/9/01.

Guests at the FDR WH: Hayes, 215–216; Fontaine, 128; Jessel, *This Way, Miss*, 167–168.

"Let's see. . .": Fontaine, 238.

Joan Crawford at LBJ dinner: Carpenter, 201–202; Bess Abell OH III, 7/1/69, 21, LBJL.

Woody Allen at LBJ dinner: Lax, *Woody Allen*, 210–211; Claudia T. Johnson, 223.

"You must remember. . .": WP, 1/31/75.

Pearl Bailey at Ford dinner: WP, 5/16/75.

Marty Allen at Ford dinner: WS, 9/22/76; Maria Downs, *Mostly Wine and Roses* (unpublished, undated memoir by Ford WH social secretary), 93, Maria Downs Papers, Box 1, GRFL.

Dancing with Fred Astaire, Ginger Rogers: Betty Ford, 229; WP, 3/30/81.

Queen Elizabeth in California: WP, 3/1/83 and 3/5/83.

Michael J. Fox, Sylvester Stallone as WH guests: WP, 10/9/85.

"I just wish my mother. . .": Barbara Bush, 397–398.

Don Rickles, Leslie Nielsen at the Bush WH: WP, 5/16/90 and 10/23/91.

"She seemed feisty. . .": Barbara Bush, 383–384.

Sophia Loren at Clinton dinner: WP, 4/3/96.

Clinton dinner for Tony Blair: TNY, 2/16/91; NYT, 2/18/98.

Celebrities at FDR inaugurals: WP, 3/5/33, 1/20/41, and 1/20/45; NYT, 1/20/41.

Celebrities at Truman inaugural: WP, 1/20/49.

Celebrities at Eisenhower inaugurals: WP, 1/20/53 and 1/20/57.

Celebrities at JFK inaugural: BG, 1/20/61; DV, 1/20/61; WP, 1/20/61; Merman, 211–212.

Celebrities at LBJ Inaugural: WP, 1/9/65; Kilgallen quoted in Spada, *Streisand*, 160.

Celebrities at Nixon inaugurals: WP, 1/20/69 and 1/20/73.

Sinatra at 1973 Inaugural: Kitty Kelley, 411–413; Cheshire, 125.

Celebrities at 1977 Inaugural: Inaugural Gala videotape, JCL; WP, 1/21/77.

Sinatra at 1981 Inaugural: CBS, 1/12/81; Inaugural Gala videotape, RRL.

Dean Martin at 1981 Inaugural: WP, 1/20/81; Heston, 526.

Sinatra, controversies at 1985 inaugural: ABC, 1/19/85; Inaugural Gala videotape, 1/19/85, RRL.

Celebrities at 1989 Inaugural: Inaugural gala videotape, GBL.

Celebrities at 2001 Inaugural: WP, 1/18/01; LAT, 1/19/01.

Clinton's 1993 inaugural: NYT, 1/10/93; Author interview with Thomason; *Time*, 2/1/93; *Harper's*, April 93; DV, 1/20/93; WP, 1/21/93.

"There is this mutual. . .": NYT, 1/20/93.

Chapter 7: Groupies, Aficionados, and Philistines: Presidents as Fans

Rock 'n' Roll President: VH1, 6/3/97.

"Clinton listens. . .": Collins, 296.

Clinton's Dolly Parton poster: Morris, 48.

"I'm pretty certain there has never. . .": NYT, 8/23/92.

"I was notable. . .": WP, 10/8/93.

"For me personally it was. . .": BG, 12/4/92.

Elvis Presley and Clinton: *Rock 'n' Roll President*; Maraniss, 352; NBC *Today*, 12/20/99; Marcus, *Double Trouble*, 50.

"Before John F. Kennedy rode. . .": Virginia Kelley, 88.

"I have always aspired. . .": LAT, 9/18/92.

Clinton and Harrison Ford, Mel Brooks, and Roberto Benigni: NYDN, 2/8/98 and 10/5/99; CST, 2/3/00.

The description of Clinton as a movie lover comes from various sources, including interviews Clinton gave to Roger Ebert (CST, 2/3/00) and Gene Siskel (*CBS Morning News*, 8/12/97); LAT 12/5/93 and 3/20/94; and Author interview with Harry Thomason, 7/8/03.

"an inexhaustible supply of home entertainment. . .": Rose Kennedy, 117.

JFK as a movie lover: Hamilton, 182; Bradlee, *A Good Life*, 208; Evelyn Lincoln, 25; Blair, 516; Manchester, 26–27; Spalding OH, 106–7, JFKL; Bradlee, *Conversations with Kennedy*, 128; Fay, 109–112.

Tony Curtis, Kirk Douglas at the WH: Curtis and Paris, 190; Kirk Douglas, *The Ragman's Son*, 349; Suid, 203.

"Now perhaps he was interested. . .": Peter Lawford OH, 3–5, JFKL.

JFK's musical preferences: Letter, Evelyn Lincoln to Helga Sandburg, 5/3/62, President's Office Files, Box 130, Personal Secretary's Files, JFKL; Anthony, *The Kennedy White House*, 188; Bradlee, *Conversations*, 136.

Television at the JFK WH: Sanders, 277; Anthony, *The Kennedy White House*, 67; Schroeder, 5.

Jacqueline Kennedy's film preferences: Anthony, *The Kennedy White House*, 69.

JFK and James Bond: Bradlee, *Conversations*, 227; Anthony, *The Kennedy White House*, 150.

FDR as a movie lover: NYT, 1/31/37; Eleanor Roosevelt, *This I Remember*, 117; Letter, FDR to Walt Disney, 3/4/40, FDRL; Nesbitt, 59; Massey, 254.

FDR and Myrna Loy: Tully, 85; Kotsilibas-Davis and Loy, 179.

Jack Warner and FDR: Telegram, Warner to FDR, 3/3/42, and Memorandum, FDR to Lowell Mellett, 11/9/42, PPF File 1050, FDRL; Telegram, Warner to Stephen Early, 3/17/41, and Telegram, Early to Warner, 6/19/41, FDR Scrapbook, Box 11, Jack Warner Collection, USC.

"I am very glad to see. . .": Letter, FDR to Will Rogers, 10/8/34, FDR Clipping File, MHL.

"Invariably, he would suggest. . .": Tully, 13.

FDR's screenwriting endeavors: Tully, 13; *Journal of the WGA, West*, Dec./Jan. 1991, MHL; Eugene Zukor OH, 252, MHL; Brownstein, 75–76.

The President's Mystery: Clipping file, MHL.

Woodrow Wilson and *The Birth of a Nation*: Schickel, *D. W. Griffith*, 268–271, 298.

"Amusement and relaxation. . .": *NY Graphic*, Dec. 1925, clipping from Scrapbook 1, CCL.

Calvin Coolidge as a movie fan: WS, 7/25/26; WP, 9/20/27 and 2/3/29; other clippings, CCL.

Carter, Truman, and classical music: Kirk, 338, 255.

Truman's critique of Charles Chaplin: Letter, HST to James P. O'Donnell, 8/21/57, Quotations File-Truman, HSTL.

Nixon as music lover: Nixon, 9, 335, 715; Reeves, *President Nixon*, 20.

Nixon's attitude toward movies and TV: Nixon, 539; LAT, 8/28/72.

Nixon and *All in the Family*: WP, 3/21/00.

Nixon and westerns: NYT, 8/4/70; Ambrose, *Nixon, Volume Two*, 323.

Nixon and Patton: Suid, 263–264; Kissinger, 498.

Eisenhower's taste in music, TV, and movies: Kirk, 267–268; *Dinner with the President*, CBS, 11/23/53; West, 157–158, 161; Lester and Irene David, 194–195; Talbot, 407.

Prescott Bush: Green, 2.

Bush and *Forever Plaid*: WP, 8/7/91 and 8/30/91; NYT, 8/31/91; SPT, 10/21/93.

Bush and Anne Murray: WP, 4/7/92; Fitzwater, 341; NYT, 5/1/90.

"Who was that beautiful girl. . .": Deaver, *Behind the Scenes*, 11.

"What writing does it take. . .": LAT, 10/4/69.

Film and TV viewing at the Reagan WH: *Interview*, Dec. 1981; Deaver, *Behind the Scenes*, 101–102; NYT, 12/8/81; Nancy Reagan, 252.

"Well, Jim, *The Sound of Music*. . .": Cannon, 56–57.

LBJ's dislike of entertainment: Sam Houston Johnson, 228; Kearns, 332; Paar, 137; Beschloss, 318.

"I've known Jerry Ford. . .": NYT, 9/14/75.

"If they won't play some music. . .": Betty Ford, 230.

George W. Bush's lack of interest in pop culture: Bruni, 126–127; NYDN, 5/4/00; USAT, 1/19/01.

Bush and comedy: *Baltimore Sun*, 2/20/01; WP, 7/23/02.

Bush TV and movie screenings: WP, 2/2/01 and 7/22/03; AP, 2/26/02; LAT, 4/25/02.

Bush and Stevie Wonder: WP, 3/6/02.

Chapter 8: "Happy Birthday, Mr. President": Entertainers as Friends and Lovers

Gene Tierney and JFK: Tierney, 141–147, 152–156.

"I've met this extra. . .": Hamilton, 157.

JFK on meeting Spencer Tracy, Clark Gable: Hamilton, 380.

Robert Stack and JFK: Stack, 72.

"He leaned toward her. . .": Blair, 368.

JFK and June Allyson, Hedy Lamarr, and Zsa Zsa Gabor: Allyson, 44; Lamarr, 84; WP, 4/2/90.

"Jack would ask me. . .": Vidal, 358–359.

Peter Lawford as JFK's procurer: Patricia Seaton Lawford, 134; Sammy Davis, 108.

Angie Dickinson and JFK: Reeves, *President Kennedy*, 35; SLPD, 5/10/89; TS, 8/6/96.

Jayne Mansfield and JFK: Strait, 108–110.

Marlene Dietrich and JFK: Tynan, 38–39.

JFK and Sophia Loren, Jean Simmons, and Edie Adams: Cheshire, 55–56; Granger, 380; Adams, 346.

Ann-Margret and JFK: Ann-Margret, 104–106; Fisher, 221.

Grace Kelly and JFK: Princess Grace OH, 6, JFKL; Vidal, 373–374; Baldrige, 191–192.

Marilyn Monroe and JFK: Blair, 494; Spada, *Peter Lawford*, 188; Spoto, *Marilyn*, 486–487.

Marilyn Monroe at Madison Square Garden: Spoto, *Marilyn*, 519; Schlesinger, 590; Hersh, 336; John H. Davis, 390.

Adlai Stevenson and Lauren Bacall, other actresses: Bacall, 225, 235–236; Kotsilibas-Davis and Loy, 278; Fontaine, 239–240; Shirley Temple Black, 438–439.

"He never asked me. . .": Hart, 227.

Bob Kerrey and Debra Winger: NW, 10/28/85.

Helen Gahagan Douglas and LBJ: Califano, 337, 381; Beschloss, 137–138.

"She was very young. . .": Ronald Reagan, 88.

Jane Wyman and Reagan: Cannon, 225–228; LAT, 12/5/47.

Doris Day and Reagan: Hotchner, 121.

Vikki Carr and Ford: WS, 11/13/74; Betty Ford, 195; Gerald Ford, *A Time to Heal*, 206–207; Nessen, 24.

Ford and Elke Sommer, Zsa Zsa Gabor, and Phyllis George: Nessen, 25; Gabor, 254.

Betty Ford and Burt Reynolds: Maria Downs, *Mostly Wine and Roses*, 80, Maria Downs Papers, Box 1, GRFL.

"I wanted to be Humphrey Bogart. . .": Paris, 346–347.

Clark Gable, Carole Lombard, and FDR: Letter, Carole and Clark Gable to FDR, 12/10/41, Letter, FDR to Carole and Clark Gable, 12/16/41, Telegram, FDR to Clark Gable, 1/18/42, PPF File 7874, FDRL.

Death of FDR: DV, 4/13/45; *Motion Picture Daily*, 4/13/45; Geddes, 53–54.

"We sized each other up. . .": Benny, 228.

Truman and the Marx Brothers: Raymond H. Geselbracht, "Mutual Admiration and a Few Jokes: The Correspondence of Harry Truman with Groucho and Harpo Marx," *Prologue: Quarterly of the National Archives and Records Administration*, Spring 2001, Vol. 33, No. 1, pp. 46–50.

"I felt I could unbend. . .": Hayes, 216–217.

"so-called 'stars'. . .": Galambos, 439.

"That's about a three-word. . .": Hamilton, 684.

Jack and Jackie Kennedy at Marion Davies's house: Letter, Jacqueline Kennedy to Marion Davies, postmarked 9/26/53, Marion Davies Collection, Folder 125: "Kennedy Family," MHL.

Surprise party for JFK: Niven, 357; Bradlee, *A Good Life*, 234.

JFK's friendship with Judy Garland: Clarke, 348; Frank, 462; Paar, 156; Luft, 52–53, 104–106; Sanders, 274–278, 295–303; Torme, 113, 135–140, 156–160.

Hollywood and the JFK assassination: Ann-Margret, 121; DV, 11/25/63; NYT, 12/1/63.

"just from watching. . .": Autry, 108–109.

"Don't ask Ronnie what time. . .": Allyson, 96.

The Reagans and William Holden: Patti Davis, 30–31; Speakes, 93.

The Reagans and Robert Taylor: LAT, 6/12/69; Deaver, *A Different Drummer*, 53.

"After he was elected. . .": Brochu, 125.

Gene Kelly's advice to Reagan: Michael Reagan, 157.

James Stewart and Reagan: Fishgall, 362.

Bette Davis and Reagan: Hadleigh, 201; Stine, 265.

Kirk Douglas and the Reagans: Kirk Douglas, 494; Letter, Douglas to Nancy Reagan, 6/2/81, WHORM Alphabetical File, Kirk Douglas, RRL.

Rock Hudson and the Reagans: WP, 7/24/85; LAT, 9/20/85; *Seattle Times*, 8/31/89.

Mary Steenburgen and Clinton: WP, 1/31/92 and 1/14/94; LAT, 7/14/92.

Kevin Spacey and Clinton: NYDN, 10/8/00; NYT, 10/3/02; Leaming, 293.

Gregory Peck and LBJ: Claudia T. Johnson, 324; Valenti, 176–177; film footage, LBJ Ranch, 5/31/68, LBJL; Freedland, 197.

"unless there's a bomb. . .": David, 122.

"I never saw either of them. . .": Moore, 227–228.

Joe Garagiola, Pearl Bailey as Ford campaigners: Election Eve political broadcast, 11/3/76, GRFL.

Weintraub party: George Bush, 525–527; Barbara Bush, 417; Videotape of Weintraub party, GBL.

Chapter 9: Secrets of the Stars: Entertainers as Professional Associates

The account of Robert Montgomery and Eisenhower is taken from: Montgomery, 62–63; *Life*, 4/19/54; NYT, 3/1/56; Memo, Montgomery to Mr. Hughes, 7/14/53, Central Files PPF, Box 415, Folder: "Broadcasting by the President," DDEL; Letter, Eisenhower to Montgomery, 1/5/54, Central Files PPF, Box 964, "Robert Montgomery" folder, DDEL.

Nixon in the 1960 debates: Allen, 174; Montgomery, 69–72.

Don Penny and Ford: WP, 5/9/76 and 8/21/76; *Chicago Tribune*, 4/19/76; WS, 5/9/76; Gerald Ford, 376.

Orson Welles and FDR's Fala speech: Leaming, 292–293.

Mort Sahl and JFK: *Time*, 8/15/60; WP, 10/15/78; Sahl, 89.

LBJ's jokewriters: Carpenter, 250–251; Hope, *Dear Prez*, 66.

"A lot of people can write. . .": LAT, 5/2/93.

1995 Clinton Gridiron video: NYT, 3/27/95.

Sources for Clinton and Harry and Linda Thomason include Author interview with Thomason, 2/17/03; LAT, 7/25/92; LAT, 9/27/92; *Time*, 1/18/93; USAT, 5/25/93.

John Wayne and George Wallace: Roberts and Olson, 566–567; *Playboy*, May 1971, 86.

Douglas Fairbanks Jr. in South America: WH Press Release, 4/10/41, Memorandum, Sumner Welles to FDR, 1/24/41; Letter, Fairbanks to FDR, 7/12/41, PPF File 7130, FDRL; Fairbanks, 382–383.

"I was privileged to know. . .": ABC, 12/8/69.

Pearl Bailey, Paul Newman at the United Nations: SPT, 1/1/88; WP, 5/26/78.

Ambassador John Gavin: NYT, 3/14/81; WP, 4/23/81; LAT, 10/26/86.

James Stewart nominated as brigadier general: Fishgall, 262–263; NW, 9/2/57.

Betty Furness as consumer advocate: WP, 5/1/67.

Shirley MacLaine and McGovern, Carter: MacLaine, 212, 225–229.

"If there is ever an occasion. . .": Letter, Gregory Peck to Jack Valenti, 2/19/64, LBJL.

Sinatra as a CIA volunteer, informal adviser: BG, 4/15/76; Letter, Sinatra to Reagan, 5/19/87, FO002, Folder 492280, RRL.

Entertainers writing to the White House: Ambrose, 480; Telegram, John Wayne to Carter, 12/2/78, Executive File, JCL; Letter, Robert Redford to Carter, 10/27/77, Executive File, JCL; Letter, Walter Mondale to Cary Grant, Box 9, Folder: "Walter Mondale," Cary Grant Collection, MHL.

"Knowing your facility. . .": Letter, Rudy Vallee to Nixon, 3/19/65, PPS 238, Folder 1841, RNL.

"I have one word for you. . .": Fitzwater, 348–349.

Letter from Lionel Barrymore's dog to Fala: Barrymore, 289–290.

Chapter 10: Leading Ladies, Supporting Cast: First Families in the Showbiz Presidency

"This one song. . .": Nancy Reagan, 42.

"National Crusade" against drugs: Videotape, 9/14/86, RRL.

Nancy Reagan and Frank Sinatra: CBS News, 10/19/82; Nancy Sinatra, 273; WP, 1/23/83 and 5/8/81; CBS, 5/7/81; Kitty Kelley, 492; Tina Sinatra, 178–179, 289–290.

Nancy Reagan and Mr. T: ABC, 12/12/83.

Nancy Reagan and James Stewart, Katharine Hepburn: Nancy Reagan, 79–80.

"Clark was sexy. . .": Nancy Reagan, 87.

"I think if left to his own devices. . .": *60 Minutes*, CBS, 10/10/99.

"If Ronald Reagan had married Nancy. . .": Woodward, 38.

Pat Nixon in Hollywood: ABC, 11/10/70; Julie Nixon Eisenhower, 46–48.

Eleanor Roosevelt in Hollywood: DV, 3/25/29; Roosevelt, *My Day*, 115.

Victory Caravan at the WH: WP, 5/1/42; Crosby, 277; Hope, *Dear Prez*, 22.

Eleanor Roosevelt on Gene Autry's radio show: Autry, 137.

Marian Anderson and Eleanor Roosevelt: Roosevelt, *My Day*, 113.

"Isn't what's happening to you. . .": Vidal, 284.

The Kennedys on *Person to Person*: CBS, 10/30/53, JFKL.

Jacqueline Kennedy's WH tour: CBS, 2/14/62; Charlotte Curtis, 113–114; West, 253.

Jacqueline Kennedy in *Photoplay*: *Photoplay*, June 1962, MHL.

"This woman wrote her own script. . .": NYT, 5/4/01.

Jacqueline Kennedy and Greta Garbo: Anthony, *As We Remember Her*, 297.

Betty Ford's Gridiron dance: Weidenfeld, 277–282.

Betty Ford and Woody Allen: NYT, 6/20/75; Betty Ford, 264; Weidenfeld, 148–149.

Betty Ford at AFI salute: Betty Ford, 260; WP, 3/11/76.

Betty Ford at Sammy Davis party: Weidenfeld, 309–310.

Betty Ford on *Mary Tyler Moore Show*: WP, 11/8/75; Moore, 280, 287; Weidenfeld, 217.

Betty Ford Center, TV movie: Strausbaugh, 108; NYT, 2/25/87 and 2/27/87.

James Roosevelt, Elliott Roosevelt, and Faye Emerson: *Look*, 6/6/50; Collier and Horowitz, 415–416, 426–427, 455–456; NYT, 12/29/48.

Margaret Truman's musical career: *Saturday Evening Post*, 4/22/50; *Time*, 2/26/51; NW, 11/1/51; Margaret Truman, *Souvenir*, Chapter 12: "Soprano"; Traubel, 206–216; WP, 12/6/50 and 11/27/01.

Margaret Truman's broadcast career: *The Big Show*, NBC Radio, 12/3/50, HSTL; WS, 4/27/51; *Person to Person*, CBS, 5/27/55, HSTL.

Lynda Bird Johnson and George Hamilton: NW, 4/4/66; LAT, 3/19/66; NYT, 4/19/66; Film footage at Johnson Ranch, Christmas 1966, LBJL; Wayne, 163.

Hamilton's draft status: WP, 4/11/66; NYT, 8/2/81.

Hamilton's influence on Lynda: Carpenter, 284; Bess Abell, OH, LBJL; Jan Russell, 287.

"I was one of the most photographed. . .": Maureen Reagan, 26.

"This is my show. . .": Michael Reagan, 258.

"It was an elite atmosphere. . .": Patti Davis, 27–28.

Patti Davis's career: See Davis's autobiography; *Barbara Walters Special*, ABC, 3/24/86; *Playboy*, July 1994.

Ron Reagan's career: WP, 7/29/86; *Barbara Walters Special*, ABC, 3/24/86.

Steve Ford's acting career: TS, 2/28/87.

JFK Junior: *Murphy Brown*, CBS, 9/18/95; Blow, 66–67, 90.

Chapter 11: Is Everybody Happy? Presidents as Entertainers

Ozzy Osbourne and Bush: WP, 5/6/02.

"No president really enjoys. . .": BG, 3/22/98.

"While I was doing. . .": Griffin, 69–70.

Reagan's joke about farmers: WP, 3/25/85 and 3/26/85.

"We ended the skit. . .": Fitzwater, 370.

"I'm not a bit thin-skinned. . .": Memo, Nixon to Haldeman, 5/9/71, quoted in Oudes, 250–253.

Nixon's piano duet with Agnew: Brayman, 11–13; WP, 3/26/70.

Truman's White House tour: NBC, 5/3/52, HSTL.

The Nixons' *Christmas at the WH*: CBS, 12/24/71, NPMS.

The First Family's Holiday Gift to America: Fox, 12/15/00.

"Oh, boy! Is that desperation. . .": Crowley, 90.

"Clinton looks presidential. . .": WP, 1/21/97.

"I had to give up singing. . .": NYT, 6/27/01.

Reagan's Hollywood career: Ronald Reagan, 81; Wills, *Reagan's America*, 178; Disneyland video, ABC, 7/17/55, RRL.

"I don't know. I've never played. . .": Cannon, 37.

Reagan's performance techniques: Cannon, 53; Didion, 110–111.

Reagan blending reality with movies: LAT, 12/18/85; WP, 2/5/86; Cannon, 58; Schieffer, 167–168, 178–179.

Reagan and Mikhail Gorbachev: WP, 12/2/87 and 5/31/88.

Reagan's vanity: D'Souza, 219; Deaver, *Different Drummer*, 75.

"He couldn't not do it. . .": Noonan, 154–155.

"The president always groaned. . .": Regan, 272.

"I was happy when I first heard. . .": Hope, *Dear Prez*, 135.

FDR as a performer: NYT, 1/31/37; Reinsch, xii; Burns, 447; Barrymore, 289.

"I was made an honorary. . .": *Tonight Show*, NBC, 6/16/60, JFKL.

"We wouldn't have had a prayer. . .": Barnouw, 277.

JFK press conferences: See Alan Schroeder, "Kennedy Press Conferences," in Michael D. Murray, ed., *The Encyclopedia of Television News* (Phoenix: Oryx, 1999), 119–120; Giglio, 260.

JFK as a photographic subject: *American Photography: A Century of Images*, Part 3, PBS, 1999; Bradlee, *Conversations*, 29; Sorensen, 29; Strausbaugh, 39.

JFK's sex appeal: *San Francisco Chronicle*, 10/5/56; Stack, 72–73.

Eisenhower's use of TV: Perrett, 488; Allen, 213.

"Television wasn't his friend. . .": Quoted by Lynda Bird Johnson, "Presidential Tapes Conference," JFK Library, C-SPAN, 2/16/03.

LBJ and Bob Hope: Hope, *Don't Shoot*, 280–281.

Nixon's use of TV: Safire, 55; Memo, Nixon to Haldeman, 12/1/69, quoted in Oudes, 77–78.

Nixon's WH TV office: Maltese, 59.

"We cut back Ford's attendance. . .": Nessen, 170.

Carter's use of TV: *Time*, 2/14/77; *Ask President Carter*, CBS, 3/5/77, JCL; WP, 3/8/77; Carter, 564–565.

Bush 41's use of TV: Rozell, *The Press and the Bush Presidency*, 158; Bush, *All the Best*, 562.

Bush 43 aboard the USS *Lincoln*: WP, 5/2/03; NYT, 5/7/03 and 5/11/03. For a discussion of Bush's military service record, see BG, 10/31/00.

Chapter 12: "I'm Gerald Ford, and You're Not": Presidents as Entertainment

Chevy Chase and Ford: *Saturday Night Live*, NBC, 12/20/75; *Playboy*, May 1977, 76; Gerald Ford, 47.

Chase and Ford at correspondents dinner: WP, 3/26/76.

Ron Nessen on *Saturday Night Live*: NBC, 4/17/76; Nessen, 172–176.

"I didn't want him in the White House. . .": *Westchester Wag*, Nov. 2000.

Eddie Cantor's "Dr. Roosevelt" sketch: Telegram, Cantor to FDR, 12/31/34, PPF, File 1018, FDRL.

FDR lookalike: *Hollywood Citizen-News*, 11/8/37; LAT, 11/27/37 and 7/17/38.

Theodore Roosevelt look-alike: Fielding, 51; Crowther, 68–69.

Actors playing Franklin and Eleanor Roosevelt: Ward, 750; LAT, 6/7/46; Barrymore, 290–291; WP, 2/1/67; Melvyn Douglas, 113; Hepburn, 250.

"Judging by *Gabriel*. . .": NYHT, 4/4/33.

Eisenhower biopic: Letter, Eisenhower to Milton Eisenhower, 5/31/44, quoted in Chandler, *The War Years*, 1896–1897; NYT, 7/9/45; Letter, Eisenhower to Milton Eisenhower, 7/22/45, quoted in Chandler, *Occupation*, 208.

JFK and *Navy Log*: Letter, JFK to Sam Gallu, 7/2/57, Pre-Presidential Files, Box 547, Folder: "Navy Log," JFKL.

JFK and *PT 109*: Reeves in Carnes, 233; Beatty quoted in *George*, Nov. 1995; *Time*, 6/28/63; LAHE, 7/3/63; LAT, 7/3/63.

The First Family record album: WP, 3/14/82; Sorensen, 383; Bradlee, *Conversations*, 123; Anthony, *As We Remember Her*, 133; Various items, Name File: Vaughn Meader, Box 1842, JFKL.

Vaughn Meader's career: WP, 11/4/79; LAT, 4/20/97; NYT, 11/30/63.

Frank Sinatra's assassination movies: Ferrell, 50; WP, 2/13/88; Kitty Kelley, 293–294.

George Lucas and Nixon: Biskind, 324.

"an actor's dream. . .": *People*, 8/23/99.

"I took it somewhat as a gag. . .": Letter, Nixon to Dick St. Johns, 7/13/61, PPS 238, Folder 1219, RNL.

"the blind optimism of Ronald Reagan. . .": *Inside the Actor's Studio*, Bravo, 9/8/02.

Dana Carvey and Bush: WP, 4/2/90; WH staff Christmas party videotape, 12/7/92, GBL; LAT, 10/24/94.

"Rational—and irrational. . .": NYT, 2/17/01.

Clinton as a comedic subject: WP, 5/1/00 and 1/26/99.

"Some Americans are going to say. . .": USAT, 8/21/98.

Clinton and *Primary Colors*: UPI, 9/13/96; *Time*, 8/18/97; LAT, 3/15/98 and 3/26/98; NYT, 3/15/98.

Clinton and *Contact*: WP, 7/16/97; USAT, 7/15/97.

"I have been very interested. . .": *CBS Morning News*, 8/12/97.

That's My Bush: NYT, 4/5/01 and 8/8/01.

Conclusion: The Common Vocabulary of Presidents and Entertainers

"There have been times in this office. . .": ABC, 12/22/88.

"Politicians and movie stars. . .": NYT, 9/12/96.

Alec Baldwin on the link between actors and politicians: Author interview, 10/24/02.

"Can you imagine that. . .": WP, 3/24/86.

Orson Welles as a Senate candidate: Estrin, 200.

Warren Beatty for president: NYT, 8/22/99; BG, 10/1/99; WP 6/5/72.

"Bill Clinton knew. . .": Ezterhas, 390.

"The two communities are made for each other. . .": LAT, 2/21/83.

Assassination attempt on Reagan: NYP, 4/1/81; NBC, 4/1/81; Academy Awards broadcast, ABC, 3/31/81; WP, 4/1/81 and 4/2/81; Deaver, *Different Drummer*, 140.

Selected Bibliography

Adams, Edie. *Sing a Pretty Song*. New York: William Morrow, 1990.

Allen, Craig. *Eisenhower and the Mass Media: Peace, Prosperity, and Prime-Time TV*. Chapel Hill: University of North Carolina Press, 1993.

Allyson, June, with Frances Spatz Leighton. *June Allyson*. New York: Putnam, 1982.

Ambrose, Stephen E. *Nixon, Volume Two: The Triumph of a Politician 1962–1972*. New York: Simon & Schuster, 1989.

Andersen, Christopher. *Citizen Jane: The Turbulent Life of Jane Fonda*. New York: Holt, 1990.

Andrews, Bart. *Lucy & Ricky & Fred & Ethel: The Story of I Love Lucy*. New York: Dutton, 1976.

Ann-Margret, with Todd Gold. *Ann-Margret. My Story*. New York: Putnam, 1994.

Anthony, Carl Sferrazza. *Florence Harding*. New York: William Morrow, 1998.

______. *As We Remember Her: Jacqueline Kennedy in the Words of Her Friends and Family*. New York: HarperCollins, 1997.

______. *The Kennedy White House: Family Life and Pictures, 1961–1963*. New York: Lisa Drew, 2001.

Autry, Gene. *Back in the Saddle Again*. Garden City, N.Y.: Doubleday, 1978.

Bacall, Lauren. *Lauren Bacall by Myself*. New York: Knopf, 1978.

Baldrige, Letitia. *A Lady, First*. New York: Viking, 2001.

Bankhead, Tallulah. *Tallulah: My Autobiography*. Chicago: Sears Readers Club, 1952.

Barnuow, Eric. *Tube of Plenty: The Evolution of American Television*. New York: Oxford University Press, 1975.

Barrymore, Lionel. *We Barrymores*. New York: Grosset & Dunlap, 1951.

Benny, Jack, with Joan Benny. *Sunday Nights at Seven: The Jack Benny Story*. New York: Warner, 1990.

Bergen, Candice. *Knock Wood*. New York: Simon & Schuster, 1984.

Beschloss, Michael P., ed. *Taking Charge: The Johnson White House Tapes, 1963–1964*. New York: Simon & Schuster, 1997.

Biskind, Peter. *Easy Riders, Raging Bulls: How the Sex-Drugs-and-Rock 'n' Roll Generation Saved Hollywood*. New York: Simon & Schuster, 1998.

Black, Christine M., and Thomas Oliphant. *All by Myself: The Unmaking of a Presidential Campaign*. Chester, Conn.: Globe Pequot, 1989.

Black, Shirley Temple. *Child Star: An Autobiography*. New York: McGraw-Hill, 1988.

Blair, Joan, and Clay Junior. *The Search for J.F.K.* New York: Berkley, 1976.

Blow, Richard. *American Son: A Portrait of John F. Kennedy Junior*. New York: Holt, 2002.

Bourne, Peter G. *Jimmy Carter: A Comprehensive Biography from Plains to Postpresidency*. New York:

Scribner/Lisa Drew, 1997.

Bradlee, Ben. *Conversations with Kennedy*. New York: Pocket Books, 1976.

_____. *A Good Life*. New York: Simon & Schuster, 1995.

Braudy, Leo. *The Frenzy of Renown: Fame and Its History*. New York: Vintage, 1997.

Brayman, Harold. *The President Speaks Off-the-Record: From Grover Cleveland to Gerald Ford*. Princeton, N.J.: Dow Jones Books, 1976.

Brochu, Jim. *Lucy in the Afternoon*. New York: William Morrow, 1990.

Brodie, Fawn M. *Richard Nixon: The Shaping of His Character*. New York: Norton, 1981.

Brown, James, with Bruce Tucker. *The Godfather of Soul*. New York: Macmillan, 1986.

Brownstein, Ron. *The Power and the Glitter: The Hollywood-Washington Connection*. New York: Pantheon, 1990.

Bruni, Frank. *Ambling into History: The Unlikely Odyssey of George W. Bush*. New York: Harper-Collins, 2002.

Burns, James Macgregor. *Roosevelt: The Lion and the Fox, 1882–1940*. New York: Harcourt, Brace, Jovanovich, 1956.

Bush, Barbara. *Barbara Bush: A Memoir*. New York: Scribner's, 1994.

Bush, George. *All the Best, George Bush: My Life in Letters and Other Writings*. New York: Scribner's, 1999.

Califano, Joseph. *The Triumph and Tragedy of Lyndon Johnson*. New York: Simon & Schuster, 1991.

Cannon, Lou. *President Reagan: The Role of a Lifetime*. New York: Simon & Schuster, 1991.

Carnes, Mark C., ed. *Past Imperfect: History According to Movies*. New York: Holt, 1995.

Carpenter, Liz. *Ruffles and Flourishes*. Garden City, N.Y.: Doubleday, 1970.

Carter, Jimmy. *Keeping Faith: Memoirs of a President*. New York: Bantam, 1982.

Cash, Johnny, with Patrick Carr. *Cash: The Autobiography*. New York: HarperCollins, 1997.

Chandler, Alfred D. Junior, ed. *The Papers of Dwight David Eisenhower: The War Years*. Baltimore: Johns Hopkins University Press, 1970.

_____. *The Papers of Dwight David Eisenhower: Occupation, 1945*. Baltimore: Johns Hopkins University Press, 1970.

Charles, Ray, with David Ritz. *Brother Ray: Ray Charles' Own Story*. New York: Dial, 1978.

Cheshire, Maxine, with John Greenya. *Maxine Cheshire, Reporter*. Boston: Houghton-Mifflin, 1978.

Clark, Tom, with Dick Kleiner. *Rock Hudson: Friend of Mine*. New York: Pharos, 1989.

Clarke, Gerald. *Get Happy: The Life of Judy Garland*. New York: Random House, 2000.

Clooney, Rosemary, with Joan Barthel. *Girl Singer: An Autobiography*. Garden City, N.Y.: Doubleday, 1999.

Coleman, Ray. *The Carpenters: The Untold Story*. New York: HarperCollins, 1994.

Collier, Peter, with David Horowitz. *The Roosevelts: An American Saga*. New York: Simon & Schuster, 1994.

Collins, Judy. *Singing Lessons*. New York: Pocket Books, 1998.

Crosby, Bing, as told to Pete Martin. *Call Me Lucky*. New York: Simon & Schuster, 1953.

Crowley, Monica. *Nixon off the Record*. New York: Random House, 1996.

Crowther, Bosley. *Hollywood Rajah: The Life and Times of Louis B. Mayer*. New York: Holt, Rinehart & Winston, 1960.

Curtis, Charlotte. *First Lady*. New York: Pyramid, 1962.

Curtis, Tony, and Barry Paris. *Tony Curtis: The Autobiography*. New York: Morrow, 1993.

David, Lester. *Lonely Lady at San Clemente: The Story of Pat Nixon*. New York: Thomas Y. Crowell, 1978.

David, Lester, and Irene David. *Ike and Mamie: The Story of the General and His Lady*. New York:

Putnam, 1981.

Davis, John H. *The Kennedys: Dynasty and Disaster, 1848–1983*. New York: McGraw-Hill, 1984.

Davis, Patti. *The Way I See It*. New York: Putnam, 1992.

Davis, Sammy, Jr., with Jane Boyar and Burt Boyar. *Why Me? The Sammy Davis Junior Story*. New York: Farrar, Straus & Giroux, 1989.

Davis, Tracey, with Dolores A. Barclay. *Sammy Davis Junior: My Father*. Los Angeles: General Publishing, 1996.

Deaver, Michael, with Mickey Herskowitz. *Behind the Scenes*. New York: William Morrow, 1987.

_____. *A Different Drummer: My Thirty Years with Ronald Reagan*. New York: HarperCollins, 2001.

Didion, Joan. *Political Fictions*. New York: Knopf, 2001.

Donaldson, Sam. *Hold On, Mr. President!* New York: Ballantine, 1987.

Douglas, Helen Gahagan. *A Full Life*. Garden City, N.Y.: Doubleday, 1982.

Douglas, Kirk. *The Ragman's Son: An Autobiography*. New York: Simon & Schuster, 1988.

Douglas, Melvyn, with Tom Arthur. *See You at the Movies: The Autobiography of Melvyn Douglas*. Lanham, Md.: University Press of America, 1986.

Dressler, Marie, as told to Mildred Harrington. *My Own Story*. Boston: Little, Brown, 1934.

D'Souza, Dinesh. *Ronald Reagan: How an Ordinary Man Became an Extraordinary Leader*. New York: Free Press, 1997.

Duke, Patty, with Kenneth Turan. *Call Me Anna*. New York: Bantam, 1988.

Eisenhower, Julie Nixon. *Pat Nixon: The Untold Story*. New York: Simon & Schuster, 1986.

Estrin, Mark, ed. *Orson Welles Interviews*. Jackson: University of Mississippi Press, 2002.

Ezterhas, Joe. *American Rhapsody*. New York: Knopf, 2000.

Fairbanks, Douglas, Jr. *The Salad Days*. Garden City, N.Y.: Doubleday, 1988.

Fay, Paul B., Jr. *The Pleasure of His Company*. New York: Harper & Row, 1966.

Ferrell, Robert H. *Diary of James C. Hagerty*. Bloomington: University of Indiana Press, 1983.

Fielding, Raymond. *The American Newsreel, 1911–1967*. Norman: University of Oklahoma Press, 1972.

Fields, Ronald J. *W.C. Fields by Himself: His Intended Autobiography*. Englewood Cliffs, N.J.: Prentice-Hall, 1973.

Fisher, Eddie. *Eddie: My Life, My Loves*. New York: Harper & Row, 1981.

Fishgall, Gary. *Pieces of Time: The Life of James Stewart*. New York: Scribner's, 1997.

Fitzwater, Marlin. *Call the Briefing!* New York: Times Books, 1995.

Fontaine, Joan. *No Bed of Roses: An Autobiography*. New York: William Morrow, 1978.

Ford, Betty. *The Times of My Life*. New York: Harper & Row, 1978.

Ford, Gerald R. *A Time to Heal: The Autobiography of Gerald R. Ford*. New York: Harper & Row, 1979.

_____. *Humor and the Presidency*. New York: Arbor House, 1987.

Frank, Gerold. *Judy*. New York: Harper & Row, 1975.

Freedland, Michael. *Gregory Peck*. New York: William Morrow, 1980.

Fury, David. *Chuck Connors: The Man Behind the Rifle*. Minneapolis: Artist's Press, 1997.

Gabor, Zsa Zsa, with Wendy Leigh. *One Lifetime Is Not Enough*. New York: Delacorte, 1991.

Galambos, Louis, ed. *The Papers of Dwight David Eisenhower: The Middle Way*. Vol. 14. Baltimore: Johns Hopkins University Press, 1978.

Gardner, Ava. *Ava: My Story*. New York: Bantam, 1990.

Gatlin, Larry, with Jeff Lenburg. *All the Gold in California*. Nashville: Thomas Nelson, 1998.

Geddes, Donald Porter, ed. *Franklin D. Roosevelt: A Memorial*. New York: Pitman, 1945.

Giglio, James N. *The Presidency of John F. Kennedy*. Lawrence: University of Kansas Press, 1991.

Gish, Lillian. *Lillian Gish. The Movies, Mr. Griffith, and Me*. Englewood Cliffs, N.J.: Prentice Hall,

1969.

Gold, Vic. *I Don't Need You When I'm Right: The Confessions of a Washington PR Man*. New York: William Morrow, 1975.

Granger, Stewart. *Sparks Fly Upward*. New York: Putnam, 1981.

Green, Fitzhugh. *George Bush: An Intimate Portrait*. New York: Hippocrene, 1991.

Griffin, Merv, with Peter Barsocchini. *Merv: An Autobiography*. New York: Simon & Schuster, 1980.

Hadleigh, Boze. *Bette Davis Speaks*. New York: Barricade, 1996.

Haggard, Merle, with Tom Carter. *My House of Memories: For the Record*. New York: Cliff Street, 1999.

Haldeman, H.R. *The Haldeman Diaries: Inside the Nixon White House*. New York: Random House, 1988.

Hamilton, Nigel. *JFK. Reckless Youth*. New York: Random House, 1992.

Hart, Kitty Carlisle. *Kitty: An Autobiography*. Garden City, N.Y.: Doubleday, 1988.

Hassett, William D. *Off the Record with F.D.R.* New Brunswick, N.J.: Rutgers University Press, 1958.

Hayes, Helen, with Katherine Hatch. *My Life in Three Acts*. San Diego: Harcourt Brace Jovanovich, 1990.

Hepburn, Katharine. *Me: Stories of My Life*. New York: Ballantine, 1991.

Hersh, Seymour M. *The Dark Side of Camelot*. Boston: Little, Brown, 1997.

Heston, Charlton. *In the Arena: An Autobiography*. New York: Simon & Schuster, 1995.

Hope, Bob, with Melville Shavelson. *Don't Shoot, It's Only Me: Bob Hope's Comedy History of the United States*. New York: Putnam, 1990.

Hope, Bob. *Dear Prez, I Wanna Tell Ya! Bob Hope's Presidential Jokebook*. Edited by Ward Grant. Santa Monica: General Publishing, 1996.

Hotchner, A. E. *Doris Day: Her Own Story*. New York: William Morrow, 1976.

Israel, Lee. *Miss Tallulah Bankhead*. New York: Putnam, 1972.

Jessel, George. *This Way, Miss*. New York: Holt, 1955.

Jessel, George, with John Austin. *The World I Lived In*. Chicago: Regnery, 1975.

Johnson, Claudia T. *A White House Diary*. New York: Holt, Rinehart & Winston, 1970.

Johnson, Sam Houston. *My Brother Lyndon*. New York: Cowles, 1969.

Kearns, Doris. *Lyndon Johnson and the American Dream*. New York: Harper & Row, 1976.

Kelley, Kitty. *His Way: The Unauthorized Biography of Frank Sinatra*. New York: Bantam, 1986.

Kelley, Virginia, with James Morgan. *Leading with My Heart*. New York: Simon & Schuster, 1994.

Kennedy, Rose Fitzgerald. *Times to Remember*. Garden City, N.Y.: Doubleday, 1974.

Kirk, Elise K. *Music at the White House: A History of the American Spirit*. Urbana: University of Illinois Press, 1986.

Kissinger, Henry. *White House Years*. Boston: Little, Brown, 1979.

Kitt, Eartha. *Confessions of a Sex Kitten*. Fort Lee, N.J.: Barricade, 1989.

Kotsilibas-Davis, James, and Myrna Loy. *Myrna Loy: Being and Becoming*. New York: Knopf, 1987.

Krogh, Egil "Bud." *The Day Elvis Met Nixon*. Bellevue, Wash.: Pejama, 1994.

Kuntz, Tom, and Phil Kuntz, eds. *The Sinatra Files: The Secret FBI Dossier*. New York: Three Rivers, 2000.

Lake, Veronica, with Donald Bain. *Veronica*. New York: Citadel, 1971.

Lamarr, Hedy. *Ecstasy and Me: My Life as a Woman*. London: W. H. Allen, 1967.

Lamour, Dorothy, as told to Dick McInnes. *My Side of the Road*. Englewood Cliffs, N.J.: Prentice-Hall, 1980.

Lawford, Patricia Seaton. *The Peter Lawford Story*. New York: Carroll & Graf, 1988.

Lax, Eric. *Paul Newman: A Biography*. Atlanta: Turner, 1996.

_____. *Woody Allen: A Biography.* New York: Knopf, 1991.

Leaming, Barbara. *Orson Welles: A Biography.* New York: Viking, 1985.

Leigh, Janet. *There Really Was a Hollywood.* Garden City, N.Y.: Doubleday, 1984.

Lincoln, Evelyn. *My Twelve Years with John F. Kennedy.* New York: David McKay, 1965.

Lippman, Theo, Jr. *The Squire of Warm Springs: FDR in Georgia, 1924–1945.* Chicago: Playboy Press, 1977.

Luft, Lorna. *Me and My Shadows: A Family Memoir.* New York: Pocket Books, 1998.

MacLaine, Shirley. *My Lucky Stars: A Hollywood Memoir.* New York: Bantam, 1995.

Maltese, John Anthony. *Spin Control: The White House Office of Communications and the Management of Presidential News.* Chapel Hill: University of North Carolina Press, 1992.

Manchester, William. *Portrait of a President: John F. Kennedy in Profile.* Boston: Little, Brown, 1967.

Maraniss, David. *First in His Class: A Biography of Bill Clinton.* New York: Simon & Schuster, 1995.

Marcus, Greil. *Dead Elvis.* Cambridge: Harvard University Press, 1991.

_____. *Double Trouble: Bill Clinton and Elvis Presley in a Land of No Alternatives.* New York: Holt, 2000.

Marsh, Dave. *Glory Days: Bruce Springsteen in the 1980s.* New York: Random House, 1988.

Marx, Arthur. *Red Skelton.* New York: Dutton, 1979.

Marx, Groucho. *The Groucho Phile: An Illustrated Life by Groucho Marx.* New York: Bobbs-Merrill, 1976.

Massey, Raymond. *A Hundred Different Lives.* Boston: Little, Brown, 1979.

Merman, Ethel, with George Eels. *Merman: An Autobiography.* New York: Simon & Schuster, 1978.

Montgomery, Robert. *Open Letter from a Television Viewer.* New York: Heineman, 1968.

Moore, Mary Tyler. *After All.* New York: Putnam, 1995.

Morris, Dick. *Behind the Oval Office.* New York: Random House, 1997.

Murray, Michael D., ed., *The Encyclopedia of Television News.* Phoenix: Oryx, 1999.

Nelson, Willie, with Bud Shrake. *Willie: An Autobiography.* New York: Simon & Schuster, 1988.

Nesbitt, Henrietta. *White House Diary: FDR's Housekeeper.* Garden City, N.Y.: Doubleday, 1948.

Nessen, Ron. *It Sure Looks Different from the Inside.* Chicago: Playboy Press, 1978.

Newton, Wayne. *Once Before I Go.* New York: William Morrow, 1989.

Niven, David. *The Moon's a Balloon.* New York: Putnam, 1972.

Nixon, Richard. *RN: The Memoirs of Richard Nixon.* New York: Grossett & Dunlap, 1978.

Noonan, Peggy. *What I Saw at the Revolution.* New York: Random House, 1990.

O'Donnell, Kenneth P., and David F. Powers, with Joe McCarthy. *Johnny, We Hardly Knew Ye: Memories of John Fitzgerald Kennedy.* Boston: Little, Brown, 1972.

Oudes, Bruce, ed. *From: The President: Richard Nixon's Secret Files.* New York: Harper & Row, 1989.

Paar, Jack. *P.S. Jack Paar.* Garden City, N.Y.: Doubleday, 1983.

Paris, Barry. *Audrey Hepburn.* New York: Putnam, 1996.

Perret, Geoffrey. *Eisenhower.* New York: Random House, 1999.

Pickford, Mary. *Sunshine and Shadow.* Garden City, N.Y.: Doubleday, 1954.

Quayle, Dan. *Standing Firm.* New York: HarperCollins, 1994.

Reagan, Maureen. *First Father, First Daughter.* Boston: Little, Brown, 1989.

Reagan, Michael, with Joe Hyams. *On the Outside Looking In.* New York: Kensington, 1988.

Reagan, Nancy. *My Turn: The Memoirs of Nancy Reagan.* New York: Random House, 1989.

Reagan, Ronald, with Richard G. Hubler. *Where's the Rest of Me? The Autobiography of Ronald Reagan.* New York: Duell, Sloan & Pearce, 1965.

Reeves, Richard. *President Kennedy: Profile of Power*. New York: Simon & Schuster, 1993.

_____. *President Nixon: Alone in the White House*. New York: Simon & Schuster, 2001.

Regan, Donald. *For the Record: From Wall Street to Washington*. San Diego: Harcourt Brace Jovanovich, 1988.

Reinsch, J. Leonard. *Getting Elected: From Radio and Roosevelt to Television and Reagan*. New York: Hippocrene, 1988.

Reynolds, Debbie, with David Patrick Columbia. *Debbie: My Life*. New York: William Morrow, 1988.

Roberts, Randy, and James S. Olson. *John Wayne: American*. New York: Free Press, 1995.

Rogers, Ginger. *My Story*. New York: HarperCollins, 1991.

Rooney, Mickey. *Life Is Too Short*. New York: Villard, 1991.

Roosevelt, Eleanor. *This I Remember*. New York: Harper, 1949.

_____. *Eleanor Roosevelt's My Day, 1936–1945*. New York: Pharos, 1989.

Rozell, Mark J. *The Press and the Bush Presidency*. Westport, Conn.: Praeger, 1996.

_____. *The Press and the Carter Presidency*. Boulder: Westview, 1989.

_____. *The Press and the Ford Presidency*. Ann Arbor: University of Michigan Press, 1992.

Russell, Jan Jarboe. *Lady Bird: A Biography of Mrs. Johnson*. New York: Scribner's, 1999.

Russell, Rosalind, and Chris Chase. *Life Is a Banquet*. New York: Random House, 1977.

Safire, William. *Before the Fall: An Inside View of the Pre-Watergate White House*. Garden City, N.Y.: Doubleday, 1975.

Sahl, Mort. *Heartland*. New York: Harcourt Brace Jovanovich, 1976.

Sanders, Coyne Steven. *Rainbow's End: The Judy Garland Show*. New York: William Morrow, 1990.

Schickel, Richard. *D.W. Griffith: An American Life*. New York: Simon & Schuster, 1984.

Schieffer, Bob, and Gary Paul Gates. *The Acting President*. New York: Dutton, 1989.

Schlesinger, Arthur. *Robert F. Kennedy and His Times*. Boston: Houghton Mifflin, 1978.

Schroeder, Alan. *Presidential Debates: Forty Years of High-Risk TV*. New York: Columbia University Press, 2000.

Simon, Roger. *Roadshow*. New York: Farrar, Straus, Giroux, 1990.

_____. *Show Time*. New York: Times Books, 1998.

Sinatra, Nancy. *Frank Sinatra: An American Legend*. Santa Monica: General Publishing, 1995.

Sinatra, Tina, with Jeff Coplon. *My Father's Daughter: A Memoir*. New York: Simon & Schuster, 2000.

Slick, Grace, with Andrea Cagan. *Somebody to Love? A Rock-and-Roll Memoir*. New York: Warner, 1998.

Sorensen, Theodore C. *Kennedy*. New York: Harper & Row, 1965.

Spada, James. *Peter Lawford: The Man Who Kept the Secrets*. New York: Bantam, 1991.

_____. *Streisand: Her Life*. New York: Crown, 1995.

Speakes, Larry. *Speaking Out: Inside the Reagan White House*. New York: Scribner's, 1980.

Spoto, Donald. *Marilyn Monroe: The Biography*. New York: HarperCollins, 1993.

Stack, Robert, with Mark Evans. *Straight Shooting*. New York: Macmillan, 1980.

Stenn, David. *Bombshell: The Life and Death of Jean Harlow*. Garden City, N.Y.: Doubleday, 1993.

Stine, Whitney. *I'd Love to Kiss You. . . Conversations with Bette Davis*. New York: Pocket, 1990.

Strait, Raymond. *The Tragic Secret Life of Jayne Mansfield*. Chicago: Regnery, 1974.

Strausbaugh, John. *Alone with the President*. New York: Blast, 1993.

Stroud, Kandy. *How Jimmy Won*. New York: William Morrow, 1977.

Suid, Lawrence H. *Guts and Glory: Great American War Movies*. Reading, Mass.: Addison-Wesley, 1978.

Talbott, Strobe, ed. *Khrushchev Remembers: The Last Testament*. Boston: Little, Brown, 1974.

Thomas, Tony. *The Films of Ronald Reagan*. Secaucus, N.J.: Citadel, 1980.

Tierney, Gene, with Mickey Herskowitz. *Self-Portrait*. New York: Wyden, 1979.

Torme, Mel. *The Other Side of the Rainbow: With Judy Garland on the Dawn Patrol*. New York: William Morrow, 1970.

Traubel, Helen. *St. Louis Woman*. New York: Duell, Sloan & Pearce, 1959.

Truman, Margaret. *Harry S. Truman*. New York: William Morrow, 1973.

Truman, Margaret, with Margaret Cousins. *Souvenir: Margaret Truman's Own Story*. New York: McGraw-Hill, 1956.

Tully, Grace. *F.D.R.: My Boss*. New York: Scribner's, 1949.

Turner, Lana. *Lana: The Lady, the Legend, the Truth*. New York: Dutton, 1982.

Turque, Bill. *Inventing Al Gore: A Biography*. Boston: Houghton-Mifflin, 2000.

Tynan, Kenneth. *The Diaries of Kenneth Tynan*. Edited by John Lahr. New York: Bloomsbury, 2001.

Valenti, Jack. *A Very Human President*. New York: Norton, 1975.

Vidal, Gore. *Palimpsest: A Memoir*. New York: Random House, 1995.

Ward, Geoffrey C. *A First-Class Temperament: The Emergence of Franklin Roosevelt*. New York: Harper & Row, 1989.

Wayne, Pilar. *John Wayne: My Life with the Duke*. New York: McGraw-Hill, 1987.

Weidenfeld, Sheila Rabb. *First Lady's Lady: With the Fords at the White House*. New York: Putnam, 1979.

West, J. B. *Upstairs at the White House: My Life with the First Ladies*. New York: Coward, McCann & Geoghegan, 1973.

Wiener, Jon. *Gimme Some Truth: The John Lennon FBI Files*. Berkeley: University of California Press, 1999.

Williams, Esther, with Digby Diehl. *The Million Dollar Mermaid*. New York: Simon & Schuster, 1999.

Wills, Garry. *John Wayne's America: The Politics of Celebrity*. New York: Simon & Schuster, 1997.

———. *The Kennedy Imprisonment. A Meditation on Power*. Boston: Little, Brown, 1981.

———. *Reagan's America: Innocents at Home*. Garden City, N.Y.: Doubleday, 1987.

Winters, Shelley. *Shelley II: The Middle of My Century*. New York: Simon & Schuster, 1989.

Woodward, Bob. *Veil: The Secret World of the CIA, 1981–1987*. New York: Simon & Schuster, 1987.

ACKNOWLEDGMENTS

✳✳✳✳

The research and writing of this book would not have been possible without a great deal of support. Thanks especially to my editor, Jill Rothenberg, and publicists, Greg Houle and Trish Goodrich, as well as Marietta Urban and Wendy Halitzer at Westview Press in Boulder, copy editor Chrisona Schmidt, and to my agent, Maria Massie in New York.

I would also like to acknowledge the following institutions and individuals who contributed to the effort:

- Margaret Herrick Library, Academy of Motion Picture Arts and Sciences: Barbara Hall, Linda Mehr, and staff librarians
- George Bush Presidential Library: Robert Holzweiss, Mary Finch, Matt Lee, Melissa Walker, and Debbie Carter
- Jimmy Carter Presidential Library: Robert Bohanan, David Stanhope, and Polly Nodine
- Bill Clinton Presidential Materials Project: John Keller
- Calvin Coolidge Library: Lou Knox
- Dwight Eisenhower Presidential Library: Jim Leyerzapf and Hazel Stitt
- Gerald R. Ford Presidential Library: Geir Gundersen, Kenneth Hafeli, Nancy Mirshah, and Donna Lehman
- Herbert Hoover Presidential Library: Matthew Schaefer
- John F. Kennedy Presidential Library: Stephen Plotkin, Sharon Kelly, Jim Cedrone, Jim Hill, and Allan B. Goodrich
- Lyndon B. Johnson Presidential Library: Tina Houston, Philip Scott, Shannon Jarrett, and Mary Elizabeth McLain
- Richard Nixon Library and Birthplace: Susan Naulty and Beverly Lindy

- Ronald Reagan Presidential Library: Kelly Barton, Steve Branch, and Meghan Lee
- Franklin Delano Roosevelt Presidential Library: Raymond Teichman, Mark Renovitch, Virginia Lewick, Bob Clark, and Karen Anson
- Harry S. Truman Presidential Library: Dennis Bilger, Raymond Geselbracht, Pauline Testerman, and Liz Shafly
- University of California Los Angeles Arts Library, Special Collections: Julie Graham
- University of Southern California Cinema-Television Library, Special Collections: Ned Comstock
- Vanderbilt University Television News Archives: John Lynch

Also the Boston Public Library; Cambridge Public Library; Library of Congress; Los Angeles County Public Library; and National Archives and Records Administration facility in College Park, Maryland.

This book was generously supported by a grant from the Office of the Provost at Northeastern University and by the Northeastern University School of Journalism. I am indebted to Darrell Hosea and to my faculty colleagues in Boston, and to Feby Kiragu, Christopher King, Afsha Bawany, and Kathleen Walsh for research assistance.

Thanks also to Madeleine Gruen, Mimi Pizzi, and Jonah Meyers in New York; Joshua King in Washington; Barry Paris in Pittsburgh; Namhee Han and Peter Gilhuly in Los Angeles; and Merilyn Britt in San Diego.

Finally, I would like to acknowledge the invaluable work of the scholars and writers who have previously explored this terrain, most notably Ron Brownstein, Elise K. Kirk, and John Strausbaugh. I am honored to share space on the bookshelf with them.

INDEX

✴✴✴